Nineteenth-Ce
Russian Plays

Nineteenth-Century Russian Plays

AN ANTHOLOGY

Edited, Translated, and Introduced by

F. D. REEVE

W · W · NORTON & COMPANY

New York · London

First published in the Norton Library 1973
by arrangement with Random House, Inc.

Published simultaneously in Canada
by George J. McLeod Limited, Toronto

Books That Live
The Norton imprint on a book means that in the publisher's estimation it is a book not for a single season but for the years.
W. W. Norton & Company, Inc.

Originally published under the title *An Anthology of Russian Plays, Volume I*

Library of Congress Cataloging in Publication Data
Reeve, Franklin D., 1928– comp.
Nineteenth century Russian plays.
(The Norton library)
Published in 1961 under title: An anthology of Russian plays, v. 1., which was issued in series, Vintage Russian library, V-731.
1. Russian drama—Translations into English.
2. English drama—Translations from Russian.
I. Title.
[PG3245.R4 1973] 891.7'2'008 72-13663
ISBN 0-393-00683-2

PRINTED IN THE UNITED STATES OF AMERICA

3 4 5 6 7 8 9 0

for

Elena Borisovna

and

Maksim Osipovich

Contents

Nineteenth-Century Russian Plays

INTRODUCTION

Histrionic sensibility is the human response, though a mode of action, to the modes of action which occur in present, or real, time. Perhaps you could call it mere awareness, provided you mean by that whatever appropriate reaction the awareness of any action brings.

The most celebrated theater of our time, the Moscow Art Theater, deliberately cultivated the histrionic sensibility. The purpose of Stanislavsky and Nemirovich-Danchenko's "system" was to train actors to distinguish and to imitate *action* in order to make-believe, to *play* accurately all kinds of dramatic roles. The actor was to free himself from his feelings, habits, thought, cultural environment, and imagination—to free himself from the limitations of his own personality. He was to learn to make-believe *situations* and, by mimesis, to respond significantly within any given imagined situation. He was to study highly emotional human relationships, to concentrate, as Ignatius Loyola asked his disciples to concentrate, on a total situation. He was to think not in nouns and adjectives but in infinitives—Oedipus' aim, in his condition, was not "knowledge of self" but "to find the culprit." The memory of sense impressions, of actions such as shaving or getting off a train, were used, as in the old commedia dell' arte tradition, as devices, or moments, in a technique by which the actor transfers his belief to the whole situation which he and the other actors are in.

The desire to reproduce or to imitate a certain action, preserving its original characteristics but at the same time investing it with new meaning, leads directly to the theater. This desire, which produced out of folk festival and sacred rite the great, secularized Greek theater, similarly produced out of peasant celebration and religious ritual the great Russian theater of the nineteenth century. The development of the theater in Russia is analogous to its development in France or England or Germany; only the instances are different.

As early as the third century, Tertullian, in Byzantium, wrote that the devil himself had inculcated in men the desire for theatrical productions. In the fifth century, John Chrysostomos begged that people give up the baneful habit of attending plays. The ritual of the church was threatened by the imposition of a dramatic intent. As Evreinov and others have pointed out, not only the physical similarity of the Orthodox iconostasis and ambo to the skenetheke and proscenium of the ancient Greek theater but also the similar number of priests, the role of the choir, and the plastic movements of the officiants make "the divine service a real theater." The primitive rituals which underlay the dramatic rite may be traced back to Babylon (the pageant in honor of Marduk) and were to be found, according to Vesselovsky, in Russian village rites in this century—a procession, vehicles for the god's passage over the ocean in December, etc.—a real Christmas celebration.

The origin of the theater in Russia is traceable to a religious or ritualistic state of mind the same as that in all other European countries. The forms and feasts around which the artistic forms developed were rooted in the immediacy of the histrionic sensibility.

The beginning of the theater in Russia as a sophisticated art-form is counted from the historical—not dramatic—event of Tsar Aleksei's establishment in 1672 of the Comic Theater and the performance there that year of the Book of Esther. The organizer appointed by Aleksei for his theater was a German named Gregory; the actors and directors were Germans from the bourgeois German quarter of Moscow; but the point is, not that the theater was *another* foreign borrowing, but that gradually the two main types of theater in Russia merged: the ritual theater of the peasants and the liturgy, and the formal, consciously aesthetic theater of the town, the palace, and the church schools. What is important in considering the relation between religious rite and theatrical performance is the concept of profanity—the fact that the theater is, literally, "outside the temple." The dramatizations of the liturgy finally moved out of the church altogether because the essential idea of theater contradicted the essential moral values of the service. The dramatization of *The Washing of the Disciples' Feet* lost its anagogical significance the more it became good theater. The moral of sin and betrayal, of grace and redemption, yielded to the aesthetic pleasure of a deft imitation of action.

Throughout the late Renaissance (one often forgets that the Renaissance did reach Russia) Russian travelers to the West were excited by their experience of theatrical spectacles there. One traveler reported a play in Florence in 1658 involving sea, fish, clouds, and "people sitting on the clouds." The first presentation of this kind of show in Russia had probably occurred under False Dimitri in 1605, but there had been no organization of actors. Amateur theatricals were staged throughout the seventeenth century in Moscow, especially by foreign diplomats.

Extremely important—for it contributed style and plays—was the "theater of the schools." The founding of the Kiev Academy in 1615 (Kiev was the center of culture) and the rectorship of Peter Mogila enormously encouraged the development in Russia of the Polish, Latin (Jesuit), Western cultural tradition. Teachers wrote plays for their students to perform, first in Latin, later in Russian. The material for the plays was drawn, obviously, from the Bible—in particular, from the life of Jesus. Later, there were plays on semi-religious themes, and, following Jesuit practice, a special form of panegyric drama was introduced.

These seventeenth-century school dramas were thoroughly moral. The stage was a kind of pulpit, and the plays were designed to lead to an understanding of ecclesiastical or theological subjects. The Renaissance plays that were part of Western tradition were omitted in favor of Gospel dramatizations. What was retained from the classical Renaissance theater were certain formal precedents: the device of prologue and epilogue, a division into three or five acts, and so on. What was retained from the liturgical, or medieval, theater was use of allegorical characters, metaphysical settings, and eschatological debate.

The most famous author of school dramas in the seventeenth century was Dimitri, the bishop of Rostov, whose *Nativity Play* presented somewhat secularized events and people (the shepherds, for example) from a theatrical point of view in what was basically a morally edifying spectacle. Around the turn of the century Simeon Polotsky acquired a considerable reputation and is still remembered, by some, for his *King Nebuchadnezzar, the Golden Calf and the Three Young Men in the Furnace* (a redramatization of an earlier liturgical play) and *The Parable of the Prodigal Son*, written in rhymed, syllabic verse. What these plays mark is a conscious "artificialization" of the ethical story.

The accession of Peter the Great caused the school dramas to move back to the academies. Secular dramas, chiefly translations of German or European plays, came to predominate. These plays were in prose, modeled still on the kind of plays that had long been produced in Poland.

The work of Teofan Prokopovich encouraged the secularization of the theater: action superseded dialogue, the chorus became much less important, plausible characters replaced allegorical personifications, and—most important of all—contemporary themes were made the cores of the plays. Prokopovich, in other words, took as model the classical drama of the Renaissance. His "tragi-comedy" of 1705, *Vladimir, Prince and Sovereign of the Slavo-Russian Lands, Led by the Holy Ghost from the Shades of Unbelief into the Light of the Gospel in the Year of Our Lord 988*, has as its hero not the almost legendary reformer of ancient Rus but the then contemporary Russian reformer, Peter the First. It is a kind of panegyric drama, lauding the triumph of the rational, liberal Christian over the conservative and the idolatrous. Under Peter, the theater became a literary agent for political ideas. An amusement reserved for the Court became a necessity for a civilized country. And the plays of Molière and of Shakespeare, chief among foreign authors, entered the repertoire.

The theater's competency was small. The style of playing was taken, along with the actors, mostly from Germany and consisted in declarations of attitudes rather than in dramatizations. In Russia, as elsewhere in the eighteenth century, the classic plays were chopped up, scenes were added, music was appended, and local characters were introduced. The theater was not Russian; it was simply functioning in Russia. But the elaborate settings and preparations, the didacticism of certain plays—all the theatrical (though anti-dramatic) elements serve as marks of an increasing artistic consciousness, however naïve and however second-rate.

In the middle and end of the eighteenth century, the French classical theater (the theater of Racine, of Corneille and his theory of drama) was imported and misinterpreted. The talent that in France had created and justified such a theater was in Russia absent. Sumarokov was the first famous Russian classical playwright, and he declared:

> It is I who revealed to you, o Russians, the theater of Racine;
> It is to Thee, Melpomene, that I erect this beautiful temple.

And the theory of classical art was all the more vindicated by Tredyakovsky's translation of Boileau's *The Art of Poetry*.

Classical theater was first presented to Russians in 1740 by the German actress Neiber, who put on French tragedies in the manner they were performed in France under Louis XIV. The first Russian play was Sumarokov's *Khorev*. Sumarokov belonged to a group in the Cadet Corps which spent its leisure translating and composing and which called itself "The Society of Friends of the Russian Language." He had his play printed in 1747, performed in 1749. He wrote his *Hamlet* in 1748, and a succession of classical tragedies after that. What he did to *Hamlet* measures his vitality: he eradicated all supernatural elements (since French theory held that the miraculous was properly part only of epic poetry), reduced the number of characters to five (Claudius, Gertrude, Polonius, Ophelia, and Hamlet), and added two confidantes and a page. The play was made into a love story between Ophelia and Hamlet, who seeks revenge on Polonius for the murder of his father. Gertrude, out of remorse, enters a convent, and Claudius is ready to marry Ophelia, but she refuses. The play ends with Ophelia and Hamlet alive and happy. "His tragedies," Pushkin said of Sumarokov, "filled with misunderstandings and misconstructions, written in a barbaric and sentimental language, pleased Elizabeth's Court as much by their novelty as by their imitation of Parisian spectacles."

Knyazhnin, also, wrote plays (*Vadim*), but not very well. Lomonosov's plays are less important than his other work, scientific and poetic. His tragedy *Tamira and Selim*, written at royal command in 1750, is "correct," based on an historical event, and with an admixture of classical characters and classical diction:

> What can I do now? He is leaving me.
> My dream has already pursued him along the shore.
> Together we fend off the waves of the sea.
> The peaks of the Crimea have vanished in the distance—
> But what cold, what mist envelops my thoughts!
> He leaves, undissuaded by my flaming passion,
> And my tears henceforth will never move him.

In classical fashion, Lomonosov distinguished three levels of diction, which he called high (Church Slavonic forms), middle (Russian forms), and low (dialect forms and corruptions of standard speech). His syntax was overly elaborate (he had less of a "feel" for language than Tredyakovsky) and was influential only for a short while. His distinction of levels of diction soon became archaic, but his broad, talented use of syllabo-tonic verse (chiefly, iambic) changed Russian concepts of poetry. His *Manual of Rhetoric*, conforming to Quintilian's principles, describes, through its catalogue of gestures, the classic manner and the self-conscious artificiality of the new, rich, socially predominant individual:

> During a speech which is ordinary and depicts no unusual passion, one must stand erect and not move. . . . When one stretches out both hands together toward Heaven, one addresses a prayer to God or else one takes an oath; when one stretches forward one's open hands, one entreats or one rejects; . . . By turning one's head and face up, one expresses a magnificent thing or pride; by lowering one's head, treachery and humiliation; by shaking it, refusal. Hunched shoulders are a sign of fear, or of doubt and of refusal.

The culture of the eighteenth century in Russia, as in the rest of Europe, was an upper-class culture. A man was thought of primarily as a gentle-man, and the center of life was the most refined: the Court.

Comedy suited the time. The talk of the educated (the most significant sign of their differentiation from the masses) was the substance of the stage. An extravagance of words was used rationally to dissect and evaluate man and society.

In this deliberately artificial world of life-and-stage, language became declamatory, decorative, superficial, and rhetorical (in the bad sense). Heroic tragedy vanished into factitiousness, bombast, an implausible hierarchy of social values. Emotionalism replaced emotion; sentimentality replaced poetry. The pattern became not one of life but of "art"—a verbal pattern existing for its own sake without any necessary relation to a perceptual mode. The import of the theater was the success of its novelty—that is, of the wit with which it unmasked, or ridiculed, the convention upon which, in fact, it depended for its life. The misinterpretation the comic plot worked out suggested, then as now, the correct, conventional interpretation. And the serious task of comedy was, as it has always been, to restore the world and its "hero" to their proper condition.

Fonvizin is the first great Russian writer of comedy. Both his plays are famous for their merit and their anti-French attitude, though both are based on precisely what might be called the French attitude toward comedy. "I see that you know our customs well," Panin wrote to Fonvizin apropos of Fonvizin's *The Brigadier General*, "because the wife of your general is completely familiar to us; no one among us can deny having a grandmother or an aunt of the same sort. You have written our first comedy of manners." The play mocks the attitude, then fashionable, that without French rules for behavior "we wouldn't know how to dance, how to enter a room, how to bow, how to perfume ourselves, how to put a hat on, and, when excited, how to express our passions and the state of our heart." Fonvizin's *The Minor* expresses more successfully the attitude that lies behind one of his own letters from abroad: "I've seen that in all countries there is more evil than good, that men are everywhere men, that intelligent people are always rare, that there are crowds of fools everywhere, and, in a word, that our nation is no worse than another and that we can, in this country, enjoy true good without having to seek it elsewhere."

The play is a study of a family. There are, to be sure, the usual lovers, and their relationships to each other and to others in the play are usual. What moves the play is the way the family—the Prostakovs—is anatomized. The mother is a bully obsessed with her son (that he get enough to eat and marry an heiress); her brother is more like a pig (as his name suggests) than a man; her husband is sheepish; the nurse spoils the boy; and the boy beats her and is wildly selfish and stupid. The play's virtue (its success) is that all these beasts speak well. The conventionally artificial talk of the lovers all the more reinforces the illusion of reality of the ordinary fools. In contrast to Mitrofan, who is shaving before he has learned the alphabet, stands dashing Milon, the typical hero who "has learned German, French, Italian, arithmetic, geometry, trigonometry, fortification, architecture, history, geography, dancing, fencing, dressage, and has mastered several sciences, and even knows how to play several musical instruments."

The play is a series of scenes more or less picturesque depending on who is in them. Some scenes are open criticism of Catherine's reign, of Court life and its perquisites. Some are satires against the barbarity of semi-conscious, self-important, antiquely moral lives:

SKOTININ: . . . when I go into the sties and don't find them in order, I get real annoyed. Like you, and this is between you and I, once you got here, found my sister's house no better off than the sties, and you got annoyed.

STARODUM: You are more fortunate than I. People affect me.

SKOTININ: But pigs, me.

The wit, the humor, and the naturalism of Fonvizin's "local-color" dialogues and the characterization developed through them moved the theater considerably closer to the possibility of great comedy—which *was* written in the early and middle nineteenth century. Of course, light comedy, or "vaudeville," continued—for example, the work of Shakhovskoi—up to the 1850's, but a serious tradition (a theater of meaning) had been established which later work could draw on.

Important, and symptomatic in its importance, was the birth of the great actor Shchepkin in 1788. Born a serf, he followed a career of acting through the serf-theaters maintained by noblemen on their private estates and through the private and governmental provincial theaters, to end as the principal actor of the Maly Theater in Moscow, still known as "The House of Shchepkin." By his commanding talent he fashioned Russian realistic acting.

Shchepkin eschewed the artificial style then in vogue. One day, he says in his memoirs, playing Sganarelle, "I realized that I had pronounced some words in a perfectly ordinary way, a way so ordinary that if this had been real life and not a play I still wouldn't have spoken them any differently."

Shchepkin worked long and hard for such a discovery—to find, by systematic search, a style of acting which, adapted to each play, would create for the audience a serious illusion of reality. It was hard work. "What would art be," he wrote a friend, "if it came to us without labor? . . . The actor must work much more than one thinks. He must begin by extinguishing himself, by extinguishing his personality, his particular characteristics, and become the figure that the author wanted." Second-rate actors try for success by selling their personalities. Shchepkin, like all great actors, insisted on the opposite: that the actor take his individuality from the techniques of playing he has talent for. The individuality of the actor, like that of the poet, resides in the integrity of excellence.

This presumes that a play is not merely literature—not merely verse dressed up as dialogue. And there can then no longer be any *one* way of playing a role. All ways that work are plausible. The delimitations are imposed by the organic harmony of the total idea the play represents, by that central, invisible action which, Aristotle said, is the soul of the tragedy. "I, perhaps, might speak well enough in my way," said Shchepkin, "and you might speak better in yours: let everyone follow that manner which belongs to him alone. . . . No matter how apt the emotion is, if it transcends the limits of the central, or over-all, idea, it loses that harmony which is part of the play and which is common to all art."

The first book on the theater published in Russia came out in 1781: *Garrick, or the English Actor*, and the author said that: "Everybody shouts, 'You must play naturalistically,' but nobody explains what he means." Shchepkin explained. Some actors followed him; some followed the semi-classical style of Dmitrevsky; and some persisted in the outrageously classical eighteenth-century style. Finally, in the early nineteenth century, the playwrights came along with the necessary new drama.

Griboyedov's *The Trouble with Reason*, although not produced until many years after it was written, was circulated in manuscript after 1823 and partly published (heavily censored). It was the first great play realistically to mirror indigenous Russian manners and morals.

It is a comedy, organized and composed as you would expect a comedy to be: a pair of lovers—the straight men—advances a relatively docile plot through a society of artificial characters—the comics—who are composed of attitudes and who speak a colloquial language (but in verse, and the "classical unities" are faithfully observed). Griboyedov's success is his ability to present an attitude or an idea as a person, not as a personification. The hero of the play (like a Molière hero) is the idea of society behind it. In *The Trouble with Reason*, Chatsky is not only not an idealistic reformer but also not the hero: his fault is that he is too honest and too generous, and the hero is that already envisioned new, or reformed, society in which generosity is not incompatible with criticism.

"Art," said Wilde, "is only one of the forms of exaggeration." The classical form of Griboyedov's play looks like the form of Molière's: a social satire; a conflict between noble and vicious people; an unsatisfactory love affair; dramatic unity of time, place, and action; a strict, exacting metrical form; alternating scenes of slapstick, social comment, and love. In Griboyedov's play the form itself is exploited as a kind of disciplined, inverted lyric—which is what satire *is*. The author is making a game not only of his stage dolls but also with them. We assent to the conventions by which the characters present themselves, but we are astounded, I think, to find reality in the highly artificial, unreal, literary forms through which the author has arranged the "show" for *his* purpose. We are astounded, but in this play we take these forms themselves as what is meaningful. For example, in the speech in which Repetilov asserts the measure of his friendship for Chatsky, we discover our sense of frustration in "friendship," but we know, in fact, that what we are actually taking as real is Griboyedov's language in which our frustration is consumed.

It is the transforming power of language that preserves the play as the greatest Russian "classic," that turns it from a period piece (like the other plays Griboyedov collaborated on and like the other plays of his time) into a profound portrait of a complex society. Nobody in the play talks profoundly, as they do in *Faust* or in *Major Barbara:* Liza worries about the time and the footman Petrushka; Sofiya talks about romances and Molchalin and parties; Famusov remembers the good old days and the papers he has to sign; and Chatsky observes and comments and observes and comments. They all talk "small," and the unwinding skein of their conversation is the weaving of our understanding of *them*—their positions, their attitudes, their conventions, and, most importantly, their stature as human beings. This is the profundity of the play: that their talk (which to each of them has, at most, only inchoate meaning, though they *mean* all they say very seriously) shapes a pattern of language, even an aesthetically formal pattern, in which we experience a delight in words and see the values which move men. Famusov may hope to carry on the good old days by catching Skalozub for his daughter (and we know what sort of husband Skalozub would be, for we know the sort of general he is), but his attempt to "seduce" Skalozub also exposes the inadequacy of the convention of marriage in terms of which he thinks. Of course, the romantic, intellectual, imaginative Chatsky stands as contrast to the safe, dull, promotion-conscious Skalozub, but he is not "right," either, though for different reasons. Once, Sofiya was more than interested in Chatsky (real-life little Liza, to whom he is inaccessible, still is), but now she has picked up her father's secretary, Molchalin. When Molchalin stands finally exposed by Chatsky, Sofiya still refuses "the hero." She scorns Molchalin (ladies love nobility in a man more than the man, the convention runs), but she declines to reward Chatsky. This would be puzzling (who is more "noble" than Chatsky?) if two things were not clear: 1) that Chatsky has moved outside the circle in which the usual conventions apply (for example, his long speech on Russian manners), and 2) what these figures say adds up to more than they can handle. Chatsky has literally talked himself out of upper-class society—he is still admitted, but deeply distrusted—but he is unprepared to lead any *other* kind of life. He knows he is right, but he does not know where he is, except when with those who are wrong. The language of the play is not only bright, witty, poignant, moving, and proverbial, but it also contains, by its own extraordinary excellence, both the characters of the real world and those images of ultimate freedom which make that world important to us. This is the great and subtle art of the play.

It was awareness of language, of its uses and power, that attracted Pushkin to Shakespeare and that prompted him to comment, "How miserable is the tragic Byron in comparison to him." Elsewhere, he wrote about Shakespeare that, "He creates a character in the fullness of life, because he is sure of finding the kind of language which suits that character and which belongs to the conditions of the place and the time. . . . Shakespeare's characters, unlike Molière's, are not types of one sort of passion or another . . . , but living beings filled with a mire of passions . . . ; the action unravels before the spectator the variety and complexity of the characters."

Pushkin insisted that the subject, or substance, of literature was all the property of civilization. He wanted to honor the many—"The new history is the history of Christianity. . . . The history of the nation belongs to the poet"—but he knew that his ultimate appeal was to "the approval of a small number of selected persons." As he wrote in a preface to *Boris Godunov:*

> Strongly convinced that the obsolete forms of our theater demand transformation, I made my tragedy *Boris Godunov* in the manner of our father Shakespeare and offered as sacrifice to him before his altar the two classical unities. . . . There is [also] a unity which the French critic doesn't even mention—the unity of style, the fourth unavoidable requirement of French tragedy from which the Spanish, the English, and the German theaters have escaped. . . . The honored Alexandrine verse I have changed to the pentameter of blank verse; in certain scenes I have even lowered myself to base prose. I haven't divided my tragedy into acts—and I have even thought that the public will thank me. . . . I have tried to replace the obvious inadequacy [of not following the usual style] by a faithful portrayal of characters, of the period, of the development of historical figures and events. In a word, I have written a truly romantic tragedy.

Pushkin knew that drama originated in the market place and must be entertaining and "truthful"—that it must be completely adequate to its situation; that it must show "the truth of passions and the reality of emotions in any given circumstances." And he knew, also, that, although the actors on the stage are "real," the words they speak cannot be, that the words must fit other conventions.

Pushkin, like Eliot's Elizabethans, lacked a dramatic convention. The weakness of his play is not its absence of "realism" but its attempts at it. On the contrary, the establishment of convention is what distinguished Griboyedov's *The Trouble with Reason* and Gogol's *The Inspector General.* The intense search for realism and the inceptive notion of literature as a form of knowledge not only altered the subject matter of plays (and books) and the possibilities for relationships within them but also emphasized the limiting compass a work of art must carry with itself. Gogol played his society against his art to the incalculable advantage of art.

Out of fear and scorn for society's inanition he wrote *The Inspector General,* the end of which is its beginning. The world that is examined in the play is a world that bothered Gogol: the preposterous world of the hollow bureaucrat whose power, like his position, proceeds from convention. But the artistic convention does not follow from the social and does not depend on it for value. What gives us pleasure in the play comes from the play's conventions, not from society's.

The subjects of the play are not lovely. "The more common the subject," Gogol said, "the greater the poet must be in order to extract from it everything that is unusual." The hero is a nonentity, in the literal sense. He comes from nowhere, takes a position on rumor, and vanishes at the end as if he had never been. Unlike Mark Twain's "The Man Who Corrupted Hadleyburg," his presence among the townspeople is without moral significance: *he* does not persuade them to anything. *They,* on the contrary, persuade him into a certain position, and then they go on from there in terms of the hero *their* conventions and need for conventions have impelled them to establish. The plot is, literally, nothing. What succeeds about the play is its effort to avoid realism, to assert *itself* as real on top of the ordinary assumptions we make about people. What usually happens, of course, is that the audience gets fooled, as Kotlyarevsky was fooled by Gogol's little farce *The Marriage:* "He was the first to recognize that the theater exists above all to present life as it is, without flourishes or exaggeration, and he was the first to formulate aesthetically the identity of the theater with real life."

What is required is that the play be perceived as an artificial unity any part of which is informed on only by another equally artificial part. Any fracture of this general illusion immediately postulates the standards of real life, and the play of the actors becomes a silly pantomime. The play is a world on the stage opposite to the actual world in which the stage is located and which is inimical to the stage—a hypostatized world the reality of which we are deceived into presuming by the fact that its relationships appear to be analogous to ours. The end of the game—the end of the play—is the beginning of actuality. That is, the reality of life takes its meaning from the reality of art; here, *The Inspector General ends* with the arrival of the Inspector General. The hero of the imposition is, in terms of that imposition, himself an impostor.

The joke begins at once. And to reassert the illusion within illusion, Dobchinsky and Bobchinsky each haggles with the other to keep him out of *his* conversation, as if, by keeping what are in fact the same words separate, they could separate themselves. Since each character takes all the others seriously, each nicely describes himself by expressing his interpretation of the communal problem which animates the play, by setting his ambitions and opinions of himself off against the hollow core. By gestures such as their responses to the Postmaster's early information, the characters become committed to each other, and their vain world is defined.

That their world is the world of convention, regulated by rules and tracing assigned behavioral patterns (and not the actual world of action, confusion, repetition, and incoherence)—that the world of the play is the disciplined world of art is demonstrated again by the reading of Khlestakov's captured letter. The Postmaster's pretense of a feeling of impropriety illuminates, by opposition, the regulations of this conventional world to which all the actors belong and which is set off from our world, perhaps in the sense that in *Oliver Twist* Fagin's is set off from the normal. In other words, for the Postmaster *not* to open and read the letter would be, for him, the real violation:

MAYOR: But how did you dare unseal the letter of an important person with such authorization?

POSTMASTER: That's just it—he's not authorized, and he's not an important person.

The denial of Khlestakov's imposture affirms the necessity of the unusual pretense. Ironically, since the unusual pretense is built on the ordinary (since, to become what we desire, we must first pretend to it), the collapse of the ordinary pretense threatens the whole imaginative structure. A letter is, of course, a device for turning a plot, as in the well-made plays of Scribe or Pinero. Here, it *seems* to be used for turning the plot, but it does not. The letter forces a kind of unmasking, but it alters none of the characters and none of their relationships. They argue unattractively with each other, but they come to no further perceptions. They cannot; their world is fixed, and they must patch it up. The effort of the quarreling is to recement their relationships threatened by an intruder. The letter actually belongs to their world: it is the kind of report they make about each other. All that is different is that someone *outside* their world wrote it, someone who seems to be halfway between the world on the stage and the world of the audience. You could say that this is the symbol of the author, but what is relevant is how that symbol functions in the play—how Khlestakov stumbles onto his pretense and how, by exploiting it, he compels the others to insist more carefully on theirs.

The letter reveals almost nothing—only Khlestakov's arbitrary judgments. The characters reveal themselves through their responses to it. Khlestakov's own pretense is much less significant than theirs, simply because his is fragmentary, a sort of accidental method of operation that can have no meaning because it is not part of a whole, or complete, convention.

So he goes. He vanishes into nowhere, just as he appeared from nowhere. He disappears into a fabulous letter, just as he appeared via a fabulous rumor.

The end of the play is terrifying. At a stroke, the convention is smashed, the community is dissolved, the comedy vanishes. But the *play* is over: the actors stand in frozen pantomime. The conventions of the play are relieved by the conventions of the audience (comedy presumes an immediate audience). The make-believe is over. The people in the play were equal precisely because they had the convention of power but no power. The Inspector General has power. Facing real, incomprehensible odds, the mysterious power which will ruin him, the man who has lived by his dreams can only mock himself, terrified, in apology for the way of life that was real for him but which, when questioned, is incredible.

Ostrovsky's *The Storm* is a dramatization of a way of life in which neither social convention nor stage convention takes on independence. The ethical attitude presented in the play's action is, I think, like Ibsen's. The effort is the same and the structure is similar, though the carefully elaborated intrigue, essential to Ibsen's intellectual moralism, is absent. The symbol of the thunderstorm itself stands as a poetic symbol of a total attitude rather than as a dramatic symbol of a total action or complete plot. It does not function in the play like the pistols in *Hedda Gabler*, nor is it something the characters associate themselves with dramatically, like the bird in *The Wild Duck*. It is a symbol of the play itself, something that we, in the audience, appropriate as a general representation of the central conflict.

The play is moved by an opposition of morals: the older people insist on predominant power; the younger search for delight and self-fulfillment. The usual habits of society are not, ultimately, sufficient to satisfy either side, since the expense of each person involved is not compensated by any discovery. What Kabanov learns from his wife's suicide is negligible. He does not gravely threaten his mother by shouting that she killed his wife; and he has only moved into Katerina's position when, at the end, he laments that he remains to suffer. The irony in this limited reversal is not deep irony: too few knew who Katerina was, too little depended on her life. This, of course, is the real horror, but it is something *we* perceive, if it is perceived at all.

The characters move *against* each other. In the center is the triangle, the impetus of the playing, and the rest are grouped and regrouped around it. The first group you see on stage are, in one way or another, attached to each other by attachment to money (they desire money and power); the second is held together by the power each has and by various degrees of blood relationship (they scorn and fear the young). The groups are connected by the stranger Boris, whose speech to Kuligin takes you into the closed-off world of these spiritually crippled people. Katerina's memories of her childhood, Kuligin's ambition to write great civic poetry, Kudryash's music, the threat of the power of nature—all these encircle the corrupt world and the moralities in conflict.

The outsider outlandishly desires another man's wife, whose desirability is enforced by her access to a mystical, beautiful, natural world which none of the other characters (including the old mad witch) can reach. It is from this enchanting, mystical world that literally, as experience, and dramatically, as symbol, the storm comes. The violation of the sanctity of this world—you might almost say virginity—reinvokes the antique curse and calls down social disfigurement on the person who tried to reach it but could not get free of society. Unlike Icarus, here nobody goes too high; nobody can get away at all. Katerina suffers passively "like a bird," an easy victim in a storm. It is better, she says, not to live at all than to live in this merchants' world. Katerina needs *another* world, just as she needs another language to communicate her sense of reality to those around her. We know what she means and we feel sorry for her, but we cannot take her world upon ourselves. Merchants or not, we, too, belong to this one.

The Power of Darkness points this out, scene after scene, and points to our almost intransigent ambition to affirm pleasure by power. We manipulate social conventions to express our superiority or, worse, merely to enjoy ourselves. Indeed, the judgments to which we apply the modes of conventions are no judgments at all—like Aksiniya's complaints against old Pyotr, or Nikita's against Marina, they are merely rationalizations of self-indulgence, the petulance of an irresponsible lust. And the convention Tolstoy uses to expose what he believes is the hollow heart of men and the evil use of institutions to conceal it is the convention of the realistic theater: the characters are peasants, their speech is dialect (or a literary modification of it), and the action of the play (which covers a number of years in order to show the accumulations of corruption and the consequences within the context of any man's life) is "ordinary"—that is, people get sick, die, are born, get married, as they always do. In this play, however, each new event is made the consequence of a preceding one, and the evil in the "first" builds up to a final explosion—the man can no longer contain the forces he has unwound and, destroying himself as a citizen in the name of God, confesses to his village his crimes and lusts.

The "realism" is also contained within the moral framework Akim's simple, patient theology symbolizes. The salvation in which he believes, and which seems to be promised his son after confession, is less vital, from our point of view in the theater, than the slow, constant corruption of a man caught by his lust in playing the games of this world. The "realism" of the theater exposes the "reality" of the disintegration and the inadequacy of usual conventions either to forestall or to redeem the loss.

Still, the realism of the theater is not the reality of life. The most successful presentation of it must involve making-believe a "real" situation, a "reality" analogous to life's. This is what the Moscow Art Theater did, with a rigor and brilliance that lasted some twenty-five years. Chekhov's *Sea Gull* failed when put on by Kommissarzhevskaya in 1896; restaged and restyled by the Moscow Art Theater in 1898 (though by no means completely to Chekhov's liking), the play was such an extraordinary success that the gull was adopted as the theater's emblem, embroidered on the great curtain, and worn as a lapel button by the members of the company.

But the development of the Moscow Art Theater, the histories of the great directors Meyerhold, Vakhtangov, Kommissarzhevsky, Evreinov and Tairov (all of whom had theories quite different from that of the Moscow Art), and the return of drama to its ancient, rhythmic roots in the plays of Chekhov belong to the years after 1900, to a survey of the modern Russian theater. Chekhov, Stanislavsky and Nemirovich-Danchenko, Gorky, Blok and the Symbolists, Meyerhold—the theatrical activity of these men marks the end of the "classical" period.

F. D. Reeve

The Minor

A COMEDY IN

FIVE ACTS

Denis Ivanovich Fonvizin

DRAMATIS PERSONAE

Prostakov [Mr. Simple]
Mrs. Prostakov, his wife
Mitrofan, their son, The Minor*
Eremeyevna, Mitrofan's nurse
Pravdin [Mr. Truthful]
Starodum [Mr. Oldsense]
Sofya, Starodum's niece
Milon [Mr. Dear]
Mr. Skotinin [Mr. Pig], Mrs. Prostakov's brother
Kuteikin [Mr. Carouser], a seminarian
Tsyfirkin [Mr. Number], a retired sergeant
Wrahlman [Mr. Liar], a tutor
Trishka, a tailor
Prostakov's servant
Starodum's valet

The action takes place on the Prostakovs' country estate.

* The Russian title is *Nedorosl'*, which means 1) a boy, not yet of age, who is preparing for government service, and 2) ever since this play, a stupid young man who, though from a well-to-do family, will never amount to anything.

A NOTE ON THE PLAY

The earliest known version of the play dates from approximately the 1760's, perhaps even antedating Fonvizin's other famous play *The Brigadier*, completed in 1766. *The Minor* was first presented in St. Petersburg on October 5 (September 24, Old Style), 1782, published anonymously in 1783, issued as a separate book in 1788 and reprinted in 1789 in Volume XXXI of the anthology *The Russian Theater*. The final edition, which was corrected by Fonvizin himself, appeared in 1790. Subsequent editions, following the edition of 1830, included inserted material taken from old manuscript and notebook jottings. The text used here is the last edition Fonvizin himself made (1790) as reissued in D. I. Fonvizin, *Izbrannye sochineniya i pis'ma*, Moscow: Ogiz, 1947.

Decrees relating to government service for young noblemen ("minors") appeared first during the reign of Peter the Great. Children of nobility were obliged to prepare for government posts and to study the sciences. In view of the opposition which the enactment of these laws provoked among the nobility, compulsory registration of "minors" in school and in service was prescribed. Those who concealed "minors" were subjected to punishment.

Pravdin refers to his assignment as a member of the office of the local deputy—that is, as the representative of the deputy in charge of the district. According to *The Institutions for the Direction of the Provinces*, issued by Catherine the Great in 1775, the deputy was granted broad powers to "suppress every kind of abuse . . . to curb excesses, debauchery, extravagance, tyranny and cruelty."

Fénelon's *On the Education of Young Women*, to which Sofya refers, appeared in Russia in translation in 1763.

The *Decree on the Freedom of the Nobility*, to which Mrs. Prostakov refers, was issued by Peter III in 1762 and granted the nobility many privileges, including, in particular, release from obligatory service to the state.

ACT I

MRS. PROSTAKOV, MITROFAN, EREMEYEVNA *on stage.*

MRS. PROSTAKOV (*looking over the coat on* MITROFAN). The coat's completely ruined. Eremeyevna, bring that swindler Trishka here. (EREMEYEVNA *exits*) The thief—made it too tight all over. Mitrofanushka, my dear! I bet it's squeezing you to death. Call your father in.

(MITROFAN *exits.* TRISHKA *enters.*)

MRS. PROSTAKOV (*to* TRISHKA). And you, you pig, come closer. Didn't I tell you, you plug-ugly, to make the coat wider? The child, first of all, is growing; secondly, the child's of a delicate build even without a tight coat. What've you got to say for yourself, you half-wit?

TRISHKA. As you know, madam, I learned without a teacher. I recommended to you earlier that it be given to a tailor.

MRS. PROSTAKOV. And is it absolutely essential to be a tailor to know how to sew a coat well? What piggish thinking!

TRISHKA. Yes, but a tailor has learned how, madam, and I haven't.

MRS. PROSTAKOV. He's arguing too. One tailor learned from another, the other from a third, so who did the first tailor of all learn from? Tell me, you pig.

TRISHKA. Indeed, perhaps, the first tailor sewed worse than I.

MITROFAN (*running in*). I called Father. He requested me to say: Right away.

MRS. PROSTAKOV. So go drag him out, if you can't call him out in a friendly way.

MITROFAN. Here's Father.

(PROSTAKOV *enters.*)

MRS. PROSTAKOV. What, what? Are you trying to hide from me? Look, sir, what I've come to, thanks to your connivance. What're your son's new clothes like for his uncle's engagement? What kind of a little coat did Trishka sew?

PROSTAKOV (*stammering from timidity*). A li--ttle bb-b--aggy.

MRS. PROSTAKOV. You're baggy yourself, genius.

PROSTAKOV. But I thought, Mother, it seemed that way to you.

MRS. PROSTAKOV. Have you really gone blind?

PROSTAKOV. With your eyes around, mine see nothing.

MRS. PROSTAKOV. See what kind of a mate God rewarded me with! Can't think for himself to figure out what's wide, what's narrow.

PROSTAKOV. I've always believed you, Mother, and I still believe you.

MRS. PROSTAKOV. So believe, also, that I don't intend to indulge sniveling serfs. Go, sir, and at once punish—(SKOTININ *enters.*)

SKOTININ. Whom? For what? On the day of my engagement? I beg you, Sister, on account of the holiday, postpone the punishment until tomorrow, and tomorrow, if you want, I'll gladly help myself. Don't call me Taras Skotinin if every fault ain't faulty for me. In this I always do the same as yourself, Sister. But what're you so cross about?

MRS. PROSTAKOV. Hold on, Brother, I rely on your eyes. Mitrofanushka, come here. Is this coat baggy or not?

SKOTININ. No.

PROSTAKOV. I myself, also, see now, that it's tight, Mother.

SKOTININ. I don't see that. The coat, my friend, is sewn quite well.

MRS. PROSTAKOV (*to* TRISHKA). Get the hell out, pig. (*To* EREMEYEVNA) Go, Eremeyevna, get the child's breakfast. You know, I bet the teachers'll be coming soon.

EREMEYEVNA. As it is, ma'am, he's already been pleased to eat up five rolls.

MRS. PROSTAKOV. And so you grudge the sixth, you ogre? What diligence! You better watch out.

EREMEYEVNA. For good health, ma'am. I mean I said that for Mitrofan Terentevich. He was miserable until morning.

MRS. PROSTAKOV. Ah, Jesus, Mary and Joseph! What happened to you, Mitrofanushka?

MITROFAN. Well, Mother, yesterday after supper it started.

SKOTININ. So, obviously, my boy, you ate heartily.

MITROFAN. But, Uncle, I hardly ate at all.

PROSTAKOV. As I recall, my dear, you were pleased to eat up a bit.

MITROFAN. Says you! Three slices of corned beef and five, I don't remember, maybe six, pies.

EREMEYEVNA. All night he continually asked for a drink. He drank up a whole pitcher of kvass.

MITROFAN. And now I go around like crazy, I saw such stuff in my dreams all night.

MRS. PROSTAKOV. What kind of stuff, Mitrofanushka?

MITROFAN. Well, you, Mother, and Father.

MRS. PROSTAKOV. How so?

MITROFAN. I just begin to fall asleep when I see you, Mother, seeming to beat Father.

PROSTAKOV (*aside*). Well! Just my luck! The dream's true!

MITROFAN (*relaxing*). So I got sorry.

MRS. PROSTAKOV (*with sorrow*). For whom, Mitrofanushka?

MITROFAN. For you, Mother. You were so tired, pummeling Father.

MRS. PROSTAKOV. Embrace me, my dearest! That's my boy, my only consolation.

SKOTININ. Well, Mitrofanushka! I see you're Mother's boy, and not Daddy's.

PROSTAKOV. At least, I love him, as a father should—such an intelligent child, so reasonable, a cheerful boy, a real joker. Sometimes I'm beside myself because of him, and from joy honestly can't believe that he's my son.

SKOTININ. But now our cheerful boy looks pretty surly.

MRS. PROSTAKOV. Shouldn't we send to town for a doctor?

MITROFAN. No, no, Mother. I'd rather get better myself. I'll just run down to the dovecote, so perhaps may—

MRS. PROSTAKOV. So perhaps may God be merciful. Go, play around, Mitrofanushka.

(MITROFAN *and* EREMEYEVNA *exit.*)

SKOTININ. Why don't I see my bride? Where is she? The engagement's this evening, so isn't it time to tell her she's going to be married?

MRS. PROSTAKOV. We'll make it, Brother. If you tell her ahead of time, she could still think that we're making up to her. Although by marriage, however, I'm her relative. And I like strangers, too, to obey me.

PROSTAKOV (*to* SKOTININ). To tell the truth, we treated Sofyushka like a real orphan. She was still a child when her father died. And six months later her mother, my in-law, had a stroke—

MRS. PROSTAKOV (*pretending to cross herself*). The Lord be with us.

PROSTAKOV. From which she went to her long home. Her

uncle, Mr. Starodum, went to Siberia, and for a number of years there hasn't been a word, a whisper, about him, so we've given him up for dead. Seeing she was left alone, we brought her to our little estate and have looked after her place as if it were our own.

MRS. PROSTAKOV. Why're you telling such wild stories today, Father dear? Why, Brother here'll think we took her in for our own advantage.

PROSTAKOV. Why, Mother, how could he think that? You know we can't move Sofyushka's immovables over.

SKOTININ. And even if the movable has moved, I'm not a petitioner. I don't like to litigate; in fact, I'm afraid to. No matter how my neighbors have offended me, no matter what losses they've caused, I've never litigated with nobody, but every loss, instead of chasing after it, I make up off my peasants, and nobody's the wiser.

PROSTAKOV. That's true: the whole neighborhood says that you take in the rent masterfully.

MRS. PROSTAKOV. If only you'd show us how, Brother dear. We just can't do it. Ever since we took away everything the peasants had, we haven't been able to collect a thing. Such a shame!

SKOTININ. I'll teach you, Sister, if you want. I'll teach you if you'll just marry me to Sofyushka.

MRS. PROSTAKOV. Does the little girl really please you so much?

SKOTININ. No, it's not the girl pleases me.

MRS. PROSTAKOV. Or the nearness of her estate?

SKOTININ. And not the estate, but something that goes on on her estate, and that's my heart's desire.

MRS. PROSTAKOV. What's that, Brother?

SKOTININ. I love pigs, Sister, and in our neighborhood we have such fine pigs that there isn't one of them, stood on its hind legs, wouldn't be taller by a head than any of us.

(SOFYA *enters, holding a letter in her hand, with a gay expression.*)

MRS. PROSTAKOV (*to* SOFYA). Why so gay, dear? What's made you happy?

SOFYA. I have just received joyful news. My uncle from whom we have so long heard nothing and whom I love and honor as my father, has recently arrived in Moscow. Here's the letter I just received from him.

MRS. PROSTAKOV (*frightened, spitefully*). What! Starodum, your uncle, is alive! And you're pleased to suggest that he's risen from the dead! What a handsome lie!

SOFYA. But he never died.

MRS. PROSTAKOV. Didn't die! And *can't* he die? No, young lady, it's all your invention to scare us with your uncle so we give you your freedom. Your uncle, see, is a clever man; seeing me in other people's hands, he'll find a way of rescuing me. That's what you're happy about, young lady. But don't be too chipper, I'd say; your uncle, of course, hasn't risen from the dead.

SKOTININ. Sister, what if he didn't die?

PROSTAKOV. God spare us, if he didn't die.

MRS. PROSTAKOV (*to her husband*). How didn't die? You trying to pull my leg? Don't you know that for several years I had him remembered in masses for the repose of his soul? So didn't my sinful prayers get there that way? (*To* SOFYA) The letter, please. (*Practically snatches it*) I'll bet it's a love letter. And I can guess who from. It's from that officer who wanted to marry you and who you wanted to marry yourself. What ogre gives you letters without my permission? I'll find out. That's what we've come to. They write letters to girls. Girls know how to read and write!

SOFYA. Read it yourself, madam. You will see that nothing could be more innocent.

MRS. PROSTAKOV. Read it yourself! No, madam, I, thank God, am not so brought up. I may receive letters but I always have someone else read them. (*To her husband*) Read it.

PROSTAKOV (*looking long at it*). It's hard.

MRS. PROSTAKOV. And obviously you, Father dear, were brought up like a fair young thing. Brother, read it, try.

SKOTININ. I've never read anything since birth, Sister. God spared me that boredom.

SOFYA. Allow me to read it.

MRS. PROSTAKOV. Oh, heavens! I know you're an expert, but I don't trust you very far. I expect Mitrofanushka's teacher'll come soon. I'll order him—

SKOTININ. And has the boy already been set to reading and writing?

MRS. PROSTAKOV. Brother dear! He's been studying for four years already. You can't say we haven't tried to educate

Mitrofanushka. We pay three teachers good money. The sexton from Pokrov, Kuteikin, comes for reading and writing. He's taught arimmetic by a retired sergeant, Tsyfirkin. They both come out here from town. You see, the town's just three versts away. The German Adam Adamych Wrahlman teaches him French and all the sciences. He gets three hundred rubles a year. We seat him at the table with ourselves. Our old women wash his laundry. Wherever he wants to go he has a horse. A glass of wine during the meal. A tallow candle to go to bed by, and our own Fomka combs his wig for nothing. To tell the truth, we're pleased with him, Brother. He doesn't force the child. You see, my dear, as long as Mitrofanushka is still a minor, we must go easy on him. But a dozen years from now, when, God forbid, he goes into the service, he'll put up with everything. Some are born lucky, Brother. Look at the Prostakovs, who, without lifting a finger, climbed up the ladder. How's Mitrofanushka worse than they? Ah, here comes our dear lodger just in time.

(PRAVDIN *enters.*)

MRS. PROSTAKOV. Brother dear! I commend our dear guest to you, Mr. Pravdin; to you, dear sir, I commend my brother.

PRAVDIN. I'm delighted to have made your acquaintance.

SKOTININ. Well said, dear sir! What's your name? I didn't catch it.

PRAVDIN. I am called Truthful, so you get it.

SKOTININ. A native of where, dear sir? Where's your place?

PRAVDIN. I was born in Moscow, if you must know, but my estate is in this district.

SKOTININ. And do I dare ask, sir—I don't know your first name—do you keep pigs on your place?

MRS. PROSTAKOV. Enough, Brother, don't start off on the pigs. It'd be better to talk about our troubles. (*To* PRAVDIN) It's like this, friend! God ordered us to take the care of a young girl into our own hands. She thinks it's fine to get written things from her uncles. Her uncles write her from their long home. Be so good, kind friend, as to take the trouble of reading this aloud to us all.

PRAVDIN. Forgive me, madam. I never read letters without the permission of those to whom they are addressed.

SOFYA. I beg you to do so. You will be doing me a great favor.

PRAVDIN. If you so command. (*Reads*) "Dearest Niece! My affairs compelled me to live for a number of years apart from those dear to me, and distance deprived me of the pleasure of having news of you all. I am now in Moscow, having spent several years in Siberia. I may serve as an example that by work and honesty a man may make his fortune. By these means, with the aid of good luck, I acquired an income of ten thousand rubles—"

SKOTININ *and both* PROSTAKOVS. Ten thousand!

PRAVDIN (*reads*). "Of which I make you, my dearest niece, the heiress—"

MRS. PROSTAKOV. You the heiress!
PROSTAKOV. Sofya the heiress! (*Together*)
SKOTININ. Her the heiress!

MRS. PROSTAKOV (*throwing herself on* SOFYA). Congratulations, Sofyushka! Congratulations, my darling! I'm wild with joy! Now you must have a husband. I, I couldn't wish Mitrofanushka a better bride. That's a real uncle! What did I tell you, a real father! I always did think that God'd watch over him, that he was still with us.

SKOTININ (*holding out his hand*). So, Sister, it's a deal.

MRS. PROSTAKOV (*to* SKOTININ *quietly*). Hold it, Brother. First we have to ask her if she still wants to marry you.

SKOTININ. What? What a question! Are you going to start playing up to her now?

PRAVDIN. Will you allow me to finish reading the letter?

SKOTININ. What for? Even if you read for five years, you won't get to anything better than ten thousand.

MRS. PROSTAKOV (*to* SOFYA). Sofyushka, my pet! Let's go into my bedroom. I've a terrible need of chatting with you. (*Leads* SOFYA *off*)

SKOTININ. Bah! I see there'll hardly be an engagement today. (*Servant enters.*)

SERVANT (*to* PROSTAKOV, *panting*). Master! Master! Soldiers have come, stopped at our place.

PROSTAKOV. What a shame! They'll ruin us completely.

PRAVDIN. What are you frightened by?

PROSTAKOV. Oh, dear friend! We've seen lots of things. I don't dare show up.

PRAVDIN. Don't be afraid. Of course, an officer's in charge of them, who won't permit the slightest impudence. Let's go to him together. I'm certain that you're nervous over nothing. (PRAVDIN, PROSTAKOV *and the servant exit*)

SKOTININ. They've all left me alone. Might just as well take a walk to the pigsty.

ACT II

PRAVDIN *and* MILON *on stage.*

MILON. How happy I am, my dear friend, that we've unexpectedly run into each other! Tell me, what happened—?

PRAVDIN. Being a friend, I'll let you know the reason for my staying here. I've been made a member of the local deputy's office. I have instructions to travel round the local district. And besides, from the integrity of my heart I cannot give up pointing out those immoral know-nothings who, having absolute power over their people, use it for inhuman evil. You know the cast of mind of our governor. With what ardor he helps suffering humanity! With what zeal by the same token he fulfills the humane policy of a higher authority! In our own country we have experienced that, where the governor is one such as is described as desired in the *Institutions*, there the well-being of the inhabitants is safe and assured. I've been here three days already. I found the landowner a hopeless fool; his wife, a most wicked virago whose hellish disposition is the bane of the entire house. And what are you thinking about, my friend? Tell me. Will you stay here long?

MILON. I'm going away in a few hours.

PRAVDIN. Why so soon? Rest a bit.

MILON. I can't. I'm under orders to lead the soldiers on without delay. Besides which, I myself burn impatiently to be in Moscow.

PRAVDIN. What's the reason?

MILON. I'll open my heart's secret to you, my dear friend. I'm in love, and have the great fortune of being loved. It's over half a year since I've been away from the one who is dearer to me than anything in the world, and, what is sadder still, I've heard nothing of her all that time. Frequently, ascribing her silence to coldness, I've been tormented with grief, but suddenly I received news which astounded me. They wrote me that, following her mother's death, some distant relative took her off to her estate. I don't know who or where. Perhaps she's now in the hands of some selfish people who, taking advantage of her orphanhood, tyrannize her. This thought drives me nearly out of my mind.

PRAVDIN. I see just such inhumanity in this house here. I fondly hope, however, soon to put an end to the malice of the wife and to the stupidity of the husband. I have already informed our chief of everything and do not doubt that measures will be taken to calm them down.

MILON. You are fortunate, my friend, being in a position to ease the lot of the unfortunate. I don't know what to do in my unhappy position.

PRAVDIN. Allow me to ask her name.

MILON (*in ecstasy*). Ah! Here she is herself.

(SOFYA *enters.*)

SOFYA. Milon! Is it really you?

PRAVDIN. What happiness!

MILON. Here is she who has my heart. Dearest Sofya! Tell me, by what chance do I find you here?

SOFYA. I've endured so many misfortunes since the day we parted! My unscrupulous relatives—

PRAVDIN. My friend, don't inquire about what is so sorrowful for her. You'll learn from me what crudenesses—

MILON. Vulgar people!

SOFYA. Today, however, for the first time the mistress here changed her attitude toward me. Having heard that my uncle has made me his beneficiary, suddenly she turned from a coarse and cursing woman into the most gentle, and I see from all her hedging that she intends me to be her son's bride.

MILON (*impatiently*). And didn't you right away show her complete contempt?

SOFYA. No—

MILON. And didn't you tell her that your heart is promised, that—?

SOFYA. No—

MILON. Now I see my undoing. My rival is happy! I don't deny all virtues in him. He, perhaps, is rational, enlightened, courteous, but that he could be compared with me in my love for you, that—

SOFYA (*laughing*). My Lord! If you saw him your jealousy would lead you to extremes!

MILON (*indignantly*). I conceive all his merits—

SOFYA. You can't conceive them *all*. He's only sixteen, but he's already reached the final stage of his perfection and will go no farther.

PRAVDIN. Why won't he go farther, madam? He's finishing up the breviary, and then, one would suppose, he'll take up the psalter.

MILON. What! That's my rival? Dearest Sofya, why are you torturing me with your jokes? You know how easily a passionate man gets upset by even the slightest suspicion. Tell me, how did you answer her?

(*At this point* SKOTININ *comes on stage, lost in thought, and no one sees him.*)

SOFYA. I said that my fate depends on my uncle's wishes, that he himself promised to come here in his letter which (*to* PRAVDIN) Mr. Skotinin didn't let us finish reading.

MILON. Skotinin!

SKOTININ. Me!

PRAVDIN. How you sneaked up, Mr. Skotinin! I wouldn't have expected it of you.

SKOTININ. I was just going past you, heard my name called, so I called back. That's the way I do it: whoever calls—Skotinin!—I say to him—Me! Why, friends, do you mean that? I myself served in the Guard and retired a corporal. Time was, drawn up for roll-call, they'd call out: Taras Skotinin! and I at the top of my voice: Me!

PRAVDIN. We didn't call you just now, and you may go where you were going.

SKOTININ. I wasn't going anywhere, just wandering, thinking. That's the way I do it, so whatever I take into my head you can't knock out with a hammer. Whatever's gone into my mind, see, is settled down there for keeps. So all my mind's on the thing I see in dreams like awake and awake like in dreams.

PRAVDIN. What might so occupy you now?

SKOTININ. You're a clever man, figure it out. My sister brought me over to get married. Now she herself's come up with an excuse. "What do you want a wife for?" she says. "You want a good pig, Brother," she says. No, Sister! I want to raise my own pigs. You can't fool me.

PRAVDIN. It seems to *me*, Mr. Skotinin, that your sister is contemplating a wedding, only not yours.

SKOTININ. What a story! I'm in nobody's way. Let everyone

marry his own bride. I won't touch anyone else's, and let nobody else touch mine. (*To* SOFYA) Don't you fear, sweetie. Nobody'll get you away from me.

SOFYA. What does that mean? That's something new!

MILON (*shouts*). What impudence!

SKOTININ (*to* SOFYA). What'd you get scared for?

PRAVDIN (*to* MILON). How can you get angry at Skotinin?

SOFYA (*to* SKOTININ). Am I really fated to be your wife?

MILON. I can hardly hold back!

SKOTININ. You won't get around your promised husband, sweetie, even on horseback. It's a sin for you to complain about good fortune. You and me'll be living in a bed of roses. Ten thousand your income! That's happiness piled high. Why, I never saw so much since the day I was born. Why, with that I'll buy up all the pigs in the whole wide world. Why, see, I'll do what they'll all sound off about: Life in this here district's for pigs only.

PRAVDIN. If only the pigs can be happy at your place, why, then your wife will have little peace from them and from you.

SKOTININ. Little peace! Bah! bah! bah! Haven't I got enough nice sunny rooms? Just for herself I'll give up the corner one with the stove-couch. My dearest friend, if though I've nothing now and still each pig has its own sty, why, sure I'll find my wife a little sunny spot.

MILON. What a piggish comparison!

PRAVDIN (*to* SKOTININ). Nothing will come of it, Mr. Skotinin! I see that your sister is playing with you like a ball.

SKOTININ (*bitterly*). Like a ball? God save us, I myself'll throw her so far you won't find her in the whole estate in a week of looking.

PRAVDIN. I know for a fact that she's planning to marry her to her own son.

SKOTININ. What! The nephew get in ahead of the uncle! Why, as soon as I see him I'll smash him to pieces. Let me be a son of a pig if I don't be her husband, or Mitrofan ain't a plug-ugly.

(EREMEYEVNA *and* MITROFAN *enter*.)

EREMEYEVNA. Study, even if just a teensy-weensy bit.

MITROFAN. Say another word, you old bag, and I'll fix you.

I'll complain to Mother again, and she'll give you a drubbing like yesterday again.

SKOTININ. Come over here, my boy.

EREMEYEVNA. Go over to your uncle.

MITROFAN. Hey, Uncle! What've you got your back up for?

SKOTININ. Mitrofan. Look me in the eye.

EREMEYEVNA. Look at him, master.

MITROFAN (*to* EREMEYEVNA). What kind of a wonder's my uncle? What do you see in him?

SKOTININ. Once more: Look me in the eye.

EREMEYEVNA. Don't make your uncle angry. Back, see how he's been staring and you stare like him.

(SKOTININ *and* MITROFAN, *popping their eyes, stare at each other.*)

MILON. What a fine understanding!

PRAVDIN. How'll it end?

SKOTININ. Mitrofan! You're a hair's breadth from death this moment. Tell the whole truth. If I weren't scared of sin, without another word more I'd take you by the legs and smash your head in the corner. I don't want to ruin my soul without finding who's guilty.

EREMEYEVNA (*trembling*). Oh, he's coming for him! Where can my poor head hide?

MITROFAN. What's up, Uncle? Are you off your rocker? I sure don't know what you've pounced on me for.

SKOTININ. Look out, don't deny it, so's in a fit I don't beat the stuffing out of you with one blow. You won't even get your hands up. My fault. Guilty before God and sovereign. Look out, don't start accusing yourself, so's not to take an unfair beating.

EREMEYEVNA. God spare us from unfairness!

SKOTININ. Do you want to get married?

MITROFAN (*relaxing*). Well, for a long time, Uncle, the desire—

SKOTININ (*rushing at* MITROFAN). Ah, you damned pig!

PRAVDIN (*blocking* SKOTININ). Mr. Skotinin! Put down your hands.

MITROFAN. Nanny, protect me!

EREMEYEVNA (*protecting* MITROFAN, *becoming frenzied and raising her fists*). I'll drop on the spot, but I won't give up the child. Hit me, sir, just you please, hit. I'll scratch out your old wall-eyes, I will.

SKOTININ (*trembling and shaking his fists, exits*). I'll eat you up.

EREMEYEVNA (*trembling, after him*). My claws is real sharp, too!

MITROFAN (*after* SKOTININ). Beat it, Uncle! Make yourself scarce!

(*Both* PROSTAKOVS *enter.*)

MRS. PROSTAKOV (*to her husband, entering*). There was nothing to mix up. You've gone around your whole life, sir, swallowing whatever you're told.

MR. PROSTAKOV. But he himself and Pravdin disappeared from before my very eyes and vanished. How's it my fault?

MRS. PROSTAKOV (*to* MILON). Oh! My dear sir, Mr. Officer! I've just been looking for you all over the place. I ran the legs off my husband for him to bring you humblest gratitude for a good troop.

MILON. For what, madam?

MRS. PROSTAKOV. What do you mean for what, my dear sir? Such good soldiers. So far not a one's touched a hair. Don't get angry, dear fellow, that my black sheep slipped away. From the day he was born he hasn't understood about entertaining anyone. He was born such a dawdler, sir.

MILON. I haven't the slightest complaint, madam.

MRS. PROSTAKOV. He goes around, sir, in such a, as we say here, fog. Sometimes he just stands a whole hour with his eyes popped out, rooted to the spot. What I haven't tried to do with him! What he's had to put up with from me! Nothing works. If the fog clears, dear sir, you get such a lot of nonsense you're ready to beg God for the fog back.

PRAVDIN. At least, madam, you cannot complain about his wicked disposition. He's meek—

MRS. PROSTAKOV. As a calf, dear sir, which is why in our house everything's so easy and carefree. You know he hasn't the faintest idea of there being strictness in a house so the guilty get punished. I run everything myself, sir. From morning to night, swinging like a clapper, I never sit down: I scold, I slap them, and that's what keeps the house together, sir!

PRAVDIN (*aside*). Soon it will be kept by other means.

MITROFAN. And today Mother spent the whole morning working with the servants.

MRS. PROSTAKOV (*to* SOFYA). I was straightening things up for your good uncle. I'm dying to see this splendid old fellow. I've heard a lot about him. Even those who don't like him just say he's a teensy bit gloomy, but such a remarkably intelligent man, they say, that if he likes someone, they say, he really likes him.

PRAVDIN. And whoever he dislikes is really an evil man. (*To* SOFYA) I myself have the honor of knowing your uncle. Moreover I have heard from many people such things about him that have implanted in me a genuine respect for him. What in him are called sullenness, coarseness are the direct result of his straightforwardness. From the day he was born his tongue has never said yes when his heart felt no.

SOFYA. However, he had to win his happiness by hard work.

MRS. PROSTAKOV. God's blessing on us that he made it. There's nothing I want so much as his paternal blessing on Mitrofanushka. Sofyushka, my sweet, won't you go look at your uncle's room? (SOFYA *exits*) Again you're standing with your mouth open, old boy. Please, sir, escort her. Your legs didn't fall off.

PROSTAKOV (*going*). Didn't fall off, but they buckled.

MRS. PROSTAKOV (*to the guests*). My only concern, my only joy, is Mitrofanushka. My time is running out. I'm preparing him for the world.

(*Here* KUTEIKIN *appears with a breviary, and* TSYFIRKIN, *with a slate and a slate pencil. By gestures they ask* EREMEYEVNA: *May we come in? She waves them in, but* MITROFAN *waves them out.*)

MRS. PROSTAKOV (*not seeing them, goes on*). If God's just merciful, maybe he's fated for happiness.

PRAVDIN. Look around, madam, at what's going on behind you!

MRS. PROSTAKOV. Oh! It's Mitrofanushka's teachers, sir, Sidorich Kuteikin—

EREMEYEVNA. And Pafnutich Tsyfirkin.

MITROFAN (*aside*). Let them go to hell, and Eremeyevna, too.

KUTEIKIN. Peace to the house of the master and long life to his sons and his household.

TSYFIRKIN. We wish your excellency good health a hundred

years, nay twenty more, then fifteen more, indeed countless years.

MILON. A brother-in-arms! Where did you come from, my friend?

TSYFIRKIN. Did garrison duty, your excellency. But now I've retired.

MILON. What do you do?

TSYFIRKIN. One thing and another, your excellency. I can make out a little arithmetic, so I make my way around in town doing accounting for different offices. The Lord didn't give science to everyone, so whoever can't figure things out himself gets me in to check the figures or add it all up. So I make out. I don't like to live doing nothing. In my free time I give kids lessons. This is my third year here at his excellency's with this fellow here racking our brains over fractions, but it hardly sticks. But then it's true, no two are alike.

MRS. PROSTAKOV. What? What's this nonsense, Pafnutich? I wasn't paying attention.

TSYFIRKIN. Nothing. I was just telling his excellency that in ten years you can't pound into one stump what another'll catch on the wing.

PRAVDIN (*to* KUTEIKIN). But aren't you, Mr. Kuteikin, a man of letters?

KUTEIKIN. A man of letters, your honor. From the seminary of the local diocese. Got to rhetoric, but, God's will be done, turned back. Sent a petition to the consistory, in which I wrote out: "Such-and-such a seminarist, from a church family, fearing the depths of great wisdom, requests release from it." To which a gracious resolution soon came in answer, with the note: "Such-and-such a seminarist is released from all study; for it is written, cast not pearls before swine, lest they trample them underfoot."

MRS. PROSTAKOV. And where's our Adam Adamych?

EREMEYEVNA. I'd started to go in to him, but I could hardly walk away. The smoke's so thick you could cut it. He smothered me, damn him, with his old tobacco. What a sinner!

KUTEIKIN. Nonsense, Eremeyevna. There's no sin in smoking.

PRAVDIN (*aside*). Kuteikin's getting brighter!

KUTEIKIN. It's allowed in many books. In the Psalter it says exactly: "And herb for the service of man."

PRAVDIN. Well, and where else?

KUTEIKIN. And in another psalter the same thing's written. Our archpriest has a little octavo one, and it's in that, too.

PRAVDIN (*to* MRS. PROSTAKOV). I do not wish to interfere with your son's exercises. Your humble servant.

MILON. Nor do I, madam.

MRS. PROSTAKOV. Sir, sir, where are you going?

PRAVDIN. I'm taking him to my room. Friends who have not seen each other for a long time have much to talk about.

MRS. PROSTAKOV. Where would you wish to eat, with us or in your own room? There's only just the family at table, and Sofyushka—

MILON. With you, with you, madam.

PRAVDIN. We both shall have the honor.

(PRAVDIN *and* MILON *exit.*)

MRS. PROSTAKOV. So, now read your assignments, Mitrofanushka, even if in Russian.

MITROFAN. But the assignments, I don't want to.

MRS. PROSTAKOV. You live and learn, my dearest. That's the way it is.

MITROFAN. Not at all! Studying goes to your head. You might have brought even more uncles here!

MRS. PROSTAKOV. What? What're you talking about?

MITROFAN. Yes! Look what a pummeling I can get from an uncle. And already, from his fists and the breviary—thanks, but no thanks. I've had it.

MRS. PROSTAKOV (*frightened*). What—what do you want to do? Think a minute, sweetie.

MITROFAN. You know the river's close. I'll dive in, and then they'll remember what they called me.

MRS. PROSTAKOV (*beside herself*). You've killed me! You've killed me! God save you!

EREMEYEVNA. His uncle just scared him. Almost had him by the hair. For nothing—over nothing—

MRS. PROSTAKOV (*spitefully*). Well—

EREMEYEVNA. Came up to him: "Do you want to get married?"

MRS. PROSTAKOV. Well—

EREMEYEVNA. The child didn't hide it; for a long time, he says, Uncle, I've had the desire. How he got mad, madam, how he rushed—

MRS. PROSTAKOV (*shaking*). Well—and you, you ogre, got petrified, and you didn't punch him in the puss, and you didn't twist his snout back to his ears—

EREMEYEVNA. I was about to! Oh, sure, I was about to—

MRS. PROSTAKOV. Yes—yes, sure—but it's not your child, you ogre! You'd let them beat the child to death.

EREMEYEVNA. Oh, Creator, bless us and save us! Indeed, if your brother hadn't got out that very same moment, why, I'd have pounded away with him. Whatever God's price. These would of got dull (*showing her nails*), and I wouldn't of kept back my fangs neither.

MRS. PROSTAKOV. All you, you ogres, get mad only in words, and never really—

EREMEYEVNA (*crying*). I don't seem eager to you, madam? I don't know how to serve better—I'd be happy not only just—it's not your life you worry about—but nothing pleases them.

KUTEIKIN. Are you ordering us to go home?
TSYFIRKIN. Where are we to march, your excellency? } (*Together*)

MRS. PROSTAKOV. You, you old witch, started another good howl. Go, feed them and yourself, and right after you eat come back here. (*To* MITROFAN) Come with me, Mitrofanushka. Now I won't let you out of my sight. I'll tell you a little something, and it'll be all nice again. You won't, my dear, you won't spend all your life studying. You, thank God, already understand so much you yourself can bring up kids. (*To* EREMEYEVNA) I'll have a talk with my brother different than yours. Let all good people see who's the nurse and who's the real mother.
(*Exits with* MITROFAN.)

KUTEIKIN. Your life, Eremeyevna, is absolute darkness. Let's go have a bite, but first drink a cup against grief—

TSYFIRKIN. And then a second. There's multiplication for you.

EREMEYEVNA (*in tears*). Nobody wants me. I've served her forty years, and her kindness is still the same—

KUTEIKIN. And are the wages good?

EREMEYEVNA. Five rubles a year, and five slaps in the face a day.

(KUTEIKIN *and* TSYFIRKIN *lead her out, holding her by her arms.*)

TSYFIRKIN. We'll figure out at table what you make in a full year.

ACT III

STARODUM *and* PRAVDIN *on stage.*

PRAVDIN. We had just risen from table when I, going over to the window, caught sight of your carriage and, saying nothing to anyone, ran out to meet you, to embrace you with all my heart. My warmest regards to you—

STARODUM. That means much to me, believe me.

PRAVDIN. Your friendship for me is the more flattering for your not being able to have it for others, except those who—

STARODUM. Are like you. I speak without ceremony. Stand on ceremony, and sincerity stops.

PRAVDIN. Your manner—

STARODUM. Many laugh at it. I know that. Let them. My father brought me up the old-fashioned way, and I haven't found any need for re-educating myself. He served Peter the Great. In those days a man was addressed as "thou" and not "you." In those days they still didn't know how to contaminate people so much that each would think of himself as plural. But the many now aren't worth one then. In Peter the Great's Court my father—

PRAVDIN. I heard that he was in military service—

STARODUM. In those times the courtiers were soldiers, and not the soldiers courtiers. The upbringing given me by my father was the very best of its day. At that time there were few ways of getting an education, and people still didn't know how to stuff an empty head with someone else's intelligence.

PRAVDIN. Education then actually consisted of a few rules—

STARODUM. Of one. My father ceaselessly said one and the same thing to me: Have a heart, have a soul, and you'll be a man all the time. Everything else is a fad: wit's a fad, knowledge is a fad, like buckles and buttons.

PRAVDIN. You speak the truth. The true worth of a man is his soul—

STARODUM. Without it the most educated wise man is a pitiful creature. (*With feeling*) An ignoramus without it is a beast. The pettiest act leads him into all sorts of crime. He has no way to balance what he does against what he is doing it for.

It's from just such animals that I've come to liberate—

PRAVDIN. Your niece. I know that. She's here. Let's go—

STARODUM. Stop. My heart still seethes with indignation at the unworthy action of our present hosts. Let's stay here a few minutes. I have a rule: Don't start anything on impulse.

PRAVDIN. Few are able to observe your rule.

STARODUM. The experiences of my life have schooled me to it. If only I had known how to be master of myself sooner, I would have had the pleasure of serving my country longer.

PRAVDIN. In what way? No one can be indifferent to the story of what has happened to a man of your qualities. You would oblige me greatly if you would tell—

STARODUM. I conceal it from no one so that others in a similar situation may find themselves more capable than I. Having gone into military service, I became acquainted with a young Count whose name I don't even want to recall. He was my junior in service, a man whose father had made a brilliant career, brought up in high society, and one who had particular occasion to learn what had not yet gone into my education. I employed all my powers to win his friendship in order to endow the inadequacies of my upbringing with his continual relationship. At the very same time that our mutual friendship was being established, we heard unexpectedly that war had been declared. I rushed to embrace him with delight. "Dearest Count! Here is a chance to distinguish ourselves. Let's go into the line immediately and make ourselves worthy of the title of nobility which our birth gave us." My friend the Count frowned deeply and, having embraced me, said drily: "A happy journey to you," and added: "But I cherish the thought that my old man wouldn't want me to part from him." There is nothing to compare with the scorn which I felt for him in that moment. I suddenly saw that there sometimes is an immeasurable difference between lucky men and honorable men, that the most petty souls are in high society, and that with much education one may be a great skinflint.

PRAVDIN. Absolutely true.

STARODUM. Having left him, I proceeded immediately where duty called me. I had many opportunities for distinguishing myself. My wounds show that I did not let them go by.

The good opinion of me on the part of my superiors and the troops was the gracious reward of my service, when suddenly I received the news that the Count, my former comrade, whose memory I shunned, had been promoted and I had been passed over—I who at that time lay desperately ill from my wounds. Such injustice rent my heart, and I immediately resigned.

PRAVDIN. And what else could you have done?

STARODUM. I should have come to my senses. I did not know how to be chary of the first impulses of my irritated self-respect. Fervor did not allow me to reason then that a properly self-respecting man envies deeds, not rank; that rank is not infrequently solicited, but that true respect is inevitably won by merit; and that it is much more honorable to be passed over without fault than to be favored without merit.

PRAVDIN. But isn't a noble not permitted to resign under any circumstances?

STARODUM. Under one only: when he is absolutely convinced in his heart of hearts that his service is of no immediate use to his country. Then, get out.

PRAVDIN. You make me sensible of the real essence of a nobleman's duty.

STARODUM. Having resigned, I went to Petersburg. There blind chance led me to a place where I had never thought I would be.

PRAVDIN. Where?

STARODUM. The Court. I was admitted to the Court. Well? What do you think of that?

PRAVDIN. How did it strike you?

STARODUM. Curious. It at first seemed strange to me that in this Court world almost no one goes by the straight and open road, but that everyone follows a detour around, hoping to arrive that much sooner.

PRAVDIN. Although a detour, is the road wide?

STARODUM. It's so wide that two men, meeting, can't pass. One knocks the other down, and the one who's standing up never picks up the one on the ground.

PRAVDIN. So that, there, there is self-esteem—

STARODUM. There is no self-esteem there, but rather, you might say, self-love. There people love themselves excellently; they care for only themselves; they think only of the present hour. You won't believe me. I saw there a great number of people who not once in all their lives had thought of their ancestors or of their descendants.

PRAVDIN. But those worthy people who serve the state at Court—

STARODUM. Oh! Those don't leave the Court, because they're useful to it; and the rest don't leave, because the Court's useful to them. I was not among the former and didn't wish to be among the latter.

PRAVDIN. They, of course, didn't pay attention to you at Court?

STARODUM. It was better for me that way. I managed to get away without commotion; otherwise, they would have squeezed me out in one of two ways.

PRAVDIN. What are they?

STARODUM. They squeeze you out of the Court, my friend, in two ways. Either they get angry at you or they get you angry. I didn't want to wait for one or the other. I realized that it was better to lead my life in my own house than in someone else's vestibule.

PRAVDIN. And so you left the Court empty-handed? (*Opens his snuffbox*)

STARODUM (*taking a pinch from* PRAVDIN). What do you mean empty-handed? The price of a snuffbox is five hundred rubles, say. Two men go into a store. One, having paid cash, takes his snuffbox home. The other goes home without a snuffbox. And you think that he goes home empty-handed? You're wrong. He brought back his five hundred rubles intact. I left the Court without estates, without decorations, without rank, but I brought myself home unharmed—my soul, my honor, my principles.

PRAVDIN. One should not let people with your principles go from the Court but should summon them to it.

STARODUM. Summon them? What for?

PRAVDIN. For the same reason people summon a doctor for the sick.

STARODUM. My friend! You're wrong. It's folly to call a doctor to the incurably ill. The doctor can do no good and will himself get infected.

(SOFYA *enters.*)

SOFYA (*to* PRAVDIN). I'm worn out from their noise.

STARODUM (*aside*). Those are the features of her mother's face. That is my Sofya.

SOFYA (*looking at* STARODUM). My Lord! He said my name. My heart does not deceive me—

STARODUM (*embracing her*). No. You are my sister's daughter, the daughter of my heart!

SOFYA (*throwing herself into his arms*). Uncle! I'm wild with joy!

STARODUM. Dearest Sofya! I found out in Moscow that you're living here against your will. I've been in the world for sixty years. Often I've had occasion to be irritated, sometimes satisfied, with myself. Nothing has so torn my heart as innocence in the web of perfidy. I was never so satisfied as when I managed to tear the victim from the clutches of vice.

PRAVDIN. How pleasant to be a witness to this!

SOFYA. Uncle! Your kindness toward me—

STARODUM. You know that I am held to life by you alone. You must be the consolation of my old age, and my care of you must bring your happiness. Upon resigning from the service, I laid the foundation for your education, but I could not secure your fortune other than by separating myself from your mother and yourself.

SOFYA. Your absence grieved us unspeakably.

STARODUM (*to* PRAVDIN). In order to protect her from lacking in the necessities of life, I decided to go away for several years to that part of the country where money is gotten without exchanging it for conscience, without dishonest service, and without robbing my country; where money is drawn from the earth itself, which, more just than men, does not know partiality but faithfully and liberally pays labor alone.

PRAVDIN. You could have become, so I heard, incomparably richer still.

STARODUM. But for what?

PRAVDIN. To be a rich man, like others.

STARODUM. A rich man! But who's rich? Do you realize that all Siberia is too small for one man's fancies? My friend! Everything depends on imagination. Follow nature and you'll never be poor. Follow public opinion and you'll never be rich.

SOFYA. Uncle, what you say is so true!

STARODUM. I earned just so much so that, when you get married, the poverty of a worthy suitor would not give us pause.

SOFYA. Your will will be my law throughout my life.

PRAVDIN. But, having given her away, it wouldn't be amiss to leave the children—

STARODUM. The children? Leave wealth to children? Not on your life. If they're clever, they'll get on without it; and wealth is no help to a dumb son. I've seen youngsters in gold brocade coats but with pig-iron heads. No, my friend! Ready cash is not ready virtue. A gold fool is still a fool.

PRAVDIN. For all this, we see that money often leads to promotions, promotions usually to nobility, and nobles are shown respect.

STARODUM. Respect! The only respect that should be gratifying to a man is that of the heart; and only he is worthy of heartfelt respect who does not owe his promotions to money or his nobility to promotions.

PRAVDIN. Your conclusion is irrefutable.

STARODUM. Hey! What's that noise!

(MRS. PROSTAKOV, SKOTININ, *and* MILON *enter.* MILON *pulls* MRS. PROSTAKOV *and* SKOTININ.)

MRS. PROSTAKOV. Let me go, let me go! Let me at his ugly puss, that ugly puss—

MILON. I will not, madam. Do not get angry!

SKOTININ (*vehemently, straightening his wig*). Leave me alone, Sister! It'll come to bone-breaking, and I'll fold you in two so's you begin to crack.

MILON (*to* MRS. PROSTAKOV). And you've forgotten that he's your brother!

MRS. PROSTAKOV. Oh, young man! My heart's set, let's have at it!

MILON (*to* SKOTININ). And isn't she your sister?

SKOTININ. Got to admit it, from the very same litter. Just look how she squeals.

STARODUM (*unable to keep from laughing, to* PRAVDIN). I was afraid of getting angry. Now I'm being carried away with laughter.

MRS. PROSTAKOV. Who's being? At who? Who's this newcomer?

STARODUM. Don't get angry, madam. I've never in my life seen anything funnier.

SKOTININ (*hand on his neck*). It's funny to him, but it's no joke to me.

MILON. She didn't hurt you, did she?

SKOTININ. I got the front covered with both hands, but she caught ahold of the back of my neck—

PRAVDIN. So it hurt?

SKOTININ. She scratched through the nape a bit.

(*During the following speech by* MRS. PROSTAKOV, SOFYA *tells* MILON *by glances that* STARODUM *is in front of him.*)

MRS. PROSTAKOV. Scratched through! No, pal, you ought to pray for thanks to Mr. Officer, for if it wasn't for him you'd of never covered up from me. I'll defend my boy. Won't let his own father. (*To* STARODUM) There's nothing funny in this, sir. Don't get angry. I've a mother's heart. Did you ever hear of a bitch giving up her own pups? Besides, nobody knows who you are or what you're here for.

STARODUM (*pointing to* SOFYA). Her uncle, Starodum, has come to see her.

MRS. PROSTAKOV (*growing timid and frightened*). What! It's you! You, sir! Our priceless guest! Ah, I'm an endless idiot! This is hardly the way you're supposed to meet your own father, who all hopes are on, who's all we have, the apple of our eye. Sir! Forgive me! I'm an idiot. I can't come to my senses. Where's my husband! Where's my son! Like if you'd come to an empty house! God's punishment! Everybody's gone mad! Wench! Wench! Palashka! You wench!

SKOTININ (*aside*). So that's the one's the uncle! So!

(EREMEYEVNA *enters.*)

EREMEYEVNA. What do you want?

MRS. PROSTAKOV. And are you the wench, you lousy bitch? Don't I have maids in my house besides your nasty muzzle? Where's Palashka?

EREMEYEVNA. She's got sick, ma'am; in bed since morning.

MRS. PROSTAKOV. In bed! Oh, she's an ogre! In bed! Just like a lady!

EREMEYEVNA. Such a fever came on, ma'am, she rants on without stopping—

MRS. PROSTAKOV. Rants, the ogre! Just like a lady! Call my husband, my son. Tell them that by divine mercy we've finished waiting for the uncle of our dearest Sofyushka. Well—run, scram.

STARODUM. Why be so concerned, madam, when by divine mercy I am not acquainted with you at all?

MRS. PROSTAKOV. Your sudden coming, sir, took away my wits. So, our benefactor, let's just really embrace.

(PROSTAKOV *and* MITROFAN *enter. During* STARODUM'S *following speech,* PROSTAKOV *and his son, who have entered through the center door, stand behind* STARODUM. *The father is ready to embrace him as soon as his turn comes; the son, to kiss his hand.* EREMEYEVNA *takes a place on one side and, arms folded, stands rooted to the spot staring at* STARODUM, *in slavish servility.*)

STARODUM (*reluctantly embracing* MRS. PROSTAKOV). A completely superfluous kindness, madam! I could get on perfectly easily without it. (*Having torn himself from her arms, he turns around to the other side where* SKOTININ, *standing with outstretched arms, at once seizes him*) Who's this I've fallen into?

SKOTININ. It's me, my sister's brother.

STARODUM (*seeing two more, impatiently*). And who are these?

PROSTAKOV (*embracing him*). I'm my wife's husband. } (*Together*)
MITROFAN (*catching his hand*). And I'm Mother's boy. }

MILON (*to* PRAVDIN). I won't introduce myself now.

PRAVDIN (*to* MILON). I'll find a chance to introduce you later.

STARODUM (*not giving his hand to* MITROFAN). This one's trying to catch my hand to kiss it. Obviously a great soul is being formed in him.

MRS. PROSTAKOV. Speak up, Mitrofanushka. Say: How, sir, couldn't I kiss your little hand? You're my second father.

MITROFAN. How couldn't a person kiss your little hand, Uncle? You're my— (*To his mother*) Which one now?

MRS. PROSTAKOV. Second.

MITROFAN. Second? Second father, Uncle.

STARODUM. I, sir, am neither father nor uncle to you.

MRS. PROSTAKOV. Sir, maybe the child, see, is just foretelling his happiness: perhaps maybe God'll make it so he's really your little nephew.

SKOTININ. Really! And why'm I not nephew? Hey, Sister!

MRS. PROSTAKOV. I'm not going to start arguing with you, Brother. (*To* STARODUM) I've never since the day I was born, my dear, gone around calling someone else names. That's the way I am. Go ahead, even curse me; I'll never say a word. Let him think he's smart; God'll pay back whoever insults a poor woman like me.

STARODUM. I observed this the moment you appeared in the doorway, madam.

PRAVDIN. And I've been a witness of her fine behavior three full days.

STARODUM. I cannot have this amusement so long. Sofyushka, my dear, tomorrow morning you and I are going to Moscow.

MRS. PROSTAKOV. Ah, dear sir! Why such anger?

PROSTAKOV. Why the harshness?

MRS. PROSTAKOV. What! For us to part with Sofyushka! With our dear, dear friend! I'll lose my appetite from loneliness.

PROSTAKOV. And I'm already done in.

STARODUM. Oh! Since you love her so, I must then make you rejoice. I'm taking her to Moscow to guarantee her happiness. I've been introduced to a certain young man of great merit from among her suitors. I will give her away to him.

MRS. PROSTAKOV. Ah, he's the death of me!
MILON. What do I hear!
(SOFYA *looks astounded.*)
SKOTININ. So that's it!
(PROSTAKOV *clasps his hands.*)
MITROFAN. Well, I'll be damned!!
(*Together*)

(EREMEYEVNA *shakes her head sadly.* PRAVDIN *shows pained surprise.*)

STARODUM (*observing everyone's confusion*). What does this mean? (*To* SOFYA) Sofyushka, my dear, even you seem to me upset. Did my intention really grieve you? I've taken the place of your father. Believe me, I know a father's rights. They go no further than averting an unhappy inclination on the part of the daughter, for the choice of a worthy man depends entirely on her heart. Be calm, my dear! Your husband, worthy of you, whoever he may be, will find in me a sincere friend. Marry whom you wish. (*All look cheerful.*)

SOFYA. Uncle! Don't doubt my obedience.

MILON (*aside*). Estimable man!

MRS. PROSTAKOV (*with a cheerful expression*). That's a father! Just listen to that! Marry whom you wish, just so's the man's up to her. Right, my dear fellow, right. Only now you don't want to let the suitor slip through. As there is within sight a nobleman, a nice young fellow—

SKOTININ. Who long ago grew up—

MRS. PROSTAKOV. Who's got a nice income, even if not a big one—

SKOTININ. Yes, and a pig farm that isn't bad—

MRS. PROSTAKOV. And good luck—it's Judgment Day. (*Together*)

SKOTININ. And let's have a real feast—at my wedding. (*Together*)

STARODUM. Your recommendations are impartial. That I see.

SKOTININ. You'll see more soon's you get to know me closer See, there's just a ruckus here. Another hour or so I'll come see you alone. Then we'll wind up the business. I tell you, no boasting, people like me, really, are scarce. (*Exits*)

STARODUM. That's most probable.

MRS. PROSTAKOV. You, dear, don't get surprised that my own brother—

STARODUM. Your own—

MRS. PROSTAKOV. Right, dear. Sure, I'm a Skotinin on my father's side. My late father married my late mother. She was a Priplodin [Fruitful]. There were eighteen of us children. In fact, except my brother and me, they all, by God's grace, died off. Some they pulled out of the tub dead. Three, who gulped down milk from a copper pot, passed away. Two during Holy Week fell out of the bell tower. And the rest just couldn't keep up, dear!

STARODUM. I see what sort of people your parents were.

MRS. PROSTAKOV. Old-fashioned people, dear! Times weren't like now. They didn't teach us a thing. Sometimes good-intentioned people'd come to my old man, wheedle and wheedle so's he'd send my brother out to school. Luck would have it, the dear departed—may his soul rest in peace—would sometimes shout, stamping and waving his arms: "I'll curse the child who takes in something from the pagans, and let there never be a Skotinin who wants to learn anything."

PRAVDIN. You, however, are teaching your boy something.

MRS. PROSTAKOV. But it's another time, dear! (*To* STARODUM) We don't spare the least thing just so they teach the boy everything. He'll be sixteen, you know, dear, around St. Nicholas' Day. He's a suitor for any girl, and still the teachers come, he doesn't waste an hour, and right now two of them are waiting in the hall. (*Winks to* EREMEYEVNA *to call them in*) In Moscow we hired a foreigner for five years, and so's the others don't lure him off we made the contract in the police office. He haggled about what we wanted him to teach, but we said teach whatever you can. We did our whole parental duty, took on a German, and pay him his money a third in advance. I really heartily wish that you yourself, dear, 'd take a good, long look at Mitrofanushka and see what he's learned.

STARODUM. I'm a bad judge of that, madam.

MRS. PROSTAKOV (*catching sight of* KUTEIKIN *and* TSYFIRKIN). Here're the teachers! My Mitrofanushka gets no peace day or night. It's bad to praise your own child, but she who God brings him as wife won't be a bit unhappy.

PRAVDIN. This is all very well, but don't forget, however, madam, that your guest has just arrived from Moscow, and that he needs quiet much more than hearing praises of your son.

STARODUM. I confess I'd be glad to rest both from the journey and from everything I've heard and seen.

MRS. PROSTAKOV. Ah, my dear! It's all set. I tidied up the room for you myself.

STARODUM. Much appreciate it. (*To* PRAVDIN) When will we meet? When I've rested a bit, I'll come down here.

PRAVDIN. So I will have the honor of seeing you here, too.

STARODUM. Delighted. (*Catching sight of* MILON, *who bows respectfully to him, he returns the bow courteously*)

MRS. PROSTAKOV. Come with me.

(*All exit, except the teachers.* PRAVDIN *and* MILON *go out one side; the rest, the other.*)

KUTEIKIN. What an old devil! You can't make any sense of it from the beginning of the morning. Here everything blossoms and dies every morning.

TSYFIRKIN. Fellows like us have lived like this a hundred years. Don't work today, you can't run away. What's the trouble for fellows like us is how bad they feed you, like today for dinner here there was no chow left.

KUTEIKIN. Yeah, and if the Lord hadn't put me wise, coming here, to stop in at the crossroads at the woman who bakes the communion bread, I'd of starved like a dog at evening.

TSYFIRKIN. These people here are real good commanders.

KUTEIKIN. Have you heard, my friend, what life's like for the servants here? Means nothing you were in service, in battles, still fear and trembling will overcome you—

TSYFIRKIN. That's just it! Have I heard? I myself've seen the gunfire here three hours at a stretch out of twenty-four. (*Sighing*) Oh, oh, it's sad. You get really sad.

KUTEIKIN (*sighing*). Oh, woe is me, sinner that I am!

TSYFIRKIN. What'd you sigh about, Sidorych?

KUTEIKIN. And does the heart shrink within you, Pafnutevich?

TSYFIRKIN. You can't help thinking—God gave me a pupil, a boyar's boy. I'm struggling along with him the third year now: he can't count to three.

KUTEIKIN. We got the same sorrow. It's the fourth year now I'm torturing my life. You sit an hour, and except the review, he can't figure out a new line, and besides he mumbles the review stuff, God forgive us, rhyme and reason all mixed up.

TSYFIRKIN. But whose fault is it? He gets the pencil in hand, and the German's in the door. He scrams from the board and pushes me on the way.

KUTEIKIN. Is it my fault? He gets the pointer in his fingers, and the pagan shows up. The pupil gets patted, and I get it in the neck.

TSYFIRKIN (*heatedly*). I'd let them cut off my ear if only this sponger got schooled like a soldier.

KUTEIKIN. Let them even whip me right now, if only they break his sinful neck.

(MRS. PROSTAKOV *and* MITROFAN *enter*.)

MRS. PROSTAKOV. While he rests, dear, make it look like you're studying, so he'll get to hear how hard you work, Mitrofanushka.

MITROFAN. Well! And then what?

MRS. PROSTAKOV. And then you'll marry.

MITROFAN. All right, Mother dear, I'll go along with you. I'll study a bit, but only on the condition that this is the last time and that the engagement's today.

MRS. PROSTAKOV. God's will'll be done in time.

MITROFAN. My will's being done. I don't want to study, I want to get married. You've egged me on, blame yourself. There, I've sat down.

(TSYFIRKIN *sharpens the slate pencil.*)

MRS. PROSTAKOV. And I'll sit down here. I'll knit you a purse, my dear. Sofyushka's money needs a place to be put in.

MITROFAN. Well! Let's have the slate, you old pack rat! Tell me what I'm to write.

TSYFIRKIN. Your excellency, you're always barking for no reason.

MRS. PROSTAKOV (*working*). Ah, my Lord! The child shouldn't scold Pafnutich. Already he's got angry.

TSYFIRKIN. Why get angry, your excellency? We have a Russian proverb: The dog barks, the wind carries.

MITROFAN. Give me the review stuff; get going.

TSYFIRKIN. All the review work, your excellency. Knowing just the review you'll stay a century behind.

MRS. PROSTAKOV. That's not your business, Pafnutich. It's touching to me that Mitrofanushka doesn't like to get ahead. Why, with his intelligence, God forbid he goes too far.

TSYFIRKIN. The problem. You're coming, just for example, along the road with me. Well, and let's just take Sidorych with us. We three find—

MITROFAN (*writes*). Three.

TSYFIRKIN. On the road, still as example, three hundred rubles.

MITROFAN (*writes*). Three hundred.

TSYFIRKIN. It comes time to divvy them up. Figure out, how much to each?

MITROFAN (*figuring, whispering*). One times three is three. One times zero is zero. One times zero is zero.

MRS. PROSTAKOV. What, what? To divvy what up?

MITROFAN. See, the three hundred rubles we found are to be divvied up among the three of us.

MRS. PROSTAKOV. That's absurd, my dearest. When you find money don't share it with anyone. Take it all yourself, Mitrofanushka. Don't study this foolish science.

MITROFAN. You hear, Pafnutich? Give me another one.

TSYFIRKIN. Write it down, your excellency. For teaching I'm granted ten rubles a year.

MITROFAN. Ten.

TSYFIRKIN. At the moment, it's true, for nothing, but if on you, sir, *any*thing rubbed off, it wouldn't be a sin to add ten more.

MITROFAN. Okay, ten.

TSYFIRKIN. How much would that be for the year?

MITROFAN (*figuring, whispers*). Zero and zero are zero. One and one— (*Gets lost in thought*)

MRS. PROSTAKOV. Don't labor over nothing, my dear. I won't add a kopek; no reason to. Science isn't like that. It's torture for you, and, I see, it's all nothing. If there's no money, what's there to count? If there is money, we'll count it even without Pafnutich real well.

KUTEIKIN. That's enough, really, Pafnutich. Two problems are worked out. They surely won't insist on checking them.

MITROFAN. No fear, friend. Mother herself here don't make mistakes. Come on yourself, now, Kuteikin, teach me yesterday's stuff.

KUTEIKIN (*opens a breviary.* MITROFAN *takes the pointer*). We'll begin with the blessing. After me, attentively. "I am a worm—"

MITROFAN. "I am a worm—"

KUTEIKIN. A worm, in other words that is, a barnyard beast, a pig. In other words that is: I am a pig.

MITROFAN. I am a pig.

KUTEIKIN (*in a sing-song voice*). "And not a man."

MITROFAN (*the same way*). "And not a man."

KUTEIKIN. "The defamation of men."

MITROFAN. "The defamation of men."

KUTEIKIN. "And the humi—"

(WRAHLMAN *enters.*)

WRAHLMAN. Ai, ai ai! Und now I see! Dey vant to kill de

chilt! Oh, modder, modder! Haf peety ofer your voom, veech draggt out nine monts—how you say, de ate vunder uf de vorlt. Gif de liberty to dese cursed rascals. Iss chust de headt dat makes such cherk? Die disposition iss so. Everytink iss so.

MRS. PROSTAKOV. Right. How right you are, Adam Adamych! Mitrofanushka, my dear, since studying is so dangerous for your head, I think you ought to stop.

MITROFAN. I thought so long ago.

KUTEIKIN (*closing the breviary*). The end, and glory be to God.

MRS. PROSTAKOV. The Lord preserve him, Adam Adamych, dear! As it is, he didn't eat much of a supper last night.

WRAHLMAN. Chust tink, my dear, he stuffed de belly ofermuch. A peety. Und you know hiss leetle headt iss veaker much dan belly. Stuff eet ofermuch, und Got forbeedt.

MRS. PROSTAKOV. How right you are, Adam Adamych, but what are you going to do? Send a child who hasn't studied into Petersburg, and they'll say he's a fool. There's lots of clever people around now. I'm scared of them.

WRAHLMAN. Vy be frait, my dear? Intellichent man von't nefer start de arkument, und he better not get mixed up mit de clefer people, und den dere'll pe real peace on ers.

MRS. PROSTAKOV. That's how you ought to live in this world, Mitrofanushka!

MITROFAN. I myself don't go for the clever people, Mother. Your own's always better.

WRAHLMAN. Alvays stick mit your own!

MRS. PROSTAKOV. Adam Adamych, who should you pick them from?

WRAHLMAN. Don't ket vorriet, modder, don't ket vorriet. Chust like your precious son dere iss millions in de vorlt, iss millions. He can't help put chooss hiss own.

MRS. PROSTAKOV. Then it means nothing that my son, such a quick-witted boy, is so clever.

WRAHLMAN. De trouple iss, maype dey ruin him py teachink? Russian's gramma! Arismetic! Mein Got, mein Got, how keep pody un soul togedder! Iss chust like eef Russian noblesman couldn't in de vorlt avanzier mitout de Russian's gramma!

KUTEIKIN (*aside*). May your tongue be struck dumb.

WRAHLMAN. Like eef everypody vas unendet fools pefore der vas arismetic!

TSYFIRKIN (*aside*). I'm counting up your ribs. Just come near me.

WRAHLMAN. He must know how de vay dey lif in de vorlt. I know de vorlt py heart. Myself I am olt shoe.

MRS. PROSTAKOV. How couldn't you know the ways of high society, Adam Adamych? Why, I bet that just in Petersburg you got a good look at everything.

WRAHLMAN. Enuff, my dear, enuff. I vas alvays enkshus to look ofer de public goot. In olt times on de holidays der come to Katrinkoff many carriches mit ladies und gentlemens. I vas alvays lookink on dem. In olt times I didn't get off de coach-pox efen for vun minute.

MRS. PROSTAKOV. What coach-box?

WRAHLMAN (*aside*). Ai, ai, ai, ai! Vat I let out! (*Aloud*) You know, my dear, iss alvays easier to look from de up apofe. So vat I uset to do vas sit myself on de carrich off a frient, and dere from de coach-pox I look on de high society.

MRS. PROSTAKOV. A better view, of course. A clever man always knows where to climb.

WRAHLMAN. Your dearest poy some day like dat vill also look on society, ja to see und to pe seen. De daredefil! (MITROFAN, *standing in the same place, turns around*) Daredefil! He nefer stands on de place, like vilt horss mitout de pridle. Moof! Vort!

(MITROFAN *runs out.*)

MRS. PROSTAKOV (*laughing happily*). A child, really, though also a bridegroom. I should go after him, however, so he doesn't get our guest angry with a careless bit of playfulness.

WRAHLMAN. Ko, my dear! A real kame pirt! You haf to keep de eyes on him!

MRS. PROSTAKOV. Good-bye now, Adam Adamych! (*Exits*)

TSYFIRKIN (*laughing*). What a specimen!

KUTEIKIN (*laughing*). The talk of the town!

WRAHLMAN. Vat for you pare your teet, you poors?

TSYFIRKIN (*slapping him on the shoulder*). And what're you frowning so for, you old Finnish owl!

WRAHLMAN. Oi, oi! de iron pawss!

KUTEIKIN (*slapping him on the shoulder*). You old cursèd eagle-owl! What're you batting your eyelids at?

WRAHLMAN (*quietly*). I'm lost. (*Aloud*) Vat for you make fun, children, uff me?

TSYFIRKIN. You eat your fill for doing nothing and give others nothing to do. Just wait—you won't stick out your puss.

KUTEIKIN. Your lips have always uttered proud things, you godless man.

WRAHLMAN (*pulling himself together*). How can you dare pe so poorish pefore a learnèd personich? I will shout de guart.

TSYFIRKIN. And we'll salute you farewell. I with the slate—

KUTEIKIN. And I with the breviary.

WRAHLMAN. I vill sent de madam on you.

TSYFIRKIN (*brandishing the slate*). I'll open your puss like a can

KUTEIKIN (*brandishing the breviary*). I'll knock out the sinner's teeth. (*Together*)

(WRAHLMAN *runs out.*)

TSYFIRKIN. Ah! The coward beat it!

KUTEIKIN. Hasten your footsteps, damned man!

WRAHLMAN (*at the door*). Vat you got, okres? Come ofer here.

TSYFIRKIN. He squeaked in! We'd of given you what's coming!

WRAHLMAN. I don't pe frait of dem now, I don't pe frait.

KUTEIKIN. The lawless man found refuge! Are there a lot of you there, you pagans? Send 'em all out!

WRAHLMAN. You coultn't to mit vun! You kot me, hey, frient?

TSYFIRKIN. I'll knock off a dozen!

KUTEIKIN. On the morrow I will raze all the sinful earth! (*All suddenly shout*)

ACT IV

SOFYA *alone on stage.*

SOFYA (*alone, looking at the clock*). My uncle ought to come down soon. (*Sits*) I'll wait for him here. (*Takes out a little book and reads a bit*) That's true. How can one's heart not be content when one's conscience is at peace? (*Having read a bit more*) It's impossible not to love the rules of virtue. They are the means to happiness. (*Reads a bit more, looks up, and, having seen* STARODUM, *runs up to him*)

(STARODUM *enters.*)

STARODUM. Ah, you're already here, my dearest!

SOFYA. I was waiting for you, Uncle. I was just now reading a book.

STARODUM. Which?

SOFYA. A French book. Fénelon, *On the Education of Young Women.*

STARODUM. Fénelon? The author of *Télémaque?* Very good. I don't know your book, but read it, read it. The man who wrote *Télémaque* isn't going to undermine manners and morals by his pen. On your behalf I'm afraid of contemporary wizards. I've had occasion to read everything of theirs which has been translated into Russian. To be sure, they powerfully eradicate prejudices, but they also turn virtue from its roots. Let's sit down. (*They both sit*) My sincere desire is to see you as happy as a person can be in this world.

SOFYA. Your precepts, Uncle, will constitute my whole well-being. Tell me the rules I must follow. Direct my heart. It is ready to obey you.

STARODUM. The inclination of your heart is pleasing to me. I'll give you my advice with delight. Listen to me as attentively as I sincerely speak. Closer.

(SOFYA *moves her chair over.*)

SOFYA. Uncle! Each word of yours will be engraved on my heart.

STARODUM (*with weighty candor*). You are now at the age when the soul wishes to enjoy its existence to the full, the mind desires to know and the heart to feel. You're going into the world now, where often the first step decides the outcome of one's whole life, where most often of all the first encounter occurs—minds, corrupted in their concepts; hearts, depraved in their emotions. Oh, my dear! Know how to distinguish, know how to stay with those whose friendship is trustworthy confirmation of your intelligence and heart.

SOFYA. I will bend all my efforts to merit the good opinion of worthy people. But how shall I avoid that those who see how I withdraw from them will not start to think maliciously of me? Isn't it possible, Uncle, to find some way so that no one in the world would wish me evil?

STARODUM. The evil disposition of people unworthy of respect must not be distressing. Know that they never wish evil to those they scorn, but usually wish evil to those who have the right to scorn them. People do not envy only wealth or only nobility; virtue, too, has those who envy it.

SOFYA. Is it really possible, Uncle, that there are in the world such pitiful people in whom a nasty feeling develops because there is good in others? A virtuous man must feel sorry for such miserable people.

STARODUM. They are pitiful, that's true. However, a virtuous man does not because of this stop going his own way. Consider what a misfortune it would be if the sun stopped shining in order not to blind weak eyes.

SOFYA. Yes, but tell me, please, are they to blame? Can every man be virtuous?

STARODUM. Believe me. Any man can find enough strength in himself to be virtuous. One must desire decisively, and then it is easier not to do what would cause remorse.

SOFYA. Who watches over a man, who doesn't let him do what later will torment his conscience?

STARODUM. Who watches over him? That same conscience. Know that conscience, as a friend, always gives warning before it, as a judge, passes sentence.

SOFYA. Then it must follow that every honest man is actually fit for scorn when he does evil, having known what he was doing. His soul must be very base if it's not above base action—

STARODUM. And his reason must not be right reason when it proposes that his happiness lies not in what is proper.

SOFYA. It seemed to me, Uncle, that all people were agreed in what their happiness lies. Nobility, wealth—

STARODUM. Yes, and I agree to call the noble and the rich happy. Let's first agree who is noble and who is rich. I have my own reckoning. I reckon the degree of nobility according to the number of deeds which an important man has done for his country, and not according to the number of deeds which he has latched onto out of arrogance; not according to the number of servants who loaf about in his vestibule, but according to the number of servants pleased by his conduct and actions. My noble man, of course, is happy. My rich man is, also. According to my reckoning, he is not rich who counts out his money to hide it in a chest but he who counts out his extra money in order to help someone in need.

SOFYA. How just this is! How appearance blinds us! I myself have had occasion to see many, many times how people envy whoever at the Court petitions and carries weight—

STARODUM. But they don't know that at the Court every man has some weight and seeks something. They don't know that at the Court everyone's a courtier and everyone has courtiers. No, there's nothing to envy in that. Without noble deeds a position of nobility is nothing.

SOFYA. Of course, Uncle! And such a noble makes no one happy except himself alone.

STARODUM. So right! And is he happy who's happy all by himself? Know that, no matter how noble he may be, his soul does not taste real pleasure. Imagine a man who directed all his nobility only to the end that he alone was well-off, who even reached the point where there was nothing more for him to wish himself. You know that then his whole being would be occupied with one emotion, one disease: sooner or later falling down. Tell me, my dear, is he happy who has nothing to desire but something to fear?

SOFYA. I see what a difference there is between seeming happy and really being so. It's incomprehensible to me, Uncle, how a man can think only of himself. Really, don't people reflect how each is obligated to the next? Where is that intelligence for which they are so celebrated?

STARODUM. How be celebrated for intelligence, my dear! Intelligence, insofar as it is only intelligence, is the merest trifle. We see the keenest minds in bad husbands, bad fathers, bad citizens. Good conduct gives it real value. Without such conduct an intelligent man is a monster. It is above all intellectual wit. Anyone may easily understand this who thinks on it well. There are many minds, and all are different. One may easily excuse an intelligent man for not having a certain intellectual quality. One may never forgive an honorable man for lacking a certain spiritual quality. He absolutely must have them all. The virtue of the heart is indivisible. An honorable man must be a completely honorable man.

SOFYA. Your explication, Uncle, corresponds with what I feel inside, which I couldn't express. I now vividly feel both the worth of an honorable man and his duty.

STARODUM. Duty! Ah, my dear! How this word's on everyone's tongue and how few understand it! The hourly use of this word has so accustomed us to it that, saying it, a man means nothing by it, feels nothing, though if people sensed its significance none could utter it without sincere respect. Just think what duty is. It is that sacred vow by which we all are bound to those we live with and on whom we depend. If people did their duty the way they talk about it, every estate in life would have its proper honor and would be completely happy. The noble, for example, would consider it the prime dishonor to do nothing when there is so much for him to do: people to help and his country to serve. Then there would be no such nobles whose nobility, one may say, lies buried with their ancestors. A noble unworthy of being a noble! I know of nothing in the world fouler than that!

SOFYA. Is it possible for a man so to debase himself?

STARODUM. My dear! What I said about the nobleman we may now extend to man in general. Everyone has his duties. Let's see how they're fulfilled: what, for example, the greater part of today's husbands are like and, let's not forget, what their wives are like. Oh, my dear friend! Now I require all your attention. Let's take as example an unhappy home, of which there are many, where the wife has no kind of genuine friendship for the husband and he has no faith in his wife; where each, for his own part, has fallen from the path of virtue. Instead of a sincere and indulgent friend, the wife sees in her own husband a vulgar, corrupted tyrant. On the other hand, instead of gentleness, open-heartedness, the accomplishments of a virtuous wife, the husband sees in his wife only self-centered impudence, and impudence in a woman is the sign of depraved conduct. They both become an unbearable burden on each other. Neither has a good name in anything, for both have lost it. Can there be a position more terrible than this? The house is lost. Its servants forget the duty of obedience, seeing in their own master a slave of vile passions. The estate is squandered: it becomes nobody's for its lord is not his own master. The children, their unhappy children, are orphaned even while their mother and father live. The father, having no respect for his wife, can hardly embrace them, can hardly yield to the tenderest emotions of the human heart. The innocent young are also deprived of a mother's warmth. She, unworthy of having children, shuns their caresses, seeing in them either the cause of her anxieties or the reproach for her depravity. And what sort of upbringing can children expect from a mother who has lost virtue? How can she teach them good behavior, of which she has none? In those moments when their thought turns to their position, what hell must not the husband and wife suffer?

SOFYA. My God! Why are there such terrible woes!

STARODUM. Because, my dear, in marriages nowadays people rarely consult the heart. The issue is all: is the man noble, is he rich? is the bride pretty? is she rich? There is no issue of right conduct. It doesn't enter anyone's head that in the eyes of thoughtful people an honest man without great rank is greater than a person of technical nobility, that virtue takes precedence over all, but that nothing can take the place of virtue. I confess to you that my heart will be at rest only when I see you married to a man worthy of your heart, when your mutual love—

SOFYA. Yes, how can one not intimately love a worthy husband?

STARODUM. Right. Only please don't have for your husband a love that resembles friendship. Have for him the friendship that resembles love. This is much more lasting. Then, after twenty years of marriage, you each will still find in your hearts your former bonds with the other. A prudent husband! A virtuous wife! What can be more honorable! Your husband, my dear, must bow to reason, and you, to your husband, and you both will be completely happy—

SOFYA. Everything you say touches my heart—

STARODUM (*with tenderest warmth*). And mine is delighted at your responsiveness. Your happiness depends on yourself. God gave you all the charms of your sex. I see in you the heart of an honest person. You, my dearest, unite in yourself the perfections of both sexes. I flatter myself that my zeal does not deceive me, that virtue—

SOFYA. You have suffused all my emotions with it. (*Rushing to kiss his hand*) Where may it be?

STARODUM (*himself kissing her hands*). It is in your soul. I thank God that in yourself I find the firm foundation of your happiness. It will not depend either on nobility or on wealth. All this may come to you, but you have a happiness still greater than all this. It is to feel yourself worthy of all blessings which you may enjoy—

SOFYA. Uncle! My real happiness is that I have you. I know the value—

(*A valet enters, hands* STARODUM *a letter.*)

STARODUM. Where from?

VALET. From Moscow, by special delivery. (*Exits*)

STARODUM (*breaking the seal and looking at the signature*). Count Chestan. Ah! (*Beginning to read, indicates that he cannot see the writing*) Sofyushka! My glasses are on the table, in the book.

SOFYA (*going*). Right away, Uncle! (*Exits*)

STARODUM (*alone*). He, of course, writes me about what he proposed in Moscow. I don't know Milon, but since his uncle, my true friend, since everybody considers him an honest and worthy man— If her heart is free—

(SOFYA *returns.*)

SOFYA (*handing him the glasses*). I found them, Uncle.

STARODUM (*reads*). ". . . I only now found out . . . he is bringing his command to Moscow. . . . He must meet you. . . . I will be sincerely happy if he meets you. . . . Take the trouble to find out his cast of mind." (*Aside*) Of course. Without that I won't give her away. "You'll find . . . Yours most sincerely . . ." Good. This letter concerns you. I have told you that a young man of laudable qualities, introduced— My words embarrass you, my dearest. I noticed this not long ago, and see it now. Your trust in me—

SOFYA. Can I conceal anything in my heart from you? No, Uncle. I'll frankly tell you—

(PRAVDIN *and* MILON *enter.*)

PRAVDIN. Allow me to introduce to you Mr. Milon, my true friend.

STARODUM (*aside*). Milon!

MILON. I shall consider it my real fortune if I be found worthy of your good opinion, your favor—

STARODUM. Isn't Count Chestan a relative of yours by marriage?

MILON. He's my uncle.

STARODUM. I'm very pleased to have met a man of your qualities. Your uncle spoke to me about you. He renders you full justice. Particular merits—

MILON. That is his kindness to me. At my age and in my position it would be unforgivable arrogance to consider everything deserved by which worthy men encourage a young man.

PRAVDIN. I'm certain beforehand that my friend will win your favor when you know him better. He was often in your sister's house—

(STARODUM *looks at* SOFYA.)

SOFYA (*quietly to* STARODUM *and very timidly*). And Mother loved him like a son.

STARODUM (*to* SOFYA). This pleases me greatly. (*To* MILON) I've heard that you were in the army. Your bravery—

MILON. I did my duty. Neither my age, nor rank, nor position has yet allowed me to show real bravery, if indeed it is in me.

STARODUM. What! Being in battles and going through—

MILON. I went through what others did. Courage was that quality of heart which the commander ordered the soldier to have but which was the officer's honor.

STARODUM. I'm most curious to know what you consider real bravery is.

MILON. If I may express my thoughts on this, I mean real

bravery of soul and not of heart. The man who has a brave soul has, without any doubt, a courageous heart. In our military business the soldier must be courageous; the commander, brave. He weighs all the dangers in cold blood, takes the necessary measures, prefers his glory more than life, but above all he is not scared to forget his personal glory for the good of his country. His bravery, consequently, does not lie in scorn for his life. He never just ventures it. He knows how to sacrifice it.

STARODUM. Quite right. You assert real bravery in the commander. Is it appropriate to others?

MILON. It is virtue. Consequently, there is no person who may not be distinguished by it. It seems to me that courage shows itself in the hour of battle; but bravery, in all the trials and tribulations of life. What a difference there is between the courage of the soldier who in attack risks his life along with others and the bravery of the civil servant who tells the Tsar the truth, risking his anger. The judge who, fearing neither the vengeance nor the threats of the powerful man, administers justice to the helpless is in my eyes a hero. How small is the man who calls a duel over a trifle compared to the man who intercedes for a man whose honor, in his absence, is torn to shreds by slanderers. I understand bravery—

STARODUM. As it must be understood by one who is. Embrace me, dear friend! Forgive my simplicity. I am a friend to honest people. This feeling is rooted in my upbringing. In yours I see and esteem virtue embellished with enlightened reason.

MILON. Noble soul! No—I can no longer conceal what my heart feels. No. Your virtue itself calls forth all the secrets of my heart. If my heart is virtuous, if it is worthy of being happy, its happiness depends on you. I can conceive it only in having as a wife your dearest niece. Our mutual inclination—

STARODUM (*to* SOFYA, *joyfully*). What! Your heart knew how to single out the one I myself intended for you? Here's the groom I offer you—

SOFYA. And I love him sincerely.

STARODUM. You each are worthy of the other. (*In delight,*

joining their hands) With all my heart I give you my consent.

MILON (*embracing* STARODUM). My happiness is immeasurable! } (*Together*)

SOFYA (*kissing* STARODUM'S *hands*). Who can be happier than I! } (*Together*)

PRAVDIN. How sincerely glad I am!

(SKOTININ *enters*.)

SKOTININ. Here's me.

STARODUM. What did you come in for?

SKOTININ. For what I need.

STARODUM. And what may I do for you?

SKOTININ. Say two words.

STARODUM. Which are?

SKOTININ. Embracing me tightly, say: Sofyushka's yours.

STARODUM. Aren't you undertaking the impossible? Consider well.

SKOTININ. I never think, and I'm sure ahead of time that if you don't think about it either, why, Sofyushka's mine.

STARODUM. How can you wish me to give my niece away to someone I don't know?

SKOTININ. Don't know me; well, I'll tell you. I'm Taras Skotinin, and not the last of my line. The Skotinin line is great and ancient. You'll never find our ancestors in the Heralds' College.

PRAVDIN (*laughing*). And so you assure us that it's older than Adam?

SKOTININ. What do you think? Although a bit—

STARODUM (*laughing*). That is, your ancestor was created even on the sixth day, just a little bit before Adam?

SKOTININ. No, really? So you've a good opinion about the ancientness of my line?

STARODUM. Oh, such a good opinion that I'm surprised a man in your position can choose a wife from a family other than Skotinin.

SKOTININ. Well, just think what a joy for Sofyushka it'll be to be married to me. She's only of Court nobility.

STARODUM. What a man! That's exactly why you're not her suitor.

SKOTININ. Now I've done it. Let 'em talk about Skotinin's

marrying a little noblewoman. It's all the same to me.

STARODUM. But it's not all the same to her when people will say that a noblewoman married a Skotinin.

MILON. Such inequality would make you both unhappy.

SKOTININ. Naw! Besides what's he competing here for? (*To* STARODUM *quietly*) He's not beating me, is he?

STARODUM (*quietly to* SKOTININ). It seems to me he is.

SKOTININ (*same tone*). I'll be damned!

STARODUM (*same tone*). It's rough.

SKOTININ (*loudly, pointing to* MILON). Which of us is ridiculous? Ha, ha, ha, ha!

STARODUM (*laughing*). I see who's ridiculous.

SOFYA. Uncle! I'm so glad you're happy.

SKOTININ (*to* STARODUM). Yeah, you're a real joker. Not long ago I used to think a fellow couldn't get near you. You wouldn't say a word to me, and now here you're laughing away with me.

STARODUM. That's what man is, my friend. We're not the same from one minute to the next.

SKOTININ. That's clear. But not long ago I was the same Skotinin, and you got angry.

STARODUM. There was a reason.

SKOTININ. I know it. That's just the way I am, too. At home, when I go into the sties and don't find them in order, I get real annoyed. Like you, and this is just between you and I, once you got here, you found my sister's house no better off than the sties, and you got annoyed.

STARODUM. You're more fortunate than I. People affect me.

SKOTININ. But pigs, me.

(MRS. PROSTAKOV, PROSTAKOV, MITROFAN *and* EREMEYEVNA *enter.*)

MRS. PROSTAKOV (*entering*). You got everything, Mitrofanushka?

MITROFAN. Yeah, don't worry.

MRS. PROSTAKOV (*to* STARODUM). We came, dear, to impose on you now our common request. (*To her husband and son*) Bow.

STARODUM. What's that, madam?

MRS. PROSTAKOV. First, I beg everyone to sit down. (*All sit except* MITROFAN *and* EREMEYEVNA) This is what it's all about, dear. In answer to our parents' prayers—for how could we sinners have ever demanded it—God bestowed Mitrofanushka on us. We have done everything so he'd be just the way you see him. Wouldn't you like, dear sir, to take the trouble of seeing how well he's been schooled here?

STARODUM. Oh, madam! It has already reached my ears that he only now may be weaned from learning. I have found out who his teachers are. I can already see what reading he must know, studying with Kuteikin; and what mathematics, studying with Tsyfirkin. (*To* PRAVDIN) I'd be most curious to hear what the German taught him.

MRS. PROSTAKOV. All the sciences, dear.
PROSTAKOV. Everything, old man.
MITROFAN. Anything you want.
PRAVDIN (*to* MITROFAN). What, for example?
(*Together*)

MITROFAN (*hands him a book*). Here, grammar.

PRAVDIN (*taking the book*). I see. This is a grammar book. What do you know in it?

MITROFAN. Lots. Nominals and adjèctivals—

PRAVDIN. Door, for example, is a substantive or an adjective?

MITROFAN. Door, which door?

PRAVDIN. Which door! That door.

MITROFAN. That one? Adjectival.

PRAVDIN. Why?

MITROFAN. Cause it's adjected to its place. Up in the storeroom the door's not been hung six weeks now, so for the time being it's nominal.

STARODUM. Therefore, as far as you're concerned, the word fool is an attributive because it's attributed to a stupid man?

MITROFAN. That's correct.

MRS. PROSTAKOV. Well, how about it, my dear?

PROSTAKOV. How about it, old man?

PRAVDIN. Couldn't be better. He's strong in grammar.

MILON. I'm sure he's no weaker in history.

MRS. PROSTAKOV. Oh, sir, from the time he was little he was a lover of stories.

SKOTININ. Mitrofan takes after me. I myself always gotta keep on the lookout so's the county delegate don't put one over on me. A master, the son of a bitch; where does he get it from?

MRS. PROSTAKOV. However, all the same he can't beat Adam Adamych.

PRAVDIN (*to* MITROFAN). And have you gone deeply into history?

MITROFAN. Deeply? That's a fine story. In another you go miles and miles, to the other end of the world.

PRAVDIN. Ah! So that's the history Wrahlman teaches you?

STARODUM. Wrahlman? The name's somehow familiar.

PRAVDIN. You don't happen to know geography just as well, do you?

MRS. PROSTAKOV (*to her son*). You hear, my dearest? What sort of a science is that?

MITROFAN (*quietly to his mother*). How should I know?

MRS. PROSTAKOV (*quietly to* MITROFAN). Don't be stubborn, sweetie. Now's the time to show your stuff.

MITROFAN (*quietly to his mother*). But I can't make any sense out of what they're asking about.

MRS. PROSTAKOV (*to* PRAVDIN). What, dear, did you call this science?

PRAVDIN. Geography.

MRS. PROSTAKOV (*to* MITROFAN). You hear, ejography.

MITROFAN. What the hell's that? My God! He's got his knife at my throat.

MRS. PROSTAKOV (*to* PRAVDIN). Correct, dear. But tell him, be so kind, what kind of science this is, and he'll recite it.

PRAVDIN. Description of the earth.

MRS. PROSTAKOV (*to* STARODUM). And what's the first thing it's good for?

STARODUM. The first thing it's good for is, if you have occasion to travel, you can know where you're going.

MRS. PROSTAKOV. Ah, my dear! But what are the cabbies for? That's their job. So it's not the kind of science for nobles. The noble just says: Take me there. And they take you where you want. Believe me, dear, that of course what Mitrofanushka doesn't know is junk.

STARODUM. Of course, madam. In human ignorance it is very reassuring to consider junk everything you don't know.

SKOTININ. That studying is junk my late uncle Vavila Faleleyevich proved incontrovertibly. Nobody never heard a word from him about reading, and he never wanted to hear nothing about it from nobody. And what a head he had!

PRAVDIN. How's that?

SKOTININ. Well, this is what was bound to happen to him and did. Sitting on a real fast pacer he was drunk and was jumping through a stone gate. The man was tall, the gate was low, he forgot to bend. And just the minute he catches his forehead on the lintel, he gets knocked ass-over-teakettle and the fiery steed carried him out of the gate right to the porch flat on his back. I'd like to know if there's a scholarly head in the world which wouldn't of been busted from such a swat. And my uncle, God bless him, sobering up asked only if the gate was still in one piece.

MILON. You, Mr. Skotinin, yourself admit you're not a scholarly person; however, I think that in such an instance your forehead would be no firmer than that of a scholar.

STARODUM (*to* MILON). Don't bet on it. I think all the Skotinins are hard-headed by birth.

MRS. PROSTAKOV. Dear sir! What joy is there in learning? (*To* PRAVDIN) You yourself, dear, are cleverer than the rest and look how you work! Why just now, coming here, I noticed they were taking some kind of package to you.

PRAVDIN. A package for me? And no one tells me! (*Rising*) I beg you to excuse me. Perhaps I have received some instructions from the deputy.

STARODUM (*rises, and they all rise*). Go, my friend. But I won't bid you good-bye.

PRAVDIN. I'll see you again. You're leaving tomorrow morning?

STARODUM. At seven.

(PRAVDIN *exits.*)

MILON. And after I've seen you off tomorrow, I'll lead my command on. Now I must go give directions for that. (*He exits, saying good-bye to* SOFYA *by glances*)

MRS. PROSTAKOV (*to* STARODUM). Well, dear! You seen enough of what Mitrofanushka's like?

SKOTININ. Well, my dear friend? You see what I'm like?

STARODUM. I know you both, couldn't know you better.

SKOTININ. Is Sofyushka going to be mine?

STARODUM. No, she isn't.

MRS. PROSTAKOV. Is Mitrofanushka her groom?

STARODUM. Not her groom.

MRS. PROSTAKOV. Well, what happened? } (*Together*)
SKOTININ. What's the trouble?

STARODUM (*drawing them together*). I can tell only you what the secret is. She's promised. (*Exits and indicates to* SOFYA *to follow him*)

MRS. PROSTAKOV. The rat!

SKOTININ. He's off his rocker.

MRS. PROSTAKOV (*impatiently*). When are they leaving?

SKOTININ. You heard yourself. Seven in the morning.

MRS. PROSTAKOV. Seven o'clock.

SKOTININ. Tomorrow all of a sudden I'll wake up with the sun. Let him be as smart as he pleases, but you don't get away from a Skotinin so easy. (*Exits*)

MRS. PROSTAKOV (*running back and forth, cross and thoughtful*). Seven o'clock. We'll get up earlier—what I wanted, I'll bet on— You all come here. (*All run up to her. To her husband*) Tomorrow at six get the carriage up to the back porch. You hear? Don't fail.

PROSTAKOV. I hear you, Mother.

MRS. PROSTAKOV (*to* EREMEYEVNA). Don't you dare even drowse all night outside Sofya's door. Just ever she wakes, run to me.

EREMEYEVNA. Won't bat a lid, my dear.

MRS. PROSTAKOV (*to her son*). You, dear friend, be completely ready at six o'clock and don't let your servants out of the room.

MITROFAN. All'll be done.

MRS. PROSTAKOV. God be with you. (*All exeunt*) I already know what's to be done. Where there's anger there's mercy. The old guy'll get angry and then he'll forgive, can't help himself. And we'll get ours.

ACT V

STARODUM *and* PRAVDIN *on stage.*

PRAVDIN. This was that package which our hostess told me about yesterday in your presence.

STARODUM. So now you have the means of bringing an end to the inhumanity of this evil lady landowner?

PRAVDIN. I'm instructed to take into custody the house and the village at the first frenzy from which the people under her might suffer.

STARODUM. Thanks be to God that humanity can find defense! Believe me, where the sovereign thinks, where he knows in what his real glory lies, there mankind cannot *not* recover its rights. There all soon feel that each must seek his happiness and benefit in what is lawful—and that it is unlawful to oppress your equals by slavery.

PRAVDIN. In this I agree with you. How hard it is to exterminate those deep-set prejudices in which base souls discover their advantage!

STARODUM. Listen, my friend! A great sovereign is the wisest. His function is to show people their immediate good. The glory of his wisdom is that of ruling men, for there is no wisdom in managing statues. The peasant who is lowest in the village is generally chosen to shepherd the flocks, because not much intelligence is required to shepherd animals. A sovereign worthy of the throne endeavors to elevate the spirit of his subjects. We see this with our very own eyes.

PRAVDIN. The pleasure which sovereigns enjoy who possess free subjects must be so great that I don't understand what inducements could distract—

STARODUM. How great a soul must the sovereign have to hold to the path of truth and never veer from it! First, there's the mob of stingy flatterers—

PRAVDIN. Without real scorn one cannot even imagine what a flatterer is.

STARODUM. A flatterer is a creature who has a bad opinion not only of others but also of himself. His whole desire is first to blind a man's mind and then make him into what he needs. He's a thief by night who first puts out the candle and then begins to steal.

PRAVDIN. People's misfortune is, of course, caused by their own corruption; but the means to make people happy—

STARODUM. Are in the sovereign's hands. As soon as everyone sees that without virtuous conduct no one can get on in society, that neither by base service nor for any amount of money can what merit deserves be bought, that people are chosen for positions and not positions abducted by people—then each will find it his advantage to be decent and each will become good.

PRAVDIN. Right. A great sovereign gives—

STARODUM. Favor and friendship to whom he pleases; positions and privilege to who is worthy.

PRAVDIN. So that there'll be no dearth of worthy people a special effort is presently being made in education—

STARODUM. It must be the security of the state's prosperity. We see all the unhappy consequences of a bad upbringing. What can accrue to our country from Mitrofanushka, for whom his boorish parents pay hard cash to boorish teachers? How many noblemen-fathers there are who entrust the moral education of their boy to their serf! Fifteen years from now and there'll be two serfs instead of one, the old tutor and the young lord.

PRAVDIN. But people of the upper class enlighten their children—

STARODUM. Quite true. Indeed, I might wish that in the course of all studies the chief aim of all human knowledge were never forgotten—virtuous conduct. Believe me that learning in a corrupt man is a fierce weapon for evil. Education elevates only the virtuous soul. I wish, for example, that in the process of educating the son of a noble gentleman, the tutor would every day open out his history book and show him two places in it: one, how great men served their country's good, and the other; how an important but unworthy person, using his confidence and power for evil ends, fell from the luxurious heights of his nobility into the abyss of scorn and defamation.

PRAVDIN. What is really needed is that every class of people have its own adequate education. Then one could be certain— What's the noise?

STARODUM. What's going on?

(MILON, SOFYA, *and* EREMEYEVNA *enter.*)

MILON (*pushing* EREMEYEVNA *from* SOFYA, EREMEYEVNA *having just about fastened on to her; shouts to his men, holding his bare sword in his hand*). No one dare come near me!

SOFYA (*throwing herself at* STARODUM). Uncle! Save me!

STARODUM. My dear! What is it?
PRAVDIN. What crime now?!?
SOFYA. My heart's trembling!
EREMEYEVNA. I've had it now.
(*Together*)

MILON. Criminals! Coming here, I see a lot of people who, grabbing her under her arms, despite her resistance and shouting, carry her off the porch toward a carriage.

SOFYA. He's my savior!

STARODUM. My dear friend!

PRAVDIN (*to* EREMEYEVNA). Tell us at once, where did they want to take her, or like a criminal—?

EREMEYEVNA. To get married, dear sir, to get married!!

MRS. PROSTAKOV (*from the wings*). Cheats! Thieves! Swindlers! I'll have you all crucified!

(MRS. PROSTAKOV, PROSTAKOV, *and* MITROFAN *enter.*)

MRS. PROSTAKOV. I'm not even the boss in my own house! (*Pointing to* MILON) A stranger makes threats, but my order means nothing.

PRAVDIN. The foul play of which I was a witness gives you, as uncle, and you, as future husband, the right—

MRS. PROSTAKOV. Future husband!
PROSTAKOV. We're real good!
MITROFAN. God damn you all!
(*Together*)

PRAVDIN. Of requesting of the government that the insult she has inflicted be punished with the full severity of the law. I will myself summon her to Court as a disturber of the civil peace.

MRS. PROSTAKOV (*falling on her knees*). Dear sir, forgive me!

PRAVDIN. The husband and son could not but abet the foul business—

PROSTAKOV. Guilty but guiltless.
MITROFAN. Forgive me, Uncle.
(*Together, falling on their knees*)

MRS. PROSTAKOV. I'll be god-damned! What I've done!

(SKOTININ *enters.*)

SKOTININ. Well, Sister, a joke'd be all right— What's this? All our people on their knees!

MRS. PROSTAKOV (*kneeling*). Ah, my dears, the sword can't cut off a shriven head. It's all my fault! Don't ruin me. (*To* SOFYA) My dearest lady, forgive me. Have mercy on me and (*pointing to her husband and son*) on these poor orphans.

SKOTININ. Sister! You in your right mind?

PRAVDIN. Silence, Skotinin.

MRS. PROSTAKOV. God will give you real happiness with your dear husband, so what do you want my head for?

SOFYA (*to* STARODUM). Uncle! I will forget the insult.

MRS. PROSTAKOV (*raising her arms to* STARODUM). Dear sir! Forgive me, miserable sinner that I am. I'm only human, not an angel.

STARODUM. I know, I know, man can't be an angel, but that doesn't mean he has to be a devil.

MILON. Both the crime and her remorse are fit for contempt.

PRAVDIN (*to* STARODUM). Your slightest complaint, just one word from you to the government—and she can't be saved.

STARODUM. I don't wish anyone's ruin. I forgive her.

(*All jump up off their knees.*)

MRS. PROSTAKOV. He forgave me! Ah, dear! Well, and now I'll go give a once-over to these rascals of mine. Now I'll sort 'em all out one by one. Now I'll find out who let her get away. No, swindlers! No, thieves! Not for the rest of my life I won't forgive you, won't forgive this mockery.

PRAVDIN. And just what do you want to punish your servants for?

MRS. PROSTAKOV. Ah, dear, what kind of question's that? Don't I have the last word over my servants?

PRAVDIN. So you consider you have the right to beat them whenever you take it into your head to?

SKOTININ. Yeah, isn't the noble free to beat his servant when he feels like it?

PRAVDIN. When he feels like it! What kind of feeling is that? You're a real Pigster. (*To* MRS. PROSTAKOV) No, madam, no one is free to tyrannize anyone.

MRS. PROSTAKOV. Not free! The noble, when he feels like it,

isn't free to beat up his servant? Then what's this directive about the freedom of the nobility given us for?

STARODUM. A past master in discussing directives!

MRS. PROSTAKOV. You can jeer, but now I'm going out and knock everybody's head together. (*Tries to leave*)

PRAVDIN (*stopping her*). Stop, madam. (*Taking out a sheet of paper, and in an important tone to* PROSTAKOV) In the name of the government I order you this very moment to convoke your people and your serfs to announce to them the decree that, due to the inhumanity of your wife, in which she was tolerated and abetted by your extreme weakness of mind, the government instructs me to take into custody your house and your villages.

PROSTAKOV. What have we come to!?

MRS. PROSTAKOV. What! More trouble!? What for, dear? That I'm the mistress in my own house—

PRAVDIN. An inhumane mistress whose evil conduct in our benevolent state can no longer be tolerated. (*To* PROSTAKOV) Go.

PROSTAKOV (*exits, wringing his hands*). Who's done this, Mother?

MRS. PROSTAKOV (*anguished*). Oh, miserable, miserable! Oh, so sad!

SKOTININ. Pah, pah, pah! Yeah, and then they'll come after me, too. Yeah, and that's the way every Skotinin can fall into custody. I'll slip out of here while I'm still in one piece.

MRS. PROSTAKOV. I've lost everything. I'm completely ruined.

SKOTININ (*to* STARODUM). I was coming to you to find out the story. The suitor—

STARODUM (*pointing to* MILON). Is there.

SKOTININ. Ah! Ha! So there's nothing for me to do around here. Hitch up the wagon and a—

PRAVDIN. Yes, go to your sties. I advise you, however, to proceed with caution. I have heard that you get on incomparably better with your pigs than with people.

SKOTININ (*leaving timidly*). My dearest sir, how can I ever have the heart for people? People are so clever in front of me, but among pigs I'm the smartest of all.

MRS. PROSTAKOV (*to* PRAVDIN). Dear sir, don't ruin me. What's in it for you? Can't a person somehow change the decree just a little? Are all decrees really carried out?

PRAVDIN. I will in no way fail to do my duty.

MRS. PROSTAKOV. Give me a chance, just three days. (*Aside*) They'd see what I can do.

PRAVDIN. Not even three hours.

STARODUM. Yes, my friend! In three hours she'd do such mischief you couldn't straighten it out in a hundred years.

MRS. PROSTAKOV. But how can you, dear sir, take care of the details?

PRAVDIN. That's my business. The things that aren't yours will be returned to their proper owners, and—

MRS. PROSTAKOV. And you'll divvy up the debts? The teachers aren't paid up—

PRAVDIN. The teachers? (*To* EREMEYEVNA) Are they here? Show them in.

EREMEYEVNA. I figure they're waiting. And the German one, sir?

PRAVDIN. Call them all. (EREMEYEVNA *exits*) Don't worry about anything, madam, for I will satisfy everyone.

STARODUM (*seeing* MRS. PROSTAKOV *depressed*). Madam! You yourself will feel much better for having lost the power of harming others.

MRS. PROSTAKOV. Thanks for the kindness! What am I good for, when in my own house my hands are tied?

(EREMEYEVNA *returns with* WRAHLMAN, KUTEIKIN, *and* TSYFIRKIN.)

EREMEYEVNA (*showing the teachers to* PRAVDIN). Here you have all the bums, sir.

WRAHLMAN (*to* PRAVDIN). Your most eshteemed hexèllency. Ver you pleast to ask for me?

KUTEIKIN (*to* PRAVDIN). They called unto me, and I came.

TSYFIRKIN (*to* PRAVDIN). What'll the order be, your excellency?

STARODUM (*studying* WRAHLMAN *from the time he entered*). Is it you, Wrahlman?

WRAHLMAN (*recognizing* STARODUM). Ai, ai, ai, ai, ai! It's you, my most gravious mester! (*Kissing the hem of* STARODUM'S *coat*) Iss evrytink koink mit you, our fadder, real vell?

PRAVDIN. What? Do you know him?

STARODUM. How couldn't I? He was my coachman for three years.

(*All show amazement.*)

PRAVDIN. A fine teacher!

STARODUM. Are you here as a teacher, Wrahlman? I thought, really, you were an honest man and wouldn't claim what isn't yours.

WRAHLMAN. Vat's to pe done, sir? I'm not de first, I'm not de last. Tree monts I kicked arount Moscaw mitout a place, a coachmen isn't neetet anyver. For me it vass eeter to die off hunger or be a teecher—

PRAVDIN (*to the teachers*). By order of the government custodian of this house, I dismiss you.

TSYFIRKIN. Couldn't be better.

KUTEIKIN. You have the kindness to dismiss us? But let's first settle things—

PRAVDIN. And what do you want?

KUTEIKIN. No, kind sir, my account's nothing like short. For teaching for half a year, for the footwear I've gone through in three years, for standing idle—you'd often come here, you know, for nothing—for—

MRS. PROSTAKOV. Greedy man! Carouser! What's this for?

PRAVDIN. Don't interfere, madam, I beg you.

MRS. PROSTAKOV. When it comes right down to it, what'd you teach Mitrofanushka?

KUTEIKIN. That's his business, not mine.

PRAVDIN (*to* KUTEIKIN). Very well, very well. (*To* TSYFIRKIN) Is there much to be paid you?

TSYFIRKIN. Me? Nothing.

MRS. PROSTAKOV. He was given, dear, ten rubles one year, but for the last year he didn't get two kopeks.

TSYFIRKIN. Right. Those ten rubles cover the boots I wore out in two years. We're quits.

PRAVDIN. But for teaching?

TSYFIRKIN. Nothing.

STARODUM. How, nothing?

TSYFIRKIN. I won't take anything. He didn't take anything in.

STARODUM. But all the same one must pay you.

TSYFIRKIN. Not a bit. I served the Tsar over twenty years. Took money for serving, never took it for nothing, and won't.

STARODUM. That's a really honest man!!

(STARODUM *and* MILON *take money out of their purses.*)

PRAVDIN. Aren't you ashamed, Kuteikin?

KUTEIKIN (*dropping his head*). I'm disgraced, cursed man that I am.

STARODUM (*to* TSYFIRKIN). Here you are, my man, for an honest soul.

TSYFIRKIN. Thanks, your excellency. I'm grateful. You're free to give me something. As long as I don't deserve it, I'll never in my life ask for it.

MILON (*giving him money*). Here's some more for you, my friend!

TSYFIRKIN. And thanks again. (PRAVDIN *also gives him some money*) But what are you so kind for, your excellency?

PRAVDIN. For the fact that you're not like Kuteikin.

TSYFIRKIN. Your excellency! I'm a soldier!

PRAVDIN (*to* TSYFIRKIN). God be with you, my friend. (TSYFIRKIN *exits*) But, Kuteikin, you please be here tomorrow, and try to settle your account with the madam herself.

KUTEIKIN (*running out*). With herself! I give it all up.

WRAHLMAN (*to* STARODUM). Do not leef your olt serfant, your hexellency. Take me back mit you akin.

STARODUM. But you, Wrahlman, I expect, are no longer used to horses?

WRAHLMAN. Ei, no, sir! Leefink mit dese people, seems, I leef all de time mit horses.

(*Valet enters.*)

VALET (*to* STARODUM). Your carriage is ready.

WRAHLMAN. Vill you order me to drife you?

STARODUM. Go sit on the box.

(WRAHLMAN *exits.*)

STARODUM (*to* PRAVDIN, *holding* SOFYA *and* MILON'S *hands*). Well, my friend! We're going. Wish us—

PRAVDIN. All the best, as true hearts have the right to have.

MRS. PROSTAKOV (*throwing herself on her son*). Only you're left to me, my dearest Mitrofanushka!

MITROFAN. Leave me alone, Mother. I'm fed up with you—

MRS. PROSTAKOV. You, too! You, too, are deserting me! Thankless— (*Falls in a faint*)

SOFYA (*running over to her*). My Lord! She's unconscious.

STARODUM (*to* SOFYA). Help her, help her.

(SOFYA *and* EREMEYEVNA *lend a hand.*)

PRAVDIN (*to* MITROFAN). Good-for-nothing! How can you insult your mother? Her insane love for you is what more than anything else brought her to a bad end.

MITROFAN. Yeah, she somehow mysteriously—

PRAVDIN. Boor!

STARODUM (*to* EREMEYEVNA). How's she now? How is she?

EREMEYEVNA (*looking intently at* MRS. PROSTAKOV *and wringing her hands*). She's coming to, sir, coming to.

PRAVDIN (*to* MITROFAN). I know what to do with you, young man. Into the service—

MITROFAN (*waving his hand*). As for me, whatever they say—

MRS. PROSTAKOV (*coming to, in despair*). I'm completely ruined! My power's gone! I can't show myself for shame no place! My boy's gone!

STARODUM (*pointing to* MRS. PROSTAKOV). These are the fruits of evil conduct!

The Trouble with Reason

A COMEDY IN
FOUR ACTS
IN VERSE

Aleksandr Sergeyevich Griboyedov

DRAMATIS PERSONAE

Pavel Afanasyevich Famusov, manager of a government office
Sofya [Sofiya] Pavlovna, his daughter
Lizanka [Liza], a maid
Aleksei Stepanovich Molchalin, Famusov's secretary, resident in his house
Aleksandr Andreyevich Chatsky
Colonel Sergei Sergeyevich Skalozub
Natalya Dmitriyevna Gorich, a young lady
Platon Mikhailovich, her husband
Prince Tugoukhovsky and his wife, the Princess, with six daughters
The grandmother, Countess Khryumin
The granddaughter, Countess Khryumin
Anton Antonovich Zagoretsky
Old Lady Khlyostov, Famusov's sister-in-law [his wife's sister]
Mr. N.
Mr. D.
Repetilov
Petrushka and several servants with speaking roles
A number of guests of every description and their footmen
Famusov's stewards

The action takes place in Famusov's house in Moscow.

A NOTE ON SOME OF THE NAMES

FÁMUSOV. From the Latin *fama* (rumor) or *famosus* (well known). A fictitious character but based, at least in part, on Griboyedov's uncle.

SÓFYA PÁVLOVNA. Sofya is a typical, classical heroine's name.

MOLCHÁLIN. From *molchat'*, *molchanie*, *molchalivy* (to keep quiet, silence, taciturn).

CHÁTSKY. In one manuscript spelled *Chadsky* and therefore sometimes said to come from *chad* (fumes, dazedness).

SKALOZÚB. From *skalit' zuby* (to grin, to show one's teeth).

TUGOÚKHOVSKY. From *túgo* (tight, taut) and *úkho* (ear), as in the phrase *tugói ná ukho* (hard of hearing).

KHRYÚMIN. Perhaps a combination of *khryúkat'* (to grunt) and *ugryúmy* (sullen).

ZAGORÉTSKY. Suggests *zagoret'/zagoret'sya* (to bake in the sun, to catch fire, to light up, to be all eager).

KHLYÓSTOV. From *khlyostky* (trenchant). A portrait of Natalya Dmitriyevna Ofrosimova, portrayed in *War and Peace* as Akhrosimova.

REPETÍLOV. From the Latin *repeto* (I repeat) and Shatilov, a contemporary of Griboyedov's, who was the prototype of the dramatic character.

A NOTE ON THE PLAY

Pushkin wrote in a letter in January, 1825, after he had read a manuscript of Griboyedov's play, that half the lines were bound to become proverbs. In May, Odoyevsky said that almost all the lines already had—though the play was not printed until 1833, and then in a cut and censored form. At the end of the century, a scholar computed that over sixty phrases or aphorisms from the play had in fact become proverbial—that is, were cited by people who had never read or seen it. The play was widely circulated in manuscript copies. The Academy edition of Groboyedov's complete works (1911–17, ed. N. K. Piksanov) was the first publication of an authoritative text.

Groboyedov's other work is fragmentary and unimportant: a series of dramatic collaborations which produced comedies based usually on French sources, and some critical essays in literary magazines (1815–18). His work on *The Trouble with Reason* started sometime during his service under Ermolov in Tiflis in 1823 and was completed during his residency near Moscow between March, 1823, and May, 1824. The first and third acts of the play were published in *Russkaya Taliya* in 1825, but heavily censored. Griboyedov himself, a friend of almost all the important literary and social figures of the time, was implicated in the 1825 Decembrist uprising, imprisoned, finally exonerated and recompensed, and appointed Minister to Persia. In a violent anti-Russian riot in Teheran on January 30, 1829, all the Russian legation staff except one were massacred and mutilated, Griboyedov among them.

Russians and Russian writers since 1824 have turned to this play again and again as their greatest classic drama. Blok even said that it was perhaps the greatest work in Russian literature. Goncharov said (1871) that the figures in the play would live forever and had already outlasted Pushkin's Onegin, Lermontov's Pechorin, and the works of the age of Gogol. There are several reasons for such estimates:

First, the language of the play is, in Russian, brilliant. It is easy, colloquial, fluid, witty, aphoristic, poignant. The play is written in "free iambics," in rhymed lines of from one to thirteen syllables, over half of which are regular alexandrines. As example, Chatsky's last eight lines in transliteration:

> Vy právy: iz ognýa tot vyídet nevredím,
> Kto s vámi dén' probýt' uspéyet,
> Podýshit vózdukhom odním,
> I v nyóm rassúdok utseléyet.
> Vón iz Moskvý! syudá ya ból'she ne ezdók.
> Begú, ne oglyanús', poidú iskát' po svétu,
> Gde oskorblyónnomu est' chúvstvu ugolók!—
> Karétu mné, karétu!

Further, there are several "levels" of language in the play, all worked in together: the "sublime" or Slavonic, as the eighteenth century distinguished it; the Frenchified Russian of the upper class; the official or bureaucratic; the colloquial; and the substandard, popular speech (as of the servants). The play is very much a study of Russian language, life, and literary canons.

Secondly, the play is unique. There were, of course, both tragedies and comedies written in verse since the very beginning of the eighteenth century, but none used such an elaborate form, such a skilled, elegant combination of styles of speech and manners, and none presented such a dramatic development of character and action. The play was the first of its kind—and also the last, for after it, comedy was written mostly in prose (for example, *The Inspector General*) and tragedy in prose or in blank verse (for example, *Boris Godunov*).

Thirdly, although the play is classical in form (the unities are observed), it depicts the world contemporary with it. It is a deft portrait—and critique—of the life of Moscow society around 1820.

Fourthly, it is much more than an eighteenth- or early nineteenth-century satire or comedy of manners. It presents a complex group of complex characters, none of whom can be satisfactorily reduced to a prevailing "humor." The "problems" the play sets up are not "resolved."

The text used is that of the Academy edition as reprinted in A. S. Griboyedov, *Gore ot uma* (N. Piksanov and V.

Filippov, eds.), Moscow, 1946. The same text is also that of the Oxford University Press edition, 1951, with extensive notes in English by D. Costello, some of which I found extremely helpful.

ACT I

The living room, a large clock in it; on the right, a door leads into SOFIYA'S *bedroom, from which a piano and flute are heard and then fall silent.* LIZA *is asleep in the middle of the room, spread out over the armchairs.*

Morning; day is just beginning to break.

LIZA (*suddenly wakes up, gets up from the chairs, looks around*).
It's getting light! . . . How fast the night went by!
Wanted to sleep last night—no go,
"Expect my friend."—Keep an eye out,
Stay awake as long as you don't tumble off the chair.
Now I just had a little nap—
It's day already! . . . Better tell them.
(*Knocks on* SOFIYA'S *door.*)
You people there,
Hey Sofya Pavlovna, be careful.
All your talk outdid the night.
You deaf?—Aleksei Stepanoch!
Madam!—They haven't even any fear!
(*Goes away from the door.*)
Now, like an uninvited guest,
Your father, maybe, will come in!
What it is to serve a girl in love!
(*Goes back to the door.*)
Come on, leave off. It's morning.—What?

SOFIYA'S VOICE. What time is it?

LIZA. The whole house is up.

SOFIYA (*from her room*). What time is it?

LIZA. Seven, eight; nine.

SOFIYA (*from the same place*). That's not true.

LIZA (*going away from the door*). Oh! damned Cupid!
They hear you but don't want to listen,
But oughtn't they open up the shutters?
I'll set the clock ahead, though there will be a fuss,
I'll set it so it chimes.
(*Climbs on a chair, moves the hand, the clock strikes and chimes.* FAMUSOV *enters.*)

LIZA. Oh! Sir!

FAMUSOV. Sir, indeed.

(*Stops the clock's chiming.*)

What a naughty little girl you are.
I couldn't figure out what was going on!
I think I hear a flute, and then it seems a piano;
And it's too soon for Sofya, now?

LIZA. No, sir, I . . . just accidentally . . .

FAMUSOV. Accidentally, exactly, have to keep an eye
On you; bet you meant to.

(*Presses close to her and makes advances.*)

Oi! Imp! You little scamp!

LIZA. You're the scamp; these antics hardly suit you!

FAMUSOV. Modest girl, but nothing save
Mischief in your empty head.

LIZA. You're the empty-headed one, yourself,
Remember now, you are an old man . . .

FAMUSOV. Almost.

LIZA. Now if someone comes, where will we go?

FAMUSOV. Who's going to come?
Isn't Sofya sleeping?

LIZA. Just fell asleep.

FAMUSOV. Just now! And in the night?

LIZA. She read all night.

FAMUSOV. See what sort of whims are all the rage!

LIZA. She's always reading aloud in French, locked in her room.

FAMUSOV. So tell her there's no point in ruining her eyes,
And no great use in reading;
French books keep her up all night,
And Russian ones put me to sleep.

LIZA. Soon as she's up, I'll tell her.
But you go, please; I am afraid you'll wake her up.

FAMUSOV. What do you mean, wake up? You're winding up the clock
Yourself, thundering through all the neighborhood.

LIZA (*as loud as possible*). Oh stop that, sir!

FAMUSOV (*claps his hand over her mouth*).

Heavens! how you shout!

Are you going crazy?

LIZA. I'm afraid it all may end up part of that . . .

FAMUSOV. What?

LIZA. It's time for you to know, sir, you're not a child;

Girls' morning sleep is something very light;
You hardly squeak the door and whisper;
They hear it all . . .

FAMUSOV. You're always lying.

SOFIYA'S VOICE. Oh, Liza!

FAMUSOV (*hurriedly*). Pssst!

(*Steals out of the room on tiptoe.*)

LIZA (*alone*). Gone . . . Ah! Better to keep away from the master;
You have to be all set for trouble any time,
Let's hope that, even more than all
Our sorrows, the master's anger and his love will pass.

(SOFIYA *enters with a candle;* MOLCHALIN *behind her.*)

SOFIYA. What's got into you, Liza?
You're making noise . . .

LIZA. Of course, it's hard for you to part?
Locked in till daylight, and still it seems too little?

SOFIYA. Ah, it's grown light indeed!

(*Puts the candle out.*)

The light, the sadness. How short the nights!

LIZA. Go on and grieve, it's all too much for me,
Your old man came in here, I got petrified,
Put on an act for him, forget the lies I told;
Well, why don't you two do something? Make a bow, sir.
Get out, I'm scared to death.
See what time it is, look out the window;
The crowd's been straggling down the street
For hours now; and in the house they're tidying up.

SOFIYA. Happy people do not count the hours.

LIZA. Don't count them then; that's up to you;
But of course it's me who's got to answer for you.

SOFIYA (*to* MOLCHALIN). Go on, we must put up with boredom one more day.

LIZA. Good-bye to you; take your hands away.

(*Separates them;* MOLCHALIN *bumps into* FAMUSOV *in the doorway.*)

FAMUSOV. What a surprise! Molchalin, is it really you?

MOLCHALIN. Me.

FAMUSOV. Why here? and now, at this time?
And Sofya! . . . Good morning, Sofya, why
Did you get up so early? hey? what bothered you?

And how come you two got together now?
SOFIYA. He just came in this minute.
MOLCHALIN. Just came from a walk.
FAMUSOV. My friend, can't walks be taken
In alleyways a little farther off?
And, madam, you are hardly out of bed—and with
A man! a young man!—What business for a girl!
All night reads fantastic stories,
And here's the fruit of all these books!
It's the doings of Kuznetsky Street[1] and the eternal Frenchmen,
Where all these fads come from to us, writers, artists:
Undoers of our hearts and pocketbooks!
When will the Creator set us free
Of all their hats! and caps! the bonnets and the pins!
And bookstores, and little pastry shops!
SOFIYA. Excuse me, Father, I feel very dizzy;
I can hardly catch my breath from fright;
You came running in so quickly
I'm all upset.
FAMUSOV. Humbly thank you, humbly,
I ran in too fast!
I interfered! I frightened her!
I'm all upset myself, Sofya Pavlovna, I run
Around all day without a rest, just like a madman.
The fuss and bother of my job is such—
One pesters me, another, all of them want something!
But did I expect fresh troubles? To be deceived . . .
SOFIYA (*in tears*). By whom, Father?
FAMUSOV. Now I'm getting a dressing down
For always scolding for no reason.
Don't cry, I'm talking seriously:
Haven't we done everything
To bring you up right, from the cradle?
Your mother died: I managed to engage
A second mother in Madame Rosier.
I gave the nice old lady the job of taking care of you:

[1] *Kuznetsky most*, a Moscow street famous from the eighteenth century until the Revolution for elegant French shops; literally, "Blacksmith Bridge," so called because once a river ran there, a bridge crossed it, and there was a smithy there.

She was clever, quiet, a woman of rare scruple.
One thing doesn't do her honor, though:
For five hundred rubles more a year
She let herself be lured away by others.
But Madame is not the point.
You don't need any other model when
You have your father here before you.
You look at me now: I don't boast about my build,
Yet I am hale and hearty, hair grown gray . . .
Free, widower, the master of myself . . .
Famous for my ascetic life!

LIZA. May I make bold, sir . . .

FAMUSOV. Silence!
A dreadful age! You don't know what to do!
Everybody's gotten overwise.
Our daughters worst of all! And we ourselves are idiots—
These foreign things have taken hold!
After all, we take the tramps to live in and give lessons,[2]
To teach our daughters everything, everything—
Dancing, singing, courteousness, and even sighing,
As if we're getting set to marry them to jesters!
You, visitor, what do you want? What are you here for, sir?
I sheltered you, an orphan, and took you in my household.
I got you major's rank and took you as my secretary;
With my assistance you were transferred to Moscow;
If it weren't for me, you'd still be slaving out in Tver.

SOFIYA. I cannot understand the reason for your anger.
He lives here in our house—what terrible disaster!
Walking toward one room, he got into another.

FAMUSOV. Got, or did he want to go?
Indeed, how come you are together? Can't be accidental—

SOFIYA. Well, this is how the whole thing happened:
When you and Liza were here just now
Your voice frightened me terrifically,
And I ducked in as quickly as I could.

FAMUSOV. Why, really, she will blame the fuss on me:
My voice caused them alarm inopportunely!

SOFIYA. After a restless night, even a little thing's alarming;
Shall I tell you my dream? Then you'll understand.

[2] A reference to the foreign, usually French, tutors. Some lived with the family; others came in to give lessons.

FAMUSOV. What was it all about?
SOFIYA. Shall I tell you?
FAMUSOV. Of course.
(*Sits down.*)
SOFIYA. Now . . . you see . . . at first
A flowering meadow; I was searching
For an herb,
Some herb—awake, I can't remember which.
Suddenly a kind, sweet man—one of those
We see and feel we've always known—
Appeared right here beside me, ingratiating, clever,
But modest . . . You know, a man who was born in poverty . . .
FAMUSOV. Ah, my dear, don't finish off the blow!
A man who's poor is not a match for you.
SOFIYA. Then everything got lost: the meadows and the sky—
We're in a darkened room. To crown the miracle,
The floor split open—and you came up
As pale as death and all your hair on end!
Then something neither beast nor man
Flung the doors back like a clap of thunder.
It dragged us apart and tortured the man who had been sitting with me.
He seems to me more dear than any treasure,
I want to go to him—you drag me off with you.
The monster's moaning, whistling, howls and laughing follow us.
He's shouting at us!
I woke up. —Somebody was talking:
It's your voice—why so early, I wonder?
I run in here—and find the two of you.
FAMUSOV. Indeed, a nasty dream, now that
I look at it; it's full of things,
If it is really true—love and devils, fear and flowers.
Well, sir, and how about you?
MOLCHALIN. I heard your voice.
FAMUSOV. That's funny.
They got all wrapped up in my voice. How diligently it reaches
Everyone and keeps them all together until dawn!
You hurried when you heard me, what for? what for?

Speak up.

MOLCHALIN. Your papers, sir.

FAMUSOV. Indeed! That's all we needed.

For goodness' sake, how come this sudden zeal

For doing all the paperwork!

(*Gets up.*)

Well, Sonyushka, now I'll leave you alone:

Dreams are often strange, but reality is stranger;

You tried to find yourself an herb,

You quickly came upon a friend;

Put all this nonsense out of mind;

There's little sense in miracles—

Go, lie down again, and sleep.

(*To* MOLCHALIN.)

Let's go take care of the papers.

MOLCHALIN. I was just bringing them to tell you

They can't be sent along without some going over;

There are some contradictions, and a lot's not clear.

FAMUSOV. I'm mortally afraid of one thing only,

That most of them will get piled up; if you

Had your way, the whole business would bog down;

But as for me, whatever sense it makes,

This is the way I do things:

Once it's signed it's out of sight.

(*Goes out with* MOLCHALIN, *letting him pass through the doorway first.*)

LIZA. Well, here's a circus for you! now, here's some fun!

Not really, though; this isn't to be laughed at;

It goes dark before your eyes, your heart stops beating;

A sin is no misfortune, but talk is bad.

SOFIYA. What's talk to me? Let them think whatever they want,

Yet father is enough to make you thoughtful:

He always was a grumpy, restless,

Hasty man, but from now on . . .

You can size things up . . .

LIZA. I don't go by stories;

He might lock you up—that's all right if it's us both—

But what, God save us, if he sends

Molchalin, me and all the rest off packing.

SOFIYA. Just think, happiness is so capricious!

We get away with much worse things;
No misery could have crossed our minds,
We lost ourselves in music, and the time went by
So smoothly, fate seemed guarding us,
No difficulties and no doubts . . .
But grief lay waiting round the corner.
LIZA. That's just it, you never pay attention to
My silly thoughts:
And then there's trouble.
How could you want a better prophet?
I kept repeating, this love will never come to anything.
Not forever and ever.
Your father's just the same as all the Muscovites:
He'd like a son-in-law with lots of rank and medals,
(But, just between ourselves, not every hero's rich);
Of course, he's also got to have
Some money to live well, so he can offer balls;
Why take, for example, Colonel Skalozub,
A moneybags, and one who's out to be a general.
SOFIYA. How very cute! I'm terribly delighted
To hear all about the battle-lines and columns;
He hasn't said a clever word since he was born—
It's the same to me: to marry him or drown.
LIZA. Yes, ma'am, a talker, sure, but really very simple;
No matter he's a soldier or civilian
Who's so light-hearted, sensitive and witty
As Aleksandr Andreich Chatsky!
I don't say this just to make you blush!
It's all long past and can't come back,
But I recall . . .
SOFIYA. Now what do you recall?
He really knows how to laugh at all
The rest; he jokes and chatters—it's
Quite amusing; he'll laugh along with anyone.
LIZA. No more than that? So you're pretending? He cried and cried,
Poor man, I remember, when you and he were parting—
"Why are you crying, sir? Live merrily and laugh."
And then he says: "I have a reason, Liza,
For who knows what I'll find when I come back?
And how much, perhaps, I will have lost?"

The poor man seemed to know some three years later that . . .
SOFIYA. Listen, don't take too many liberties with me.
Maybe I behaved quite thoughtlessly,
I know it and I'm sorry; but how did I betray him?
Who's he that I be censured for infidelity?!
Why, of course, it's true that I grew up with Chatsky;
The habit of being together always every day
Bound us in a childhood friendship, but afterwards
He left the house—our place seemed very boring to him—
And he rarely came to visit us;
Later, he pretended he was in love,
Again demanding and distressed!
Witty, clever, eloquent,
Especially happy in a crowd,
He got a fancy notion of himself . . .
A real desire for traveling came over him.
Oh, if a person loves someone,
Why search for wit and go on such a lengthy trip?
LIZA. Where's he running around? What sort of places?
He took the cure, they say, at a Caucasian spa,
Not from disease, I bet, but (much more likely) boredom!
SOFIYA. And delighted any place where people are ridiculous.
The one I love is not like that:
Molchalin's ready to forget himself for others;
The foe of impudence, he always is reserved and shy . . .
How easy to spend the night with such a man!
We're sitting still, though it's already getting light
Outside—and what do you think we're doing?
LIZA. God knows,
Dear lady! Is it any of my business?
SOFIYA. He presses my hand against his breast,
Sighs from the bottom of his heart,
Without a word too forward, and so the whole night goes,
Hand in hand, his eyes not leaving mine—
You're laughing! How can you! What basis did I give
You for such a burst of laughter?
LIZA. Me–ee? I was just now thinking of your aunt,
When the young Frenchman ran away from her,
The dear! she wanted so to bury
Sorrow—couldn't do it:
She forgot to dye her hair,

And in three days turned gray:
(Continues laughing loudly.)
SOFIYA *(with chagrin)*. And that's the way they'll later start to talk about me.
LIZA. Forgive me, really, holy God,
I only wished this silly laughter
Would help to cheer you up a bit.
*(A servant enters, behind him—*CHATSKY.*)*
SERVANT. Aleksandr Andreich Chatsky has arrived.
(Goes out.)
CHATSKY. It's hardly light—you're already up! And I bow down before you.
(Enthusiastically kisses her hand.)
So, kiss me in return! You didn't expect me? Tell me!
Well, glad? Or not? Look me in the face.
Surprised? That's all? Well, what a welcome!
As if not even a week had passed,
As if yesterday we two together
Had completely bored each other to death.
Not a touch of love! Oh, what a fine young lady!
And meanwhile I, mindless of myself,
And out of my mind, have covered over seven hundred
Versts in forty-five hours without a wink of sleep . . .
The wind and storm . . . I got completely lost and fell
So often!—and this is my reward!
SOFIYA. Oh, Chatsky, I am glad to see you.
CHATSKY. You're glad! Well, that's good news.
But who sincerely does rejoice like this?
It seems to me that after all
By freezing both my men and horses
I only entertained myself.
LIZA. Why, sir, if only you had been behind the door,
Honest to God, not five minutes back,
How we two talked about you here!
Madam, you tell him yourself.
SOFIYA. We always have; not merely now.
You have nothing to reproach me for.
If someone hurries by, peeps in the door,
Just passing through, by chance, from foreign lands afar,
Even if he is a sailor, I ask him
Hasn't he somewhere perhaps met you in a stagecoach?

CHATSKY. Let's assume that's so.
The believers are the blessed; the world is good to them!
Oh, my God, am I really here again
In Moscow? at your place? I wouldn't know you!
Where did time go? Where is that age of innocence
When on long evenings you and I
Would run in and out, here and there, appear and vanish,
Playing and shouting among the chairs and tables?
But here your father and *madame* sit down to piquet;
We're in a darkened corner, and I think that this . . .
Do you remember? We'd shudder if the table squeaked, the door . . .

SOFIYA. Child's play!

CHATSKY. Oh, yes, but now . . .
At seventeen you've blossomed charmingly,
Inimitably, as you well know,
And so you're modest and don't eye society.
Aren't you in love? I beg you, answer me,
Without reflecting, end this confusion.

SOFIYA. If hasty questions and
An inquisitive glance should fluster anyone . . .

CHATSKY. Come now: what shall I admire if not you?
What novelty will Moscow show to me?
Yesterday, a ball; tomorrow, two.
One proposed—and made it; another failed.
It's all the same, the same poems in the albums.[3]

SOFIYA. Driven into Moscow! That is to see the world!
Where is it better?

CHATSKY. Where we aren't.
Well, how's your father? Still the old-line faithful member
Of the English Club until the grave?[4]
Your uncle's scampered off to his long home?
And that—what's his name? a Turk or Greek?—
That swarthy, darkish fellow on the cranelike legs,
I don't know his name, just that
Wherever you go, he's already there,

[3] Young people often kept albums, like autograph books now, in which they and their friends wrote down poems, etc. Real books at this time were few and very expensive.

[4] An aristocratic Moscow club, so called because it was patterned after the famous London clubs.

In the dining and the drawing rooms.
And what of those three *boulevard* lovelies
Who've kept on looking young some fifty years?
They have a million relatives, and with their sisters'
Help they'll be related to all Europe.
And what about our leading light,
Our treasure? It's written on his forehead: Theater Tonight.[5]
His house is all done up in green, like trees . . .
Fat himself, his actors all are lean . . .
Once at a ball, remember? we together found,
Behind the wings, in one of the more hidden rooms,
A man concealed and trilling like a nightingale—
A winter singer of the summer.
And what about that consumptive relative of yours,
The foe of books, who got onto the Scholarly
Committee and shouted out for oaths
That none know how, and no one learn, to read and write?[6]
Again it is my destiny to have to see them!
I'm sick and tired of them, but who hasn't got some faults?
But after you've been traveling and come back home,
Even your country's smoke is sweet and pleasant.
SOFIYA. You and my aunt ought to get
Together and go over all your friends.
CHATSKY. How is your aunt? Still like a girl Minerva?
Still maid-of-honor for Catherine the First?
Her house still full of little girls and pugs?
Oh, let's talk of education.
Are things now still the way they were?
Are they trying to recruit regiments of teachers,
As many and as cheaply as they can?
Not that they're so far behind in science:
In Russia, under pain of penalty,
We're ordered to acknowledge any man
A geographer or an historian.
Our mentor—remember how his cap, his smock,

[5] Both this reference and the "Turk or Greek" seem to be to real, contemporary figures. Some rich noblemen had private theaters and personal troupes of serf actors.

[6] The *Uchonyi komitet*, established in 1817, was under the Ministry of Ecclesiastical Affairs and National Education and had broad powers of censorship.

His index finger—all the signs of learning—
So terrified our timid minds?
How soon we got accustomed to believe
That without the Germans we were lost?
And Guillaumé, the Frenchman, the empty-headed fool?
He isn't married yet?
SOFIYA. To whom?
CHATSKY. Perhaps to some sort of princess, say,
To Pulkheriya Andrevna, for example?
SOFIYA. A dancing master! Impossible!
CHATSKY. Why? He's a fine partner.
We have to have an estate or some high rank,
But Guillaumé! —Is that the way things go now?
At the assemblies, at the great ones, on the parish holidays,
Does it still prevail—that confusion of French
And the dialect of the town?
SOFIYA. A mixture of languages?
CHATSKY. Yes, of two; can't do without it.
LIZA. But it'd be hard to cut one out of both, like yours.
CHATSKY. At least, it's not blown up.
Why, this is new! —I enjoy this minute,
Excited by my seeing you,
And talkative, but aren't there times when
I'm duller than Molchalin? Where is he, anyway?
He still hasn't broken the seal of silence?
Used to be he'd see a book of the latest songs
And badger friends: kindly have a copy made for me.
By the way, he'll get on quite handsomely—
Nowadays they like the mute.
SOFIYA (*aside*). A viper, not a man!
(*Loudly and constrainedly*) I want to ask you something:
Has it ever happened that, while laughing or while crying,
Or even by mistake, you said some good about someone?
Not lately even, but in childhood, maybe?
CHATSKY. When everything's so soft, so gentle, and so green?
Why go back so far? Here's a good deed for you:
Keeping the sleigh-bells jingling all
The time both day and night across the snowy waste,
I hurried on to you at breakneck speed.
And how do I find you? all seriousness and pomp!
I've put up with your aloofness a full half-hour!

Your face is like the holiest pilgrim's!
And all the same I love you passionately—
(*A momentary silence.*)
Listen, is everything I say indeed so harsh?
And does it tend to do some person harm?
For if that's so, my mind and heart are split.
I laugh once at the oddities
Of these eccentrics and then forget them;
Order me into fire—I'll go as in to dinner.

SOFIYA. Well enough if you burn up, but if you don't?
[FAMUSOV *enters.*]

FAMUSOV. Now here's another!

SOFIYA. Oh, Father, the dream came true!
(*Goes out.*)

FAMUSOV (*in a low voice, after her*). Damned dream!
(CHATSKY *looks toward the door where* SOFIYA *went out.*)
Well, what a trick you played!
Didn't write a word in three years
And suddenly dropped in as if from the sky!
(*They embrace.*)
Hello, my friend, hello, and welcome, greetings!
Tell me all, for I expect you have
A mighty fine collection of news.
Sit down, now; hurry up and tell me.
(*They sit down.*)

CHATSKY (*absent-mindedly*). Sofya Pavlovna has become so beautiful!

FAMUSOV. You young men have nothing else to do
But keep your eye on lovely young girls;
She said something casually,
And you, carried away with hope no doubt, have been enchanted.

CHATSKY. Oh, no! I have been little spoiled by hope.

FAMUSOV. "The dream came true," she whispered in my ear,
Now you've imagined . . .

CHATSKY. Me? Nothing!

FAMUSOV. Who did she dream about? What was it?

CHATSKY. I'm no interpreter of dreams.

FAMUSOV. Don't believe her. It's nonsense.

CHATSKY. I believe what my eyes see;
In all my life I never met—

I guarantee it—a creature anything like her!

FAMUSOV. How he keeps on! Come, tell me in detail
Where you went, how long you knocked around?
Where have you come from now?

CHATSKY. I'm in no mood to talk.
I wanted to go around the world
And didn't go around a hundredth part.
(*Hurriedly gets up.*)
Good-bye! I was in a hurry to see you first
And didn't stop at home. Good-bye! I'll come back
An hour from now, I won't forget the least detail,
And tell you first, and later you can tell it round.
(*In the doorway.*)
So beautiful!
(*Goes out.*)

FAMUSOV (*alone*). Which one of the two?
"Oh, Father, the dream came true!"
And then she tells me this out loud!
So, I was wrong. How far off the track I was!
Molchalin recently made me uneasy.
Now . . . out of the frying pan into the fire:
The one's a beggar, the other's a dandy,
Acknowledged a spendthrift and a rakehell . . .
What a job it is, oh, Lord,
To be the father of a grown-up girl!
(*Goes out.*)

ACT II

[FAMUSOV *and a servant.*]

FAMUSOV. Petrushka, you are always in
A new coat with tattered elbows. Get me the calendar;
Don't read it the way the sexton does,
But with feeling, sense and proper pauses.
No, wait. Write down on the blank page
Opposite next week:
Invited to Praskovya Fyodorovna's
House on Tuesday to eat trout.[7]
How come the world's so strangely made?
Philosophize—your head gets turned;
One minute, diet; the next, a feast.
You eat three hours and can't digest it in three days!
Make a note: that very day . . . No, no . . .
On Thursday asked to a funeral.
Oh, human kind! You have forgot
That every man himself must crawl in there,
Into that casket where no one stands or sits.
But for anyone who, by an illustrious life, would leave
Behind a glorious memory here's an example:
The late-departed was an honored kammerherr,[8]
With the symbolic key, which he passed on to his son;
A rich man, married to a woman who was rich;
Married off his children, grandchildren;
And died—and everyone remembers him with grief;
Kuzma Petrovich! God rest his soul!
What big shots live and die in Moscow!
Write down: on Thursday, one thing after another,
But perhaps on Friday, or maybe even Saturday—
I must go to the doctor's widow's christening.
She hasn't given birth, but according to
My reckoning she ought.
[CHATSKY *enters.*]

[7] A delicacy; trout are not found in Central Russia.

[8] A gold key was embroidered on the back of the kammerherr's dress uniform to symbolize his right of access to the Tsar's chambers.

Ah! Aleksandr Andreich, welcome,
Come in, sit down.
CHATSKY. You aren't busy?
FAMUSOV (*to the servant*). You may go.
(*The servant goes out.*)
Yes, we've been noting various matters down to help remember.
One forgets if one's not careful.
CHATSKY. You've somehow lost a little gaiety;
Tell me, why? Was my arrival inopportune?
Can some kind of sorrow have befallen
Sofya Pavlovna?
Worry's written on your face, in all your movements.
FAMUSOV. My friend! You've hit upon the mystery:
I am not gay! . . . At my age in life
I cannot try to dance the heel-and-toe!
CHATSKY. Nobody is asking you;
I only asked a little question
About Sofya Pavlovna: perhaps she isn't well?
FAMUSOV. Bah, Lord forgive us! five thousand times
He says the same old thing!
First, nothing's comelier than Sofya Pavlovna,
Then, Sofya Pavlovna is sick.
Tell me, do you find her pleasing?
You've seen the world—don't you want to marry?
CHATSKY. What's that to you?
FAMUSOV. Wouldn't be so bad to ask me first,
For after all I am related to her.
At the very least, there is some reason
They've called me Father all these years.
CHATSKY. Suppose I asked to marry her, what would you say?
FAMUSOV. I'd say, first thing: don't be so negligent;
Don't run your estate, my friend, so carelessly;
But, most importantly, go serve the government.
CHATSKY. I would be glad to serve, but servility is sickening!
FAMUSOV. That's just the point, you all are proud!
You ought to ask what did your fathers do?
You ought to learn by copying your elders.
For example, now, myself, or my late uncle,
Maksim Petrovich: he did not dine on merely silver,
But on gold; had a hundred servants in attendance;

All covered with medals, went driving with a six-in-hand.
A life spent at the Court, and what a Court!
Now things are not like then;
He served under the sovereign *Catherine*.
In those days everyone was someone! Weighed half a ton . . .
You'd bow your greetings to them—they wouldn't nod.
A noble was unlike the rest—
Lived differently, especially if in favor.
And my uncle now! What's your prince to him!
A serious man, both grave and proud!
When it came time to curry favor,
Even he would bend down twice:
Once at a Court reception he chanced to stumble—
He fell so hard he nearly cracked his skull;
The old man started groaning hoarsely;
Her Majesty bestowed the favor of a smile—
She chose to laugh; and what did he do then?
He got up, straightened out his coat, and started bowing—
And fell again—this time on purpose!
More laughter still. He fell once more exactly so.
Well? What do you think? . . . I think he was quite clever.
He fell down badly, got up well.
For this who used to be most often asked to whist?
Who always used to get a friendly word at Court?
Maksim Petrovich! Who was honored first of all?
Maksim Petrovich! Something!
Who handed out promotions? Who gave out pensions?
Maksim Petrovich! Right! What do you youngsters say to that?

CHATSKY. You may say with a sigh—"Indeed
The world has started getting dull"—
When you look closely and compare
The present age and times gone by—
The legacy is fresh, but no one honors it;
Then he in fact was praised who most often bowed his head,
Then men won the day not by a front attack
But bent their foreheads to the floor!
Who was in need met arrogance—he lay in the dirt—
But those who were above were laced with flattery.
An age of real submissiveness and fear

And all beneath the mask of devotion to the Tsar!
I am not speaking of your uncle—I
Do not wish to disturb his ashes—
But all the same, who's likely to desire now,
Even in the most ardent fawning,
Just to make the people laugh,
To bravely sacrifice his skull?
And any man his age or even
Some old man disintegrating
In his skin who saw this leap
Undoubtedly presumed: if only I could, too!
Although everywhere there are some men who love to grovel,
Nowadays they're scared of ridicule, and shame
Holds them in check: that's why the sovereign pays them badly.

FAMUSOV. Oh, for God's sake! He's a Carbonarist![9]

CHATSKY. No, nowadays the world is changed.

FAMUSOV. A dangerous man to know.

CHATSKY. Each man breathes more freely
And doesn't rush to join the regiment of fools.

FAMUSOV. The way he talks! as if it were in writing!

CHATSKY. Stares at the ceiling in his patrons' houses,
Shows up just to sit, shuffle his feet, eat dinner,
Hold someone's chair, pick up a handkerchief.

FAMUSOV. He's out to propagate new freedom!

CHATSKY. Some men go traveling, some live on their estates . . .[10]

FAMUSOV. Why, he denies authority!

CHATSKY. They serve a cause, and not a master . . .

FAMUSOV. I would most stringently prevent these gentlemen
From getting within gunshot of the capitals.[11]

CHATSKY. I won't disturb you any more . . .

FAMUSOV. No strength, no patience left—annoying!

CHATSKY. I have abused your time relentlessly,

[9] A secret political organization first set up in Italy about 1811 with the aim of establishing a republic. Later the movement spread to other countries, especially France.

[10] The general presumption was that the man who left his estate to travel was a radical.

[11] Both Moscow and St. Petersburg were considered capital cities, although of course St. Petersburg was the seat of the central government.

I now give you authority:
Subtract a bit
And even add it on to ours—
Go ahead, I won't mind at all.
FAMUSOV. I don't even want to know you; I loathe depravity.
CHATSKY. I've finished talking.
FAMUSOV. Good enough, I closed my ears.
CHATSKY. But why? I'm not offending them.
FAMUSOV (*patteringly*). Now here they roam around the world, waste their time,
Come back—and how can one expect a decent thing from them?
CHATSKY. I am all through . . .
FAMUSOV. Spare me, if you please.
CHATSKY. I have no wish to keep on arguing.
FAMUSOV. Just let me go in peace.
SERVANT (*enters*). Colonel Skalozub.
FAMUSOV (*sees and hears nothing*). They'll surely drag you off
To Court; you mark my words.
CHATSKY. Somebody has come to see you.
FAMUSOV. Never mind—off to Court!
CHATSKY. Your man's announced someone.
FAMUSOV. Never mind—off to Court! To Court!
CHATSKY. But turn around—they're calling you.
FAMUSOV (*turns around*). What? Riot? Well, I'm all prepared for Sodom.
SERVANT. Colonel Skalozub. Shall I show him in?
FAMUSOV (*gets up*). Jackasses! Have I got to repeat
It a hundred times? Admit him, call him, beg him, tell him
That I'm at home and very pleased. Hurry up.
(*Servant goes out.*)
Now, sir, if you please, be careful in his presence:
He's quite well known, of consequence,
And has collected hordes of decorations!
Young for his rank, which one may envy,
Any day he'll be a general.
I beg you, be most unassuming in his presence.
Oh, Aleksandr Andreich, it's no good!
He regularly comes to see me;
You know I'm glad to see them all.
In Moscow people exaggerate:

They're saying that he'll marry Sonyushka. Absurd!
He, perhaps, would be sincerely pleased,
But I myself don't see a great or pressing need
To marry off my daughter now or later;
Why, Sofya still is young. Besides, it's as God wills.
But, please now, don't argue right and left with him,
And drop these wild, nonsensical ideas of yours.
But he's not here! What could the reason be . . .
Oh! He must have gone to see me in the other wing.
(*Hurriedly goes out.*)

CHATSKY. What a fuss he makes! What energy!
And Sofya? Isn't this, perhaps, indeed a suitor?
How long they've shunned me now as if I were a stranger!
How can she not be here?
Who is this Skalozub? The father raves about him,
And very possibly not just the father . . .
Oh! he must say good-bye to love
Who goes away for several years.
[FAMUSOV *and* SKALOZUB *enter.*]

FAMUSOV. Sergei Sergeich, come in, please do,
I humbly beg you, it's warmer here;
You're frozen through, we'll warm you up;
I'll open up the draft some more at once.

SKALOZUB (*in a thick bass*). Why should I bother you, by God!
I feel embarrassed, as an upright officer.

FAMUSOV. Can't I do a thing to help my friends?
My dear Sergei Sergeich!
Put down your hat, take off your sword;
There is the sofa, stretch out at leisure.

SKALOZUB. Wherever you would have me, as long as I may sit.
(*All three sit down,* CHATSKY *some distance from them.*)

FAMUSOV. Oh, Lord, I'd better mention it before
I forget: you know we're relatives,
Though distant— nothing to divide between us—
You didn't know (still less did I)
Your cousin, whom I thank, explained the whole thing to me—
How Nastasya Nikolavna is related to you.

SKALOZUB. I didn't know, I'm sorry:
She and I never served together.

FAMUSOV. Sergei Sergeich, is that like you?
Oh no! I'm always out to help a relative;
I'll spot him even in the sea!
Very few from other families serve under me;
They're mostly my sister's children, or of the sister of my wife;
Molchalin only isn't mine,
And, therefore, certainly efficient.
When you must recommend one for a medal or a job,
How can you not oblige a man who is your own?
Your relative, however, is close to me, and said
That he'd received from you real help in his career.
SKALOZUB. In 'thirteen my cousin and I won honors for ourselves
In the Thirtieth Chasseurs, then in the Forty-fifth.[12]
FAMUSOV. Happy is the man who has a son like that!
He has, hasn't he, a little medal on his chest?[13]
SKALOZUB. For August third;[14] we held out in the trenches:
He got a ribbon; I, a star around my neck.
FAMUSOV. A very pleasant man, and when you think of it,
A real gay blade; your cousin is a splendid man.
SKALOZUB. But now he's all involved in new ideas and rules;
Up for promotion, he suddenly left the service
And started reading books at his estate.
FAMUSOV. That's youth for you! . . . Reading! . . . And then—boom!
You have comported yourself industriously—
Not long in service, but a colonel now a long time.
SKALOZUB. I am quite fortunate in all my friends and cohorts—
The vacancies have opened just as they should:
Some of the older men have been let go,
And others, then again, have been killed off.
FAMUSOV. Yes, God picks out His own for different rewards.
SKALOZUB. Sometimes other men have happier luck than I:
Just in our own Fifteenth, to go no further afield,

[12] Both these regiments were in reserve throughout the war.

[13] Costello points out that "the badge of Russian orders of the first class was a star and a broad ribbon; that of orders of the intermediate classes was a cross worn at the opening of the collar; of the lowest class, a cross suspended from a ribbon tied in a bow and worn on the breast."

[14] On August 3, 1813, a truce was in effect on all fronts.

To speak about, say, none but our own brigadier.
FAMUSOV. But, come now, what is it you're lacking?
SKALOZUB. No complaints, they haven't passed me over;
However, I've had to wait two years to get a regiment.
FAMUSOV. You chasing after a regiment?
Although, of course, in other respects,
The others can't keep up with you.
SKALOZUB. No, sir, there are men senior to me in the corps;
I've been in service since Oughty-nine;
Of course, there are a lot of ways to get advanced;
Like a true philosopher, I study them—
I only want to be a general.
FAMUSOV. And may God grant you health to study gloriously
And get to general; and after that—
Why put it off a moment longer,
Shouldn't one discuss a general's wife?
SKALOZUB. Get married? I have nothing against it.
FAMUSOV. Really? Different men have sisters, nieces, daughters;
In Moscow there's no lack of marriageable girls;
Why, they're propagated every year!
Oh, sir, admit, there's hardly anywhere
A man will find a capital like Moscow.
SKALOZUB. It's way far out in front of all the rest.
FAMUSOV. She has her own laws, sir, for taste, for manners
Most refined—for everything:
For example, now, it is our old, old custom that
A son is honored according to what his father has:
So, though he's mentally retarded, if he gets
A couple of thousand family serfs,
Why, he's a good suitor.
Another might be quicker but all filled with pride;
So what if he is called a famous thinker?
He won't get taken in the family—can't blame us—
For after all it's *here* nobility is valued!
Is that the only thing? Why, take our hospitality:
Anyone who wants to see us—let him come,
The door is open for the uninvited, too,
Especially for foreigners;
Whether he's an honest man or not—
It's all the same to us, there's food set out for all.

Just take a person, size the whole man up:
All the Muscovites have an especial mark.
Just take a look at all our youngsters, please,
At all our sons and grandsons—
We scold them hard, but if you study it
You'll see they could teach the teachers at fifteen!
And what about the old folks? —When they've got something up,
They'll judge the matter: once something's said it's like a verdict!
Why, they're of ancient pedigree, don't care a hoot.
Sometimes they say such things about the government[15]
That if anybody overheard . . . look out!
Not that they'd introduce new ways or things—oh, never.
God save us that! . . . Oh, no! But they will squabble
Over this and that, and often over nothing
They'll fight and shout and . . . go their separate ways.
They're real, retired chancellors when it comes to brains.
I'll tell you this, that obviously the time
Is not yet ripe, but the thing can't be done without them.
The ladies? —Let someone try to get the better of them!
Everywhere the judges of everything, they have no judges
Over them; if they set up commotion playing cards—
God grant you patience then! So, I've been married, too.
Order them to lead the troops' parade!
Send them to their places in the Senate!
Irina Vlasyevna! Lukeriya Aleksevna!
Tatyana Yuryevna! Pulkheriya Andrevna!
But whoever's seen our daughters must bow his head!
His Majesty the Prussian king was here;[16]
He was astounded at our Moscow girls—
Not just their looks, but their sweet grace.
Indeed, can any be more well-brought-up than they?
They really know how to dress themselves in collars
Of taffeta and velvet flowers and veils.
They won't just say a simple word, but shape it roundly;
They'll sing you lovely French romances

[15] The following lines describe the "cantankerous spirit of opposition" characteristic of the English Club and the degree to which the atmosphere of the time was filled with conspiracy.

[16] Frederick William III, in 1818.

And trill the upper notes;
They simply run after uniforms,
Which is because they're patriotic.
I really mean it: nowhere hardly
Can you find another capital like Moscow.

SKALOZUB. In my opinion
The fire helped a lot to make it look much better.[17]

FAMUSOV. Don't remind us of it, they've croaked enough about it!
Since then the sidewalks and the streets,
The houses and everything are new.

CHATSKY. The houses now are new; the prejudices, old.
Rejoice that, after all, the years
And fashions and the fires can't get rid of them.

FAMUSOV (*to* CHATSKY). Hey, tie a string around your finger to remind you:
I asked you to keep quiet, not too much to ask.
(*To* SKALOZUB) Allow me, sir; this is my friend young Chatsky,
The late Andrei Ilyich's boy;
He's not in service, for he sees no point in it,
But if he wanted to, he'd be a great success.
Too bad, too bad; he is a smart young lad,
Writes splendidly and translates.
Can't help feel sorry that a man with such a mind . . .

CHATSKY. Can't you feel sorry for someone else instead?
Your praises even make me quite annoyed.

FAMUSOV. It's not just me; everybody says it.

CHATSKY. But who're the judges? Because of their antiquity,
Their hostility toward a freer life is implacable;
They dig their opinions up out of old, forgotten papers
On the Conquest of Crimea and the Ochakov Siege.[18]
Always ready for nagging,
They sing the same old song:
Not noticing about themselves
That whatever gets older gets worse.

[17] The fire of 1812, after which Moscow was painstakingly rebuilt.

[18] The Crimea was annexed to Russia in 1783; Ochakov was a Turkish fortress at the mouth of the Dnepr River captured by the Russian army under Suvorov in 1788.

You show us where our country's fathers are
Whom we must now accept as paragons!
Aren't these the men, made rich by robbery,
Who found a way around the law through friendships and
Relations, after they had built themselves real mansions
Where they go on and on in feasts and dissipation
And where their foreign clients try unsuccessfully
To revive the foulest features of a by-gone age?
And who in Moscow hasn't had his mouth stopped up
With dinners, snacks and dancing?
Aren't they like the one you took me to, for some
Strange reasons of your own, when I was very little,
To pay respects to?
That Nestor of the noble no-goods[19]
Surrounded by a crowd of servants?
Diligent and honest, they had saved his life
And honor many times when he was drunk and brawling;
And suddenly he swapped them for three greyhounds!
Or take that other one[20] who for his own amusement,
For his serf ballet, filled up a lot of wagons
With children torn away from their mothers and their fathers!
His mind on nothing but his Zephyrs and his Cupids,
He made all Moscow marvel at their grace;
But his creditors would not postpone his payment—
The Cupids and the Zephyrs all
Were sold off one by one.[21]
Those are the men who lived to a ripe old age!
Those are the ones whom we, for want of real men, must admire!
Those are our judges, the ones who watch us critically!
Just let a young man now, one of
The younger generation, be against all flattery,
Not looking for a job, nor for promotion to high rank—
A man whose mind's on study, a man who yearns to know,
Or one within whose soul the Lord Himself inspired

[19] Believed to be a reference to L. D. Izmailov, a very rich land owner and general, famous for his terrible abuse of serfs.

[20] Believed to be a reference to Prince A. N. Golitsyn, who so loved the theater and theatrical performances he squandered a huge fortune and died in poverty.

[21] To sell serfs "singly," unattached to land, was termed an abuse by the State Council in 1820.

A passion for creative art, beautiful, exalted—
And they shout out: Fire! theft!
And he gets known among them as a dangerous dreamer.
The uniform! The uniform alone! Before,
It used to cover up with its embroidery and beauty
Their feeble-heartedness and intellectual wastes;
And we're supposed to take after them!?
And the women and the girls are wild for uniforms.
Is it so long since I myself renounced my fondness for it?
Though there is little chance of my being so childish now,
Who at that time wouldn't have followed the rest?
Whenever some of the Guards, or someone from the Court,
Came for a visit here,
All the women cried: Hurrah!
And tossed their caps into the air!

FAMUSOV (*to himself*). He's going to get me into trouble.
(*Loudly*) Sergei Sergeich, I'm going now;
I'll be waiting for you in the study.
(*Goes out.*)

SKALOZUB. I'm very pleased by the artful way
In your appraisal you touched upon
The predilection Moscow has
For favorites, the Guards and Grenadiers;
They marvel at their epaulettes and gold as at the sun!
And when were we First Army men behind? In what?
It's all so trimly cut, the waists so tightly fitted,
And we could list you officers
Who—some of them—can even speak in French.
[SOFIYA *and* LIZA *enter.*]

SOFIYA (*runs to the window*). Oh, my God! He fell! He's killed himself!
(*Faints.*)

CHATSKY. Who?
Who did?

SKALOZUB. Who's had a fall?

CHATSKY. She's scared to death.

SKALOZUB. But who? What's going on?

CHATSKY. Hurt himself on what?

SKALOZUB. Maybe our old man has bungled?

LIZA (*bustles around her mistress*).
The man whose fate is fixed can't change his destiny!

Molchalin mounted on the horse, put foot in stirrup,
The horse reared on its hindlegs—
Off he went and landed on his crown.

SKALOZUB. He yanked the reins; as a rider, indeed a sorry sight!
I'll take a look how he landed—on his chest or on his side?
(Goes out.)

CHATSKY. How can we help her? Tell me quickly.

LIZA. There's water there inside the door.
(CHATSKY *runs and gets it. The following is spoken in a low voice until the moment* SOFIYA *comes to.*)
Fill a glass.

CHATSKY. I just did.
Undo the lacing on her corset,
Rub her temples with vinegar,
And sprinkle water over her. Look:
She's breathing more easily now . . .
What can we fan her with?

LIZA. This fan.

CHATSKY. Look out the window—
Molchalin's been on his feet for hours!
A little thing has quite upset her.

LIZA. My lady has an unfortunate nature.
She can't just look on from the side
While people go falling headlong.

CHATSKY. Sprinkle some water on her.
That's it . . . More . . . Some more . . .

SOFIYA (*with a deep sigh*). Who's this with me?
It seems as if I'm dreaming . . .
(Quickly and loudly.)
Where is he? What's happened to him? Tell me.

CHATSKY. Let him go and break his neck—
He nearly was the death of you.

SOFIYA. You and your coldness are what's murderous!
I cannot bear to see or hear you.

CHATSKY. You want me to torment myself for him?

SOFIYA. Run out there, be there, try to help him!

CHATSKY. So you would have been left alone here helpless?

SOFIYA. What help are you?
It's all too true: others' troubles are our fun,
It's all the same if even your own father's killed.

(*To* LIZA.)
Let's go out there, let's run . . .
LIZA (*takes her aside*). Pull yourself together! Go where?
He's alive and well; look out the window here.
(SOFIYA *leans out the window.*)
CHATSKY. Flustered! fainting! in a rush! enraged and scared!
A person only feels that way
When he's about to lose his only friend.
SOFIYA. They're coming here. He cannot raise his arms!
CHATSKY. I wish I'd fallen, too . . .
LIZA. To keep him company?
SOFIYA. No, no; no more than just a wish.
[SKALOZUB *and* MOLCHALIN *enter,* MOLCHALIN *with a bandaged arm.*]
SKALOZUB. Arisen and unharmed! The arm's
Been hurt a little.
But otherwise it was a false alarm.
MOLCHALIN. I frightened you; forgive me, please, I beg you.
SKALOZUB. Well, I surely didn't know that you
Would be disturbed by this—you ran in in a panic,
We shivered, and you fell down in a faint.
And so? —Your fear was all for nothing.
SOFIYA (*not looking at anyone*). Oh, I well see there's nothing to it—
But still I'm quivering all over.
CHATSKY (*to himself*). Not a word now to Molchalin!
SOFIYA (*as before*). However, I will say I'm not
Cowardly about myself. Sometimes
The carriage breaks, they raise it, and I'm ready
To gallop along the road once more.
But the littlest things to others frighten me—
Even if they are not a grave misfortune,
Even if I don't know the man—that's beside the point.
CHATSKY (*to himself*). Now she's begging for his pardon
She once felt sorry for someone.
SKALOZUB. Let me, I beg you, tell you something.
There is a certain Princess Lasov here,
A widow and a horsewoman, but no reports
That many cavaliers go riding out with her.
The other day she really fell:
The groom was clearly just wool-gathering, didn't hold her,

And anyway, I've heard, she's very awkward.
Now one rib's missing, so
She's looking for a husband for support.
SOFIYA. Ah! Aleksandr Andreich! There,
Now be magnanimous indeed:
You are so interested in the misfortunes of your friends!
CHATSKY. Indeed, I just now showed I am
By my sincerest efforts,
By sprinkling and by wiping—
I've no idea for whom, but I brought you back to life.
(*Takes his hat and goes out.*)
SOFIYA. You'll be coming over here tonight?
SKALOZUB. How soon?
SOFIYA. Soon as you can. Some family friends are coming
For a little dancing to the piano.
We are in mourning, so there can't be a ball.
SKALOZUB. I'll come, but I have promised to call on your father . . .
Meantime, good-bye.
SOFIYA. Good-bye.
SKALOZUB (*shakes* MOLCHALIN'*s hand*). Your servant.
(*Goes out.*)
SOFIYA. Molchalin! I don't know how I've kept my wits together!
Of course, you know how much you mean to me!
Why gamble with your life—so carelessly?
Tell me, what happened to your arm?
Don't you want some drops? Shouldn't you lie down?
Let's call the doctor: nothing must be neglected.
MOLCHALIN. I bound it with my handkerchief—since then it hasn't hurt.
LIZA. I'll bet you anything it's fake,
And there needn't be a bandage, except it looks so good.
But there's no fooling that you won't avoid publicity:
Look out now, Chatsky'll make a laughingstock of you.
And Skalozub, as soon as he starts gossiping,
Will tell about the fainting and paint it in bright colors.
He, too, is great at joking—who isn't nowadays?
SOFIYA. What do I care for the two of them?
I love whom I want, I'll tell if I want to.
Molchalin! didn't I really make an effort?

You came in and I said nothing;
While they were here, I didn't dare
Say anything or breathe or look!

MOLCHALIN. Yes, Sofya Pavlovna, you're much too candid . . .

SOFIYA. How could I suddenly be reticent?
I was all set to jump to you out through the window.
What do I care for all the rest? for the whole wide world?
Ridiculous—well, let them laugh; a shame—well, let them scold.

MOLCHALIN. So long as candidness does us no harm.

SOFIYA. You think that they would challenge you to a duel?

MOLCHALIN. Oh! Wicked tongues are far more terrible than pistols . . .

LIZA. They're sitting in your father's study now:
If only you'd flit through the door
Lightly, with a happy face . . .
When people tell us what we want
How eagerly it gets believed!
And when you're with Aleksandr Andreich—
You should let yourself relax in talking
With him about old times and pranks;
A little smile, three little words—
And a man in love will do anything.

MOLCHALIN. I do not dare give you advice.
(*Kisses her hand.*)

SOFIYA. You want me to? . . . I'll go and be polite through tears.
I am afraid I don't know how to keep pretending.
Why did God bring Chatsky, anyway!
(*Goes out.*)

MOLCHALIN. You're a gay and lively little thing!

LIZA. Please leave me alone: there are two of you already.

MOLCHALIN. What a pretty little face you have!
How much I love you!

LIZA. What about my lady?

MOLCHALIN. I love
Her as my duty, you . . .
(*Tries to embrace her.*)

LIZA. For something to do?
Please keep your hands off me.

MOLCHALIN. I have three lovely little things:

A dressing table of expert workmanship!
A little mirror on the top and one inside,
With fretwork and gold leafing all around;
A cushion with a pattern in pearl beads,
And a toilet set in mother-of-pearl;
A needlecase and little scissors—both so darling!
Little pearls ground into white facial powder!
I have some lipstick, too, which you can use as rouge;
Some little phials of perfume: mignonette and jasmine.
LIZA. You know I'll not be tempted by a lot of gifts;
Rather, you now tell me why
You're modest with the lady, but with the maid, a rake?
MOLCHALIN. I feel unwell today; I won't take off my bandage.
Come stay with me at dinnertime.
I'll let you know the whole truth then.
(*Goes out the side door.*)
[SOFIYA *enters.*]
SOFIYA. I went to Father's room—there's no one there at all.
I feel unwell today and won't come down to dinner.
Please tell Molchalin this and tell him that I want
For him to come and see me later.
(*Goes into her room.*)
LIZA. Oh, what the people here are like!
She's after him, and he wants me!
And I . . . Only I am scared to death of love!
And yet—how can a girl not love the butler Petrùsha!?

ACT III

[CHATSKY *on stage.*]

CHATSKY. I'll wait for her and make her speak her mind:
Which one does she prefer? Molchalin? Skalozub?
Molchalin used to be so dull!
A miserable sort of man!
Can he really have grown clever? . . . The other's
Completely hoarse, half choked to death, a bassoon,
A constellation of maneuvers and mazurkas!
It is love's fate to play at blind man's buff.
And mine . . .
(SOFIYA *enters.*)
You're here? I'm very glad.
I hoped for this.

SOFIYA (*to herself*). And most inopportunely.

CHATSKY. Of course it wasn't me you looked for?

SOFIYA. I wasn't looking for you.

CHATSKY. May I inquire, please—
Even if inopportune, it makes no difference—
Who is the one you love?

SOFIYA. Ah! my Lord! The world.

CHATSKY. But whom do you prefer?

SOFIYA. Oh, many—relatives . . .

CHATSKY. All more than you do me?

SOFIYA. It's different.

CHATSKY. And what can I presume, when everything's decided?
If I'd hang myself she'd think it funny.

SOFIYA. You want to know the whole truth in two words?
If anyone shows but the slightest eccentricity,
Your merry mood is hardly modest,
You're ready right away with witty jokes,
Though you yourself . . .

CHATSKY. Myself? ridiculous, am I not?

SOFIYA. Indeed! A dreadful glance, a caustic tone,
There is no end to all your peculiarities.
How very useful, though, the criticism of oneself.

CHATSKY. I'm odd? But who is not a little?

Only he who's like the other fools—
Molchalin, for example . . .
SOFIYA. Your examples are not new;
It's clear you're ready to vent your spleen on everyone,
But I, in order not to interfere, am leaving.
CHATSKY (*restrains her*). But wait!
(*Aside.*)
For once in my life I'll make believe.
(*Loudly.*)
Let's stop this bickering.
I'm not right about Molchalin, I confess;
Perhaps he's not the way he was three years ago;
There are such transformations in the world
Of trends and climates, of moralities and minds;
There are important people who are considered fools:
One—a military man, another—a bad poet,
Another . . . I don't dare say who, but all the world
Asserts, especially in recent years,
That they've grown very, very clever.
Perhaps Molchalin has a ready wit and daring,
But does he have such passion, feeling, fervency
So that except for you the world
Appears to him completely worthless?
So that the beating of his heart
Is quickened by his love for you?
So that the center of his thoughts, of all he does,
Is you and how to make you happy?
I feel this on my part but have no way to prove it;
I would not wish on even my worst enemy
What seethes inside of me, what burns and drives me mad.
But he? . . . He doesn't speak, he hangs his head.
Of course he's humble—they're all of them demure;
God knows what mystery is hid in him.
God knows what you've thought up on his account,
What never has occurred to him in all his life.
Attracted by him, perhaps you have
Assigned to him a host of your own virtues.
It's not at all his fault; you're a hundred times more wrong.
No, no! Assume he's clever, getting smarter every minute,
Still, is he worthy of you? That is the question for you.
That I may bear my loss with more equanimity,

Let me, as one who shared your childhood with you,
A friend of yours, a brother,
Let me be certain now of this—
And then
I can beware of madness afterwards;
I will go far away, grow cold, indifferent,
And never think of love; there I will know how,
While wandering through the world, to forget and entertain myself.

SOFIYA (*to herself*). Unknowingly I drove him mad!
(*Aloud.*) Why make believe?
Molchalin just now might have smashed his arm,
And I was really worried over him;
But you, who happened to be here just then,
Didn't even bother to consider
You could help others out without analyzing it.
Perhaps there is some truth in your surmises,
And I stand up for him most warmly now!
Why be—I'll tell you quite straightforwardly—
So talkative and critical?
So open in your scorn of people?
Why grant the humblest, too, no quarter? . . . What for?
If someone happens to mention him,
The biting hail of your remarks, your jokes, starts falling.
Make fun, make fun for all your life! —How can you do it?

CHATSKY. Oh, Lord, am I really one of those
Whose only aim in life is laughing?
I enjoy myself when I meet the silly fools,
But I find them mostly very boring.

SOFIYA. You're wrong. All of this applies to other men.
Molchalin hardly could be tiresome
If you really knew him better.

CHATSKY (*heatedly*). What have you grown to know him so well for?

SOFIYA. I didn't try: chance brought us two together.
Just look, he's won the friendship of everyone in the house:
He's worked for Father three years now,
And Father often gets mad at nothing,
But he disarms him by his silence and forgives
Him from the goodness of his heart;
By the way, he could,

Of course, look for amusements, but—
He doesn't. He'll never overstep his elders' bounds.
We joke and laugh together—
But he will sit with them all day, happy or not,
Playing . . .

CHATSKY. He plays with them all day!
He keeps quiet when he's being cursed!
(*Aside.*)
She has no respect for him at all.

SOFIYA. Of course, he doesn't have that sort of mind
Which is the genius of some men, the pestilence of others;
Which is both swift and brilliant but soon unpleasant;
Which outright takes the world to task
So that the world at least will pay attention;
Is that the kind of mind to make a family happy?

CHATSKY. A satire and a moral—is that the meaning of all this?
(*Aside.*)
She doesn't care two beans for him.

SOFIYA. But after all he is a man of
Most marvelous virtue: pliant, modest, quiet,
Not a trace of anxiety on his face,
And not a false or foul step in his heart.
He doesn't chop strangers into pieces—
That's what I really love him for.

CHATSKY (*aside*). She's fooling! She's not in love with him.
(*Aloud.*)
I'll give you a hand to finish up
Your picture of Molchalin—but
What about Skalozub? There's a feast
For sore eyes! He stands up for the army
And holds himself erect,
In what he says and seems the hero . . .

SOFIYA. But not of my romance.

CHATSKY. But not of yours? Whoever can make you out?
[LIZA *enters.*]

LIZA (*in a whisper*). Madam, Aleksei Stepanych
Is coming right behind me to see you.

SOFIYA. Excuse me, I must hurry up, be on my way.

CHATSKY. Where to?

SOFIYA. The hairdresser's.

CHATSKY. Forget it.

SOFIYA. His curling-irons will get cold.

CHATSKY. Let them . . .

SOFIYA. I can't, we're having guests tonight.

CHATSKY. Lord, never mind! Again I'm left with my enigma.
However, let me steal for just a moment
Into your old room and look around:
The walls, the air—it's all so pleasant there! . . .
The memories of what now never will come back
Warm me, animate me, and give me peace!
I won't stay long; I'll just go in a couple of minutes . . .
And then—just think!—as a member of the English Club,
I'll give up whole days there to talking of
Molchalin's wit and Skalozub's intelligence.

(SOFIYA *shrugs her shoulders and,* LIZA *behind her, goes into her room and locks the door.*)

CHATSKY. Oh! Sofya! Has she really chosen this Molchalin!
Why isn't he fit husband? He isn't very smart.
But whoever wanted wit
Just in order to have children?
Obliging, frugal, a little color in his face . . .

(MOLCHALIN *enters.*)

Here he comes on tiptoe, a man not rich in words . . .
What black magic did he use to creep into her heart?

(*Turns to him.*)

You and I, Aleksei Stepanych,
Haven't managed to exchange two words.
Well, how're things going for you now?
No troubles nowadays? no sorrow?

MOLCHALIN. As always, sir.

CHATSKY. And how did you get on before?

MOLCHALIN. From day to day, today as yesterday.

CHATSKY. To pen from cards, and from the cards to the pen?
The hour fixed for both the high tide and the low?

MOLCHALIN. According to my work and effort,
Since I've been serving in the Archives,
I have received three decorations.

CHATSKY. You wheedled out respect and rank?

MOLCHALIN. No, sir, each has his talent . . .

CHATSKY. And yours?

MOLCHALIN. Two, sir:

Temperance and tidiness.

CHATSKY. The two most wonderful! Worth all the rest of ours.

MOLCHALIN. You didn't get promoted—for failure in your duties?

CHATSKY. Promotions come from people
And people sometimes can be wrong.

MOLCHALIN. How much surprised we were!

CHATSKY. What is so surprising?

MOLCHALIN. We're sorry for you.

CHATSKY. Wasted effort.

MOLCHALIN. Tatyana Yurevna was saying something just the other day
Coming back from Petersburg
About your connections with the Cabinet
And then your break . . .

CHATSKY. What does it matter to her?

MOLCHALIN. To Tatyana Yurevna?

CHATSKY. I've never even met her.

MOLCHALIN. Not Tatyana Yurevna?

CHATSKY. I haven't in my life;
I've heard she's very foolish.

MOLCHALIN. Are we talking about the same?
Tatyana Yurevna . . . is quite well known . . . besides
High officials and functionaries
All are her friends and close to her:
You ought to stop in once at Tatyana Yurevna's . . .

CHATSKY. For what?

MOLCHALIN. Well! There we very often
Find patronage and favor in places we weren't looking.

CHATSKY. I often call on women but not with that in mind.

MOLCHALIN. How urbane and good she is! How kind and simple!
Gives balls as lavish as could be
From Christmastime right up to Lent,
And summer parties at her dacha.
Now, really, why not enter service here in Moscow?
Get lots of decorations and start living big?

CHATSKY. When I am working, I avoid amusement;
When it's time to play the fool, I play it;
But there's a host of past masters at the art
Of mixing these two jobs; I am not one of them.

MOLCHALIN. Pardon me. All the same, I see no crime:
Why, take Foma Fomich—perhaps you know him?
CHATSKY. So?
MOLCHALIN. He's been department head under three ministers;
He was transferred here . . .
CHATSKY. Excellent!
A very shallow man, one of the most muddle-headed.
MOLCHALIN. How can you? His style is here set up as an example!
You've read his things?
CHATSKY. I never read such rubbish,
Especially of its best examples.
MOLCHALIN. No, but, on the contrary, I chanced to read them through with pleasure.
I'm not a writer . . .
CHATSKY. One can see that right away.
MOLCHALIN. I do not dare express my personal judgment . . .
CHATSKY. But why so secretive?
MOLCHALIN. A man of my age mustn't
Dare form a personal judgment.
CHATSKY. For Heaven's sake, you and I aren't children;
Why are only other men's opinions sacred?
MOLCHALIN. You know one must depend on what others think.
CHATSKY. And why this "must?"
MOLCHALIN. We're not so high in rank.
CHATSKY (*almost shouting*). With such a heart! With such emotions!
Beloved! . . . The fraudulent lady was making fun of me!
[*Servants enter.*]
(*Evening. All the doors are wide open, except the one into* SOFIYA'S *room. A series of brightly lit rooms extends into the distance in perspective. The servants bustle about; one of them, the most important, speaks:*)
Hey, Filler, Fomka, step it up!
Tables for cards, chalk, brushes and the candles!
(*Knocks on* SOFIYA'S *door.*)
Hurry up and tell our mistress, Lizaveta,
Natalya Dmitriyevna and her husband, too, are here,
And another carriage is at the porch.
(*They disperse;* CHATSKY *remains alone.*)
[NATALYA DMITRIYEVNA, *a young lady, enters.*]

NATALYA DMITRIYEVNA. Can I be mistaken? . . . Indeed, it's he, the face . . .

Ah, Aleksandr Andreich, it's you?

CHATSKY. You're looking me over from foot to head skeptically;

Have three years really made such changes in me?

NATALYA DMITRIYEVNA. I kept thinking you were very far from Moscow.

Are you back long?

CHATSKY. Just today . . .

NATALYA DMITRIYEVNA. For long?

CHATSKY. Depends.

But who wouldn't be amazed to look at you?

You have filled out; you have grown terribly attractive;

You look much younger, much more alive:

A spark, some color, laughter, liveliness all over.

NATALYA DMITRIYEVNA. I'm married.

CHATSKY. You should have said so long ago!

NATALYA DMITRIYEVNA. My husband is an ideal husband—he's coming now.

I'll introduce you—may I?

CHATSKY. Please do.

NATALYA DMITRIYEVNA. I know ahead of time

That you will like him. You look and be the judge.

CHATSKY. I believe you: he's your husband.

NATALYA DMITRIYEVNA. Oh, no; not for that,

All by himself, his character and mind,

Platon Mikhailych is my one and only jewel!

Retired now, he was a soldier,

And everybody says, who ever knew him then,

That with his bravery, his talent,

If he had stayed on in the service,

He would, of course, have been the Moscow commandant.

[PLATON MIKHAILOVICH *enters.*]

Here's my Platon Mikhailych.

CHATSKY. Heavens!

My old friend! We've known each other for years! That's fate for you!

PLATON M. Hello, dear Chatsky!

CHATSKY. Wonderful, Platon, my friend!

You ought to get a gold star: you've done this excellently.

PLATON M. Just as you see:

A Moscow resident and married.

CHATSKY. The barrack noise is gone, your comrades all forgotten?

You're peaceful now and lazy?

PLATON M. No, there are some things to do:

I'm learning how to play the A-minor duet

On the flute . . .

CHATSKY. The one you always played five years ago?

Well, a husband's constant taste is the dearest thing of all.

PLATON M. My friend, when you get married keep me in mind!

From boredom you'll be whistling the one and the same thing.

CHATSKY. From boredom? What? You already really pay her tribute?

NATALYA DMITRIYEVNA. *My* Platon Mikhailych likes various things to do

Which he can't now: likes studying and reviews,

Manège . . . so sometimes in the morning he is bored.

CHATSKY. But who, good friend, commands you to be idle?

To arms! You'll get a troop. You're a field officer or staff?

NATALYA DMITRIYEVNA. *My* Platon Mikhailych isn't very well.

CHATSKY. Not very well? For long?

NATALYA DMITRIYEVNA. The same old rheumatism and the headaches.

CHATSKY. More exercise. To the country, to a warmer clime,

Spend more time on horseback. In summer the country is divine.

NATALYA DMITRIYEVNA. Platon Mikhailych loves the city,

Loves Moscow; why should he waste his life in a faraway place?

CHATSKY. The city, Moscow . . . You're a queer one!

Remember how it was?

PLATON M. But, friend, now things have changed . . .

NATALYA DMITRIYEVNA. Ah! my dearest!

It's so chilly here one cannot stand it;

You've opened up completely and undone your vest.

PLATON M. I'm not now, friend, the man I was . . .

NATALYA DMITRIYEVNA. Listen, just a minute;

My darling—be careful, button up.

PLATON M (*coldly*). Right away.

NATALYA DMITRIYEVNA. And move a little farther from the door.
A draught is blowing on your back!
PLATON M. I'm not now, friend, the man I was . . .
NATALYA DMITRIYEVNA. My angel, for God's sake
Move back a little from the door!
PLATON M (*his eyes turned up*). Ah, wife of mine!
CHATSKY. Well, let God be your judge;
You didn't take much time to become the man you weren't!
Wasn't it last year, at the end,
I knew you in the regiment? Barely dawn
And you'd be off upon a nimble stallion;
Never mind the autumn wind in you face or on your back.
PLATON M (*sighs*). Ah, friend, that was indeed a splendid life.

[PRINCE TUGOUKHOVSKY, *the* PRINCESS *and their six daughters enter.*]

NATALYA DMITRIYEVNA (*in a little, thin voice*). Pyotr Ilyich, and Princess! Oh, my Lord!
And Princess Zizi! Mimi!

(*Loud kisses, after which they sit down and look each other up and down from head to foot.*)

1ST Princess. What a lovely cut!
2ND PRINCESS. What marvelous little pleats!
1ST PRINCESS. Trimmed all around with fringe.
NATALYA DMITRIYEVNA. If you only could see my satiny mantilla!
3RD PRINCESS. And what an *écharpe* I was given by my *cousin!*
4TH PRINCESS. Oh, yes!—of real *barège!*
5TH PRINCESS. Delightful!
6TH PRINCESS. Just darling!
PRINCESS. Shh! Who's in the corner there? And bowed when we came in?
NATALYA DMITRIYEVNA. Chatsky, a visitor.
PRINCESS. Re-tir-ed?
NATALYA DMITRIYEVNA. Yes, he was on a trip, came back not long ago.
PRINCESS. A ba-che-lor?
NATALYA DMITRIYEVNA. Yes, he's unmarried.
PRINCESS. Prince, Prince! Come here! Come quickly!
PRINCE (*turns his ear trumpet toward her*). O-hm!

PRINCESS. Hurry up and ask Natalya Dmitriyevna's
Friend to come to see us Thursday evening; there he is!
PRINCE. EE-hm!
(*Goes off, hovers around* CHATSKY *and coughs.*)
PRINCESS. That's what it means—children!
They have a ball and the father must come along to pay respects:
Partners have been so awfully scarce!
He's a Kammer-junker?[22]
NATALYA DMITRIYEVNA No.
PRINCESS. Ri-ich?
NATALYA DMITRIYEVNA. Oh, no!
PRINCESS (*loudly, with all her might*). Prince! Prince! Come back!
[*The* COUNTESSES KHRYUMIN, *grandmother and granddaughter, enter.*]
COUNTESS GRANDDAUGHTER. Ah, *grand'maman!* Whoever comes so early!
We're the first!
(*Disappears into a neighboring room.*)
PRINCESS. How rude she is!
The first one here, and she pretends we're nobody!
Nasty girl, an old maid all her life; may God forgive her!
COUNTESS GRANDDAUGHTER (*returning, looking at* CHATSKY *through her lorgnette*).
Monsieur Chatsky! You, in Moscow? And are you still the same?
CHATSKY. Why should I have changed?
COUNTESS GRANDDAUGHTER. You returned a bachelor?
CHATSKY. Whom should I have married?
COUNTESS GRANDDAUGHTER. There must be lots abroad.
Oh! Many of our men, not asking who,
Get married there and make us relatives
Of seamstresses in fashion shops.
CHATSKY. Unfortunate! Must we endure reproach
From ladies copying their milliners?
Just because we dared prefer
The real thing to the imitation?
(*Many other guests* [*enter*]. *Among others,* ZAGORET-

[22] A Court rank just below Kammerherr. Pushkin was a Kammer-junker.

SKY. *Men appear, bow, move aside, go in and out from room to room, etc.* SOFIYA *comes out from her room. All go to meet her.*)

COUNTESS GRANDDAUGHTER. *Eh! bon soir! vous voilà! Jamais trop diligente*
Vous nous donnez toujours le plaisir de l'attente.

ZAGORETSKY (*to* SOFIYA). Do you have a ticket to the theater tomorrow night?

SOFIYA. No.

ZAGORETSKY. Let me give you one; another man would have
In vain tried to oblige you. However,
Where I didn't run!
The office—all were taken—
To the director—he's my friend—
Since six o'clock this morning—was it worth while?
Since evening nobody could get a thing;
This one, that one—I hounded all of them;
And finally I snatched this forcibly
From some old, sickly man—a friend
Of mine, a well-known stay-at-home:
So let him stay at home in peace.

SOFIYA. Thank you kindly for the ticket,
And doubly for all you did.

(*Still more people come in. At the same time,* ZAGORETSKY *moves over to the men.*)

ZAGORETSKY. Platon Mikhailych . . .

PLATON M. Go away!
Go over to the women, tease *them*, and pull their leg.
I could tell such tales about you which
Would be far worse than any lie. My friend,

(*To* CHATSKY.)

I commend him to you!
How does one address these people more civilly,
More kindly? He's a society man,
A thorough swindler and a cheat:
Anton Antonych Zagoretsky.
Be careful when he's around: he's great at carrying tales.
And don't play cards with him: he'll skin you!

ZAGORETSKY. What a funny fellow! Grumpy, but without the slightest malice.

CHATSKY. And it'd be absurd for you to take offense;

Besides honesty there is a host of comforts:
One place they curse you, but the next they're grateful.

PLATON M. Oh, no, my friend! Here, they curse you
Everywhere and everywhere accept you.

(ZAGORETSKY *moves into the crowd.*)

[KHLYOSTOV *comes forward.*]

KHLYOSTOV. Do you think it's easy at sixty-five
For me to drag myself to your house, niece? It's torture!
I drove an *hour* from Pokrovka[23]—too much for me!
It's night—the dying of the light!
To keep me company I took
Along my Negro girl and little dog.
Have them given a bite to eat, my dear, in a little while,
Send down some leftovers from supper.
Princess, how do you do!

(*Sits down.*)

So, Sofyushka, my dear,
What a splendid little Negro girl I have!
Curly-headed, hunchbacked, too!
An angry thing, all kittenish ways.
And black, so black! So terrifying!
Just think, the Lord created such a breed!
A devil really! She's in the servants' room—
Shall I call her?

SOFIYA. Not now; some other time.

KHLYOSTOV. Imagine: they show them off like animals,
I've heard, there . . . there is some Turkish city . . .
You know who got her for me?
Anton Antonych Zagoretsky.

(ZAGORETSKY *comes forward.*)

He's a liar, a gambler, and a thief.

(ZAGORETSKY *disappears.*)

I was just about to lock the door on him for good,
But he knows how to help you: he got a pair
Of little Negroes for me and my sister at the fair.
Bought them, he says—I bet he cheated playing cards;
But he gave me a little present, God grant him all the best!

CHATSKY (*laughing, to* PLATON MIKHAILOVICH).
He won't get any good from just that kind of praise.
And that was more than Zagoretsky himself could face.

[23] Pokrovka—a street in Moscow.

KHLYOSTOV. Who's this cheerful man? What's his position?
SOFIYA. That man there? Chatsky.
KHLYOSTOV. So? What did he find funny?
What pleases him? What's so laughable?
It's very wrong to laugh at older people.
I remember, as a child, you often used to dance with him,
I used to box his ears—but not enough.

[FAMUSOV *enters.*]

FAMUSOV (*loudly*). We're waiting for Prince Pyotr Ilyich,
And the Prince is here already!—and I'd closeted myself
In the study.[24] Where's Skalozub, Sergei Sergeich?
Not here? It seems he isn't. He's an outstanding man,
Sergei Sergeich Skalozub.
KHLYOSTOV. Creator above! He deafened me: louder than trumpets!

[SKALOZUB *enters, then* MOLCHALIN.]

FAMUSOV. Sergei Sergeich, you are late!
And we have waited, waited, waited!

(*Escorts him over to* KHLYOSTOV.)

My dear sister-in-law,[25] who long, long since
Has heard about you!
KHLYOSTOV (*seated*). You were here before in the regiment . . . in . . . grenadiers?
SKALOZUB (*in a bass voice*). In His Highness' regiment, you mean,
The Novozemlyansky musketeers.
KHLYOSTOV. I'm not an expert in sorting out these regiments.
SKALOZUB. But there are differences in uniform:
The piping on the full-dress coats, the shoulder straps, the buttonholes.
FAMUSOV. Let's go in, old friend, I'll amuse you there;
We play a funny whist. Prince, I beg you, come!

(*Leads them both out.*)

KHLYOSTOV (*to* SOFIYA). Whew! I really did just barely escape the noose!

[24] In Russian, *portrétnaya*, which was the "study" in which the family portraits hung.

[25] In Russian, *névestushka*, which means his brother's wife. Khlyostov (in Russian, nom. sg., of course, Khlyostova) is his wife's sister. Filippov says it was an old custom in Moscow to give relatives, in their presence, a closer relationship than they actually had.

Of course, your father is half-witted:
He's taken a liking to this six-foot daredevil
And shows him round without inquiring do we want to or not?

MOLCHALIN (*hands her a card*). I have set up your foursome: Monsieur Coq,
Foma Fomich, and I.

KHLYOSTOV. Thank you, my dear!

(*Rises.*)

MOLCHALIN. Your spitz is just adorable! No bigger than a thimble!
I petted him all over; his fur is just like silk!

KHLYOSTOV. Thank you, my dear!

(*Goes out,* MOLCHALIN *and many others behind her.*)

[CHATSKY, SOFIYA *and several bystanders come forward. During the next few speeches, they all disperse.*]

CHATSKY. Well! He chased the clouds away . . .

SOFIYA. But still can't we go on?

CHATSKY. How did I frighten you?
Because he mollified the guest who had grown angry,
I meant to praise . . .

SOFIYA. And would have ended spitefully.

CHATSKY. Shall I tell you what I thought?
Old women are an angry bunch:
It wasn't bad that here their celebrated lackey
Stood like a lightning rod—
Molchalin! —Who else could settle things so peacefully?
He'll pet a pug at the right time,
He'll shove the right card in your hand,
Zagoretsky will live on in him!
You recently enumerated all his points
To me, but forgot a lot—right?

(*Goes out.*)

SOFIYA (*to herself*). Oh! This man always is the cause
Of great uneasiness for me!
He's glad to humiliate and sting—an envious, proud and evil man!

MR. N. (*comes up to her*). You're thinking now . . .

SOFIYA. About Chatsky.

MR. N. What did he strike you like when he got back?

SOFIYA. He's not in his right mind.

MR. N. He really has gone mad?

SOFIYA (*after a pause*). Well, not exactly that . . .

MR. N. However, there are symptoms?

SOFIYA (*stares at him*). It seems to me . . .

MR. N. How so, at such an age!

SOFIYA. What can you do?

(*Aside.*)

He's ready to believe it!

Ah, Chatsky! You who want to turn them into fools—

Will you first try it on for size?

(*Goes out.*)

MR. N. He's really mad, she thinks . . . Well, there you are!

Therefore, there's something to it . . . Where could she have got it?

[MR. D. *enters.*]

You heard it?

MR. D. What?

MR. N. About Chatsky?

MR. D. What?

MR. N. He's really mad.

MR. D. Absurd!

MR. N. I didn't make it up; others say so.

MR. D. But you approve of spreading it?

MR. N. I'll go find out; why, *some*body must know.

(*Goes out.*)

MR. D. Believe a gossip!

He hears some nonsense and repeats it right away!

[ZAGORETSKY *comes in.*]

You know the news of Chatsky?

ZAGORETSKY. No . . . ?

MR. D. He's really mad!

ZAGORETSKY. Oh, I know, I do remember, heard it.

How couldn't I? An amazing thing occurred:

His crooked uncle locked him up with crazy men.

They stuck him in a madhouse and put him on a chain.

MR. D. For Heaven's sake, he just was in this room.

ZAGORETSKY. Well, then, they must have let him out.

MR. D. Oh, so, dear friend, no need for newspapers with you.

I'll go and stretch myself a bit

And ask them all. But meanwhile—shh!—this is a secret!

ZAGORETSKY. Which Chatsky is it? . . . I think I've heard the name . . .

There was a Chatsky I was acquainted with.

[*The* COUNTESS GRANDDAUGHTER *enters.*]

You've heard of him?

COUNTESS GRANDDAUGHTER. Of whom?

ZAGORETSKY. Of Chatsky. He was in this room just now.

COUNTESS GRANDDAUGHTER. I know,
I was talking to him.

ZAGORETSKY. Then I congratulate you:
He's a crazy man.

COUNTESS GRANDDAUGHTER. What?

ZAGORESTKY. Yes, he really has gone mad!

COUNTESS GRANDDAUGHTER. Think of that. I noticed it myself!
I might have bet—you took the words right out of my mouth.

[*The* COUNTESS GRANDMOTHER *enters.*]

Ah! *grand'maman!* Here's something really amazing!
You haven't heard what's happened here?
Just listen! It's so wonderful—divine!

COUNTESS GRANDMOTHER. My dear, my ears are blocked;
Talk louder . . .

COUNTESS GRANDDAUGHTER. But there isn't time!

(*Points to* ZAGORETSKY.)

Il vous dira toute l'histoire . . .
I'll go find out.

(*Goes out.*)

COUNTESS GRANDMOTHER. Well? What? Perhaps there is a fire?

ZAGORETSKY. No, Chatsky was the cause of all this wild commotion.

COUNTESS GRANDMOTHER. What? Who put Chatsky into prison?

ZAGORETSKY. Badly wounded in the forehead once, he lost his reason.

COUNTESS GRANDMOTHER. What? Gone to the Freemasons' club? He has turned heathen?[26]

ZAGORETSKY. She'll never understand.

(*Goes out.*)

COUNTESS GRANDMOTHER. Anton Antonych! Ah!
He, too, is in a hurry; they're all in panic.

[PRINCE TUGOUKHOVSKY *enters.*]

Prince, Prince! Oh, that Prince! He comes to balls, can hardly breathe!

[26] Freemasonry was outlawed in Russia in 1822.

Prince, have you heard?

PRINCE. AH-hm!

COUNTESS GRANDMOTHER. He doesn't hear a thing!

At least, perhaps, you noticed if the chief of police was here?

PRINCE. EH-hm!

COUNTESS GRANDMOTHER. Who was it, Prince, took Chatsky off to jail?

PRINCE. EE-hm!

COUNTESS GRANDMOTHER. A broadsword and a knapsack,

He's been made a private, really—changed his church![27]

A Russian Orthodox could not at this time leave his faith.

PRINCE. OO-hm!

COUNTESS GRANDMOTHER. Truly! . . . He's become a heathen!

Ah! The damned Voltairian!

What? eh? Deaf, my dear; go, get your ear trumpet.

Oh! deafness is a handicap!

(KHLYOSTOV, SOFIYA, MOLCHALIN, PLATON MIKHAILOVICH, NATALYA DMITRIYEVNA, *the* COUNTESS GRANDDAUGHTER, *the* PRINCESS *with the* [*six*] *daughters*, ZAGORETSKY [*and*] SKALOZUB [*enter, followed by*] FAMUSOV *and many others.*)

KHLYOSTOV. He has gone mad? That's really something!

So suddenly! And just like that!

Sofya, did you hear?

PLATON M. Who was the first to let it out?

NATALYA DMITRIYEVNA. Ah, my dear, we all!

PLATON M. Well, then, we can't help but believe it.

But, still I'm skeptical.

FAMUSOV (*entering*). Of what, of Chatsky, now?

How so—skeptical? I was the first, I discovered it.

I've been amazed a long time now that no one locked him up.

Just talk about the powers that be—God knows what he'll say!

And let a man bow low, just bend himself in two,

Even if before the monarch,

Why, he will call him a toady scoundrel! . . .

KHLYOSTOV. Then too, he likes to laugh.

I had hardly said a word—and he began guffawing.

[27] Nobles and men of "high society" were, if found guilty, often sentenced by the courts to compulsory military service in the ranks.

MOLCHALIN. He counseled me to serve in Moscow in the Archives.

COUNTESS GRANDDAUGHTER. And deigned to honor me with the title—milliner!

NATALYA DMITRIYEVNA. And gave my husband the advice of living in the country.

ZAGORETSKY. Everything shows he's mad!

COUNTESS GRANDDAUGHTER. I saw it in his eyes!

FAMUSOV. Takes after his mother, after Anna Aleksevna;
The dear-departed went insane eight times.

KHLYOSTOV. The world is full of wonderful adventures!
At his age, now, he has gone crazy!
I bet he drank beyond his years?

PRINCESS. Oh, sure . . .

COUNTESS GRANDDAUGHTER. No doubt.

KHLYOSTOV. Guzzled down champagne by tumblerfuls.

NATALYA DMITRIYEVNA. By bottlefuls—the very biggest.

ZAGORETSKY (*heatedly*). No, by forty-bucket barrelfuls.

FAMUSOV. Well, now! It's no great shame, indeed,
For a man to take a drop too much!
Study—that's the plague; learning—that's the reason
That nowadays there are more madmen
And crazy things and thoughts than there ever were before.

KHLYOSTOV. And really all these things are enough to drive you mad,
These boarding-schools, lycées—what are their names, again?—
And then these Landcruiser Mutual Teaching things.[28]

PRINCESS. Now, in Petersburg there is the Ped-
A-go-gic Institute—I think that's what it's called?—
There professors practice away at schism-making
And lack of faith.[29] A relative of ours went there—

[28] In 1819, the *Obshchestvo uchilishch vzaimnogo obucheniya* was established, modeled on the Lancaster, or *Lankasterskaya*, system of mutual instruction. Khlyostov uses, instead, the word *land-kartochn*[*aya*], which means "map." The system was popular among liberals. Like some of the boarding-schools and lycées, it was considered by the government and by conservatives as a breeding ground of dangerous ideas.

[29] Costello points out that "in 1821 four professors of the Pedagogical Institute were accused of atheism and subversive activities and lost their jobs."

When he came out, he might as well have been a pharmacist's
Apprentice. He avoids all women, even me!
Pays no regard to rank! A botanist, a chemist—
That's Fyodor, my nephew and a prince.
SKALOZUB. I have good news for you: everybody's saying
There is a plan afoot for all lycées and schools:
Then they'll do the teaching there our way: left! right!
And books will be reserved just for the big occasions.
FAMUSOV. Sergei Sergeich, no! If the evil is to be undone
The books must all be gathered up and burned.
ZAGORETSKY (*meekly*). No, sir, there are all kinds of books.
But, just between us,
If I were made the censor now,
I'd give it to the fables. Oh—fables are my death!
Eternal making-fun of eagles and of lions!
Whatever you may say,
Although they're beasts, they still are really kings!
KHLYOSTOV. My dears, my dears, now if a man's deranged,
It doesn't matter whether it's from books or drink;
But I feel sorry for Chatsky.
Why, he is worthy of our Christian pity now;
He was a witty man and had three hundred serfs.
FAMUSOV. Four.
KHLYOSTOV. Three, good sir.
FAMUSOV. Four hundred.
KHLYOSTOV. No, only three.
FAMUSOV. Now, on my calendar . . .
KHLYOSTOV. Suddenly these calendars!
FAMUSOV. Exactly four! Oh, what a loud-voiced arguer!
KHLYOSTOV. No, three; you think I know nothing about other people's estates?
FAMUSOV. Four hundred, I beg you understand.
KHLYOSTOV. No, three, three, three!
[CHATSKY *enters.*]
NATALYA DMITRIYEVNA. He's here!
COUNTESS GRANDDAUGHTER. Shsh!
ALL. Shsh!
(*They move away from* [CHATSKY] *toward the opposite side.*)
KHLYOSTOV. Now, what if in his madness
He wants to start a fight and settle things with us!

FAMUSOV. O, Lord! have mercy on us sinners!
(*Cautiously.*)
My dearest friend, you're not at all yourself.
After your journey, you need to rest. Your pulse—you are unwell.
CHATSKY. True, I can stand no more! A thousand torments are
In my breast from the clutches of my friends,
In my feet from shuffling, in my ears from exclamations,
And most of all inside my head from all these nothings.
(*Goes up to* SOFIYA.)
The heart in me is heavy with some kind of grief,
And I am lost in all these people; I'm not myself.
No, I'm displeased with Moscow!
KHLYOSTOV. Moscow, see, is guilty.
FAMUSOV. Get back from him!
(*Makes a sign to* SOFIYA.)
Hm, Sofya!—She isn't looking!
SOFIYA (*to* CHATSKY). Tell us: what is it makes you angry?
CHATSKY. I had a silly encounter in that room:
A Frenchman from Bordeaux, unburdening his heart,
Drew a sort of meeting around himself
And kept repeating how he prepared to go
To Russia, to the barbarians, in fear and trembling;
Arrived and found there was no end of kindness,
And didn't hear a Russian sound or see
A Russian face—as if he were at home, with friends—
In his own provinces! Just look: each evening he
Feels himself a little king among us:
The ladies make no more sense, dress the same . . .
He's glad, but we are not.
He stopped, and then on every side
There were groans and moans and yearning:
"Ah, France! There isn't a better country in the world!"
Two princesses decided, sisters, just repeating
The lesson that was pounded into them since childhood.
Where can you get away from princesses?
I, at a distance, raised the wish—
A humble wish but said out loud—
That God exterminate this evil spirit
Of empty, servile, blind, foul imitation;
That He implant a spark in someone with a heart

Who could by word and deed
Restrain us, as if by taut, stout reins,
From miserable longing for what isn't ours.
Let everyone call me an Old Believer;[30]
Our North is a hundred times much worse for me
Since it exchanged the things it had for this modernity—
Its morals, manners, and its language, revered traditions,
Even its majestic dress, for something foreign
That's like a jester's costume:
A tail behind, some weird excision up in front—
Against all reason and in defiance of the elements;
The gestures, hobbled; no beauty in the face:
The gray, absurd, and beardless chins! . . .
Like the hairdos and the dresses, so the minds are short![31]
Ah! If we have been born to pick up everything,
We might at least adopt a little of the Chinese
Very sage ignorance of men of other lands!
Will we ever come out from under the foreign rule of fashions,
So that our wise and valiant people
Will, even just by language, not think that we are Germans?
"How can you put what's European on a level
With what's national—that's somehow odd!
How can you translate, say, *madame* and *mademoiselle?*
Now, really, not just 'madam!'?" someone mumbled to me.
Just imagine, everybody
Burst out laughing at my expense.
"Madam! ha! ha! ha! ha! Splendid!
Madam! ha! ha! ha! ha! Dreadful!"—
Growing angry and cursing life,
I had a devastating answer ready,
But everyone moved back from me.
That's what happened to me once—nothing new.
In Moscow, Petersburg, in all of Russia, you
Will find that a man from the city of Bordeaux,
Just once he's opened his mouth, can win
All the little princesses' compassion.

[30] Technically, one of the dissident sects which refused to support the church reforms in the 17th century; hence, loosely, an old-fashioned conservative.

[31] The proverb is: "A woman's hair is long, but her mind is short."

And in Petersburg and, also, Moscow,
Who hates imported faces, freaks, and fancy words,
Who has unhappily in his head
Some five or six sensible ideas,
And who dares openly express them, suddenly—
See . . .

(He looks around. Everyone is whirling around in a waltz with the greatest enthusiasm. The old men have sat down at the card tables.)

ACT IV

The front hall of FAMUSOV'S *house. A large stairway leading down from the second floor. Many side rooms on the mezzanine open onto it. Downstairs, stage right the exit to the porch and the porter's lodge; stage left, on the same level,* MOLCHALIN'S *room. Night. The lights are dim. Some footmen bustle about; others sleep while waiting for their masters.*

[*The* COUNTESS GRANDMOTHER *and* COUNTESS GRANDDAUGHTER *enter, preceded by their footman.*]

FOOTMAN. Countess Khryumin's carriage.
COUNTESS GRANDDAUGHTER (*while she is being bundled up*).
The ball! Oh, Famusov! How he collects the guests!
Some sort of freaks from beyond the grave,
And nobody to talk to, nobody to dance with.
COUNTESS GRANDMOTHER. Let's go, my dear. It really was too much for me!
Some day I'll go from a ball straight to my grave.
(*Both drive off.* PLATON MIKHAILOVICH *and* NATALYA DMITRIYEVNA [*enter*]; *one footman bustles around them, another in the doorway shouts:*)
The Gorichs' carriage.
NATALYA DMITRIYEVNA. My angel, oh, my life,
My priceless, darling Poposh,[32] why are you so sad?
(*Kisses her husband's forehead.*)
Admit we had a merry time at Famusov's.
PLATON M. Natasha, darling, I always doze at balls;
I'm one who really doesn't care for them,
But I don't object—I am your man—
I stand the watch to midnight, then
To please you, however sad I am,
You give the order, and I dance.
NATALYA DMITRIYEVNA. You're just pretending, and quite unskilfully;
You want terrifically to be considered old.
(*Goes out with the footman.*)

[32] A Frenchified diminutive of Platon.

PLATON M. (*coldly*). A ball is something good, but bondage, something bitter;
And who compels us to get married?
Some men, of course, are fated at their birth . . .
FOOTMAN (*from the porch*).
Your lady's in the carriage, sir, and growing angry.
PLATON M. (*with a sigh*). Coming, coming!
(*Drives off.*)
(CHATSKY [*enters*], *preceded by his footman.*)
CHATSKY. Call and tell them to hurry up.
(*The footman goes out.*)
Well, there it is—the day is gone
And all the specters with it, all
The smoke and fumes of all the hopes I cherished . . .
What did I expect? What would I find?
Where is this charm of meeting? Real sympathy in whom?
A shout! Delight! Embrace! —Nothing there!
Sitting idly in a carriage,
Traveling across a boundless plain,
Something seems to lie ahead:
It's bright, it's blue, it's various . . .
And you drive on an hour, or two, all day. Then suddenly
You've galloped up to your resting place. You spend the night.
No matter where you look, there is the same flat steppe;
It's empty, and it's dead . . . Oh, Lord! Too much! The more you think . . .
(*The footman returns.*)
It's ready?
FOOTMAN. Nobody can find the coachman, sir.
CHATSKY. Get going, search. This isn't the place to spend the night.
(*The footman goes out again.* REPETILOV *runs in from the porch. Right in the doorway he falls flat on his face and hurriedly picks himself up.*)
REPETILOV. Damn! I slipped! Ah! Lord in Heaven!
Let me wipe my eyes . . . How come you're here? my friend!
My old-time friend! My dearest friend! *mon cher!*
Now, I've been given goings-over groundlessly
For being a tattle-tale, for being stupid, superstitious,
For having premonitions all the time, and omens—
Right now . . . I must explain the way

I seemed to know that hurrying here,
Crash! —I'd trip across the sill
And sprawl out on the floor.
You may make fun of me,
Say Repetilov's lying, Repetilov's dumb,
But I have a great desire to see you, a sort of illness,
A sort of love—indeed, a passion.
I'm ready now to stake my life
That in the world you'll never find yourself a friend
So true as me, honestly;
May I lose my wife and children,
Be abandoned by the world,
May I die right on the spot,
May God tear my soul to pieces . . .

CHATSKY. Oh, stop this stupid nonsense.

REPETILOV. You don't like me—most natural, indeed:
With others I am free and easy,
With you I talk too timidly;
I'm pitiful, I'm silly, a fool, an ignoramus . . .

CHATSKY. Now, there you have strange self-abasement!

REPETILOV. Curse me out; I curse my birth myself,
When I begin to think how I have killed the time:
But, tell me, what time is it?

CHATSKY. It's time to go to bed:
Now that you've shown up to dance,
You can go home again.

REPETILOV. What is a dance, my friend? Where we, all night till dawn,
Shackled by decorum, can't escape the yoke?!
You've read about it? . . . There is a book . . .

CHATSKY. But did you read it? That's what troubles me.
You're really Repetilov?

REPETILOV. Call me vandal, then—
I have deserved that name:
I valued hollow, worthless men
And dreamed my life away with dinners and with balls!
Forgot about the children and deceived my wife!
I played! I lost! They tried to take my property!
I keep a ballerina—and not just one—
But three at once!
I drank myself dead drunk and didn't sleep two weeks!

I flaunted everything: the laws, my conscience, and my faith.

CHATSKY. Now listen: lie, but know the limits.
This is enough to make a man despair.

REPETILOV. But wish me well: now I am acquainted with
The very cleverest people! I don't wander all night long.

CHATSKY. Say, today, for example?

REPETILOV. What's one night? Doesn't count.
But ask me where I've been.

CHATSKY. I can guess that for myself.
In the club, I bet.

REPETILOV. In the English Club. To start my story—
From a very noisy gathering . . .
Now, please, be quiet—I gave my word of honor, too . . .
We have a group, and we hold secret meetings
Every Thursday.[33] The most secret kind of group . . .

CHATSKY. Ah, friend, I am afraid.
Really, in the club?

REPETILOV. Right in it.

CHATSKY. What a splendid way
To get yourselves and all your secrets bounced right out.

REPETILOV. It's wrong for you to be afraid.
We speak up openly and loudly—no one understands.
Myself, when it comes down to Senate rooms and jurors,
To Byron—well, and to important things,
I often listen without opening my mouth;
It's way beyond me, friend; and I feel dumb.
Ah, *Alexandre!* You were all the things we lacked.
Now listen, friend of mine, do me just a tiny favor:
Let's go right now—luckily we're on our way—
The kind of people I will introduce
You to! . . . They're not at all like me in any way.
What people there, *mon cher!* The cream of the bright young crowd!

CHATSKY. God take care of them—and you. Where shall I go?
What for? Into the dead of night? . . . No, home—I want to sleep.

[33] A parody of the "secret societies" of the time. Pushkin's anti-society society *Arzamas*, to which, as Costello points out, Griboyedov was unsympathetic, was itself such a parody and met on Thursday.

REPETILOV. Oh, stop it! Who sleeps nowadays? Enough, without more preludes,
Decide, and we . . . we have . . . decisive people,
A dozen brilliant hotheads!
We shout—you'd think there were a hundred talking!
CHATSKY. And what's the reason that you rave so much?
REPETILOV. We always have a row . . .
CHATSKY. You have a row—that's all?
REPETILOV. This isn't the place now to explain, and I haven't time,
But it's about the government:
You see, it hasn't been defined—
You can't suddenly . . .
What people there, *mon cher!* Without another word,
I'll tell you straight: first, Prince Grigory!
A real, unique eccentric, makes us die from laughter!
Lived with the English long, has the English temper,
And talks through his teeth just the way they do,
And wears his hair cut short, just the way they do.[34]
You don't know him? Oh, try to get to meet him.
Vorkulov Evdokim is another.
You never heard the way he sings? Marvelous!
Go hear him, friend, especially
His one most favorite thing:
"*Ah, non lasciarmi, no, no, no!*"[35]
And then there are the brothers
Levon and Borinka—wonderful young boys!
You just can't think of what to say—
And if you want me to include a genius—
There's Udushev, Ippolit Markelych!
Have you read anything
He's written? Just a little bit?
Oh, read it, friend! He doesn't write just nothing.
Why, people of that sort should be

[34] In Russian, *obstrizhen dlya poryadka.* If applied to a serf, this would mean "cropped for the sake of law and order," that is, after having been caught as a runaway. In other words, to have a foreign haircut is no more than to behave like a runaway serf.

[35] Baldassare Galuppi, *Didone abbandonata.* Galuppi was invited to Russia from Venice in 1766–68 by Catherine. His operas were well received, and he influenced Russian church music.

At one and the same time whipped and told: write, write,
write!
However, you can find among the magazines
His fragment: A View and *Some*thing.
What's *Some*thing on?—on everything;
He knows it all; we're keeping him for a rainy day.
But chief among us is a man unique in Russia—
Don't have to say his name, you'll recognize his portrait:
A midnight robber, duelist;
Once exiled to Kamchatka, he came back as an Aleutian;[36]
And terrifically dishonest;
But, sure, a clever man can't help but be a cheat!
Whenever he discusses lofty honesty,
He seems inspired by a demon:
His eyes are bloodshot; his face, on fire;
Himself, he weeps; and we weep with him.
Those are men—are there any others like them? Hardly.
Well, in such company, of course, I'm mediocre,
A bit behind, and lazy—awful to think how!
However, once my little mind's at work, I'll sit down
With them, and before an hour's up,
Just somehow, by some chance, I'll suddenly get off a pun.
The others then latch on to this idea of mine
And, presto, half-a-dozen knock a farce together;[37]
Half-a-dozen others add the music;
And others clap and cheer when it's put on . . .
Laugh, my friend, but it's all very pleasant!
God did not endow me with ability,
But gave me a good heart, and that's why people like me;
I pile it on, but they don't mind.

FOOTMAN (*in the doorway*). The carriage of Skalozub.

[36] The "portrait" is of Count Fyodor Evanovich Tolstoy (1782–1846), a distant relative of Lev Nikolayevich. He led a wild life, spent some time in the Aleutians and Russian possessions in America (was nicknamed "The American"), and, after having sailed to Kamchatka, returned to St. Petersburg across Siberia mostly on foot. He was a distinguished soldier, a notorious card-sharp, a scandalous duellist (he killed eleven men), and a friend of the leading intellectual and literary figures of his time.

[37] The word here translated "farce" is in the Russian *vodevil'chik*, or "vaudeville," a light musical comedy, such as those written by Shakhovskoy, very popular until the middle of the nineteenth century.

REPETILOV. Whose?

(SKALOZUB *comes down the stairs.* REPETILOV *goes to meet him.*)

Ah, Skalozub, my dearest friend!
Wait, where are you off to? Do me the kindness!

(*Squeezes him to his heart.*)

CHATSKY. Where can I go to get away from them?

(*Goes out into the vestibule.*)

REPETILOV (*to* SKALOZUB). The talk about you long ago died down.
They said that you went off to join your regiment.
You two have met?

(*Looks around for* CHATSKY.)

The stubborn man! He skipped away!
It doesn't matter, I've found you accidentally,
And we all beg you come with me at once, and no excuses!
Prince Grigory has a crowd of people now,
You'll find some forty of us there.
Whew! How much wit and reason there!
They talk all night, and no one's bored;
First, they're pouring out champagne to make us burst,[38]
And secondly they're teaching us such things
As you and I, of course, could never dream of.

SKALOZUB. Let me alone. You'll not fool me with scholarship.
Go call the others; and if you wish
I'll send Prince Grigory and you
A master sergeant to be Voltaire:
He'll line you up three ranks abreast,
And if you peep, he'll shut you up real fast.

REPETILOV. Always thinking of your work! *Mon cher*, look here:
I also would have won high rank but met bad luck,
Perhaps the kind that no one ever has.
I was on the civil side. At that time
Baron von Klotz was aiming for minister,
And I
To be his son-in-law
Point-blank, without a further thought;
I sat down to play reversi with his wife and him,

[38] The Russian is: *napoyat shampanskim na uboi*, which is a play on the phrase *otkarmlivat' na uboi*, "to fatten [animals] for slaughter."

And gambled away to him and her
So much, so much—God preserve me!
He lived on Fontanka quai; I built a house beside it;
With columns, too, enormous! How much it cost!
And finally I did get married to his daughter,
Drew for dowry—a pinch, and for a job—a blank.[39]
The father-in-law's a German, so what's the use?
He was afraid, see, of being reproached
For what might seem weakness for his relatives.
He was afraid—the hell with him—did that help me?
All his aids are boors, all—mercenary,
Lousy men, scribbling vermin,
All—self-made aristocrats, all—self-important.
Just look in the official listings . . .
Damn! Service, ranks, and medals are the soul's ordeals:
Aleksei Lakhmotyev puts it wonderfully
That radical medication's needed now, because
The stomach won't digest any more . . .
(*Pauses, having noticed that* ZAGORETSKY *has replaced* SKALOZUB, *who has meanwhile driven off.*)

ZAGORETSKY. Oh, please, go on. I must confess to you sincerely
How, like yourself, I'm just a terrible liberal!
And since I'm very frank and boldly speak my mind,
How much—how *very* much—I've lost!

REPETILOV (*sadly*). All are apart without a word!
One man's hardly out of sight, the next's already gone.
Chatsky was here—left suddenly, then—Skalozub . . .

ZAGORETSKY. What's your opinion, now, on Chatsky?

REPETILOV. He's not dumb;
We just ran into each other; there was a lot of chit-chat,[40]
And a clever conversation on vaudeville started up . . .
Yes, vaudeville's really something, but all the rest is *nil!*
He and I . . . We have . . . one and the same taste.

ZAGORETSKY. And did you notice that he is
Really afflicted in his reason?

[39] The word translated "pinch" is, in the Russian, *shish*, which means 1) the gesture of putting the thumb between the first and second fingers, and 2) literally, next to nothing.

[40] In Russian, *turusy* ["chit-chat"] *na kolyosakh* means "nonsense," "cock-and-bull stories," "empty talk."

REPETILOV. What a lot of nonsense!

ZAGORETSKY. Everyone has this opinion.

REPETILOV. Absurd!

ZAGORETSKY. Ask anyone.

REPETILOV. Chimeras!

ZAGORETSKY. But, fortunately, here's Prince Pyotor Ilyich,
The Princess, and the Princesses.

REPETILOV. Nonsense.[41]

[*The* PRINCESS *and her six daughters enter . . . The footmen are bustling around.*]

ZAGORETSKY. Sweet princesses, I beg you, what is your opinion?
Is Chatsky mad or not?

1ST PRINCESS. How can there be a doubt of this?

2ND PRINCESS. The whole world knows about it all.

3RD PRINCESS. The Dryanskys, Khvorovs, Varlyanskys and Skachkovs . . .

4TH PRINCESS. Ah, that's old stuff. Who can think it's news?

5TH PRINCESS. Who is in doubt?

ZAGORETSKY. Nobody believes it . . .

6TH PRINCESS. You!

ALL (*together*). Monsieur Repetilov, hey, Monsieur Repetilov!
How *can* you?
How do you do it! Can you go against everyone?
And how come you're involved? Fie, shame and ridicule.

REPETILOV (*plugs his ears*). Excuse me, I didn't know that this is widely known.

PRINCESS. I should say it is! It's dangerous to talk
To him: he should have been locked up
A long time ago; just listen how his little finger
Is the smartest thing of all, including Prince Pyotr!
I think he simply is a Jacobin,
Your Chatsky. Let's go. Prince, you might escort
Katish or Zizi; we will take the six-seater.

KHLYOSOTOV (*entering down the front stairs;* MOLCHALIN *escorts her on his arm. From the stairs:*)
Princess, the little debt from playing?

PRINCESS. I'll owe it to you, dear.

[41] In Russian, the word *dich'* means both "nonsense" and "gamebirds."

ALL (*to each other*). Good-bye.

(*The* PRINCESS' *family drives off, and* ZAGORETSKY, *too.*)

REPETILOV. Heavenly Father!
Amfisa Nilovna! Ah, Chatsky—the poor man . . .
What is all this intelligence? These thousand and one concerns?
Tell me, why do we strive so in this world?

KHLYOSTOV. That's what God decreed for him; besides,
I bet they'll treat—and cure—him!
But you, sir, are incurable, no matter what.
You showed up at the proper time!
Molchalin, there's your little room in there.
No one has to show you; go, God bless you.

(MOLCHALIN *goes to his room.*)

Good-bye, my friend; it's time you stopped behaving wildly.

(*Drives off.*)

REPETILOV (*with his footman*). Now where's a place for me to go?
It's already getting on toward dawn.
Come, put me in the carriage
And take me somewhere.

(*Drives off. The last light goes out.*)

CHATKSY (*comes out of the vestibule*).
What's this? Did I really hear all this with my own ears?
This isn't humor, but clearly malice. What miracles,
What sort of witchery do they use
To—all together—spread absurd reports of me?
Some feel as if they've won a victory,
And others seem to sympathize . . .
Oh! *If* one could see through people!
Which is worse in them—their heart or tongue?
Whose invention is this?
The fools believe it all, and then they pass it on—
At once old ladies sound the alarm—
And here's your general opinion!
And here's that homeland! . . . No, by my arrival today
I see that I will soon grow sick and tired of it.
But Sofya—does she know?—Of course, they must have told her.
She isn't one, I think, who just to do me harm

Would thus amuse herself, and right or wrong—
She doesn't care whether it's me or someone else—
To tell the truth, she doesn't care for anyone.
But where did this fainting come from, this unconsciousness?
Hypersensitive nerves, caprice—
A little thing upsets them, and a little thing will calm them—
I took to be the sign of actual passions. Not a bit!
Of course, her strength would fail her just as well
If ever someone stepped
On a cat's, or on a dog's, tail.

SOFIYA (*on the stairs on the second floor, holding a candle*). Molchalin, is that you?

(*The door hurriedly shuts again.*)

CHATSKY. It's she! Herself!
Ah, my head's on fire, all my blood is pounding;
She came! She's gone! Was it really just a vision?
Have I, indeed, gone really mad?
I certainly am ready for whatever comes,
But there's no phantom here—the hour of meeting is set.
What's the point of my trying to deceive myself?
She called Molchalin—and there's his room.

[HIS] FOOTMAN (*from the porch*). The carri . . .

CHATSKY. Shsh!

(*Pushes him out.*)

I'll stay right here and never wink an eye,
Even if till dawn. If one must down one's sorrow,
It's better all at once
Than to delay, for troubles do not fade away.
The door is opening.

(*Hides behind a pillar.*)

LIZA (*comes in with a candle*). I haven't the strength, I'm scared!
In an empty hall, at night! You're scared of ghosts!
You're scared of the living, too!
My lady, my tormentor, Oh, God help her!
And Chatsky like a mote in her eye.
Now, she thought he was somewhere here downstairs.

(*Looks around.*)

Oh, sure! A lot he wants to wander around the hall!
I bet he drove off long ago,

Saved his love up for tomorrow,
Went home—and went to bed.
However, now I must knock on the beloved's door.
(*Knocks on* MOLCHALIN'*s door.*)
Listen, sir! It's time for you to wake up, please:
Your lady's calling you . . . You hear—your lady's calling . . .
Now hurry up, so they don't catch . . .
(CHATSKY [*remains*] *behind the pillar;* MOLCHALIN [*comes out*], *stretches and yawns;* SOFIYA *creeps cautiously down the stairs.*)
You are a stone, sir! You are ice!

MOLCHALIN. Ah. Lizanka, is that your feeling?

LIZA. My lady's, sir.

MOLCHALIN. Who would have guessed
That through these little cheeks, these veins,
The crimson blush of love has not yet run?
Is all you want to be just running errands?

LIZA. But you, you courters of young girls,
Should not sit back, and shouldn't yawn;
He's nice and handsome who eats a bite
And sleeps but little until the wedding.

MOLCHALIN. What wedding's this? With whom?

LIZA. And with my lady?

MOLCHALIN. Go on!
I've high, high hopes ahead of me—
I'll get by without a wedding.

LIZA. How can you, sir! Who do you think
She plans to marry if not you?

MOLCHALIN. I don't know. But I sometimes shudder so
And get so frightened by the thought
That Pavel Afanasich once,
Just once, will catch the two of us,
And throw us out and curse us! . . . Why? Shall I tell you all?
I don't see a single thing to envy in
Sofya Pavlovna. God grant her health and wealth.
She used to love Chatsky once;
She'll stop loving me the same as him.
My little angel, I could wish I felt
For her a half of what I feel for you.
But no: no matter what I tell

Myself, how much I try—I see her and grow cold.
SOFIYA (*aside*). How despicable!
CHATSKY (*behind the pillar*). The dog!
LIZA. And you are not ashamed?
MOLCHALIN. My father's last advice was:
First of all, please everyone without exception—
The master of the house in which you live,
The office chief with whom I'm going to serve,
His valet who brushes off my clothes,
The doorman and the super—to avoid unpleasantness—
The superintendent's dog, so it is mild and kind.
LIZA. I must say, sir, you've got a very big concern!
MOLCHALIN. And so I make-believe I'm madly in love
To satisfy the daughter of such a man . . .
LIZA. Who gives you room, and board besides;
Who'll sometimes hand you out promotion, too?
Well, then, come on; we've talked now long enough.
MOLCHALIN. Let's go divide the love of our lamenting lady.
Come, let me hug you from the fullness of my heart.
(LIZA *does not yield.*)
Oh, why can't she be you?
(*Starts to go.* SOFIYA *does not let him.*)
SOFIYA (*almost in a whisper; the whole scene is in a low voice*).
Don't go any farther, I've overheard a lot . . .
You wretched man! I'm so ashamed the walls must blush.
MOLCHALIN. What! . . . Sofya Pavlovna!
SOFIYA. Don't talk, for God's sake!
Keep quiet—I might dare the worst!
MOLCHALIN (*falls on his knees.* SOFIYA *pushes him away*).
Oh, remember! Don't be angry, look at me! . . .
SOFIYA. I remember nothing, don't annoy me!
My memories! . . . How like a keen-edged knife they are . . .
MOLCHALIN (*groveling at her feet*).
Be merciful . . .
SOFIYA. Don't act meanly; get up!
I don't want an answer—I know what you will say;
You'll lie . . . .
MOLCHALIN. Just do me now the kindness . . .
SOFIYA. No, no, no!
MOLCHALIN. I was joking, and I didn't say a thing, except . . .
SOFIYA. Stop it now, I say; or else

I'll shout and wake up all the house,
And ruin both myself and you.
(MOLCHALIN *gets up.*)
From this time on it's just as if I'd never known you.
Don't you dare expect from me
Reproach, complaints, or tears—you're not worth them.
See that the daylight never finds us here in the house
And that I never hear another word about you!

MOLCHALIN. Anything you say.

SOFIYA. Or else I'll tell
My father everything in sorrow.
You know that I don't value my own self.
Go on.—No, wait! . . . Be very pleased
That in the midnight meetings between the two of us
You were much more—and naturally—reserved than now
In the light of day, in front of people, actually.
You have less impudence than deviousness of heart.
Myself I'm pleased that I found out everything at night:
There are no hostile witnesses before me now,
As recently, when I grew faint and fell—
Then Chatsky was here . . .

CHATSKY (*jumps in between them*). He is now, you hypocrite!

LIZA *and* SOFIYA. Ah! Ah!
(LIZA *drops the candle in fright;* MOLCHALIN *runs off into his room.*)

CHATSKY. Hurry up and faint! Now it's quite in order:
There is more reason for it than there was before.
Now, at last, the riddle has been solved!
Here's the one I have been sacrificed to!
I've no idea how I held back the madness in me!
I looked and saw and wouldn't believe!
And the one she loved, for whom she left
Her former friend, her woman's fear, and even shame,
Runs off behind the door, afraid to answer to it.
Ah! How can we grasp the game of fate?
She plagues and persecutes the sensitive!
Molchalins really prosper in this world!

SOFIYA (*completely in tears*).
Don't go on; I am entirely to blame.
But whoever would have thought he would be so deceitful!

LIZA. Pounding! Noise! Ah, my God, they *all* are coming!

Your father! He'll be very grateful!

[FAMUSOV *and a crowd of servants with candles enter.*]

FAMUSOV. This way! Follow me, and hurry!
More candles and more lanterns, quick!
Where are the ghosts? Pah! All the faces are well known.
My girl! . . . Sofya Pavlovna! . . . For shame!
You shameless thing! With whom? And where? Exactly like
Her mother, my dear-departed wife;
Used to be, I'd barely leave my better half
And she'd be some place with a man!
Have you no fear of God! What? How did he allure you?
You yourself said that he was crazy . . .
No! Stupidity and blindness struck me down!
All this was just a plot, and he himself was in
On it, and all the pests. Why am I punished so?

CHATSKY (*to* SOFIYA). So I have you to thank for this invention, too?

FAMUSOV. My boy, don't wriggle: I won't be deceived!
Fight together—I won't believe it.
You, Filka, you real blockhead!
I made a stupid lazybones the porter!
Doesn't know a thing, doesn't sense it, either!
Where were you? Where did you go?
How come you didn't lock the doors?
And why didn't you inspect? How come you didn't hear?
Hard labor for you! Exile to my country place.
All set to sell me for a penny!
You, bright eyes! It's all because of your caprices!
There it is, Kuznetsky Street, the fashions and the clothing.
There you learned to play the panderer.
But wait! I'll straighten you out yet:
Go to a peasant's hut—now march!—and watch the chickens!
And you, my friend, my daughter, I'll not forget you, either:
Have patience for a day or two—
You'll not stay on in Moscow, live with decent people,
But far away from cavaliers—
To the country with you, to Saratov, to your aunt's!
There you can grieve your sorrows out,
Do your embroidery, and fall asleep while reading
In the Scriptures. You, sir, I plainly ask
Never to come here by highway or by byway;

And such was this, the final thing you did,
That now, I'm sure, all doors will be shut tight against you!
I'll do my best, I'll pound on the alarum,
I'll make real trouble for you everywhere in town,
And tell the whole wide world about you:
I'll protest to the Senate, the ministers, the Tsar . . .

CHATSKY (*after a brief silence*).
I can't make sense of this . . . my fault!
I listen—and don't understand,
As if they still were trying to explain to me . . .
I'm quite distraught . . . There's something I expect . . .
(*Heatedly.*)
Blind man! In whom did I seek reward for all my labors!
I hurried! . . . Flew! I trembled! . . . Happiness seemed near!
Whom did I recently so passionately and humbly
Waste tender words upon!
And you! O God in Heaven! *Whom* have you picked out!
When I consider it, why *whom* have you preferred!
Why did you lead me on to keep up hope?
Why didn't you say candidly
That you had turned our whole past into ridicule?!
That you find hateful now the memory
Of those emotions and the movements of our hearts
Which even distance didn't cool in me,
Nor new diversions, nor a change of scene!
I breathed them, lived them, always was filled up with them!
You should have said that my arrival—unexpected—
My look and speech, my actions—were repulsive to you:
I would at once have broken off relations with you,
And before I'd taken leave of you forever
Would not have tried much to find out
Who is this man you love . . .
(*Derisively.*)
Will you become his friend again after full consideration?
What's the point of ruining oneself?
Just think, you always can take care of him,
And diaper him and send him on an errand.
To be a boy and servant, a little lady's page—
This is the ideal of all the Moscow men!
Enough! . . . I pride myself on breaking off with you.

And you, sir, father, you devotee of rank:
I wish that you may slumber on in blissful ignorance.
I do not threaten you with any courtship more.
You'll find another, well behaved,
A toady and a cheap careerist,
At last the equal, by his merits,
Of his future father-in-law.
So now! I've sobered up completely,
The scales have fallen from my eyes, the dreams are gone!
It would not be a bad thing now
To vent my spleen and all
My spite on both the daughter
And the father, the stupid lover and the world together!
Whom was I with? Where did my fate land me?
Everybody shoves and shouts! A crowd of torturers,
Of traitors in their love, endless in their hate,
Indomitable storytellers,
Incoherent wits, conniving simpletons,
Sinister old hags, old men
Growing decrepit over lies and nonsense!
All of you in chorus glorified my madness—
And you are right: he will pass through fire unharmed
Who manages a day with you,
Who breathes the same air that you breathe
And whose intelligence stays whole.
Away from Moscow! I will not come back again.
I'm off, I won't look back, I'll go search through the world
To find a little corner for a wounded heart!
My carriage, now, my carriage!
(*Drives off.*)

FAMUSOV. Well, now? And don't you see, he really did go mad?
Tell me seriously:
Crazy! What a lot of nonsense he was talking!
A toady! Father-in-law! And so menacing on Moscow!
And you've resolved to put me in my grave?
Oh, isn't what I bear lamentable?
My Lord, my Lord! Whatever will
Princess Marya Aleksevna say?

Boris Godunov

Aleksandr Sergeyevich Pushkin

Aleksandr Pushkin,
inspired by his genius,
dedicates this work
with reverence and with gratitude
to the memory,
precious to Russians,
of

NIKOLAI MIKHAILOVICH
KARAMZIN

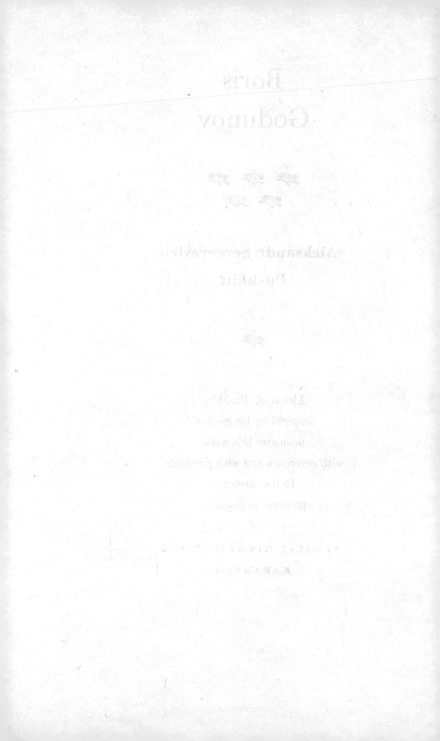

DRAMATIS PERSONAE
[not in the original]

Boris Godunov, a boyar; later, Tsar
Irena, the Tsaritsa; widow of Tsar Fyodor, sister of Boris
Feodor, the Tsarevich
Kseniya, the Tsarevna
Prince Vasily Shuisky, Prince Vorotynsky } of the royal dynasty of Rurik
Shchelkalov, Clerk of the State Council
Basmanov, Trubetskoi } boyars
Afanasy Pushkin, a noble
Gavrila Pushkin, his nephew
Semyo Godunov, a relative of Boris's, in charge of the secret police
The Patriarch of the Russian Church
The Abbot of the Chudovy Monastery
Pimen, a monk
Grigory Otrepev, a monk; later, the Impostor Dimitry
Misayil and Varlaam, mendicant friars
The Proprietress of an inn
Czernikowski, a priest
A poet
Prince Kurbsky
Pan Sobanski, a Polish landowner
Pyotr Khrushchov, a Russian gentleman
Andrei Karela, a Cossack ataman
Mniszek, a Polish military governor
Marina, his daughter
Prince Adam Wiśniowiecki
The People, including various voices from the crowd and a Woman carrying a baby
A crowd of Russians and Poles
Boyars, including various voices
Stewards in the Tsar's palace
Kseniya's nurse
Policemen
Guests at Shuisky's party, at Mniszek's ball
Margeret, Rosen } officers with the Polish forces
Rozhnov, a captured Russian noble
Russian and Polish soldiers
A gang of boys
An old woman
A beggar
A *yurodivy*
Masalski

A NOTE ON THE PLAY

Boris Godunov was written at Mikhailovskoe, Pushkin's country place, between December, 1824, and November 7, 1825. Based on old Russian chronicles—Pimen, for example, is Pushkin's reconstruction of the figure of the chronicler—and on the tenth and eleventh volumes of Karamzin's *History of the Russian State*, the play is an expression of Pushkin's concept of the fate of the nation, or of the people, at a crucial moment in history. It is written in unrhymed iambic pentameter, except for four scenes in prose, a panoramic drama in the style of, as Pushkin put it, "our father Shakespeare." The elimination of the classical unities, the introduction of "vulgar" elements, and the celebration of the confused but honest and fundamental force of the people prevented the play from winning approval. The Tsar himself, Nicholas I, who had undertaken to be Pushkin's personal censor, advised Pushkin to revise the play into a "historical novel in the manner of Walter Scott." Publication of the play was permitted, however, in 1830, but it was not performed until 1870 in St. Petersburg.

As in other history plays, the historical material in this play is compressed and presented from a dominant, dramatic point of view. Although the period actually covered—from early 1598 to spring, 1605—is the seven years preceding the "Time of Troubles," the play refers back through the Muscovite period even to the establishment of the "Land of Rus" and forward to ideas of sovereignty and popular will existent in the early nineteenth century. The best account of Godunov and the time is S. F. Platonov, *Boris Godunov*, in Russian (1921) and in French (1929). To sum it up very briefly: Boris, born about 1550, was not himself titled but connected to the Court by service and marriage. Close to Ivan the Terrible and closer still after 1581, when, in a quarrel, Ivan killed his oldest son, Godunov emerged as the power behind the throne in 1584 after Ivan's death and the accession of "the Angel Tsar" Fyodor [Feodor] Ivanovich. During the next fifteen years, until Fyodor's death in 1598, Boris really ruled Russia, driving always further to strengthen the power of the throne against that of the nobles and boyars. On May 15, 1591, the

Tsar's half brother, Dimitry, the heir apparent, died of what officially was described as a self-inflicted knife wound during an epileptic fit but what was popularly considered murder by assassins hired by Boris. Elected Tsar by majority vote of the State Council (*Zemsky sobor*) in the beginning of 1598 and crowned in September, Boris pursued a vigorous policy of consolidation of federal power in regard to domestic affairs and procedures, administration, foreign policy and relations with European countries, and the secular power of the Russian church (versus the power of the Orthodox Church in Byzantium and elsewhere). He was a tyrant not only in the sense that his rule was harsh but also in that his power rested on popular support and satisfaction of the pressing social needs of the people at the expense of the autonomy of the nobility. He did not promulgate sufficient reforms to hold the allegiance of the people, and the terrible famine of 1601–1603 increased their needs drastically. During 1603 the rumor spread through Russia that the Tsarevich, or heir apparent, Dimitry had not been killed in 1591 but was still alive in Poland. Boris denounced him as being merely an unfrocked monk called Grigory Otrepev. Whoever he actually was, as Dimitry I, subsequently known as False Dimitry I, he received Jesuit sponsorship in Poland, became a Catholic in April, 1604, and in the autumn of the same year moved against Boris on a campaign to Moscow with only several thousand soldiers. The success of his march and the death of Boris are told about in this play. Following Boris's death in 1605, Dimitry was crowned—and assassinated, paving the way for two more False Dimitrys, until the whole period of unrest, dissatisfaction and political upheaval was resolved by the stabilization of power and the election of Mikhail Romanov to the throne in 1613.

The text translated here is that of the Jubilee Academy edition (Moscow, 1937), available in many other subsequent editions, including that published by the Columbia University Press (New York, 1953) with extensive historical notes in English by P. L. Barbour.

SCENE I

The Kremlin Palace

(20 February 1598)

Princes Shuisky and Vorotynsky.

VOROTYNSKY. You and I are detailed to keep an eye on the town,
But, it seems, there's no one to look after.
Moscow is empty. All the people
Have followed the Patriarch toward the convent.
How do you think the excitement will end?
SHUISKY. How will it end? That's not hard to guess:
The people will wail some more and even weep;
Boris will keep on frowning for a while,
Like a drunkard at a glass of wine,
And finally, by his own graciousness,
Will with humility consent to take the crown;
And then—and then he will rule over us
As usual.
VOROTYNSKY. But a month's gone by
Since, shutting himself in the convent with his sister,
He's quit all worldly things, it seems.
Neither the Patriarch nor the Council boyars
Have so far been able to change his mind.
He doesn't heed humble exhortations,
Their supplications, the cry of all of Moscow,
Or the voice of the Great Council.
In vain they begged his sister
To bless Boris into taking power.
The mournful nun-Tsaritsa
Is firm, like him, and, like him, implacable:
Evidently Boris himself instilled this spirit in her.
What if the ruler has in fact
Grown bored with the problems of the state
And will not ascend the untenanted throne?
What would you say?
SHUISKY. I'd say that the blood
Of the boy-Tsarevich was spilled in vain;

That, if it's true, Dimitry could be living.
VOROTYNSKY. Horrible crime! No, you really mean
Boris killed the Tsarevich?
SHUISKY. Who else then?
Who bribed Chepchugov in vain?
Who secretly sent off both Bityagovskys
With Kachalov? I was dispatched to Uglich
To investigate this business on the spot:
I ran across fresh tracks;
The whole town was witness to the crime;
Its citizens all testified the same;
When I returned I could have—with one word—
Exposed the hidden criminal.
VOROTYNSKY. Then why didn't you annihilate him?
SHUISKY. He, I confess, confused me then
By his composure, by his unexpected shamelessness;
He looked me in the eye as if he were right:
He asked me many questions, went into details—
And face to face with him I repeated the nonsense
Which he himself had whispered in my ear.
VOROTYNSKY. It's dirty, Prince.
SHUISKY. And what was I to do?
Tell Feodor everything? But the Tsar
Saw everything through the eyes of Godunov,
Listened with the ears of Godunov—
Suppose I had convinced him of it all—
Boris would have dissuaded him at once,
And then I would have been put in seclusion
And, all in good time, just like my uncle,
Been put to death in some lonely jail.
I'm not boasting, and, of course, no kind
Of torture actually can make me scared.
I'm not a coward myself—but also not
A fool, and I'll not risk my neck for nothing.
VOROTYNSKY. Horrible crime! But listen, surely pangs
Of conscience terrify the murderer:
Naturally the blood of the innocent child
Hinders him in getting to the throne.
SHUISKY. He'll cross that, too; Boris is not that meek!
What honor it will be for us, for all of Rus!
A former serf, a Tartar, Malyuta's son-in-law,

The butcher's son-in-law, and himself a butcher at heart
Will take the crown and cape of Monomakh . . .
VOROTYNSKY. Sure he's not of noble birth; we're nobler.
SHUISKY. Seems so.
VOROTYNSKY. Of course the names Shuisky, Vorotynsky . . .
Can tell at once, princes by their birth.
SHUISKY. Princes by their birth, of Rurik's blood.
VOROTYNSKY. Now listen, Prince, you know we'd have the right
To follow Feodor.
SHUISKY. Oh, much more so
Than Godunov.
VOROTYNSKY. Actually, now!
SHUISKY. Well, so?
And if Boris won't leave off using cunning,
Let's skillfully get the people all stirred up;
Let them drop Godunov and leave him—
They have enough princes of their own,
Let them choose any one of them as Tsar.
VOROTYNSKY. There are lots of us, Varangian descendants,
But it's hard for us to compete with Godunov:
The people have lost the habit of seeing in us
The ancient line of its warrior lords.
Long ago we lost our principalities,
And long we've served as handymen to the Tsars,
But he's known how by fear and, also, love,
And glory, too, to captivate the people.
SHUISKY (*looks out the window*). He dared, that's all—but we . . . Enough of that.
Here, the people are coming back in batches;
Let's hurry and find out if it's decided.

SCENE II

The Red Square

The People.

ONE OF THE PEOPLE. Implacable! He dismissed the holy fathers
Of the church, the boyars and the Patriarch.
They fell on their knees before him all for nothing;
The radiance of the throne's what frightens him.
ANOTHER. O my God, who will rule over us?
Oh, woe for us!
A THIRD. Here comes the Clerk of State
To tell us the decision of the Council.
THE PEOPLE. Silence! Silence! The Clerk of the Council speaks.
Sh-sh-pay attention!
SHCHELKALOV (*from the Red Porch*). It has been enacted
By the Council to try the power of appeal
On our ruler's mournful soul one final time.
Once more tomorrow the Most Holy Patriarch,
Having gloriously sung high mass in the Kremlin,
Will rise preceded by the sacred gonfalons,
And along with him the Senate and the boyars,
A host of nobles, and the delegates,
And all the true-believing Moscow people—
We all will go once more to beg the Tsaritsa
That she take pity on our orphaned Moscow
And bless Boris' assumption of the crown.
Go now to your homes, and God be with you!
Offer your prayers, and let there rise to Heaven
One fervent prayer from all the Orthodox.
(*The People drift away.*)

SCENE III

The Maidens' Field. The Novodevichy Convent

The People.

ONE OF THE PEOPLE. Now they've gone in to the Tsaritsa's cell;
Boris and the Patriarch have gone in there
With a crowd of boyars.

ANOTHER. Any news?

A THIRD. He's still
Persistent, but still there is some hope.

A WOMAN (*with a child*). Ooh-hoo! Don't cry, don't cry; the bogyman,
The bogyman'll get you! Ooh-hoo! Don't cry!

ONE OF THE PEOPLE. Can't we steal in around behind the wall?

ANOTHER. Impossible. How? And even the field is jammed,
Not only there. Think it easy? All Moscow
Has crowded here. Look: the walls, the roofs,
All the tiers of the cathedral bell-tower,
The cupolas of the churches and the very crosses
Are studded with the people.

THE FIRST. Really something!

ONE OF THE PEOPLE. What's the noise there?

ANOTHER. Listen! What's that noise?
The people are howling; they're falling there, like waves
Row after row . . . and more . . . more still . . . Now, friend,
It's come to us, hurry! on your knees!

THE PEOPLE (*on its knees. Howling and wailing*). Oh, take pity on us, Father! Rule over us!
Be Father to us, be Tsar!

ONE OF THE PEOPLE (*quietly*). What's the wailing about?

ANOTHER. And how should we know? That's the boyars' business,
Not ours.

A WOMAN (*with a child*). Now, what? Just when he ought to cry
He quieted down! I'll give it to you! Here's
The bogy! Cry, you brat!
(*Throws it on the ground. The child squeals.*)
So, there.

ONE OF THE PEOPLE. They're all weeping.
Let's you and me start, too.

ANOTHER. I'm trying, friend,
But can't.

THE FIRST. The same with me. You haven't an onion?
Let's rub our eyes.

THE SECOND. No, I'll smear mine with spit.
Now what's that there?

THE FIRST. Oh, who can figure them out?

THE PEOPLE. The crown is his! He's Tsar! He has agreed!
Boris is Tsar! our Tsar! Long live Boris!

SCENE IV

The Kremlin Palace

Boris, the Patriarch, Boyars.

BORIS. My soul is bare before you all—you,
Father Patriarch, and you, boyars:
You saw I do accept the greatest power
In trepidation and humility.
How heavy is the obligation on me!
I follow after all the mighty Ivans—
I follow also the Angelic Tsar!
O pious man! My sovereign father! Look down
From Heaven on your faithful servant's tears
And grant to him whom you have loved, whom you
So wonderfully have extolled on earth,
Your sacred blessing on his taking power:
That I may rule my people gloriously,
And be both righteous and good, like you.
I count on your co-operation, boyars.
Serve me as you were used to serving him,

When I was one who shared your labor, too,
Not yet elected by the people's will.

BOYARS. We will not break the oath that we have given.

BORIS. Now let us go and venerate the graves
Of the deceased sovereigns of Russia,
And then—call all our people to a feast,
All, from the nobles to the poorest blind;
Let all come in, all are our dear guests.
(*Goes out, the Boyars behind him.*)

VOROTYNSKY (*stopping* SHUISKY). You guessed it.

SHUISKY. What?

VOROTYNSKY. Why, here, the other day,
Remember?

SHUISKY. No, I don't remember anything.

VOROTYNSKY. As the people were going to the Maidens' Field,
You said . . .

SHUISKY. Now's not the time to remember;
I sometimes even recommend forgetting.
Besides, I used pretended slander then
Because I wanted just to test you out,
Better to know your inner train of thought;
But here—the people are welcoming the Tsar—
My absence may be noticed by them—I
Will follow them.

VOROTYNSKY. Cunning courtier!

SCENE V

Night. A Cell in the Chudovy Monastery

(*1603*)

Father Pimen, Grigory sleeping.

PIMEN (*writes by an ikon-lamp*). One legend more, the final tale—
And then my chronicle is finished,
The duty done that God set out for me,

A sinner. It was not for nothing that the Lord
Made me a witness for so many years
And gave me knowledge in the art of books.
Sometime, perhaps, an industrious monk
Will find my zealous and anonymous work;
He, too, like me, will light his ikon-lamp
And shaking the dust of ages off the charter,
He will transcribe these truthful histories—
That the descendants of the Orthodox
Will know the bygone fate of their native land—
That they will remember their great Tsars
For all they did, their glory and their deeds—
But humbly pray the Savior to forgive
All their sins, all their evil deeds.
In my old age I'm living life again—
The past goes by before my very eyes—
Really was it long ago it passed,
Eventful, agitated like the ocean?
Now it's lying silent and so calm
Memory has preserved some faces for me,
And there are some words that find their way to me,
But all the rest is irrevocably lost . . .
But it's almost dawn, the lamp is burning out—
One legend more, the final tale. (*Writes*)

GRIGORY (*wakes up*). Still that dream! Is it possible?
Three times!
Damned dream! . . . And still the old man sits
Beside his lamp and writes—and half asleep,
It seems, but all night didn't shut his eyes.
How much I like the peaceful way he looks,
When, sunk in the past heart and soul,
He carries on his chronicle; often
I have wondered what he writes about:
Perhaps about the Tartars' dark dominion?
Perhaps the violent tortures by Ivan?
Perhaps the stormy Novgorod Assembly?
Perhaps the glory of our country? No use.
Neither on his high forehead nor in his eyes
Can a person read his secret thoughts;
Still the same majestic, meek appearance.
Just like a clerk, his hair turned gray in office,

He looks serenely at both the right and wrong,
Indifferently observing good and bad,
Not knowing pity, and not knowing rage.

PIMEN. You awake, brother?

GRIGORY. Let me have your blessing,
Honored father.

PIMEN. The Lord bless you now,
The next day, and forever and ever.

GRIGORY. You've written all the time and never slept,
But some devilish dreaming has alarmed
My soul, and the devil has stirred me up.
I dreamed a steep and sudden staircase led
Me up a tower where from the top
All Moscow seemed to me just like an anthill;
Below, the people were swarming in the square
And pointing up at me and laughing,
And I was ashamed, and it got terrifying—
And, falling headlong down, I awakened . . .
And three times I've dreamed that one, same dream.
Isn't it odd?

PIMEN. A young man's blood is lively;
Restrain yourself with fasting and with prayer,
And all your dreams will be fulfilled with easy
Visions. Still to this very day, if I,
Overcome by involuntary sleep,
Do not say a long prayer before night fall,
My aged sleep is neither calm nor sinless;
Sometimes I hear the sounds of noisy feats,
Sometimes of a war camp, or of a battle,
The reckless, senseless fun one had when young!

GRIGORY. But—how happily you spent your youth!
You fought beneath the turrets of Kazan,
Under Shuisky repulsed the Lithuanians,
And saw the splendors of the Court of Ivan!
How fortunate! But I since boyhood have
Been wandering from cell to cell, a poor monk!
Why shouldn't I enjoy my fill of battles,
And banquet at the table of the Tsar?
In old age I could manage still, like you,
To put aside all vanity and worldly cares,
To take monastic vows and shut myself

In some quiet cloister.

PIMEN. Brother, don't complain that you have early
Quit the sinful world, that the Most High
Has sent you few temptations. Believe me now:
Glory, luxury, and the devilish love
Of women seem beautiful from a distance.
I have lived long and had many pleasures;
But I have known real bliss only since
I was led into this cloister by the Lord.
Just think, my son, about the greatest Tsars:
Who's over them? Only God. Who dares
Go against them? No one. Well, so? Often
The crown of gold is much too heavy for them,
And they have changed it for the monkish cowl
Our Tsar Ivan sought peace and quietness
In imitation of monastic labors.
Full of proud favorites, his palace
Took on the new look of a monastery.
His followers, in skullcaps and hair shirts,
Appeared to be mild and obedient monks,
And the terrifying Tsar, their tranquil abbot.
Here I saw—here, in this very cell
(Long-suffering Kirill lived in it then,
A righteous man. Even then had God
Thought me, too, worthy of comprehending the
Insignificance of worldly cares), here I saw
The Tsar worn out from raging thoughts and tortures.
Lost in thought, the Terrible sat quietly
Among us; we stood in front of him not moving,
And he quietly carried on a conversation with us.
He said to the abbot and the brotherhood:
"My fathers, the longed-for day will come,
I will appear, thirsting for salvation.
You, Nikodim; you, Sergy; you, Kirill;
You all—accept my spiritual vow:
I'll come to you, a damned criminal,
And here I will receive the honest frock,
Fallen, Holy Father, at your feet."
Thus spoke our mighty sovereign,
And the words flowed sweetly from his lips,
And he was weeping. And we in tears were praying

That the Lord would send down love and peace
To his long-suffering, stormy soul.
And his son Fyodor? Once on the throne,
He longed only for the peaceful life
Of the vow of silence. He turned the chambers of
The tsarist palace into a cell for prayer;
There the heavy, sovereign sorrows
Did not disturb his saintly soul.
God fell in love with the humility of the Tsar,
And under him all Rus found comfort in
Serene glory—and in his dying hour
An unprecedented miracle occurred:
A man, in uncommon light and visible
Only to the Tsar, came to his deathbed,
And Fyodor began a conversation with him
And kept calling him the great Patriarch.
And everyone around was seized with fear,
Knowing that it was a divine vision,
Because the holy ruler was not then
Before the Tsar in that sacred chamber.
After he had passed away, the palace
Became all filled with a sweet and holy smell,
And his countenance shone as brightly as the sun—
We'll never see another Tsar like that.
O terrible, unprecedented grief!
We have made God angry, we have sinned:
We have called a murderer to ourselves to be
Our sovereign.

GRIGORY. Honored father, for a long time now
I have meant to ask you about the death
Of Tsarevich Dimitry; at that time,
They say, you were in Uglich.

PIMEN. Oh, I remember!
I was led by God to see the evil deed,
The bloody sin. At that time I had been sent
To distant Uglich for spiritual training,
And arrived at night. During mass next morning
I suddenly hear bells, the alarm is sounded,
Shouts, noise. They're running to the Tsaritsa's. I
Rush there, too—the whole town's already there.
I look: the Tsarevich is lying with his throat cut;

His Tsaritsa-mother's unconscious over him,
His nurse is sobbing in despair, and then
The people, in a frenzy, drag away
The godless traitress of a wet-nurse . . .
Suddenly among them, fierce, and white
With anger, the Judas, Bityagovsky, appears.
"There, there's the criminal!"—the shout
Rings out, and in a flash he's gone. The people
Then rush at the three fleeing murderers;
They grabbed the three escaping criminals
And brought them to the boy's still-warm body,
And—miracle—suddenly the body shook.
"Repent!" the people started shouting at them:
And in terror of the ax the criminals
Confessed—and gave Boris' name.

GRIGORY. How old then was the murdered Tsarevich?

PIMEN. Why, about seven; now he would have been—
(About ten years have passed since then . . . no, more:
Twelve years)—now he would be just your age
And reigning; but God decided otherwise.
I will conclude my chronicle with this
Sad tale; ever since that time I have
Not gone into world affairs. Brother Grigory,
You have enlightened your intelligence with learning,
I hand my labor on to you. In the hours
Free from spiritual endeavors
Write down, in an unsophisticated way,
Everything you witness in your life:
Both war and peace, the justice of the sovereigns,
The holy miracles of saintly men,
Prophecies and signs that are divine,—
But now it's time for me, it's time to rest
And put out the ikon-lamp . . . But the bells are calling
Us to matins . . . Bless Thy servants,
Lord! . . . Hand me my crutch, Grigory.
(*Goes out.*)

GRIGORY. Boris! Boris, everything trembles
Before you; no one even dares remind you
Of the fate of the unfortunate boy—
But meanwhile a hermit in a dusky cell
Here writes a terrible denunciation of you:

You will not escape the verdict of the world,
As you will not escape the judgment of God.

SCENE VI

The Patriarch's Palace

The Patriarch, the Abbot of the Chudovy Monastery.

PATRIARCH. And he escaped, Father Abbot?

ABBOT. Escaped, Holy Sire. It's already the third day now.

PATRIARCH. The rascal, damned rascal! What family is he from?

ABBOT. From the Otrepev family, descendants of Galician boyars. Became a monk in his youth, no one knows where, lived in Suzdal, in the Efimevsky Monastery, left there, wandered around among various cloisters, finally came to my Chudovy Brotherhood, and I, seeing that he was still young and foolish, put him under the supervision of Father Pimen, a gentle and humble old man. He was highly literate, read our chronicles, composed canticles to the saints, but, it seems, his learning came to him not from the Lord God . . .

PATRIARCH. I've had enough of these learnèd people! What won't he think up! *I will be Tsar in Moscow!* Ah, he's an agent of the devil! However, there's nothing here to report to the Tsar; why alarm our sovereign father? It will be sufficient to inform Clerk Smirnov or Clerk Efimev of the flight. What heresy! *I will be Tsar in Moscow!* . . . Catch him, catch this unholy fiend, and send him to Solovetsky for eternal penance. Why this is heresy, Father Abbot.

ABBOT. Heresy, Holy Sire, outright heresy.

SCENE VII

The Tsar's Palace

Two stewards.

FIRST. Where's the sovereign?
SECOND. He's locked himself in
His bedchamber with some kind of sorcerer.
FIRST. Sure, that's his favorite thing to talk about:
Magicians, fortune-tellers, sorcerers—
He's always telling fortunes, like a girl waiting
To get married. Wish I knew what now?
SECOND. Here he comes. Don't you want to ask him?
FIRST. How sullen he is!
(*They go out.*)
THE TSAR (*enters*). I've reached the highest power;
This is the sixth year of my peaceful reign.
But my heart has had no happiness. Isn't this
The way we fall in love when young and thirsty
For love's delights, but, once we satisfy
Our heart's desire by a moment of possession,
Turn cool, grow bored and languish?
Uselessly the magicians promise me
Long life, many days of tranquil reign—
Neither life nor power makes me happy now;
I have a premonition of a thunderbolt
From Heaven and of woe. I have no joy.
I thought I'd make my people easy in plenty
And in glory, win their love with bounties—
But I dispensed a pointless love:
Actual power is hated by the mob.
They can only love the dead—and we
Are mad if the splashings of the crowd
Or its raging howl excite our heart!
God sent famine down upon our land,
The people howled in the agony of death;
I opened up the granaries to them,
I scattered gold among them, I found them work—

And they, like men possessed, cursed me down!
Fire and flames wiped out all their homes,
I had new quarters built for all of them:
And they reproached me for the fire!
There's mob justice: go seek its love.
I thought I'd find comfort with my family,
Delight my daughter by giving her in marriage—
Death, like a tempest, carried off the groom . . .
And now a rumor cunningly names me,
Me, her most unhappy father,
As the culprit of my daughter's widowhood!
No matter who dies, I am the secret murderer
Of everyone: I hastened Fyodor's death,
I poisoned the Tsaritsa, my own sister,
Quiet nun she was . . . I did all that!
Ah! I feel it now: nothing can
Assuage our sorrows in this world;
Nothing, nothing . . . except perhaps our conscience.
When healthy, it triumphs over evil,
Triumphs over shady calumny . . .
But if there is a single stain on it,
A single one set there by accident,
Then there's trouble! The soul will be all burned
As by a plague, the heart will fill with poison,
Hammer its reproaches in your ears,
And everything makes you sick, your head spins,
And bloody little boys before your eyes . . .
Be glad to run, but where . . . It's terrible!
He's pitiful whose conscience is not clean.

SCENE VIII

An Inn on the Lithuanian Border

Misayil and Varlaam, mendicant friars; Grigory Otrepev, now a layman; the Proprietress.

PROPRIETRESS. What can I please you with, good friars?

VARLAAM. Whatever God provides, good mistress. Is there some wine?

PROPRIETRESS. How couldn't there be, fathers! I'll bring it right out.
(*Goes out.*)

MISAYIL. Why are you so sad, comrade? Here's the Lithuanian border you so much wanted to get to.

GRIGORY. I won't rest easy until I'm in Lithuania.

VARLAAM. Why has Lithuania such a hold on you? Take us, Father Misayil and your sinful servant, once we ran away from the monastery we hadn't a thing to think about. Lithuania, or Rus, see, *gudok* or *gusli:*[1] we have a good time, as long as there's wine . . . and here goes again!

MISAYIL. Right well done, Father Varlaam.

PROPRIETRESS (*enters*). Here you are, fathers. Drink to your health.

MISAYIL. Thanks, dear, God bless you.
(*The monks drink.* VARLAAM *strikes up the song: "It Happened in the City, the City of Kazan . . ."*)

VARLAAM (*to* GRIGORY). How come you won't sing or swig?

GRIGORY. Don't want to.

MISAYIL. Freedom for the free . . .

VARLAAM. And Heaven for the drunk, Father Misayil![2] Let's empty our goblets to the dame of this pot-house . . . But I must say, Father Misayil, when I'm drinking I don't like people thinking: it's one thing to keep toasting, but another to keep boasting; you want to live like us, you're welcome —you don't, get out, make yourself scarce: a joker's no pal for a priest.

GRIGORY. Drink, and hang on to what you think, Father Varlaam! See, I know how to talk in rhymes, too, sometimes.

VARLAAM. But what's this, hang on to what I think?

MISAYIL. Leave him alone, Father Varlaam.

VARLAAM. But what kind of a father is he? He himself latched on to our company, nobody knowing who, nobody knowing where from—and playing haughty on top of it; maybe he's had a taste of the horsehide . . .
(*Drinks and sings: "A young monk took the vows."*)

[1] The *gudok* was a sort of simple violin; the *gusli*, an instrument much like the psaltery.

[2] The saying is: "Freedom for the free, and Heaven for the blessed."

GRIGORY (*to the* PROPRIETRESS). Where does this road go?

PROPRIETRESS. To Lithuania, my man, to the Loyev Hills.

GRIGORY. And is it much farther to the Loyev Hills?

PROPRIETRESS. Not far. You could get there by nightfall if it weren't for the Tsar's border posts and the guards.

GRIGORY. What, border posts? What's that mean?

PROPRIETRESS. Somebody ran away from Moscow and they've ordered them to stop everybody and give them a good looking over.

GRIGORY (*to himself*). Now you're back where you started.[3]

VARLAAM. Hey, comrade! you've really grabbed hold of the hostess there. Seems you won't give the vodka a whirl but got to latch on to a girl; go to it, brother, that's fine! Everybody's got his own way; but Father Misayil and me's got one little worry: we drink up the glass in a hurry, we drink it and turn it up, brother, and pound on the glass for another.

MISAYIL. Right well rhymed, Father Varlaam . . .

GRIGORY. Who are they after? Who ran away from Moscow?

PROPRIETRESS. God knows, a thief maybe, a robber—only here now even honest people can't get through. And what'll it all mount up to? Nothing. They won't even catch a bald devil: as if there wasn't another way to Lithuania except the main road! Why, you could just go left from here through the pine forest on the path to the chapel, the one on Chekansky Creek, and then straight through the swamp to Khlopino, and from there to Zakharevo, where any little boy can take you to the Loyev Hills. The only thing you ever hear about these policemen is how they pester travelers and rob us poor people. (*A noise is heard*) What's there now? Ah, it's them, damn them! Doing the watch.

GRIGORY. Hostess! Isn't there another corner in this cottage?

PROPRIETRESS. Nothing, dear. Be glad to hide myself. They go round on watch just so it looks good, but you give 'em some wine and some bread and God knows what all—hope they kick the bucket, damned dogs! Hope they . . .

[3] Literally: "There you are, granny, St. George's Day." The reference is to the period around St. George's Day when, until the end of the sixteenth century, peasants could move from one landlord to another. By the nineteenth century, since the serfs were bound to the landowner, the phrase meant that the year of serfdom just completed was to be followed by another.

(*The Policemen enter.*)

POLICEMAN. Hello, hostess!

PROPRIETRESS. Welcome, dear guests, come in.

ONE POLICEMAN (*to the other*). Hey! There's a spree going on here; we can get something out of that. (*To the monks*) What kind of people are you?

VARLAAM. We're men of God, humble monks; we go among the villages and collect Christian alms for the monastery.

POLICEMAN (*to* GRIGORY). And you?

MISAYIL. Our comrade . . .

GRIGORY. A layman from the outskirts; I was accompanying the fathers to the border, and from here I'm going home.

MISAYIL. So you changed your mind . . .

GRIGORY (*quietly*). Shut up.

POLICEMAN. Hostess, bring out some more wine and we'll have a drink with the fathers here and a little talk.

THE OTHER POLICEMAN (*quietly*). The young fellow's broke, it looks, can't get nothing from him; but the fathers, on the other hand . . .

FIRST [POLICEMAN]. Quiet, we'll get to 'em right away.—So, my fathers, how've you been making out?

VARLAAM. Poorly, son, poorly! Nowadays the followers of Christ are become miserly; they love wealth, they lay their wealth away. They give God little. Great is the sin that's fallen on the pagans of this earth. They've all gone into trade, set up as publicans; they think about their worldly riches and not about salvation of the soul. You walk and walk; you beg and beg; sometimes you can't beg out three-quarters of a kopek in three days. It's a shame! A week goes by, another, you look into your little purse, but there's so little in it you're ashamed to show up in the monastery; what can you do? so out of grief you drink up what remains; it's bad, that's all there is to it.—Oh, it's bad; seems our last days're upon us . . .

PROPRIETRESS (*cries*). Lord save us and have mercy upon us!

(*During* VARLAAM'*s speech the* FIRST POLICEMAN *stares significantly at* MISAYIL.)

FIRST POLICEMAN. Alyokha! You got the Tsar's decree on you?

SECOND. Yeh, it's on me.

FIRST. Give it here.

MISAYIL. What're you staring at me so intently for?

FIRST POLICEMAN. Here's why: a certain evil heretic ran away from Moscow, Grishka Otrepev, y'heard about it?

MISAYIL. No, I hadn't.

POLICEMAN. Y'hadn't? All right. But the Tsar's ordered us to catch and hang that runaway heretic. Y'know that?

MISAYIL. No, I don't.

POLICEMAN (*to* VARLAAM). Y'know how to read?

VARLAAM. Used to know when I was young, but I've forgotten.

POLICEMAN (*to* MISAYIL). And you?

MISAYIL. The Lord didn't give me the wisdom.

POLICEMAN. So here's the Tsar's decree for you.

MISAYIL. What'll I do with it?

POLICEMAN. Seems to me this runaway heretic, thief, and swindler is you.

MISAYIL. Me? For God's sake! What're you talking about!

POLICEMAN. Wait a minute! Watch the door. Here, we'll find out right away.

PROPRIETRESS. They're damned torturers! Won't even leave an old friar in peace!

POLICEMAN. Who here can read and write?

GRIGORY (*steps forward*). I can.

POLICEMAN. Here! And who did y'learn from?

GRIGORY. From our sexton.

POLICEMAN (*gives him the decree*). Read it aloud.

GRIGORY (*reads*). "The unworthy monk Grigory, of the Otrepev family, from the Chudovy Monastery, fell into heresy and instructed by the devil, dared stir up the Holy Brotherhood with all kinds of temptations and lawlessness. From inquiry it has been found out that he, Grishka the damned, has fled toward the Lithuanian border . . ."

POLICEMAN (*to* MISAYIL). Now isn't that you?

GRIGORY. "And the Tsar has ordered that he be caught . . ."

POLICEMAN. And hanged.

GRIGORY. Doesn't say *hanged* here.

POLICEMAN. You're lying: not every word gets written in. Read: caught and hanged.

GRIGORY. "And hanged. And this thief Grishka is . . . (*looking at* VARLAAM) over fifty years old, of medium height, has a bald forehead, a gray beard, a fat potbelly . . ."
(*All look at* VARLAAM.)

FIRST POLICEMAN. Boys! Here's Grishka! Grab him, tie him up! Wouldn't of thought it, wouldn't of guessed.

VARLAAM (*snatching the paper*). Leave me alone, you sons of bitches, what the hell Grishka am I.—What's this: fifty years old, gray beard, fat belly! No, pal, you're still too young to be pulling tricks on me! I haven't done any reading for a long time and I don't make the words out so good, but I'll make 'em out now, since it's come to the noose. (*Reads syllable by syllable*). "An-d he i-s twen-ty ye-ars ol-d." —Well, my friend? Where's fifty here? See? twenty.

SECOND POLICEMAN. Yeh, I remember, twenty. That's what they told us.

FIRST POLICEMAN (*to* GRIGORY). Looks like you're a real joker, my friend.

(*During the reading,* GRIGORY *stands with his head down and his hand in his bosom.*)

VARLAAM (*continues*). "In he-igh-t he-'s sho-rt, broa-d-che-ste-d, o-ne arm sho-rt-er tha-n the o-ther, blue ey-es, red ha-ir, a wa-rt on hi-s chee-k, a-no-ther on hi-s for-e-he-ad." Why, now, my friend, isn't this you?

(GRIGORY *suddenly pulls a dagger; everyone steps back from him, and he jumps out the window.*)

POLICEMEN. Grab him! grab him!

(*All run out in confusion.*)

SCENE IX

Moscow. Shuisky's House

Shuisky, many guests. Supper.

SHUISKY. More wine.

(*He stands up; all stand up after him.*)

And now, my friends, dear guests,
The final beaker! Boy, say the prayer.

BOY. O Tsar of Heaven, Eternal, Omnipresent,
Heed Thy humble servants' supplication:

We pray to Thee to help our sovereign lord,
Help him whom Thou didst choose, a pious man,
The autocratic Tsar of every Christian.
Preserve him in his palace, on the field of battle,
And on the road, and in the room he sleeps.
Make him victorious over his enemies,
That he be glorified from sea to sea,
And may his family flourish in good health,
And may its precious branches cast their shade
Over all the world, and may he be
As bountiful as ever to ourselves,
His servants, and as gracious and forbearing,
And may the fountains of his endless wisdom
Flow forever forth and cover us;
And raising high our cup for this for him,
We pray to Thee, O Tsar of Heaven.

SHUISKY (*drinks*). Long live our great and noble sovereign!
Good night to you, my dear and precious guests;
I'm grateful to you that you did not scorn
My modest bread-and-salt. Good-bye, sleep well.
(*The guests go out, he shows them to the door.*)

PUSHKIN. I thought they'd never go. Well, Prince Vasily Ivanovich, I already started to think we wouldn't get a chance to talk things over even.

SHUISKY (*to the servants*). What're you standing there with your mouths open for? Always trying to listen in on your masters. Clear the table and get out. —What is it, Afanasy Mikhailovich?

PUSHKIN. Miracles, that's all there is to it.
Today my nephew Gavrila Pushkin sent
Me a special courier from Cracow.

SHUISKY. So?

PUSHKIN. My nephew sends strange news.
The Terrible's son . . . Wait.
(*Goes to the door and looks around.*)
The adolescent Tsar,
Killed by the trickery of Boris . . .

SHUISKY. There's nothing new in that.

PUSHKIN. Wait a minute:
Dimitry's living.

SHUISKY. Ah, so! That's news, indeed!

The Tsarevich is living! That's really miraculous.
Is that all?

PUSHKIN. Listen to it all.
Whoever he may be, the saved Tsarevich,
Or some kind of spirit going in his likeness,
An audacious knave, or an impudent impostor,
The thing is that Dimitry has appeared.

SHUISKY. Impossible.

PUSHKIN. Pushkin himself saw him
The first time he drove up to the royal palace
And walked right through the ranks of the Lithuanian
Lords straight into the King's chamber.

SHUISKY. Who is he then? Where's he from?

PUSHKIN. They don't know.
It is known, however, that he was a servant
Of Wiśniowiecki's, that on his bed of pain
He confided in his spiritual father,
That this proud lord, having found the secret out,
Took care of him, raised him from his sickbed,
And then drove off with him to Sigismund.

SHUISKY. What do people say about this daredevil?

PUSHKIN. From what one hears, he's clever, affable,
And smart, and liked by all. He's completely charmed
The Moscow refugees. The Latin priests
See eye to eye with him. The King adores him,
And, they say, has promised him his help.

SHUISKY. There's so much commotion here, my friend,
It makes your head spin round against your will.
There is no doubt that this is an impostor,
But, I must say, the danger isn't slight.
Important news! And if it gets as far
As the people, why there'll be a terrible storm.

PUSHKIN. Such a storm that Tsar Boris will hardly
Manage to keep the crown on his clever head.
And it serves him right! He rules over us
Like Tsar Ivan (may he leave us to our dreams).
What's the advantage of no public executions,
That we don't sing canticles to Christ
On a bloody stake in front of all the nation,
That we're not burned on public squares, and the Tsar
Doesn't use his warder to poke the coals?

Can we be certain of our own poor lives?
Disgrace and exile await us every day,
Prison, Siberia, a cowl, or fetters,
Then in a remote corner starvation or the noose.
Our noblest families—where are they?
Where are the Princes Sitsky, the Shestunovs,
The Romanovs, the white hope of our country?
Imprisoned, being tortured in exile.
Give yourself time: your fate will be the same.
You think it easy! At home we are besieged
By faithless servants, as if by Lithuania.
Everywhere tongues are ready to sell themselves,
Thieves bought over by the government.
Our very lives depend upon the first
Serf whom we may wish to punish.
And now he plans to stop St. George's Day.
We are no longer lords on our own land.
Don't you dare dismiss a loafer! No matter how,
You feed him; And don't you dare to try to win
A worker over! No good, you're in Serfs' Court.
Why even under Tsar Ivan did you ever
Hear such evil? And are the people better off?
Ask them. Let the impostor try
And promise them St. George's Day back,
Then the fun'll start.

SHUISKY. You're right, Pushkin.
But you know? We better keep all these things
To ourselves until the time has come.

PUSHKIN. Of course,
Do what you think best. You're a sensible man;
I'm always glad to have a talk with you,
And any time that something bothers me,
I cannot wait until I've talked to you.
Besides which, your mead and velvet-smooth beer
Very much unloosed my tongue today . . .
Good-bye, now, Prince.

SHUISKY. Good-bye, friend, see you later.
(*He escorts* PUSHKIN *out.*)

SCENE X

The Tsar's Palace

The Tsarevich is drawing a map. The Tsarevna, the Tsarevna's nurse.

KSENIYA (*kisses a portrait*). My darling groom, my handsome Prince, you were meant not for me, not for your waiting bride—but for a dark little grave in a foreign land. I can never be consoled, and I'll keep crying for you forever and ever.

NURSE. Now, Tsarevna! A young girl cries as the dew falls—out comes the sun and the dew dries. You'll have another groom, just as handsome and as nice. You'll fall in love with him, you little darling of ours, and you'll forget your Prince.

KSENIYA. No, Nanny, I'll be faithful to him even when he's dead.

(BORIS *enters.*)

TSAR. What is it, Kseniya? what is it, my darling?
Already a weeping widow but only a bride!
You're crying all the time for your dead groom.
My little child! Fate did not decree
That I should be the agent of your bliss.
I have, perhaps, made Heaven angry,
I could not bring about your happiness.
Sweet innocent, what are you suffering for?—
And you, my boy, what are you doing? What's that?

FEODOR. A drawing of the Moscow lands; our realm
From end to end. Look here: here's Moscow,
Here's Novgorod, here's Astrakhan. The sea
Is here, and here are the heavy forests of Perm,
And here's Siberia.

TSAR. And what's this here
That makes this winding pattern?

FEODOR. That's the Volga.

TSAR. How excellent! Here's the sweet fruit of learning!
You can look over all the realm at once

As from the clouds: the borders, cities, rivers.
Study, my son: learning shortens our trial-
And-error in this all-too-soon-gone life—
Some time or other, even soon, perhaps,
All the provinces and regions you
Today so deftly drew out on the paper,
All will fall beneath your hand—
Study, my son, and you'll then understand
More easily and clearly the work of ruling.
(SEMYON GODUNOV *enters.*)
Here Godunov is bringing me reports.
(*To* KSENIYA) My dear, retire to your drawing room;
Good-bye, my sweet, and may the Lord console you.
(KSENIYA *and the* NURSE *go out.*)
What news can you tell me, Semyon Nikitich?

SEMYON GODUNOV. Today
At dawn Prince Vasily's butler and
Pushkin's man brought me a denunciation.

TSAR. So?

SEMYON GODUNOV. Pushkin's man talked first, said
That early yesterday a courier from Cracow
Came to their house—and in an hour
Was sent back again without anything in writing.

TSAR. Seize the courier.

SEMYON GODUNOV. They're already after him.

TSAR. What about Shuisky?

SEMYON GODUNOV. Last night he entertained
His friends, both of the Miloslavskys,
The Buturlins, Mikhail Saltykov,
And Pushkin—and several others;
They went home very late. Only Pushkin
Stayed to talk in private with his host
And talked to him a good while longer.

TSAR. Send for Shuisky right away.

SEMYON GODUNOV. My lord!
He's already here.

TSAR. Then send him in.
([SEMYON] GODUNOV *goes out.*)
Relations with Lithuania! What's this?
I hate the whole rebellious tribe of Pushkins.
And Shuisky's not a man that you can trust:

Deferential, but both bold and cunning . . .
(SHUISKY *enters.*)
Prince, I have to have a talk with you.
But it seems that you yourself came here on business:
And I would like first to hear you out.
SHUISKY. Indeed, my lord: my duty is to tell
You important news.
TSAR. I'm listening to you.
SHUISKY (*quietly, pointing to* FEODOR). But, my lord . . .
TSAR. The Tsarevich may know all
That Prince Shuisky knows about. Go ahead.
SHUISKY. Tsar, news has reached us from Lithuania . . .
TSAR. Not the same
That the courier brought to Pushkin yesterday?
SHUISKY. He knows it all! . . . I thought, my lord,
That you did not yet know about these secrets.
TSAR. Never mind that, Prince: I want to reconsider
All the news; otherwise we'll never
Know the truth.
SHUISKY. All I know is that
An impostor has appeared in Cracow
And that the king and nobles are behind him.
TSAR. Well, what are they saying? And who is this impostor?
SHUISKY. I don't know.
TSAR. But . . . in what way is he dangerous?
SHUISKY. Of course, my lord: your state is powerful,
You by your graciousness, your zeal and bounty,
Have won over all your servants' hearts.
But you yourself know: the thoughtless mob
Is fickle, mutinous, and superstitious,
Given easily to idle hopes,
Obedient to the suggestion of the moment,
Deaf and indifferent to the actual truth,
A beast that feeds on fables.
It delights in shameless bravery.
Thus, if this mysterious tramp
Will cross the Lithuanian border,
The resurrected name Dimitry
Will draw a crowd of madmen to him.
TSAR. Dimitry! . . . What? that boy again?
Dimitry! . . . Tsarevich, leave us.

SHUISKY. His face is flushed: now the storm!

FEODOR. My lord,
Will you allow . . .

TSAR. Impossible, my son, go on.
(FEODOR *goes out.*)
Dimitry!

SHUISKY. He didn't know a thing.

TSAR. Listen, Prince: take steps at once
To fence Russia off from Lithuania
With border posts, not to let a soul
Cross this frontier line, not to let a hare
Come running here from Poland, not to let a crow
Come flying here from Cracow. Be off!

SHUISKY. I'm on my way.

TSAR. Wait. This news is very
Intriguing, isn't it? Have you ever heard
Of dead men rising from their grave
To interrogate the Tsars, the legal Tsars,
Appointed and elected by the people,
And crowned by the great Patriarch?
Ridiculous? hey? then why don't you laugh?

SHUISKY. I, my lord?

TSAR. Listen, Prince Vasily:
When I found out that this young boy had been . . .
That this young boy had somehow lost his life,
You were sent to investigate: Now
I adjure you, by God and by the Cross,
Honestly inform me of the truth:
Did you recognize the dead, young boy
And there was no substitution? Answer me.

SHUISKY. I swear to you . . .

TSAR. No, Shuisky, don't swear,
But answer me: that was the Tsarevich?

SHUISKY. It was.

TSAR. Think carefully, Prince. I promise you my favor,
I will not punish some bygone lie with useless
Banishment. But if you now
Are tricking me, then by the head of my son
I swear an evil death will fall on you,
Such a death that Tsar Ivan Vasilich
Will tremble in his grave from fear.

SHUISKY. Death is not terrible, but your disfavor is.
Would I dare play the fox in front of you?
And could I have been so blindly fooled as not
To have recognized Dimitry? I visited
His body in the cathedral three days,
Escorted there by everyone in Uglich.
He was surrounded by the thirteen bodies
The people tore to pieces, and on them
Decay had already visibly set in,
But the boyish face of the Tsarevich was clear
And fresh and calm, as if he'd fallen asleep;
The deep gash had not begun to heal,
And the features of his face had not changed at all.
No, my lord, there is no doubt: Dimitry
Is sleeping in his grave.

TSAR (*calmly*). Enough, you may go.
(SHUISKY *goes out.*)
Oh, the air is close! . . . Let me get my breath—
I felt that all my blood rushed to my face—
And then painfully subsided . . .
So that's why for thirteen years running
I've dreamed continually of the dead child!
Yes, yes—that's it! Now I understand.
But who is he, my threatening enemy?
Who comes at me? An empty name, a shadow—
Can a shadow strip the purple from me,
Or a sound deprive my children of their legacy?
I am a madman! What am I afraid of?
Blow on this ghost—and it is no more.
The thing's decided: I will not show my fear—
But nothing must be overlooked . . .
Oh, crown of Monomakh, you're heavy!

SCENE XI

Cracow. Wiśniowiecki's House

The Impostor and Pater Czernikowski.

IMPOSTOR. No, my father, there'll be no difficulty;
I know the spirit of my people well;
Piety in them does not know frenzy:
The example of their Tsar is sacred to them.
Tolerance, besides, is always indifferent.
I promise you, before two years are out,
That all my people, all the Eastern Church,
Will recognize the authority of Peter's vicar.

PATER. Saint Ignatius aid and comfort you
In other days and times. But until then
Carry in your soul, Tsarevich, the seeds
Of the bliss and grace of Heaven.
Our spiritual duty sometimes demands
That we dissemble to the foul, mad world;
The people judge your words and what you do,
God alone sees what your intentions were.

IMPOSTOR. Amen. Who's there?
(*A servant enters.*)
Tell them: we are receiving.
(*The doors open. A crowd of Russians and Poles enters.*)
Comrades all! Tomorrow we set out
From Cracow. Mniszek, I will halt for three
Days at your place in Sambor.
I know your hospitable castle
Not only shines with noble luxury
But also is renowned for its young lady—
I hope that there I'll see the beautiful
Marina. And you, my friends, you, Rus
And Lithuania, you, Slavic sons,
Who've raised fraternal banners high against
The common foe, against my perfidious
Evildoer—soon I will lead
Your terrifying troops to the longed-for battle—

But I see there are new faces in your midst.
GAVRILA PUSHKIN. They have come to beg service and a sword
In your good favor.
IMPOSTOR. Glad to have you, children.
Come here, my friends.—But, Pushkin, tell me who
Is this good-looking man?
PUSHKIN. Prince Kurbsky.
IMPOSTOR. A famous name.
(*To* KURBSKY) You're a relative of the hero of Kazan?
KURBSKY. I am his son.
IMPOSTOR. He's still alive?
KURBSKY. No, dead.
IMPOSTOR. A noble mind! A man of war and wisdom!
But since that time when he, the bitter avenger
Of his own many insults, appeared at Olga's
Ancient city with the Lithuanians,
The talk of him has quieted down.
KURBSKY. My father
Spent the remainder of his life in Volynia,
On the estates Batory granted him.
Peaceful, and in solitude, he sought
Consolation for himself in study:
But peaceful labor did not comfort him:
He still remembered the country of his youth
And longed for it until the very end.
IMPOSTOR. Unlucky captain! How brightly shone the dawn
Of his tumultuous and stormy life.
I am delighted, knight of noble birth,
That his blood now makes its peace with its fatherland.
Our fathers' sins are not to be remembered.
Peace on their graves! Draw closer, Kurbsky. Your hand!—
Isn't it odd? Whom does Kurbsky's son escort
To the throne? Indeed—the son of great Ivan . . .
All's in my favor: the people and, also, fate.
And who are you?
A POLE. Sobanski, a free squire.
IMPOSTOR. All praise and honor to you, child of freedom!
Give him a third of his wages in advance.
But who are these? I recognize on them
The clothing of my native land. They are ours.

KHRUSHCHOV (*bows humbly before him*). Indeed, my lord, our father. We are your
Diligent but persecuted servants.
Fallen into disgrace, we fled from Moscow
To you, our Tsar—ready to lay down
Our lives for you; indeed, let our bodies be
The steps for you up to the imperial throne.

IMPOSTOR. Take heart, you guiltless sufferers—
Just let me make my way to Moscow,
And then Boris will pay for everything.
And you?

KARELA. A Cossack. I've been sent to you from the Don,
From the volunteer troops, from the courageous atamans,
From both the Upper and the Lower Cossacks,
To look into your lucid, tsarist eyes
And bow low to you for them in homage.

IMPOSTOR. I knew the men of the Don. I didn't doubt
I'd see the Cossack standards in my ranks.
We give thanks to our army of the Don.
We know that nowadays the Cossacks are
Oppressed unjustly and persecuted;
But if God will assist us to ascend
Our fathers' throne, then, as in olden times,
We will favor our free and faithful Don.

A POET (*draws near, bowing deeply and seizing Grishka by the skirt of his robe*). Great Prince, most noble Royal Heir!

IMPOSTOR. What do you want?

POET (*hands him a piece of paper*). Deign to accept
This poor fruit of my diligent labor.

IMPOSTOR. What do I behold? Latin verses!
The sword and lyre be blessed a thousand times,
A single laurel wreath binds them together.
Though I was born beneath the Midnight Sun,
The Latin muse's voice is known to me,
And I adore the flowers of Parnassus.
I believe in poets' vaticinations.
No, ecstasy does not seethe in their ardent
Breasts in vain: blessèd is the exploit
Which they have sung and celebrated first!
Draw near, my friend. Accept this gift
In remembrance of me.

(*Gives him a ring.*)

When my covenant
With fate is done, when I invest the crown
Of my ancestors—I hope again to hear
Your honeyed voice, your inspired hymn.
Musa gloriam coronat, gloriaque musam.
And so, my friends, until we meet tomorrow.

ALL. Let's march, let's march! Long life to Dimitry!
Hail! Long live the Great Prince of Muscovy!

SCENE XII

Commander Mniszek's Castle in Sambor

A series of lighted rooms. Music.
Wiśniowiecki, Mniszek.

MNISZEK. He talks to nobody but my Marina,
He has the time for no one but Marina . . .
The whole thing looks a great deal like a wedding;
Now, admit it, Wiśniowiecki, did you think
My daughter would become Tsaritsa? hey?

WIŚNIOWIECKI. Why, it's marvelous . . . and, Mniszek, did you think
My servant would ascend the Moscow throne?

MNISZEK. But, admit, isn't my Marina something!
I only mentioned it to her: take care!
Don't let Dimitry get away! . . . And, look,
The whole thing's done. He's already in her meshes.
(*The music plays a polonaise. The* IMPOSTOR *comes in with* MARINA *as the first couple.*)

MARINA (*quietly to* DIMITRY). Yes, tomorrow night, at eleven o'clock,
I'll be beside the fountain in the linden lane.
(*They part. Another couple.*)

A GENTLEMAN. What did Dimitry see in her?

A LADY. Why, she's
A beauty!

GENTLEMAN. Sure, a marble nymph:

Her eyes and mouth have neither life nor humor . . .
(*A new couple.*)
LADY. He isn't handsome, but his looks are pleasant,
And you can see he is of royal blood.
(*A new couple.*)
LADY. When do you march?
GENTLEMAN. When the Tsarevich gives the order.
We are ready; but it looks as if Lady Mniszek
Were holding us prisoners with Dimitry.
LADY. A nice captivity.
GENTLEMAN. Of course, if you . .
(*They part. The rooms empty.*)
MNISZEK. Nowadays we old men do not dance,
The music's thunder does not draw us in,
We do not squeeze and kiss their charming hands—
Oh, I have not forgot the pranks we played!
Now nothing, nothing, is the way it was:
Young people, honestly, are not so bold,
And beauty is already not so gay.
Admit it, friend: it's all a little sad.
Let's leave them now; my comrade, let us go
And order them to uncork an ancient flask
Of good Hungarian wine, overgrown with grass,
And in a corner we together will
Imbibe the fragrant flow, the stream as thick
As fat, and meanwhile judge a thing or two.
Let's go, my friend.
WIŚNIOWIECKI. Indeed, my friend, let's go.

SCENE XIII

Night. A Garden. A Fountain

THE IMPOSTOR (*enters*). Here's the fountain; this is where she'll come.
It seems I wasn't born a timid man;
I have stared death closely in the face,
My heart has never shuddered at the thought of death.

I have been threatened with a life of bondage,
I've been pursued—my spirit's never faltered,
And I've escaped imprisonment, by boldness.
What is it that now cramps my breathing?
What does this irresistible shivering mean?
Is this the trembling of intense desires?
No—this is fear. All day long I've waited
For this secret meeting with Marina,
Thought over everything that I would tell her,
How I'd seduce her supercilious mind,
How I would call her Muscovy's Tsaritsa—
But the moment's come—and I remember nothing.
I cannot find the words I learned by heart;
Love has blanked my imagination . . .
But something just flashed by . . . a rustle . . . quiet!
No, that's the light of the delusive moon,
And the wind that rushed by here.

MARINA (*enters*). Tsarevich!

IMPOSTOR. It's she! . . . My blood's all frozen in me.

MARINA. Dimitry! Is that you?

IMPOSTOR. Sweet, magic voice!
(*Goes toward her*) Is it you at last? Do I see you alone
With me, beneath the canopy of the silent night?
How slowly did the dull day pass!
How slowly did the evening sun go down!
How long I waited in the dark of night!

MARINA. The hours fly, and time is dear to me—
I set this meeting here with you not
In order just to hear the tender speeches
Of a lover. Words aren't needed. I believe
You love me; but listen now: I have decided
To unite my fate with yours, tumultuous
And uncertain; in return, I have the right
To demand from you, Dimitry, just one thing:
I demand that you reveal to me now
Your soul's secret aspirations,
Intentions and, even, its misgivings;
So I may boldly, hand in hand with you,
Set out in life—not blindly like a child,
Nor as the servant of my husband's whims,
Your speechless concubine—but as

A spouse completely worthy of you,
The helpmate of the Tsar of Muscovy.

IMPOSTOR. O let me forget for but a single hour
The problems and anxieties of fate!
Yourself, forget you see the Tsarevich now
Before you. O Marina! behold in me
The lover you yourself have chosen and
Made a happy man by looking at.
Hear out love's supplications now,
Let me express the fullness of my heart.

MARINA. Now's not the time, Prince. You're dallying—
Meanwhile, the devotion of your myrmidons
Grows cool, the danger and the difficulties
Each moment grow more dangerous and difficult,
Suspicious rumors already go around,
And novelty gives way to novelty;
And Godunov is taking his own measures . . .

IMPOSTOR. Why Godunov? Is your love, my only
Bliss, under the power of Boris?
No, no. I look indifferently now
Upon his throne, his autocratic power.
Your love . . . what's life to me without it,
The gleam of glory, or the Russian realm?
In the distant steppe, in a poor mud hut—you,
You would replace the tsarist crown for me,
Your love . . .

MARINA. You ought to be ashamed; do not
Forget the high and holy task you have:
Your dignity must be more dear to you
Than any joy, than any of life's lures;
You cannot put it on a par with anything.
Know that not to some tempestuous boy,
Madly captivated by my beauty,
Do I in solemn ceremony give
My hand, but to the heir to the throne of Moscow,
To the Tsarevich saved from death by fate.

IMPOSTOR. Don't torture me, ravishing Marina,
Don't tell me that you chose my cloth and not
Myself. Marina! You can never know
How! Why if . . . o terrible misgiving!
Tell me: Suppose blind fate had not ordained

A tsarist birth for me, suppose
I had not been the son of great Ivan,
This boy whom long ago the world forgot,
Then would . . . would you love me then?

MARINA. You are Dimitry and cannot be another;
I could not love someone else.

IMPOSTOR. No! Stop:
I do not want to share with a man who's dead
The mistress that belongs to him.
No, I've had enough dissembling! I'll tell
The whole truth; know you now: your Dimitry
Perished long ago, is buried—and will
Not rise again; you wonder who I am?
Then let me tell you: I'm a poor frock-wearer;
Fed up with bondage in the monastery,
Beneath my cowl I figured out my brave
Design, prepared a wonder for the world—
And finally fled from my cell to the
Ukrainians, to their wild villages,
And learned to ride a horse and wield a sword;
I came to you; I called myself Dimitry
And deceived the bunch of brainless Poles.
Now what do you say, arrogant Marina?
Are you satisfied or not with my confession?
Why don't you speak?

MARINA. O shame! O grief! I'm lost!
(*Silence.*)

IMPOSTOR (*quietly*). What has this outburst of annoyance led me into?
Perhaps I have destroyed, once and for all,
The good fortune I built up with so much labor.
Madman, what have I done? (*Aloud*) I see, I see:
You are ashamed of an unprincely love.
So utter, then, the fatal word to me;
Now my fate is in your hands! Decide:
I wait. (*Falls on his knees*)

MARINA. Get up, you poor impostor.
Do you really think that by falling on your knees
You'll move my vainglorious heart to tears,
As if I were a gullible and feeble girl?
You're wrong, my friend: I have seen noble knights

And counts kneeling at my feet;
But I coldly turned their supplications down
Not so that some little, runaway monk . . .

IMPOSTOR (*rises*). Don't disdain the young impostor;
Valor is concealed in him, perhaps,
Worthy of the throne of Muscovy,
Worthy of your priceless hand . . .

MARINA. Worthy of the shameful noose, you boy!

IMPOSTOR. I am guilty: seized with pride, I have
Deceived my God and all the Tsars.
I've lied to all the world; but you, Marina,
Can't punish me; I have been straight with you.
No, I could not swindle you.
For me you were a unique and sacred thing
In front of which I did not dare pretend.
Love, jealous love, blind love,
Only love itself compelled me to
Let you know all.

MARINA. Look at the madman boasting!
Who asked for your confession anyway?
If you, some vagrant, tramp without a name,
Can miraculously blind two whole peoples,
Then, at the very least, you must
Be worthy of your own success
And cover up your own audacious fraud
With stubborn, deep, eternal secrecy.
Tell me, can I give myself to you?
Forgetting birth and maiden pride, can I
Bind our two fates together,
When you yourself with such simplicity
So openly expose your own disgrace?
For love of me he let the cat out of the bag!
I'm amazed: how come you haven't told
My father yet who you are, out of friendship?
Or told our King, simply from delight?
Or, even better, Wiśniowiecki
With a servant's faithful diligence?

IMPOSTOR. I swear to you that you alone
Could wring confession from my heart.
I swear to you that never, nowhere,
Neither in the mindlessness of banquets,

The intimate conversation among friends,
Under the knife, nor under the torture of the rack
Will my tongue betray these terrible secrets.

MARINA. You really swear! Well then, I must believe you.
O I believe you!—But may I know by what
It is you swear? The name of God,
As a devout, adopted, Jesuit child?
Or on your honor, as a noble knight?
Or, maybe, just only by your tsarist word,
As the Tsar's son? Is that it? Tell me.

IMPOSTOR (*proudly*). The shadow of Ivan adopted me,
From its grave gave me the name Dimitry,
Aroused the peoples all around me,
And doomed Boris as sacrifice to me—
I am Tsarevich. Enough, I am ashamed
To stoop before a haughty Polish girl—
Good-bye forever. The game of bloody war,
The vast anxieties of my fate
Will drown, I hope, the anguish of my love.
Oh, how I will begin to hate you when
The fire of my shameful passion's passed!
I'm going now—disaster or the crown
Is waiting for my head in Russia.
Whether I meet death in honest battle,
Like a soldier, or on the block, like a criminal,
You will not be my true companion,
You will not share my destiny with me.
But, perhaps, you will be sorry then
About the future you have now turned down.

MARINA. But if, before then, I exposed your bold
And insolent fraud to everyone?

IMPOSTOR. And do you think that I'm afraid of you?
That they'll believe a Polish girl rather
Than the Tsarevich of Muscovy?—Well then, know
That neither king nor Pope nor noble lord
Is thinking about the truth of what I've said.
Dimitry or not—what have they to do with that?
I am a good excuse for war and discord.
That is the only thing they need, and, believe me,
You little rebel, they'll force you to shut up.
Good-bye.

MARINA. Wait, Tsarevich. Finally
I hear a man, and not a boy, talking.
That reconciles me to you, Prince.
I am forgetting your outburst of madness
And see Dimitry once again. But—listen:
It's time, it's time! Wake up, linger no more.
Hurry, lead your regiments to Moscow;
Clean out the Kremlin, be seated on the throne—
Then send a marriage embassy to me;
But, God be my witness, until your foot
Is resting on the dais of the throne,
Until you've overthrown that Godunov,
I will not listen to your talk of love.
(*Goes out.*)

IMPOSTOR. No—it's easier for me to fight with Godunov,
Or play my tricks on a Jesuit at Court,
Than deal with a woman—curse them; I've had
Enough: she confuses things, and twists, and crawls,
Slips through your hands, hisses, threatens, and stings.
A serpent! serpent! . . . No wonder I was trembling.
She very nearly ruined me for good.
But, it's decided: the army moves in the morning.

SCENE XIV

The Lithuanian Border

(*16 October 1604*)

Prince Kurbsky and the Impostor, both on horseback.
The regiments are approaching the border.

KURBSKY (*the first to have galloped up*). There, there it is!
There's the Russian border!
Holy Rus, my fatherland! I'm yours!
Disdainfully I shake this foreign dust
Off my clothes and avidly drink in
This new, this native air! . . . Your soul, my father,
Now will be consoled, and in the grave

Your banished bones will leap up and rejoice!
Our hereditary sword is bright again,
That glorious sword, the terror of dark Kazan,
That trusty sword, the servant of the Moscow Tsars!
Now it's on a spree at its own feast
In the service of its honored sovereign!

IMPOSTOR (*riding quietly with lowered head*). How glad he is!
How his pure soul
Has broken out in glory and in joy!
O knight of mine! I envy you.
Kurbsky's son, brought up in banishment,
Forgetting the insults which your father bore,
Atoning for his sins after his death,
You're making ready to shed blood for the son
Of great Ivan, to return the rightful Tsar
To our fatherland . . . Of course, you're right,
Your soul must blaze with sweet rejoicing.

KURBSKY. But really, doesn't your spirit, too, rejoice?
There is our Rus: it's yours, Tsarevich.
There your people's hearts are waiting for you:
Your Moscow, your Kremlin, your state and power.

IMPOSTOR. O Kurbsky, Russian blood will flow!
You've raised the sword on the Tsar's behalf, you're clean.
But I—I lead you against your brothers; I called
Lithuania out against Rus; I'm showing enemies
The hallowed road to beautiful Moscow!
Yet may my sin fall not on me
But you, Boris, murderer of Tsars!
Forward!

KURBSKY. Forward! Death to Godunov!

(*They gallop on. The regiments cross the border.*)

SCENE XV

The Tsar's Council

The Tsar, the Patriarch, and Boyars.

TSAR. Is it possible? An unfrocked, runaway monk
Leads a host of criminals against us
And dares write threats to us! Enough of this,
It's time to tame the madman!—Trubetskoi,
You, and you, Basmanov, set out at once;
My zealous captains are in need of aid.
Chernigov is besieged by the insurgent.
Save the city and its citizens.

BASMANOV. My lord,
Before three months are up, even every
Rumor about the Impostor will have died away;
We'll bring him here to Moscow in an iron
Cage, like an outlandish beast. By God
I swear this to you.
(*Goes out with* TRUBETSKOI.)

TSAR. The Swedish king through his
Ambassadors has offered an alliance;
But we have no need of foreign aid: we have
Enough of our own people under arms
To drive away the traitors and the Pole.
I turned it down.
Shchelkalov! send out
Decrees to all the captains everywhere
That they mount horse and, as in the olden times,
Send their people out to do their duty;
Likewise in the monasteries single out
The lowest ranks. In former times,
When our country was threatened with misfortune,
The hermits themselves went out into battle;
But we don't wish to bother them today;
Let them pray for us—such is the Tsar's
Decree and the verdict of the boyars.
We will now decide a crucial question:

You all know that this outrageous impostor
Has let out crafty rumors everywhere;
The letters he has scattered everywhere
Have sown the seeds of anxiety and doubt;
A rebellious whisper walks the public squares,
And minds are seething . . . they must be cooled;
I would like to prevent more executions,
But how? with what? Let's now decide. You first,
Holy Father, let us have your thoughts.

PATRIARCH. Blessed be our God, Most High, Who has
Instilled into your soul, great sovereign,
The spirit of charity and meek forbearance;
You do not wish perdition for the sinner,
You calmly wait until his delusion pass:
And it will pass, and the sun of eternal truth
Will dawn on all.
Your faithful man of God,
Not a wise judge of things of this world,
Dares today to give you his opinion.
Child of a devil, a damned and unfrocked monk,
Has passed himself off as Dimitry among the people;
He has shamelessly arrayed himself in the name
Of the Tsarevich, as in a stolen chasuble:
It has only to be rent—and he
Himself will be ashamed of his nakedness.
God Himself has sent us means for this:
Know, my lord; it was six years ago,
In that very year in which our Lord did bless
Yourself onto the throne of sovereign power—
Toward evening, once, a simple shepherd came
To me—indeed, a venerable old man—
And did disclose a marvelous secret to me:
"In my young days," said he, "I lost my sight,
And since that time I've known neither day nor night
Until old age: all for nothing I tried
To cure myself by potions and secret spells;
All for nothing I went on pilgrimages
To pray the wonder-workers in the cloisters;
All for nothing did I sprinkle these
Dark eyes with water from the holy fonts—
The Lord did not send me recovery.

So, finally, I lost all hope and grew
Accustomed to my darkness, and even my dreams
No longer showed me things that I had seen,
But I had dreams of only sounds. Once,
In deepest sleep, I hear a childish voice
That says to me: 'Rise up, old man, and go
Now unto Uglich, to the Church of the Transfiguration;
There offer up your prayers above my grave,
God is merciful—and I forgive you.'—
'But who are you?'—I asked the childish voice.
'I am Tsarevich Dimitry. The Tsar of Heaven
Has placed me in his choir of angels now,
And I've become a famous wonder-worker!
Go there, old man.'—I awoke and thought:
Well, now? Perhaps the fact is God
Is granting me recovery later on.
I'll go—and set out on the distant journey.
And so I got to Uglich, come up to
The holy church and hear them singing mass,
And, my zealous heart on fire, start to weep
So sweetly that it seems the blindness
Is flowing from my eyes like tears.
When the people began to come out, I said
To my grandson: 'Ivan, take me to the grave
Of Tsarevich Dimitry.' And so the boy
Led me there—and hardly had I made
A quiet prayer there before the grave,
When my eyes recovered sight; I saw
God's world, my grandson, and the little grave."
That, my lord, is what the old man told me.
(*General confusion. During this speech,* BORIS *wipes his face with a handkerchief several times.*)
I sent someone deliberately to Uglich,
And was informed that many sufferers
Had similarly found salvation at
The plaque that marks the young Tsarevich's grave.
Here's my advice: transfer these holy relics
To the Kremlin, put them in the Archangel
Cathedral; the people then will clearly see
The fraud this godless criminal has pulled,
And the power of the devils will vanish like dust.

(*Silence.*)

PRINCE SHUISKY. Holy Father, who can know the ways
Of God Most High? It's not for me to judge Him.
He can give the young boy's last remains
Imperishable sleep and wondrous powers,
But still one must investigate the common
Rumor studiously and dispassionately;
For should we think about so great a matter
In the tempestuous times of such confusion?
Won't people say that we have boldly made
A holy thing a tool of world affairs?
As it is, the people waver madly,
And there already are enough of noisy rumors:
It's not the time to alarm the people's minds
With such a serious, unexpected thing.
Myself I see it this way: of course, the rumor
The unfrocked monk has spread must be wiped out;
But there are other means for this—and simpler.
Therefore, my lord—if you will but allow me,
I will appear myself in the public square,
Exhort them, prick their conscience with their folly,
And expose the evil fraud of the unfrocked tramp.

TSAR. Let it be thus! Patriarch, my Sire,
I beg you to attend me in my chamber:
I need to have a talk with you today.
(*Goes out. All the Boyars, also, after him.*)

ONE OF THE BOYARS (*quietly to another*). Did you notice how our sovereign paled
And big drops of sweat began to fall from his face?

ANOTHER. I—I must admit—didn't dare
Lift up my eyes, or breathe, or even move.

FIRST BOYAR. But Shuisky rescued him. What a man!

SCENE XVI

A Plain near Novgorod-Seversky

(*21 December 1604*)

A battle.

SOLDIERS (*fleeing in confusion*). We're lost, we're lost! The Tsarevich! The Poles! Here they are! Here they are!

(CAPTAINS MARGERET *and* WALTER ROSEN *enter.*)

MARGERET. Where, where you going! Allons . . . Go pack!

ONE OF THE FLEEING SOLDIERS. *Go pack* yourself, if you feel like it, you goddamned pagan!

MARGERET. Quoi? quoi?

ANOTHER. Kwa! kwa! You foreign frog, y'like to kwa-kwa at the Russian Tsarevich, but we're true-believers, see?

MARGERET. Qu'est-ce à dire *pravoslavni?* . . . Sacrés gueux maudite canaille! Mordieu, mein Herr, j'enrage, on dirait que ça n'a pas de bras pour frapper, ça n'a que des jambes pour foutre le camp.

W. ROSEN. Es ist Schande.

MARGERET. Ventre-saint-gris! je ne bouge plus d'un pas—puisque le vin est tiré, il faut le boire. Qu'en dites-vous, mein Herr?

W. ROSEN. Sie haben Recht.

MARGERET. Tudieu, il y fait chaud! Ce diable de Samozvnetz, comme ils l'appellent, est un bougre, qui a du poil au cul. Qu'en pensez-vous, mein Herr?

W. ROSEN. Oh, ja!

MARGERET. Hé! voyez donc, voyez donc! L'action s'engage sur les derrières de l'ennemi. Ce doit être le brave Basmanoff, qui aurait fait une sortie.

W. ROSEN. Ich glaube das.

(*Some Germans enter.*)

MARGERET. Ha, ha! voici nos allemands. Messieurs! . . . Mein Herr, dites-leur donc de se rallier et, sacrebleu, chargeons!

W. ROSEN. Sehr gut. Halt!

(*The Germans fall into formation.*)

Marsch!

GERMANS (*going*). Hilf Gott!

(*Fighting. The Russians flee again.*)

SOME POLES. Victory! Victory! Glory to Tsar Dimitry!

DIMITRY (*on horseback*). Sound the cease-fire! We have won. Enough; spare Russian blood. Cease fire!

(*Trumpets; drums roll.*)

SCENE XVII

The Square in Front of the Cathedral in Moscow

The People.

ONE OF THE PEOPLE. Is the Tsar going to come out of the cathedral soon?

ANOTHER. The mass is over; they're singing the thanksgiving now.

FIRST. What! They've already cursed *him?*

THE OTHER. I was standing on the church porch and I heard how the deacon began to shout: Grishka Otrepev is anathema!

FIRST. Let 'em curse all they like; the Tsarevich's got nothing to do with Otrepev.

THE OTHER. They're singing a requiem now for the Tsarevich.

FIRST. A requiem for the living! They'll get it, the damned atheists!

A THIRD. Listen! A noise. Isn't it the Tsar?

A FOURTH. No; it's a yurodivy.[4]

(*The* YURODIVY *enters, in an iron cap, chains hanging all over him, and surrounded by boys.*)

BOYS. Nikolka, Nikolka—iron nightcap! . . . Tr r r r . . .

AN OLD WOMAN. Leave the holy man alone, you little devils— Pray for me, Nikolka, for me, a poor sinner.

YURODIVY. Gimme, gimme, gimme a kopek.

[4] *Yuródivy*—a beggarly devotee of God supposed to be weak in mind, one of God's fools.

OLD WOMAN. Here's a kopek for you; remember me in your prayers.

YURODIVY (*sits down on the ground and sings*).

The moon is shining,
The kitten's crying,
Yurodivy, get up,
And pray to God!

(*The boys surround him again.*)

ONE OF THEM. Hello, Nikolka; how come you don't take your cap off? (*Gives him a tap on his iron cap*) Hey, how it rings!

YURODIVY. And I have a kopek.

BOY. 'S not true! Show me.
(*Snatches the kopek and runs off.*)

YURODIVY (*cries*). They took my kopek, hurt Nikolka's feelings!

THE PEOPLE. The Tsar, the Tsar is coming.
(*The* TSAR *comes out of the cathedral. A Boyar gives out alms to beggars in front of him. Other Boyars.*)

YURODIVY. Boris! Boris! The children hurt Nikolka's feelings.

TSAR. Give him something. What's he crying about?

YURODIVY. The little children hurt Nikolka's feelings . . . Have 'em cut their throats, the way you cut the little Tsarevich's.

BOYARS. Go away from here, you idiot! Grab the fool!

TSAR. Leave him alone. Pray for me, poor Nikolka.
(*Goes out.*)

YURODIVY (*after him*). No, no! I can't pray for a Herod-Tsar—the Mother of God won't allow it.

SCENE XVIII

Sevsk

The Impostor, surrounded by his followers.

THE IMPOSTOR. Where's the prisoner?

A POLE. Here.

IMPOSTOR. Send him in.

(*A Russian prisoner enters.*)

Who are you?

PRISONER. Rozhnov, a Moscow noble.

IMPOSTOR. You've been in service long?

PRISONER. About a month.

IMPOSTOR. Rozhnov, isn't it on your conscience that
You took arms against me?

PRISONER. Wasn't our choice.

IMPOSTOR. And did you fight at Sevsk?

PRISONER. I was there
Some two weeks after the fighting—came from Moscow.

IMPOSTOR. And Godunov?

PRISONER. He was very much alarmed
Over the loss of the encounter and the wounding
Of Mstislavsky, and so he sent off Shuisky
To take command of all the troops.

IMPOSTOR. But why
Did he call Basmanov back to Moscow?

PRISONER. The Tsar rewarded all he did with honor
And with gold. Basmanov's sitting now
In the Tsar's Council.

IMPOSTOR. He was needed more in the field.
So, what's new in Moscow?

PRISONER. Thank God, all's quiet.

IMPOSTOR. Really? Are they waiting for me?

PRISONER. God knows. There
They don't dare talk too much about you now.
Some get their tongues cut off, and some,
Their heads—they're really saying: Every day
Is execution day. The prisons are jammed.
On the square, whenever three men meet,
You turn around and a spy's already there,
And in his leisure the sovereign himself
Interrogates informers. It's really
Terrible; so it's better to keep quiet.

IMPOSTOR. How enviable the life of Boris's people!
And what about the army?

PRISONER. The army? It's clothed,
And fed, and satisfied.

IMPOSTOR. But is it large?

PRISONER. God knows.

IMPOSTOR. Maybe there'd be thirty thousand?

PRISONER. Put 'em all together, maybe fifty.

(*The* IMPOSTOR *gets lost in thought. Those around him look at each other.*)

IMPOSTOR. Well, and what do they think of me in your camp?

PRISONER. They talk about your charity and kindness,
That you, they say (don't be angry), are really a thief,
But a clever man.

IMPOSTOR (*laughing*). In fact, that is exactly
What I'll show them: friends, we will not wait
For Shuisky; I wish you all the very best:
We fight tomorrow.
(*Goes out.*)

ALL. Long live Dimitry!

A POLE. Fight tomorrow! There're fifty thousand of them,
And all of us together hardly make
Fifteen. He's out of his mind.

ANOTHER. That's nothing, friend:
One Pole can take on five hundred Muscovites.

PRISONER. Sure, take 'em on! But when it comes to blows,
You'll run away from one, you big windbag.

POLE. If you just had your sword on, y'insolent prisoner,
Why, I'd calm you down a bit (*pointing to his own sword*) with this.

PRISONER. We Russian fellows do all right without them:
Don't you want a taste of this (*showing his fist*), brainless!
(*The Pole looks at him haughtily and walks away without speaking. Everyone laughs.*)

SCENE XIX

A Forest

The False Dimitry [The Impostor], Pushkin.
In the distance a horse lies dying.

FALSE DIMITRY (IMPOSTOR). My poor horse! How briskly he galloped
Into his last battle today
And, wounded, quickly carried me.
My poor horse!

PUSHKIN (*to himself*). Look at what he regrets—
His horse! When all our army lies
Ground into dust!

IMPOSTOR. Wait a minute, perhaps,
He only merely foundered from his wound
And will rise refreshed.

PUSHKIN. How! It's dying.

IMPOSTOR (*goes to his horse*). My poor horse! . . . What'll I do? Take off
The bridle and undo the girth. Let him die
In freedom.
(*Unbridles and unsaddles the horse.*)
Greetings, gentlemen!
How come I don't see Kurbsky among you?
I saw how he cut his way through the thick of battle
Today; hosts of swords, like waving grain,
Surrounded and clung to that valiant man;
But his sword rose up higher than the rest,
And his terrifying cry drowned out the others.
Where is my knight?

A POLE. He lay on the field of death.

IMPOSTOR. Honor to the brave man and peace to his soul!
How few of us survived the battle unhurt!
The traitors! The Zaporozhian criminals,
Damned dogs! You, you ruined us.
Couldn't keep up three minutes of defense!
I'll show them! I'll decimate and hang them,
Damned robbers!

PUSHKIN. No matter who's at fault here,
All the same we're absolutely beaten,
Annihilated.

IMPOSTOR. But we won the fighting;
I just about had crushed their forward troops—
When the Germans thoroughly repelled us;
What soldiers! honest to God, what soldiers we have!
I love them for it; I certainly will set up
A bodyguard of honor from among them.

PUSHKIN. But where are we to spend the night tonight?

IMPOSTOR. Here, in the forest. Why isn't this a place
To sleep? At dawn, we'll move on and by lunch be in Rylsk.

Good night, sleep well.
(*Lies down, puts the saddle under his head and falls asleep.*)

PUSHKIN. Pleasant dreams, Tsarevich!
Utterly defeated, saved by flight,
He's as untroubled as a silly child;
Providence, of course, protects him;
And we, friends, will not lose heart.

SCENE XX

Moscow. The Tsar's Palace

Boris. Basmanov.

TSAR. He is defeated, but what's the good of it?
We've been crowned with a useless victory.
Again he's gathered his scattered army together[5]
And threatens us from the walls of Putivl.
And in the meantime what are our heroes doing?
Sitting at Kromy, where a bunch of Cossacks
Are laughing at them from behind a rotting fence.
That's glory! No, I'm much displeased with them;
I will send you to take over the command;
I'll make my general a man with brains, not of birth;
Let their arrogance grieve about the order of precedence;
It's time I disregarded the nobles' grumbling
And did away with a ruinous custom.[6]

[5] The fighting seems to have taken the following course (P. Mérimée, *Episode de l'Histoire de Russie*, Paris, 1854): After his victory at Novgorod-Seversky, December 31, 1604, Dimitry was deserted by most of his Polish allies and withdrew to Sevsk. The Russians under Shuisky attacked him near there and, aided by the Cossacks' desertion of Dimitry, won. Dimitry fled through Rylsk to Putivl. Mstislavsky, who replaced Shuisky, besieged Kromy, defended by the wily Cossack ataman Karela.

[6] The custom referred to, and sanctified by the Books of Rank, dated back to the end of the fourteenth century and meant that public offices were occupied according to rank of nobility at birth. The custom was abolished in 1682.

BASMANOV. Ah, my lord, that day be blessed a thousand times
When fire swallows up the Books of Rank
With all their discord and pedigreed pride
And they are gone.

TSAR. That day is not far off;
First just let me pacify the commotion
Of the people.

BASMANOV. Why pay any attention to it?
In its heart a people always leans toward strife:
The way a speedy horse champs at his bit;
The way a child's indignant with his father:
But so what? The rider calmly rides the horse,
And the father has command over the child.

TSAR. The horse sometimes unseats the horseman,
The son is not forever under the father's will.
We can contain the people only by
Strong and vigilant measures. Ivan thought that,
Wise autocrat and pacifier of storms,
And his ferocious grandson thought so, too.
No, the people don't respond to charity:
Do good for them—they won't say even thanks;
Steal and kill—you'll be no worse for it.
(*A Boyar enters.*)
What is it?

BOYAR. Some foreign guests have come.

TSAR. I'll go receive them; Basmanov, wait a bit,
Stay here; I have some other things I want
To say to you.
(*Goes out.*)

BASMANOV. A noble, autocratic spirit.
May God grant that he make out well with that
Damned Otrepev, and still do much,
Much more good for Russia.
A crucial thought's been born now in his mind.
It must not be allowed to cool. And what
A walk of life will open up to me
When he breaks the back of pedigreed nobility!
I have no equals on the field of battle;
I'll be the first beside the throne of the Tsar . . .
And perhaps . . . But what is that strange noise?

(*Disturbance. Boyars and court servants run in in confusion, gather together and whisper.*)

ONE OF THEM. Call a doctor!

ANOTHER. Hurry to the Patriarch!

A THIRD. He's calling the Tsarevich, the Tsarevich!

A FOURTH. His confessor!

BASMANOV. What has happened?

A FIFTH. The Tsar is ill.

A SIXTH. The Tsar is dying.

BASMANOV. My God!

THE FIFTH. He was sitting on the throne and suddenly fell;
Blood spurted from his mouth and from his ears.
(*The* TSAR *is carried in in a chair; all the* TSAR'*s household, all the Boyars.*)

TSAR. Leave, all of you—let only the Tsarevich
Remain here with me. (*All go away*) I am dying;
Let us embrace; good-bye, my son: now you
Will begin to reign . . . O my God, O my God!
Now I will appear before You—and I have
No time to purge my soul by confession.
I feel—my son, you are more dear to me
Than the salvation of my soul . . . let it be!
I was born a subject of the Tsar and should
Have died in darkness as all subjects do;
But I attained the highest power . . . how?
Don't ask. Enough: you are innocent,
You will begin to reign now rightfully,
I, I alone will answer God . . .
O my sweet son, don't be deluded falsely,
Don't blind yourself voluntarily.
You're taking power in tempestuous times:
This strange Impostor is a dangerous man,
Armed as he is with a terrifying name . . .
Long experienced in the ways of ruling,
I could contain rebellion and strife.
People shook with fear in front of me;
Treason did not dare raise its voice;
But you, a young and inexperienced ruler,
How will you govern during such a storm.
Suppress rebellion and entangle treason?
But God is great! He makes the young man wise,

He grants the weak man strength . . . Now, listen:
First select a reliable adviser,
A man of cool and mature years, beloved
By all the people—and honored by the boyars,
Also, either for his birth or fame—
Say, Shuisky. The army badly needs
A skillful leader: send Basmanov,
And meet the boyars' grumbling with firmness.
From the time you were young you sat with me in the Council,
You know the course of autocratic rule;
Don't change the way things go. Habit is
The soul of power. Recently I had
To reinstate exile and execution—
You can abolish them; you will be blessed
For that, as once your uncle was
When he ascended the throne Ivan had left.
Little by little as time goes on, again
Tighten up the reins of central power.
Relax them now, not letting go of them . . .
Be gracious, accessible to foreigners,
And trustfully accept their services.
Strictly preserve the statutes of the Church;
Be slow to talk; the voice of the Tsar must not
Be lost for nothing on the empty air;
Like a holy peal of bells, it must announce
Only great grief or great rejoicing.
O my sweet son! you are entering those years
When a woman's face stirs up our blood.
Keep and preserve your holy purity
Of innocence and proud bashfulness:
He who is accustomed to drown his feelings
In his youth in vicious entertainments,
Will, once he is a man, be bloodthirsty
And sullen, and his mind goes untimely dark;
Stand always at the head of all your household;
Respect your mother, but rule the house yourself—
You are a man and Tsar; love your sister—
You remain her only guardian.

FEODOR (*on his knees*). No, no—live and rule a long time still:
The people and we will be lost without you.

TSAR. Everything is done—my eyes are growing dark,
I feel the coldness of the grave . . .
(*The* PATRIARCH *enters, priests, and all the Boyars behind them. The* TSARITSA *is escorted in, supported under her arms, and the* TSAREVNA *is sobbing.*)
Who's there?
Ah! my cassock . . . so! the sacred tonsure . . .
The hour has struck, the Tsar becomes a monk—
And a dark grave will be my cell . . .
Wait a little, Holy Patriarch,
I am still Tsar! listen to me, boyars:
This is he to whom I hand my realm;
Kiss the cross to Feodor . . . Basmanov,
My friends . . . as I lie dying I beg you
To serve him zealously and truthfully!
He's still so young and still so uncorrupted.
Do you swear to this?

BOYARS. We do.

TSAR. I am content.
Forgive me my temptations and my sins,
The willful and the hidden wrongs I did . . .
Draw near me, holy father, I am ready.
(*The ritual of the tonsure begins. The women are carried out in a faint.*)

SCENE XXI

Headquarters

Basmanov escorts Pushkin in.

BASMANOV. Come in here and speak completely freely.
So, now, he's sending you to me?

PUSHKIN. He offers you his personal friendship
And the first place after him in the state of Moscow.

BASMANOV. But as it is I have already been
So elevated by Feodor. I command the army:
He scorned the Books of Rank on my behalf,
And the boyars' anger—I swore allegiance to him.

PUSHKIN. You swore allegiance to the legal heir
To the throne, but if another were alive,
Even more legal?

BASMANOV. Listen, Pushkin, that's enough.
Don't talk empty words to me; I know
Who he is.

PUSHKIN. Russia and Lithuania
Long ago recognized him as Dimitry,
But, anyway, I don't insist on that.
Perhaps he is the real Dimitry;
Perhaps, a mere impostor; I only
Know that at some point or another
Boris's son will surrender Moscow to him.

BASMANOV. As long as I'm behind the youthful Tsar,
So long he will not quit the throne;
We have sufficient regiments, thank God!
I will enliven them with a victory,
But who will you send out against me?
Not the Cossack ataman Karela? Mniszek?
With many soldiers? In all, eight thousand.

PUSHKIN. You're wrong; you won't find even that many.
I'll say it myself: our army's rotten,
The Cossacks only rob the villages,
The Poles just boast and keep on drinking,
And the Russians . . . but what more is there to say . . .
I'm not going to try to play tricks on you;
But you know where we are strong, Basmanov?
Not in soldiers, not in aid from Poland,
But in opinion; the opinion of the people.
You recall the triumph of Dimitry
And his pacific conquests
When everywhere without a shot
The obedient cities opened up to him
And the mob tied up their stubborn captains?
You yourself saw: were your troops eager
To fight against him? but when? When Boris was living!
But now? No, Basmanov, it's too late to argue
And fan the cold ashes of war:
With all your intelligence and iron will
You'll lose your ground; wouldn't it be better for you
To set the first sensible example,

Publicly proclaim Dimitry Tsar
And by that do him a good turn forever?
What do you think?

BASMANOV. You'll know tomorrow.

PUSHKIN. Make up your mind.

BASMANOV. Good-bye.

PUSHKIN. Think well, Basmanov.
(*Goes out.*)

BASMANOV. He's right, he's right; treason ripens everywhere,
What should I do? Really will I wait
Until the rebels tie me up, too, and hand
Me over to Otrepev? Wouldn't it be better
To prevent the stormy outburst of the current
And myself . . . But to betray my oath!
To deserve dishonor through all generations!
To pay back the trust of the young wearer of the crown
With a terrible betrayal . . .
It's easy for an exiled refugee
To think up rebellion and conspiracy,
But for me, for me, the sovereign's favorite . . .
But death . . . but power . . . but the poverty of the people . . .
(*Gets lost in thought.*)
Come here! Who's there? (*Whistles*) My horse! Sound muster . . .

SCENE XXII

The Place of Execution

Pushkin enters, surrounded by the People.

THE PEOPLE. The Tsarevich has sent a boyar to us.
Let's listen to what the boyar'll tell us.
Here! Over here!

PUSHKIN (*on a platform*). Citizens of Moscow,
The Tsarevich ordered me to greet you warmly.
(*Bows.*)
You know how Divine Providence

Saved the Tsarevich from a murderer's hand;
He was on his way to execute the criminal,
But God's judgment has already struck Boris.
Russia has submitted to Dimitry;
Basmanov himself with deep repentance
Has brought his army to swear allegiance to him.
Dimitry comes to you with love and peace.
To please the household of the Godunovs—
Is that why you're raising your hand against the legal
Tsar, the descendant of Monomakh?

THE PEOPLE. Course not.

PUSHKIN. Citizens of Moscow!
The whole world knows how much you have endured
Beneath the power of a cruel stranger:
Exile, executions, dishonor, taxes,
And toil and hunger—you experienced them all.
Dimitry does intend to favor you,
Boyars, nobles, office people, soldiers,
Visitors and merchants—all honest men.
Will you then be insanely stubborn
And conceitedly avoid his charity?
He is coming to the royal throne
Of his fathers with a terrifying escort.
Fear God, do not enrage the Tsar,
Kiss the cross in the name of your lawful sovereign;
Give in, and send the Metropolitan
At once to Dimitry's camp along with
Boyars, clerks and elected officers
To pay their homage to their lord and father.
(*Comes down. Noise of the crowd.*)

THE PEOPLE. What's there to talk about? The boyar said the truth.
Long live Dimitry! Long live our father!

A MAN ON THE PLATFORM. People, people! To the Kremlin, to the Tsar's Palace!
Come on! We got to tie up Boris's puppy!

THE PEOPLE (*rush off in a crowd*). Tie him up! Drown him! Long live Dimitry!
Down with the family of Boris Godunov!

SCENE XXIII

The Kremlin. Boris's House. The Watch on the Entrance Porch

Feodor by the window.

A BEGGAR. Something, for the Lord's sake!

THE WATCH. Go away, it's not allowed to talk to the prisoners.

FEODOR. Go on, old man, I'm poorer than you; you're free.

(KSENIYA, *with a veil, also comes up to the window.*)

ONE OF THE PEOPLE. Brother and sister! Poor children, like birdies in a cage.

ANOTHER. Who's sorry for them! Damned bunch!

THE FIRST. The father was a criminal, but the children are clean.

ANOTHER. Apples fall under the tree.

KSENIYA. Brother, brother, looks like some boyars are coming to us.

FEODOR. That's Golitsyn, and Masalski. I don't know the others.

KSENIYA. Oh, brother, my heart's sinking.

(GOLITSYN, MASALSKI, MOLCHANOV *and* SHEREFEDINOV. *Behind them, three secret bodyguards.*)

THE PEOPLE. Step back, step back! Boyars are coming.

(*They go into the house.*)

ONE OF THE PEOPLE. What have they come for?

ANOTHER. Probably to take Feodor Godunov to swear allegiance.

A THIRD. Really?—you hear what a noise there is in the house!

Commotion! They're fighting . . .

THE PEOPLE. Y'hear? A shriek!—that's a woman's voice—let's go in!—The doors're locked!—The cries have died down.

(*The doors open.* MASALSKI *appears on the porch.*)

MASALSKI. People! Mariya Godunova and her son Feodor

have killed themselves with poison. We saw their dead bodies.

(*The people are silent in horror.*)

Why are you silent? Shout out: long live Tsar Dimitry Ivanovich!

(*The people are speechless.*)

The Inspector General

A COMEDY IN

FIVE ACTS

Nikolai Vasilevich Gogol

Don't blame the mirror
for your own ugly mug.

— A FOLK SAYING —

DRAMATIS PERSONAE

Anton Antonovich Skvoznik-Dmukhanovsky, the Mayor
Anna Andreyevna, his wife
Marya Antonovna, his daughter
Luka Lukich Khlopov, the Superintendent of Schools
His wife
Ammos Fyodorovich Lyapkin-Tryapkin, the Judge
Artemy Filipovich Zemlyanika, the Trustee of Social Welfare Institutions
Ivan Kuzmich Shepkin, the Postmaster
Pyotr Ivanovich Dobchinsky, Pyotr Ivanovich Bobchinsky — landowners in the town
Ivan Aleksandrovich Khlestakov, the Official from Petersburg
Osip, his servant
Khristian Ivanovich Gibner, the District Doctor
Fyodor Andreyevich Lyulyukov, Ivan Lazarevich Rastakovsky, Stepan Ivanovich Korobkin — Retired officials, distinguished figures in the town
Stepan Ilich Ukhovertov, the Chief of Police
Svistunov, Pugovitsyn, Derzhimorda — policemen
Abdulin, a merchant
Fevronya Petrovna Poshlepkina, the locksmith's wife
The wife of a non-commissioned officer
Mishka, the Mayor's servant
A waiter in a tavern
Male and female guests, merchants, townsmen, petitioners

A NOTE ON THE PLAY

The Inspector General is Gogol's third, but only full-length, play. In a letter to Pushkin written October 7, 1835, Gogol asked Pushkin to give him a plot for a five-act comedy, which, he swore, "will be funnier than hell!" Gogol's work on it seems to have started after he received a letter from Pushkin suggesting a plot based on an adventure Pushkin himself had had on a trip to Nizhny-Novgorod and Orenburg in 1833 and on two other, very similar, mistaken-identity stories he had heard of.

Gogol worked hard on the play. Finished on December 4, 1835, it was passed by the censor in March, 1836, and given its première in the Aleksandrinsky Theater in St. Petersburg on April 19, 1836, the day the first edition of the play also appeared. The audience was hostile and considered the play a tasteless farce aimed at the government. Still, the Maly Theater in Moscow presented the play on May 25, 1836, with the great actor Shchepkin in the role of the Mayor.

The play's bad reception greatly discouraged Gogol. At the end of 1838, he turned to it again and thought of fundamentally revising it. In the spring of 1841 he sent the revisions for the second edition to Moscow from Rome. His own revised copy of this edition was the source for the third edition in 1842. In 1846, he started work on a "dénouement" which was to be incorporated into the play under the title: *The Inspector General, with a Dénouement. A Comedy in Five Acts with a Conclusion. The Works of N. Gogol. Fourth Edition, Enlarged, for the Benefit of the Poor*—but which was published only posthumously in 1856 and never considered an integral part of the play. This same fourth edition was also to include "A Forewarning," but this was not published until 1886. As late as 1851, the year before his death, Gogol made important, though not extensive, changes. Altogether, he worked on the play over a period of sixteen years.

The text of the play translated here is that of the Academy edition found in N. V. Gogol, *Polnoe sobranie sochinenii*, vol. 4, Moscow, 1951.

CHARACTERS AND COSTUMES

REMARKS FOR THE ACTORS

THE MAYOR, a man already grown old in the service and, in his own way, not stupid at all. Although a grafter, he comports himself, however, very reputably; rather serious; even something of a philosophizer; he speaks neither loudly, nor softly, nor much, nor little. His every word is important. The features of his face are coarse and harsh, like those of every man who began a long and hard career at the bottom. The transition from fear to joy, from meanness to superciliousness is rather quick, as with a man with vulgarly developed spiritual inclinations. He is dressed as is usual in his full-dress coat with embroidered buttonholes and in jackboots with spurs. His hair, touched with gray, is cut short.

ANNA ANDREYEVNA, his wife, a provincial flirt, not yet completely elderly, brought up half on novels and picture books and half on the bustling about in the larder and children's room. Very inquisitive and on occasion exhibits vanity. Sometimes gets the upper hand over her husband only because he does not know what to answer her. But this power extends only to little things and consists of reproofs and sneers. In the course of the play she changes into different dresses four times.

KHLESTAKOV, a young man, about twenty-three, slim, slender; a bit silly, and, as they say, with nothing upstairs. One of those people who in offices are called shallow. Talks and moves without any reflection. He is not able to devote uninterrupted attention to any kind of thought. His speech is curt, and words fly from his lips completely unexpectedly. The more the man playing this role exhibits candor and simplicity the more he will succeed. Dressed according to the fashion.

OSIP, servant, just as rather elderly servants usually are. Speaks gravely; rather condescending, a philosophizer, and likes to read to himself moral lectures for his master. His voice is almost always level; in conversation with his master assumes a stern, curt and even rather vulgar expression.

He is more intelligent than his master and therefore catches on more quickly, but does not like to talk much, and, keeping things to himself, is a knave. His costume is a gray or dark blue shabby frockcoat.

BOBCHINSKY and DOBCHINSKY, both stocky, short, very inquisitive; extraordinarily like one another. Both with not very big little potbellies. They patter away and support their patter extraordinarily much with gestures and their hands. Dobchinsky is a little taller, graver than Bobchinsky, but Bobchinsky is more pert and lively than Dobchinsky.

LYAPKIN-TRYAPKIN, the Judge, a man who, having read five or six books, is therefore somewhat free-thinking. A great lover of conjectures, and therefore gives weight to his every word. Whoever portrays him must always keep an important expression on his face. Speaks in a long drawn-out bass voice, with wheezing and sniffing, like an antique clock which first hisses and then strikes.

ZEMLYANIKA, the Trustee of Social Welfare Institutions, a very fat, sluggish and lumbering man; but on top of all this an intriguer and swindler. Very complaisant and fidgety.

POSTMASTER, a man simple to the point of being naïve.

The other roles do not require special explications. Their originals are almost always found before our eyes.

The actors are especially obliged to direct their attention to the final scene. The final spoken word must produce an electric shock on everyone at once, unexpectedly. The whole company must change its position in the twinkling of an eye. A sound of consternation must erupt from all the women at once, as if from one chest. Failure to observe these remarks may result in the loss of the whole effect.

ACT I

A room in the Mayor's house. The Mayor, the Trustee of Social Welfare Institutions, the Superintendent of Schools, the Judge, the Chief of Police, the District Doctor, two policemen.

MAYOR. I asked you in, gentlemen, in order to inform you of some most unpleasant news. An inspector general is coming to our town.

AMMOS FYODOROVICH. What do you mean, an inspector general?

ARTEMY FILIPOVICH. What do you mean, an inspector general?

MAYOR. An inspector general from Petersburg, incognito. And with a secret directive.

AMMOS FYODOROVICH. Well, I'll be—!

ARTEMY FILIPOVICH. We had it easy so far, so now we're going to get it.

LUKA LUKICH. My Lord, and even with a secret directive.

MAYOR. I somehow saw it coming: all last night I dreamed of some kind of a couple of strange rats. Really, I never ever saw such rats before: black, unnaturally big! They came, they sniffed—and went away. Here, I'll read you the letter which I got from Andrei Ivanovich Chmykov, whom you, Artemy Filipovich, know. Here's what he writes: "Dearest friend, neighbor, and benefactor" (*mutters, glancing over it quickly*) ". . . and to inform you." Ah! here: "I hasten by the way to inform you that an official with a directive came to look over the whole province and especially our county (*significantly raises his finger*). I learned of this from the most reliable sources, although he poses as a non-official. Since I know that you, just like any man, have some little faults, because you are an intelligent man and don't like to let go of what finds its way into your hands . . ." (*pausing*) well, here . . . "so I advise you to take precautions, for he may arrive at any moment, if he has not already arrived and is not living somewhere incognito . . . Just yesterday I . . ." Well, now this is just family affairs: "My sister Anna Kirilovna came to our place with her husband; Ivan Kirilovich has grown very fat and plays the violin all the time . . ." and so forth and so forth. So that's what the situation is.

AMMOS FYODOROVICH. Yes, that's the situation . . . unusual, simply unusual. Something not without a purpose behind it.

LUKA LUKICH. What for, Anton Antonovich, why is this? Why an inspector general to us?

MAYOR. Why? But, it's obvious, it's fate! (*Sighing*) Up to this moment, thanks be to God, they sneaked up on other towns. Now it's our turn.

AMMOS FYODOROVICH. I think, Anton Antonovich, that here there's a subtle and more political reason. Here's what I mean now: Russia . . . um, yes . . . wants to start war, and the ministry now, you see, has sent out a man to find out if there isn't treason somewhere.

MAYOR. Where'd you get that from! And an intelligent man, too. Treason in a district town! What's this, a border town? From here, even if you gallop for three years, you won't get to any other country at all.

AMMOS FYODOROVICH. No, let me tell you, you didn't get . . . You didn't . . . The authorities have sharp eyes: even if they're far away, nothing'll escape them.

MAYOR. Escape them or not, I have forewarned you, gentlemen—Watch out! in my own department I've given various instructions; I advise you to, too. Especially you, Artemy Filipovich. Without a doubt, an official passing through will want above all to look over the social welfare institutions within your jurisdiction—and therefore you arrange it so that everything is proper. The caps should be clean, and the sick shouldn't look like blacksmiths, the way they usually go around in their everyday clothes.

ARTEMY FILIPOVICH. Well, that's easy. They can even put on clean caps, most likely.

MAYOR. And then, too, you should put up at the head of each bed in Latin or some other such language—that's already in your department, Khristian Ivanovich—each illness, when the man got sick, what day of the week and date . . . It's not good that in your place the sick smoke such strong tobacco that you always sneeze and sneeze when you go in. And then it would be better if there were fewer of them: right away it will be attributed to bad supervision or to the doctor's lack of skill.

ARTEMY FILIPOVICH. Oh, about the doctoring, Khristian Ivanovich and I have taken measures: the closer to nature, the better; we don't use expensive medicines. Man is easy: if he's going to die, he'll die anyway; if he's going to get well, he'll get well anyway. Besides, it would be sort of difficult for Khristian Ivanovich to have to express himself to them—he doesn't know a word of Russian.

(KHRISTIAN IVANOVICH *lets out a sound partly similar to the letter* i *and partly to* e.)

MAYOR. I would also advise you, Ammos Fyodorovich, to direct your attention to your offices. In your vestibule there, where the petitioners usually present themselves, the doormen have acquired some domestic geese and little goslings, which keep poking about underfoot. It is, of course, laudable for every man to settle down to domestic life, and so why should not a doorman, also, settle down? just, you know, in such a place it isn't decent . . . I meant to mention this to you before, but somehow I kept forgetting.

AMMOS FYODOROVICH. I'll tell them right away today to pick them up and take them all out to the kitchen. If you want, come over for dinner.

MAYOR. In addition to which it's no good that all kinds of junk is hanging up to dry in your own office, and your hunting-crop is hung up over the filing case itself. I know you like to go hunting, but still it would be better to put it away for a while, and then, when the inspector general has gone, if you want, you can hang it up again. Also, your assessor . . . he is, of course, a very able man, but he smells so, as if he's just come out of a distillery—that's not good either. I meant to tell you about this some time ago, but I was distracted by something, I forget by what. There are remedies for this if it actually is, as he says, an odor he was born with. You can suggest he eat onions or garlic or something else. In that case Khristian Ivanovich can assist with various medications.

(KHRISTIAN IVANOVICH *lets out the same sound.*)

AMMOS FYODOROVICH. No, that's impossible to get rid of: he says his nurse bruised him when he was a child and ever since he's smelled a bit of vodka.

MAYOR. Yes, yes, I only wanted to mention it to you. Now about the internal dispositions and what Andrei Ivanovich in his letter terms little faults, I have nothing to say. Indeed, it would be unusual to say anything. There's not a man who doesn't have some kind of besetting sin. That's the way it was arranged by God Himself, and the Voltairians argue against it in vain.

AMMOS FYODOROVICH. What do you mean, Anton Antonovich, by little faults? There are all kinds of little faults. I tell everybody openly that I take bribes, but what kind of bribes? Borzoi puppies. That's a completely different thing.

MAYOR. Well, puppies or something else, bribes are bribes.

AMMOS FYODOROVICH. No, Anton Antonovich. Now, for example, somebody's fur coat might be worth five hundred rubles, but my wife has just a shawl.

MAYOR. Well, and what about your taking Borzoi puppies as bribes? Besides, you don't believe in God; you never go to church; but I, at least, am firm in my faith and get to church every Sunday. But you . . . Oh, I know you: if somebody starts talking about the creation of the world, your hair simply stands on end.

AMMOS FYODOROVICH. But of course I got where I am all by myself, by my native intelligence.

MAYOR. Well, in some cases a lot of intelligence is worse than none at all. Moreover, I only just mentioned that about the district judge in passing; but to tell the truth, probably nobody will ever look in here: it's such an enviable place; God Himself is watching over it. But now you, Luka Lukich, as the Superintendent of Schools, have to be especially concerned about the teachers. They are, of course, learned people and educated in various colleges, but they do have very odd ways, naturally inseparable from academic rank. One of them, for example, the one who has the fat face—I don't remember his name—cannot get on, after having mounted the lecture platform, without making a face. Like this (*makes a face*). And then he begins with his hand to iron out his beard from under his tie. Of course, if he makes such a face at a student, it's nothing at all, maybe even it has to be like that there, I can't judge that, but you judge for yourself, if he does it at a visitor—it could be very bad: an inspector general or somebody else who can take it to heart. God only knows what might come of it.

LUKA LUKICH. What can I, really, do about him? I've already spoken to him several times. Why only the other day, just as our marshal was about to go into the classroom, he cut a face such as I'd never seen in my life. He did it with a good heart, but I get rebuked: how come free-thinking thoughts are inculcated in the young?

MAYOR. And I must mention to you something about the teacher in the history department. He's a learned intellect—that's obvious, and has picked up piles of information, but it's just that he explains things with such passion that he completely forgets himself. I was listening to him once: well, as long as he was talking about the Assyrians and Babylonians, everything was all right, but as soon as he got up to Alexander the Great, I can't tell you what happened to him. I thought, There's a fire! Good God! he ran off the platform and with all his might pounded a chair on the floor. No doubt about it, Alexander the Great is a hero, but why break the chairs? it means a loss for the treasury.

LUKA LUKICH. Yes, he's fiery; I've already reminded him of this several times . . . He says: As you please. For learning I will not spare even life.

MAYOR. Yes. Such is indeed the inexplicable law of facts: an intelligent man or a drunk or one who'll make all sorts of faces—it outdoes the saints.

LUKA LUKICH. God save us from ever serving in academic ranks; you have to be afraid of everything. Everybody's meddling, everybody wants to show that he, too, is a clever man.

MAYOR. That's nothing. The damned incognito! Suddenly he'll pop in: and you are here, my boys! And who, he'll say, is the judge here?—Lyapkin-Tryapkin. Hand over Lyapkin-Tryapkin! And who's the Trustee of the Social Welfare Institutions?—Zemlyanika! That's what's bad.

(*The* POSTMASTER *enters.*)

POSTMASTER. Explain it to me, gentlemen, what kind of official's coming?

MAYOR. You really haven't heard?

POSTMASTER. I heard from Pyotr Ivanovich Bobchinsky. He was just over at my office in the post office.

MAYOR. Well? What do you think of it?

POSTMASTER. What do I think? There'll be war with the Turks.

AMMOS FYODOROVICH. That's it! I was thinking the same thing myself.

MAYOR. You're both way off!

POSTMASTER. Honestly, war with the Turks. It's all the Frenchman's dirty work.

MAYOR. What kind of war with the Turks! Simply it's going to be rough for us, not the Turks. That's already well known: I have a letter.

POSTMASTER. If that's so, well—there won't be war with the Turks.

MAYOR. Well now, what do you think, Ivan Kuzmich?

POSTMASTER. What do I think? What do you think, Anton Antonych?

MAYOR. What do I think? There's no danger, but, well, just a little . . . The merchants and the citizenry disturb me. They say I've given them a hard time, but if, now, good Lord, I've taken anything from anyone why, really, it was without malice. —I even think (*takes him by the arm and leads him to one side*), I even think, maybe there was some kind of denunciation of me. What, in fact, is an inspector general coming here for? listen, Ivan Kuzmich, couldn't we, for our general good, you know, take each letter, which gets to your office in the post office, incoming or outgoing, open it just a little bit and read it: doesn't it contain, maybe, some kind of report or simply correspondence? If not, why, we could seal it up again; besides, we could even return the letter just like that, opened.

POSTMASTER. I know, I know . . . You can't teach this to me, I do it myself, not as a precaution but mostly out of curiosity—I've got a passion for finding out what's new in the world. I can tell you it's the most interesting reading! You read somebody else's letter with real enjoyment. Some passages are so well written . . . and such edification . . . It's better than the *Moscow Record!*

MAYOR. Well, so, tell me: you never read anything about any sort of official from Petersburg?

POSTMASTER. No, there was nothing about one from Petersburg, but there's a lot about them from Kostrom and Saratov. It's really a great shame you don't read letters.

There are wonderful passages. Like not long ago one lieutenant wrote his friend and described a ball in the most wanton . . . very, very well: "My life, dear friend, flows on," he says, "in an empyrean realm: there are lots of young ladies, music's playing, the standard is waving" . . . described it with great, with great feeling. I've kept it on purpose. You want me to read it?

MAYOR. No, this isn't the time for that. So, do me a favor, Ivan Kuzmich: if by chance a complaint or a report turns up, hold on to it without any further scruples.

POSTMASTER. With great pleasure.

AMMOS FYODOROVICH. Be careful you don't get scolded for that some time.

POSTMASTER. Oh, goodness!

MAYOR. Nothing to it, nothing to it. It'd be completely different if you made something public of it, but you know it's all a family affair.

AMMOS FYODOROVICH. Indeed, we're in for a great deal of trouble! And, I must admit, Anton Antonovich, I was about to come over to your place to treat you to a puppy. The litter sister to that dog, you know. You surely heard that Sheptovich has concocted a lawsuit with Varkhovinsky, and I'm living in clover: I go hare-hunting on the property of both of them.

MAYOR. Gentlemen, your hare aren't very close to my heart right now. A damned incognito is sitting in my head. Here we sit and wait, and suddenly the door'll open and—bang . . .

(BOBCHINSKY *and* DOBCHINSKY *enter out of breath.*)

BOBCHINSKY. An extraordinary occurrence!

DOBCHINSKY. Unexpected news!

ALL. What? What is it?

DOBCHINSKY. An unforeseen thing: we go into the hotel . . .

BOBCHINSKY (*interrupting*). Pyotr Ivanovich and I go into the hotel . . .

DOBCHINSKY (*interrupting*). Pyotr Ivanovich, let me tell it.

BOBCHINSKY. No, let me . . . let me, let me . . . You don't have the right style . . .

DOBCHINSKY. And you'll forget and not remember everything.

BOBCHINSKY. I'll remember, honest to God, I'll remember. Don't interfere, let me tell it. Don't interfere! Gentlemen, do me the favor, tell Pyotr Ivanovich not to interfere.

MAYOR. So tell us, for God's sake, what is it? My heart's in my mouth. Sit down, gentlemen! Find yourselves chairs! Pyotr Ivanovich, here's a chair for you! (*All sit down around both* PYOTR IVANOVICHES) Well, what is it?

BOBCHINSKY. Let me, let me, I'll tell you everything in order. I had scarcely had the pleasure of leaving you after you had seen fit to be somewhat embarrassed by the letter received, indeed—so, then I ran over to . . . Now, please, don't interrupt, Pyotr Ivanovich. I know everything, everything, everything, sir. —So I, as you see, ran over to Korobkin's. But not finding Korobkin home, I headed over to Rastakovsky's, but not finding Rastakovsky, I dropped in on Ivan Kuzmich to tell him about the news you received, but on my way from there I ran into Pyotr Ivanovich . . .

DOBCHINSKY (*interrupting*). Near the stall where they sell pies.

BOBCHINSKY. Near the stall where they sell pies. And having encountered Pyotr Ivanovich, I says to him: Have you heard about the news which Anton Antonovich received in a reliable letter? But Pyotr Ivanovich had already heard about it from your housekeeper Avdotya, who I don't know why had been sent to Filip Antonovich Pochechuyev.

DOBCHINSKY (*interrupting*). For a keg for the French vodka.

BOBCHINSKY (*pushing his hands away*). For a keg for the French vodka. So Pyotr Ivanovich and I went to Pochechuyev's . . . Now, you, Pyotr Ivanovich . . . that is . . . don't interrupt, please don't interrupt! We went to Pochechuyev's, but on the way Pyotr Ivanovich says: Let's go in, he says, to the tavern. In my stomach . . . I've had nothing to eat since morning, so the rumbling of the stomach . . . indeed, in Pyotr Ivanovich's stomach. And in the tavern, he says, They've just brought in some fresh salmon, so we'll have a bite— No sooner do we get into the hotel than suddenly a young man . . .

DOBCHINSKY (*interrupting*). Of a not unattractive appearance, in special clothes . . .

BOBCHINSKY. Of a not unattractive appearance, in special clothes, walks around, you know, in the room, and on his face such deliberation . . . a physiognomy . . . a carriage . . . and here (*makes circles with his hand next to his forehead*) a lot, lots of everything. I like as had a premonition and says to Pyotr Ivanovich: This here's something out of the ordinary, sir. —Yes. And Pyotr Ivanovich beckoned with his finger and called the tavernkeeper over, Vlas, the tavernkeeper. His wife had a baby three weeks ago, and such a bouncing boy, he'll be keeping the tavern, just like his father. Having called Vlas over, Pyotr Ivanovich asks him on the quiet: Who, he says, is this young man? And Vlas says to this: This, he says— Oh, don't interrupt, Pyotr Ivanovich, please don't interrupt. You can't tell the story. Honest to God, you can't tell it, you lisp; one of your teeth in your mouth, I know, whistles. This, says he, is a young official, sir, coming from Petersburg, and his name, he says, is Ivan Aleksandrovich Khlestakov, and he's going, he says, to Saratov province, and, he says, he gives himself the oddest recommendation: it's his second week here, he doesn't go out of the tavern, takes everything on account and doesn't want to pay a kopek. As soon as he told me this, it came over me like that, as if from Heaven. Hey! I says to Pyotr Ivanovich . . .

DOBCHINSKY. No, Pyotr Ivanovich, I said that: Hey.

BOBCHINSKY. At first you said it, but then I said it, too. Hey! Pyotr Ivanovich and I said. But why is he sitting here when his road lies toward Saratov?— Indeed, sir! And so here he is, this official.

MAYOR. Who, what official?

BOBCHINSKY. That official about whom you received the notice, the inspector general.

MAYOR (*in fear*). What are you saying, Lord bless you! It's not he.

DOBCHINSKY. It is! He doesn't pay money and he doesn't go out, who would it be if not he? and he has an order for post-horses written out to Saratov.

BOBCHINSKY. It is, it is, honest to God, it is . . . So observant: he's looked everything over. He saw Pyotr Ivanovich and me eating salmon, mostly because Pyotr Ivanovich on account of his stomach . . . yes. And so he looked over at our plates. So circumspect, I was seized with fear.

MAYOR. Lord, have mercy on us sinners! Where's he staying there?

DOBCHINSKY. In number five under the stairs.

BOBCHINSKY. In the same room where the officers passing through last year had their fight.

MAYOR. Has he been here long?

DOBCHINSKY. Two weeks, already. He came on St. Vasily Egiptyanin's Day.

MAYOR. Two weeks! (*Aside*) Saints alive, take him away, you holy saints! In these two weeks the noncommissioned officer's wife was flogged! The prisoners got no food! The streets are like pigsties, filthy. Disgrace! Defamation! (*Grabs his head*)

ARTEMY FILIPOVICH. Anton Antonovich, why not all go and parade up to the hotel?

AMMOS FYODOROVICH. No, no. Let the most important go first, the clergy, merchants; that's the way it is in the book: the Acts of John the Mason . . .

MAYOR. No, no; let me go myself. I've had hard moments in my life before, they've passed, and I've even gotten thanks out of them. Maybe God will carry us over this one, too. (*Turning to* BOBCHINSKY) You say he's a young man?

BOBCHINSKY. Young, a little over about twenty-three or -four.

MAYOR. So much the better: you can smell a young man out quicker. It's hard if he's an old devil, but a young man's all on the surface. You, gentlemen, each get your own department ready, and I'll set off myself, or perhaps with Pyotr Ivanovich here, privately, for a walk to inform ourselves whether or not people passing through are experiencing any unpleasantnesses. Hey, Svistunov!

SVISTUNOV (*enters*). What would you like?

MAYOR. Go get the Chief of Police right away . . . or no, I need you. Tell somebody there to have the Chief of Police come to me as soon as he can, and you come here.

(*The Policeman,* SVISTUNOV, *runs out in a hurry.*)

ARTEMY FILIPOVICH. Let's go, let's go, Ammos Fyodorovich. In fact, there really can be trouble.

AMMOS FYODOROVICH. But what are you afraid of? Once you put clean caps on the sick, nobody'll be the wiser.

ARTEMY FILIPOVICH. What are caps! It's the regulation to give the sick oat-soup, but all the corridors stink so of cabbage you have to hold your nose.

AMMOS FYODOROVICH. But on this score I'm completely at ease. In fact, who's going to come into the district court?

And if he does take a look at some sort of documents, he'll be sorry he ever did. It's fifteen years now I've been sitting on the bench, and if I ever take a look at some memorandum—ah! I just throw up my hands. Solomon himself couldn't tell the true from the false in it.

(*The Judge, the Trustee of Social Welfare Institutions, the Superintendent of Schools and the Postmaster go out and in the doorway bump into the Policeman returning.*)

MAYOR. Well, is the cart waiting?

POLICEMAN. It is.

MAYOR. Go down to the street . . . or no, stop! Go get . . . but where are the others? You aren't really all by yourself? Why, I gave orders for Prokhorov to be here, too. Where's Prokhorov?

POLICEMAN. Prokhorov's home, but he can't be put on duty.

MAYOR. How so?

POLICEMAN. Well, so: they brought him in the morning dead-drunk. We poured two tubs of water over him, but he hasn't sobered up yet.

MAYOR (*holding his head*). Oh, my God, my God! Go down the street quickly, or no, first run into my room, you hear! and bring out my dress sword and the new hat. Well, Pyotr Ivanovich, let's go.

BOBCHINSKY. Me too, me too . . . let me, too, Anton Antonovich.

MAYOR. No, no, Pyotr Ivanovich, impossible, impossible! It would be awkward, and besides we wouldn't fit in the cart.

BOBCHINSKY. Doesn't matter, doesn't matter, I'll go like this: dog-paddle, dog-paddle. I'll run along behind if I could only just sort of peep in a little bit through a little crack in the door, how he carries himself . . .

MAYOR (*pointing his sword at the Policeman*). Now run, get the men, and let each of them take . . . Ah, the sword is all scratched up! That damned merchant Abdulin—saw the Mayor has an old sword, but didn't send over a new one. Oh, cunning people! And so, the swindlers, I bet, have got petitions all ready under their coats. Let each one take a street in his hand—God damn it, a street!—a broom, and sweep up the whole street that leads to the tavern, and sweep it clean. You hear. And watch out: you! you! I know you: you play friends there and steal silver spoons in your boots—watch out: my ears are up! . . . What did you do with the merchant Chernyayev, hey? He gave you two arshins of cloth for a tailcoat; but you walked off with the whole bolt. Watch out! You're taking things beyond your rank! Get going!

(*The Chief of Police enters.*)

MAYOR. So, Stepan Ilich, tell me for God's sake, where on earth have you been? What do you think it looks like!

CHIEF OF POLICE. I was right here behind the gate.

MAYOR. Well, listen now, Stepan Ilich! An official has come from Petersburg. How have you dealt with it there?

CHIEF OF POLICE. Just the way you ordered. I sent Officer Pugovitsyn with the men to clean up the sidewalk.

MAYOR. And where's Derzhimorda?

CHIEF OF POLICE. Derzhimorda went on the fire engine.

MAYOR. And Prokhorov's drunk?

CHIEF OF POLICE. Drunk.

MAYOR. How could you let this happen?

CHIEF OF POLICE. God knows. Yesterday there was a brawl outside of town—he went there to establish order, and came back drunk.

MAYOR. Listen now. You do as follows: Officer Pugovitsyn . . . he's tall, so let him, for the sake of town planning and organization, stand on the bridge. And quickly knock down the old fence next to the shoemaker's and put up a straw marker so it looks like a project. The more fragile it is the more it suggests the activity of the director of the town. Eh, my God, and I forgot, that next to the fence there's forty cartfuls of all kinds of rubbish piled up. What a nasty lot of people: just anywhere you put up some kind of monument or simply a fence, God knows from where and how they bring in all kinds of junk! (*Sighs*) And if the official who's coming asks our employees: Are you satisfied or not?—have them say: Completely satisfied, your excellency, and whoever isn't, why afterwards I'll give him such dissatisfaction . . . Oh, oh, ho, ho, ho! guilty, guilty of lots of things (*takes a filing folder instead of his hat*), God just grant that this is over soon, and then I'll burn a candle, such as nobody has ever yet burned: I'll order up then poods of wax for every damned merchant. Oh, my

God, my God! let's go, Pyotr Ivanovich! (*Instead of his hat, tries to put on the paper filing folder*)

CHIEF OF POLICE. Anton Antonovich, that's a box and not a hat.

MAYOR (*throws it down*). A box is a box. The hell with it! And if they ask how come we haven't finished building the church in the charitable institution, for which the money was assigned some five years ago, don't forget to say that we started to build it but it burned down. I sent in a report about it. Or else, perhaps, somebody'll forget and foolishly say it wasn't ever begun. And tell Derzhimorda not to be too ready to use his fists. Let him for the establishment of order hold a light up to everybody's face: both the innocent and the guilty. Let's go, let's go, Pyotr Ivanovich (*goes out and comes back*). And don't let the soldiers out on the street with nothing on: this worthless garrison will put on just a frockcoat on top of their shirt and nothing on below. (*All go out.* ANNA ANDREYEVNA *and* MARYA ANTONOVNA *run onto the stage.*)

ANNA ANDREYEVNA. Where are they, where? Ah, my God . . . (*opening the door*) Husband! Antosha! Anton! (*Speaks rapidly*) Always you, always after you. And you went on dawdling: "I can't find my pin, I can't find my scarf." (*Runs over to the window and shouts:*) Anton, where you going, where? What, he came? Inspector general? With a mustache! With what kind of mustache!

MAYOR'S VOICE. Later, later, Mama.

ANNA ANDREYEVNA. Later? There's news for you later! I don't want it later . . . Got to tell me just one thing: what's he, a colonel? Eh? (*Scornfully*) He's gone. I'll make you remember this! And this one all the time: "Maminka, Maminka, wait, I've got to fasten the kerchief behind; I'll be there right away." Here's your right away! We didn't find anything out, so there! And the damned flirting all the time; she heard the Postmaster was here and so she has to mince around in front of the mirror: and look at herself from this side and from that side. Imagines he's going to go running after her, but he's just going to make a face at you whenever you turn your back.

MARYA ANTONOVNA. But how can it be helped, Maminka? It's all the same: in two hours we'll find everything out.

ANNA ANDREYEVNA. In two hours! Thanks a lot. She favored me with an answer. How come you didn't think of saying that in a month we can find out even better! (*Leans out the window*) Hey, Avdotya! Hey! Avdotya, y'hear me, somebody's arrived there . . . Didn't hear? You stupid! He's waving? Let him wave, but you can still go and question him. She couldn't find out! Nothing in her head, boys sitting around all the time. Eh? Went in a hurry! You better run after the cart. Go on, go on right away! You hear, run, ask him: where did they go, and ask him properly, who's the man who came, what he's like, you hear! Look in the crack and find everything out, and what kind of eyes he has: whether black or not, and come right back this minute, you hear! Hurry, hurry, hurry, hurry.

(*She shouts until the curtain falls. Thus the curtain conceals them both, standing by the window.*)

ACT II

A little room in the hotel. A bed, a table, a suitcase, an empty bottle, boots, a clothes brush, and so forth. OSIP *lies on his master's bed.*

OSIP. God damn it but I'd like to eat, and there's such a rumbling in my belly like a whole company was blowing its trumpets. Why, we can't even just get home! What're you going to do about it? The second month he's been gone now out of Petersburg! Got rid of his money on the road, my boy did, and now sits with his tail between his legs and don't get excited about nothing. And there was enough, there was really plenty for the post-stations; but no, see, got to show himself in every town. (*Mimics him:*) "Hey, Osip, go get a room, the best, and order up the best dinner: I can't eat a bad dinner, I want the best." It'd be good, in fact, to have something substantial, but this is plain starvation. Meets up with a stranger, and then he's at cards—there you've played yourself out! Ah, I'm fed up! Really, village life is better: even if there's no grandeur to it, there's less worry, too. You get yourself a woman, and lie in bed your whole life and eat pies. But who's going to argue, of course, when it comes to the truth, that life in Peter's best of all. Just so there's money, and life's fine with lots to it: thee-aters, dogs dancing for you, and everything you want. Everybody's talking with this subtle refinement, which only the nobles can do better; you go to Shchukin—the merchants shout at you: "Honorable!" Across the water in a boat you sit down with an official: you want company—you go into a shop: then a gentleman'll tell you about the camps and explain what every star in the sky means, so you see it all, just like in your palm. An old officer's wife'll wander in; another time such a maid'll look in . . . phew, phew, phew! (*Bursts out laughing and shakes his head*) Real dandy, God damn it, ways of doing things! You'll never hear an impolite word, everybody says "sir" to you. You're tired of walking—you get a cab and you sit in it, like a lord, and you don't want to pay him—all right: every house has gates leading through and you scoot off so never a devil can find you. Only one thing's bad: one time you eat famously and the next you just about keel over from hunger, like now, for example. But it's all his fault. What can you do with him? His old man sends money and instead of holding on to it—what's he do! . . . goes out on the town: rides in a cab, gets himself a ticket to the thee-ater every night, and then after a week—you turn around and he sends his new morning coat to the second-hand market to sell. Next time, he gets rid of everything down to his last shirt, so he's got nothing left on him but his old coat and cloak, 's the truth, by God! And the cloth was something fine, real English! Hundred and fifty rubles the morning coat cost him alone, and he gets rid of it in the market for twenty, not to mention the pants—they go for nothing. On account of what? On account of he don't do nothing: instead of having a steady job, he goes walking along the av-e-noo and playing cards. Oh, if his old man knew it. He wouldn't pay no attention to your being an official, but lifting up your shirt he'd give you such a going over you wouldn't sit down for four days. If you're going to serve, go serve; like the tavernkeeper said now, he won't give you nothing to eat, till you pay up for the rest; well, and if we don't? (*With a sigh:*) Ah, my God, if there were just some kind of soup. Seems like I could eat up the whole world right now. Knocking, most likely it's him coming. (*Hurriedly scrambles off the bed*)

(KHLESTAKOV *enters.*)

KHLESTAKOV. So, take it (*hands him his cap and cane*). Ah, lying around on the bed again?

OSIP. What would I be lying around for? Never saw a bed, hey?

KHLESTAKOV. You're lying, you were on the bed; see, it's all mussed up.

OSIP. What do I need *it* for? don't know, hey, what a bed is? I got legs; I'll stand around. What do I want your bed for?

KHLESTAKOV (*walks around the room*). Look in the bag there. No tobacco?

OSIP. Where's there going to be any of this tobacco! You smoked up the last four days ago.

KHLESTAKOV (*walks around and purses his lips in various ways.*

Finally speaks in a loud and determined voice). Listen, hey, Osip!

OSIP. What d'you want?

KHLESTAKOV (*in a loud but not so determined voice*). You go down there.

OSIP. Where?

KHLESTAKOV (*in a voice not at all determined and not loud, very close to that of a request*). Downstairs, to the dining room . . . there tell them . . . to give me something to eat.

OSIP. No, I don't feel like going.

KHLESTAKOV. How do you dare, you fool!

OSIP. Oh, it's all the same if I go or not, nothing'll come of it. The landlord said he won't give you no more.

KHLESTAKOV. How can he dare not? What absurdity!

OSIP. I'll go to the Mayor even, he says; it's already the third week the master don't pay up his money. You and that master, he says, are swindlers, and your master's a cheat. We've seen, he says, such frauds and bastards before.

KHLESTAKOV. And it makes you so happy, you pig, to tell me all this now.

OSIP. He says that's the way they all come in, make theirselves at home, run up a bill, and afterwards you can't throw 'em out. I'm not joking, he says, I'm going straight with a complaint so he goes right to the clink.

KHLESTAKOV. Okay, okay, you idiot, enough of that. Go on, go on, tell him . . . What a vulgar beast!

OSIP. It'd be better I called the landlord himself up here.

KHLESTAKOV. Why the landlord? You go tell him yourself.

OSIP. But, really, sir . . .

KHLESTAKOV. Well, go on, God damn you! Call the landlord. (OSIP *goes out.*)

KHLESTAKOV (*alone*). How much I'd like something to eat. Took a little walk; thought, my appetite'll probably pass—no, God damn it, it won't. Oh, if I hadn't had myself such a time in Penza there'd have been money to get home with. That infantry captain really hooked me. Remarkable, the cheat, how he cuts the cards. Didn't sit there more than some fifteen minutes—and he'd fleeced me clean. And on top of it all I'd terribly like to fight him once more. Only never got the chance.What a rotten little town! Can't get anything on credit in the grocery stores. That's just foul. (*Begins to whistle first from* Roberta *and then "Don't You Sew Me, Mama . . .", and finally just anything*) Nobody wants to come.

(OSIP *and the Waiter enter.*)

WAITER. The landlord sent me to ask what you want.

KHLESTAKOV. Greetings, friend! Well, how are you, well?

WAITER. Thank God.

KHLESTAKOV. Well, now, how're things in the hotel? Everything going well?

WAITER. Yes, thank God, everything's fine.

KHLESTAKOV. Many travelers?

WAITER. Yes, enough.

KHLESTAKOV. Listen, my man, so far I haven't had a thing to eat, so please hurry it up, quicker, see, 'cause right after dinner I've got some things to do.

WAITER. But the landlord said he won't serve anything more. Seems he wanted to go complain to the Mayor today.

KHLESTAKOV. Complain about what? Look at it yourself, my friend, about what? You know I've got to eat. This way I can waste away completely. I'd very much like something to eat; I'm not joking when I say this.

WAITER. Yes, sir. He said: "I won't give him any dinner as long as he don't pay me up for the rest." That's what he said.

KHLESTAKOV. But you go make him listen to reason, you persuade him.

WAITER. But how can I tell him that?

KHLESTAKOV. You talk to him seriously, make him understand I've got to eat. The money'll come all by itself . . . He thinks, that just as it's nothing for him, the peasant, not to eat for a whole day, so it's nothing for others, too. That's a joke!

WAITER. Very well, I'll tell him. (*Exits with* OSIP)

KHLESTAKOV (*alone*). It'll be damned nasty, though, if he doesn't give me anything to eat. I want to eat as I've never wanted to before. Really, isn't there something in the way of clothing to pay him off with? Sell my pants, maybe. No, it's better to go hungry but arrive home in a Petersburg suit. It's a shame Tokhim wouldn't rent the carriage, for it would have been real good, God damn it, to arrive home in a carriage, roll up in style to some neighboring landowner's porch, with lanterns, and dress Osip in livery on the back. How everybody'd get excited, I bet: "Who's that, what's that?" And the footman in gold livery, goes in (*stretching out and representing the footman:*) "Ivan Aleksandrovich Khlestakov from Petersburg, shall I show him in?" They, the louts, don't even know what it means "shall I show him in?" If some old gander of a landowner drops in on them, he flops right into the living room, the bear. You go up to some pretty little daughter: "Madame, how I . . ." (*Rubs his hands and clicks his heels*) Damn (*spits*), I even feel sick, I'm so hungry.

(OSIP *enters, followed by the Waiter.*)

KHLESTAKOV. Well?

OSIP. Dinner's coming.

KHLESTAKOV (*claps his hands and jumps slightly up from his chair*). It's coming! It's coming! It's coming!

WAITER (*with plates and a napkin*). The landlord is serving you for the last time.

KHLESTAKOV. Well, the landlord, the landlord . . . I spit on your landlord! What's that there?

WAITER. Soup and meat.

KHLESTAKOV. What, only two dishes?

WAITER. Only, sir.

KHLESTAKOV. How absurd! I won't have it. You tell him: What, in fact, *is* this! . . . This is nothing.

WAITER. No, the landlord says, it's a lot.

KHLESTAKOV. But why's there no gravy?

WAITER. There is no gravy.

KHLESTAKOV. Why not! I saw myself, going past the kitchen, lots of things were cooking there. And in the dining room this morning two stubby fellows were eating salmon and a lot of other things.

WAITER. Sometimes there is, see, and sometimes not.

KHLESTAKOV. Why not?

WAITER. Already there isn't.

KHLESTAKOV. But the salmon, the fish, the chops?

WAITER. But that's for those who're straighter, sir.

KHLESTAKOV. Ah, you, you idiot!

WAITER. Yes, sir.

KHLESTAKOV. You lousy little pig . . . How come they eat,

but I don't? How come I, God damn it, can't do likewise? Aren't they just such travelers as I?

WAITER. Everybody knows they aren't.

KHLESTAKOV. What are they then?

WAITER. The regular kind! Everybody knows: they pay money.

KHLESTAKOV. I've got no intention of arguing with you, you idiot; (*pours the soup and eats*) what kind of soup's this? You just poured some water in a cup: there's no taste, it just stinks. I don't want this soup, give me another.

WAITER. We'll take it back, sir. The landlord said, if you don't want to eat, you don't have to.

KHLESTAKOV (*defending his meal with his hand*). Well, well, well . . . Leave it, idiot. You're used to behaving like that with others; I'm not that sort, my friend! With me I advise you not . . . (*Eats*) My God, what soup! (*Continues eating*) I think there's not a man in the world who's ever eaten such soup. Some kind of feathers're floating around instead of butter. (*Cuts the chicken*) Ai, ai, ai, what a chicken! Give me the meat! There's a little soup left, Osip, help yourself. (*Cuts the meat*) What kind of meat's this? This isn't meat.

WAITER. What is it then?

KHLESTAKOV. Damned if I know what it is, only it's not meat. It's an ax fried instead of beef. (*Eats*) Cheats, rats, what do people get here? Your jaws ache if you eat just one piece. (*Picks his teeth*) Bastards! . . . Just like bark, you can't get it out with anything, and your teeth turn black after it, you cheats! (*Wipes his mouth with a napkin*) There's nothing more?

WAITER. Nothing.

KHLESTAKOV. Rats! Bastards! not even some kind of gravy or pie. Good-for-nothings! They just rob the travelers. (*The Waiter, together with* OSIP, *clears the dishes and carries out the plates.*)

KHLESTAKOV. Really, might as well have not eaten; just barely got a taste for it. If I had some change, I'd send someone to the market to buy a roll, at least.

OSIP (*enters*). Some kind of Mayor came in down there, he's filling himself in on what's happened and asking about you.

KHLESTAKOV (*scared*). I'll be damned! That ogre of a tavernkeeper already managed to complain. What if, in fact, he hauls me off to jail? So what? if by some noble means I perhaps . . . no, no, I don't want to. Over in town there are officers and people hanging about, and I, just to make it worse, put on airs and winked at a certain merchant's daughter—no, don't want to. What about him, how come he dares to, in fact? What's he think I am, a merchant or a worker? (*Gets braver and straightens up*) Why, I'll tell him straight to his face: how do you dare, how do you . . . ? (*The doorknob turns; he turns pale and shrinks into himself*) *The Mayor and* DOBCHINSKY *enter. The Mayor, having gone into the room, stops. Both stare at each other in fright for several minutes, their eyes popping.*)

MAYOR (*pulling himself together somewhat and coming to attention*). I trust you are well!

KHLESTAKOV (*bows*). My compliments . . .

MAYOR. Excuse me.

KHLESTAKOV. Certainly.

MAYOR. It is my obligation, as the town-governor of this town, to be concerned that the people traveling through and all noble persons meet with no hindrances . . .

KHLESTAKOV (*at first stutters a little, but toward the end of the speech speaks loudly*). But what can I do? . . . It's not my fault . . . I'll pay, really . . . They'll send it to me from the country. (BOBCHINSKY *looks in through the door*) It's more his fault: gives me only beef as stiff as a board; and the soup—God knows what he slopped into it, I had to throw it out the window. He's starved me for days on end . . . The tea is queer; it smells like fish, not tea. For which now I . . . This is something!

MAYOR (*timidly*). Excuse me, it's not really my fault. I always have good beef in the market. The merchants from the mountains bring it in, sober people of upright character. I can't think where he got such meat. But if anything isn't just so, why . . . let me suggest that you come with me to another apartment.

KHLESTAKOV. No, don't want to. I know what you mean by another apartment: prison. What right have you! How do you dare? . . . Why now I . . . I serve in Petersburg. (*Proudly*) I, I, I . . .

MAYOR (*aside*). Oh, my God, how angry he is! He's found out everything, the damned merchants told him everything!

KHLESTAKOV (*getting braver*). Yes, even if you came here with your whole troop—I won't go! I'll go straight to the minister! (*Pounds his fist on the table*) What do you think you're doing! What do you think you're doing! What do you think you're doing!

MAYOR (*drawing himself up and shaking all over*). Have mercy, don't ruin me! My wife, my little children . . . Don't make a man miserable . . .

KHLESTAKOV. No, I don't want to. What next! What have I to do with this? Because you have a wife and children, I should go to jail, that's great! (BOBCHINSKY *looks in through the door and hides in fright*) No, thanks a lot, I don't want to.

MAYOR (*trembling*). From inexperience, honest to God, from inexperience. Insufficiency of funds. You judge for yourself, if you will, the regular salary isn't enough for just tea and sugar. If there were some kind of bribes, why just a trifle: something to put on the table and a couple of dresses. And as for the non-commissioned officer's widow who was dealing with the merchants and who I sort of had flogged, why, that's just slander, honest to God, just slander. My evil-wishers thought it up; they're such a bunch they're ready to attempt my life.

KHLESTAKOV. What? I have nothing to do with them. (*In reflection*) I don't know, however, why you talk about evil-wishers; or about some non-commissioned officer's widow . . . The non-commissioned officer's wife is another matter completely, but you daren't flog me. It's a long time before you'll get to that . . . What next! You just watch out! . . . I'll pay, I'll pay the money, but right now I haven't any! So, I sit here, because I haven't a kopek.

MAYOR (*aside*). Oh, subtle business! What's he aiming at! What a fog he's put us in! Figure it out who can! You don't know which way to take it. Well, let's try and see where it gets us! What happens happens. I'll just plunge in. (*Aloud*) If you need money specifically or anything else, why I am at your service this minute. It's my obligation to assist people traveling through.

KHLESTAKOV. Give me a loan, do; I'll pay off the tavernkeeper right away. If I could just have two hundred rubles, or even less.

MAYOR (*handing the bills over*). Exactly two hundred rubles; don't bother to count.

KHLESTAKOV (*taking the money*). I am humbly grateful. I'll send it to you from the country very soon, this has suddenly . . . I see that you are a noble man. Now things are quite different.

MAYOR (*aside*). Well, thank God! He took the money. Now, it seems, things'll go all right. After all I slipped him, instead of two hundred, four.

KHLESTAKOV. Hey, Osip! (OSIP *enters*) Call the waiter! (*To the Mayor and* DOBCHINSKY) But what are you standing for? Do me the favor, sit down; (*to* DOBCHINSKY) sit down, I humbly beg you.

MAYOR. No matter, we'll just stand.

KHLESTAKOV. Do me the favor, sit down. I now see completely the sincerity of your manner and your cordiality; but, before this, I must say, I thought you had come here to . . . (*To* DOBCHINSKY) Sit down!

(*The Mayor and* DOBCHINSKY *sit down,* BOBCHINSKY *looks in through the door and listens.*)

MAYOR (*aside*). I must be bolder. He wants to be considered incognito. All right, we'll go along with the nonsense: we'll pretend we don't know at all what kind of man he is. (*Aloud*) Pyotr Ivanovich Dobchinsky here, a local landowner, and I, going about on our proper business, came into the hotel on purpose to find out for ourselves if people passing through are well cared for or not, because I'm not like many another mayor who'll have nothing to do with anything. But I, aside from my job, out of Christian love for mankind, I want every mortal to have a good reception. And so, as if in reward, chance presented such a pleasant acquaintance.

KHLESTAKOV. I, too, am very glad. Without you, I must admit, I would have sat here a long time: I had no idea at all what I'd pay up with.

MAYOR (*aside*). Tell me another, didn't know what to pay with! (*Aloud*) May I be so bold as to ask where and to what places it's your pleasure to go?

KHLESTAKOV. I'm going to Saratov, to my own estate.

MAYOR (*aside, his face taking on an ironic expression*). To Saratov! Ah? And he doesn't blush! Oh, you have to be sharp with him. (*Aloud*) You chose to undertake a most excellent business . . . Now, with regard to the road: they say, on the one hand, there are unpleasantnesses in delays over horses. But, on the other hand, it's a diversion for the mind. Now you, I believe, are traveling more for your personal pleasure?

KHLESTAKOV. No, my old man's asking for me. The old boy got mad that so far I haven't qualified for anything in Petersburg. He thinks that as soon as you get there they stick a Vladimir[1] in your buttonhole. I ought to send him to kick around the office himself.

MAYOR (*aside*). Just look at the kind of lies he pours out! Got his old father implicated, too! (*Aloud*) And will you be traveling long?

KHLESTAKOV. Really, I don't know. My father, see, is stubborn and thick as a log. I'll tell him right to his face: whatever you want, I can't live without Petersburg. What, in fact, should I ruin my life for, among a bunch of peasants? Now there's no need to; my soul thirsts for knowledge.

MAYOR (*aside*). He did it up famously! He lies and lies and never stops! And such an uncomely fellow, you know, so insignificant. Seems you could crush him under your finger. Well, but just wait a bit! You'll let the cat out of the bag! I'll make you keep on talking! (*Aloud*) You could not have spoken truer words. What can one do in a remote hole? Or even here, now: you don't sleep at night, you do your best for your country, you don't spare a thing, but you don't know if you'll ever get your reward. (*Glances around the room*) Seems this room's a little damp.

KHLESTAKOV. A rotten room, and such bedbugs as I've never seen before—they bite like dogs.

MAYOR. You don't say! Such an eminent guest, and he endures it from whom? from some sort of worthless bedbug who never should have been born in the first place. Seems even a bit dark in this room?

KHLESTAKOV. Completely dark . . . The landlord established

[1] Vladimir—here, a government decoration, comparable to the Legion of Honor.

the habit of not giving out candles. Sometimes there's something you'd like to do—read a little, or you get the fantastic notion of writing something; I can't—it's dark, pitch-dark.

MAYOR. May I dare ask you . . . but no, I'm not worthy.

KHLESTAKOV. What?

MAYOR. No, no, I'm unworthy, unworthy!

KHLESTAKOV. What is it?

MAYOR. I would dare . . . In my house there's a wonderful room for you, light, quiet . . . But no, I sense it myself, it's much too great an honor . . . Don't be angry. Honestly, I suggested it in all the simplicity of my heart.

KHLESTAKOV. On the contrary, if you please, with pleasure. It's much more pleasant for me in a private house than in this saloon.

MAYOR. I'll be so glad! And my wife will be delighted! That's a habit I have: hospitality right from childhood; especially if the guest's an eminent man. Don't think I'm saying this just to flatter you. No, I don't have that vice; I'm expressing the fullness of my heart.

KHLESTAKOV. I am humbly grateful. I myself, also, don't like two-faced people. Your frankness and cordiality please me greatly, and I would ask for nothing more, I must say, than that you show me devotion and respect, respect and devotion.

(*The Waiter enters, accompanied by* OSIP. BOBCHINSKY *looks in through the doorway.*)

WAITER. You called?

KHLESTAKOV. Yes. Give me the bill.

WAITER. I gave you the other bill just recently.

KHLESTAKOV. I don't remember your stupid bills. Tell me, how much is it?

WAITER. You asked for dinner the first day and the next day had just a bite of salmon and after that you took everything on account.

KHLESTAKOV. Idiot! He's begun to count it all out. —How much does everything come to?

MAYOR. Please don't bother, he'll wait. (*To the Waiter*) Get the hell out, we'll call you when we need you.

KHLESTAKOV. In fact, that's very true. (*Puts his money away*)

(*The Waiter goes out.* BOBCHINSKY *peers in the door.*)

MAYOR. Would it be convenient for you now to survey some of

the institutions in our town, such as the charitable ones and others?

KHLESTAKOV. What's there?

MAYOR. And so, you could see how matters are proceeding with us . . . what sort of setup . . .

KHLESTAKOV. With great pleasure. I'm ready.

(BOBCHINSKY *pokes his head in through the door.*)

MAYOR. And also if it might be your desire to go from there to the district school, to survey the setup under which learning is taught here?

KHLESTAKOV. If you please, if you please.

MAYOR. Then, if you would wish to visit the jail and the town prisons—you would observe how criminals are treated here.

KHLESTAKOV. But why the prisons? Let's rather look over the charitable institutions.

MAYOR. As you wish. How had you planned to go, in your own carriage or together with me in the cart?

KHLESTAKOV. Yes, I better go with you in your cart.

MAYOR (*to* DOBCHINSKY). Well, Pyotr Ivanovich, now there's no place for you.

DOBCHINSKY. Doesn't matter, it's all right.

MAYOR (*Softly to* DOBCHINSKY). Listen: you run, fast as you can at full speed, and deliver two notes: one to Zemlyanika in the Charitable Institution and the other to my wife. (*To* KHLESTAKOV) May I be so bold as to request your permission to write just a line to my wife in your presence, so that she may make herself ready to receive our honored guest?

KHLESTAKOV. But what for . . . Besides, here's the ink, only I don't know about paper . . . Why not on this bill?

MAYOR. I'll write here. (*Writes and at the same time talks to himself*) Now let's see how things'll go after a bite and a fat-bottomed bottle! We have some provincial madeira, not much to look at from the outside, but it'll knock an elephant over. Only I've got to find out what he really is like and how much we've got to be careful of him.

(*Having finished writing, the Mayor gives the note to* DOBCHINSKY, *who goes toward the door, but at this moment the door falls in and* BOBCHINSKY, *who has been listening on the other side, flies with it onto the stage. All shout exclamations.* BOBCHINSKY *picks himself up.*)

KHLESTAKOV. What? You didn't hurt yourself some place?

BOBCHINSKY. It's nothing, nothing, sir, no dizziness at all, sir, just a little bump on the end of my nose. I'll run over to Khristian Ivanovich, he has just the right kind of plaster, so it'll go right away.

MAYOR (*making a sign of reproach to* BOBCHINSKY, *to* KHLESTAKOV). It's nothing, sir. I humbly beg you, please! and I'll tell your servant to bring your suitcase over. (*To* OSIP) My good man, you bring everything over to my place, to the Mayor's, anybody will show you. I humbly beg you! (*Lets* KHLESTAKOV *go first and follows behind him, but, turning around, reproaches* BOBCHINSKY) Look at you! Couldn't find another place to fall down! and sprawled out like God only knows what.

(*Goes out;* BOBCHINSKY *after him. The curtain falls.*)

ACT III

The room of Act I. ANNA ANDREYEVNA [*and*] MARYA ANTONOVNA *stand by the window in the very same positions.*

ANNA ANDREYEVNA. So, we're waiting here a whole hour already, and all the time you and your stupid mincing around: got completely dressed, but no, still have to rummage some more . . . Shouldn't listen to her at all. What a shame! not a soul, as if on purpose, as if everything's dead.

MARYA ANTONOVNA. But really, Maminka, we'll find everything out in a couple of minutes. Avdotya must come soon. (*Looks out the window and shouts:*) Maminka, Maminka! Somebody's coming, there at the end of the street.

ANNA ANDREYEVNA. Where's he coming? You're always seeing things; sure, somebody's coming. Who's coming? Of medium height . . . in a frockcoat . . . who is it? Hey? Oh, what a shame! Who could it be?

MARYA ANTONOVNA. It's Dobchinsky, Maminka.

ANNA ANDREYEVNA. What Dobchinsky? You're always imagining something like that! It's not Dobchinsky at all. (*Waves her handkerchief*) Hey you, come over here! Hurry up!

MARYA ANTONOVNA. Really, Maminka, it's Dobchinsky.

ANNA ANDREYEVNA. See here: that's deliberate, just to argue. I tell you it's not Dobchinsky.

MARYA ANTONOVNA. But what else? What else, Maminka? You see, it's Dobchinsky.

ANNA ANDREYEVNA. Well, yes, Dobchinsky, now I see; what're you arguing about? (*Shouts out the window:*) Hurry, hurry! You're going too slow. Well, so, where are they? Hey? But talk from there, it's all the same. What? Very stern? Hey? And my husband, husband? (*Moving back a little from the window, regretfully*) So stupid: won't say a thing until he's in the room. (DOBCHINSKY *enters*) Now, tell me, please: aren't you ashamed! I counted on you alone as an honest man: everybody suddenly runs out, and you go off after them! And here I can't get a bit of sense out of anyone to this very minute. Aren't you ashamed! I'm god mother to your Vanichka and your Lizanka, and this is how you treat me!

DOBCHINSKY. Honestly, neighbor, I ran so hard to present my respects that I'm all out of breath. My respects, Marya Antonovna.

MARYA ANTONOVNA. How do you do, Pyotr Ivanovich.

ANNA ANDREYEVNA. Well, so? Well, tell us: what's going on there?

DOBCHINSKY. Anton Antonovich has sent you a note.

ANNA ANDREYEVNA. Well, but what is he? A general?

DOBCHINSKY. No, not a general, but he's not inferior to a general. Such education and weighty bearing.

ANNA ANDREYEVNA. Aha! So it's the very same one my husband was written about.

DOBCHINSKY. Himself. Pyotr Ivanovich and I together were the first to discover it.

ANNA ANDREYEVNA. Well, tell us: who is he, and what's he like?

DOBCHINSKY. Thank God, everything's fine. At first he started to receive Anton Antonovich a bit sternly; yes, sir; got angry and said that everything wasn't right in the hotel, and that he wasn't going to go to his place and that he wasn't going to sit in prison instead of him, but then, after he saw Anton Antonovich's innocence and had talked to him closer, right away he changed his mind, and, thank God, everything came out fine. They've gone now to inspect the charitable institutions . . . but before, I must say, Anton Antonovich was already thinking, maybe there was a secret denunciation; myself, too, I got a little scared.

ANNA ANDREYEVNA. But what have you got to be afraid of: you're not in the service.

DOBCHINSKY. Yes, but you know, when a great man speaks, you get afraid.

ANNA ANDREYEVNA. Well, so . . . Still, it's all nonsense; tell us, what's he look like? what, is he old or young?

DOBCHINSKY. Young, a young man: about twenty-three; but talks exactly like an old man. If you please, he says, I'm going; and there, and there . . . (*Waves his hands*) so it's all terrific. I, he says, like to write and read a bit, but it bothers me, he says, that it's a bit dark in the room.

ANNA ANDREYEVNA. But what's he look like: dark or fair?

DOBCHINSKY. No, chestnut rather, and his eyes are so quick, like an animal's, so they even confuse you.

ANNA ANDREYEVNA. What's he write me in the note? (*Reads:*) "I hasten to let you know, honey, that my position was completely miserable, but, throwing myself on God's mercy, for two pickles specially done and half a serving of caviar one ruble twenty-five kopeks . . ." (*Stops*) I don't understand at all—what are the pickles and caviar doing here?

DOBCHINSKY. Ah, Anton Antonovich wrote this on scratch paper in a hurry: some kind of a bill was written there.

ANNA ANDREYEVNA. Ah yes, that's it. (*Continues reading:*) "But, throwing myself on God's mercy, it seems everything will turn out all right. Hurry up and get a room ready for a very important guest, the room covered with yellow paper. Don't worry about more for dinner because we'll have a bite in the charitable institution with Artemy Filipovich. But order lots more wine: tell the merchant Abdulin to send the very best; or else I'll rip up his whole cellar. I kiss your hand, honey, and remain your: Anton Skvoznik-Dmukhanovsky . . ." Ah, my God! but I've got to hurry up! Hey, who's there? Mishka!

DOBCHINSKY (*runs and shouts out the door*). Mishka! Mishka! Mishka!

(MISHKA *enters.*)

ANNA ANDREYEVNA. Listen: run to Abdulin's . . . wait, I'll give you a note. (*Sits down at the table, writes out a note and talks while she does:*) You give this note to the coachman Sidor, so he runs over to Abdulin's with it and brings some wine back. And yourself go right away and straighten up that room properly for the guest. Put a bed up there, and a washbasin and stand and so forth.

DOBCHINSKY. Well, Anna Andreyevna, I'll run on now quicky to see how he's surveying things there.

ANNA ANDREYEVNA. Go ahead, go ahead, I'm not keeping you. (DOBCHINSKY *exits*) Well, Mashenka, now we have to get ourselves dressed. He's from the capital; God save us from his ridiculing something. You'd look best of all if you put on your light blue dress with the little flounces.

MARYA ANTONOVNA. Oh, Maminka, the light blue! I don't like it at all: Lyapkin-Tryapkin's wife wears light blue, and

Zemlyanika's daughter, too, wears light blue. No, I'd better put on the print dress.

ANNA ANDREYEVNA. The print dress! Really, you say things just to spite me. The other'd be a lot better for you because I want to put on my pale-yellow; I love the pale-yellow.

MARYA ANTONOVNA. Oh, Maminka, the pale-yellow doesn't suit you at all!

ANNA ANDREYEVNA. The pale-yellow doesn't suit me?

MARYA ANTONOVNA. Doesn't suit you, I'll bet you anything, it doesn't suit you: for that you have to have eyes that are absolutely dark.

ANNA ANDREYEVNA. Well, all right, and my eyes aren't dark? The darkest. What nonsense she talks! What do you mean, not dark, when I always use the queen of clubs to tell my fortune.

MARYA ANTONOVNA. Oh, Maminka, you're more the queen of hearts.

ANNA ANDREYEVNA. Nonsense, absolute nonsense! I never was the queen of hearts. (*Hurriedly goes out together with* MARYA ANTONOVNA *and talks offstage*) What she'll suddenly think up! The queen of hearts! God only knows what she's talking about!

(*After their exit, the doors open and* MISHKA *throws some sweepings out through them.* OSIP *with a suitcase on his head comes in through the other door.*)

OSIP. Where now?

MISHKA. Here, uncle, here.

OSIP. Wait, gi' me a breath. Ah, you, mis'rable life! on a empty belly every load seems heavy.

MISHKA. So, tell me, uncle: the general'll be here soon?

OSIP. What general?

MISHKA. Why, your master.

OSIP. My master? What kind of general's he?

MISHKA. But ain't he a general?

OSIP. A general, but on the other hand only.

MISHKA. What's that, more or less 'n a real general?

OSIP. More.

MISHKA. Y'see! That's why he raised a real fuss here.

OSIP. Listen, friend: you're pretty nimble, I see, get me something to eat.

MISHKA. But for you, uncle, there ain't nothing ready yet:

you won't eat just plain dishes, but just as soon as your master sits down to table, you'll get some of the same.

OSIP. Well, but the something plain, you got some?

MISHKA. Soup, porridge, and pies.

OSIP. Gi' me some, soup, porridge, and pies! No matter, we'll eat it all. Well, let's move the suitcase! What, there's another way out?

MISHKA. Yep.

(*They both carry the suitcase into the adjoining room.*)

(*The Policemen open both leaves of the doors.* KHLESTAKOV *enters; behind him the Mayor, and, farther, the Trustee of Social Welfare Institutions, the Superintendent of Schools,* DOBCHINSKY *and* BOBCHINSKY *with a plaster on his nose; the Mayor indicates to the Policemen a piece of paper on the floor—they run to pick it up, bumping into each other in their hurry.*)

KHLESTAKOV. Fine institutions. I like it that here you show travelers everything in town. In other towns they didn't show me anything.

MAYOR. In other towns, may I be so bold as to report to you, the town-governors and officials are more concerned about their own, so to speak, advantage; but here, one may say, there is no thought except by honest service and vigilance to merit the attention of the authorities.

KHLESTAKOV. The lunch was very good. I overstuffed myself What, you have a lunch like that every day?

MAYOR. Expressly for so welcome a guest.

KHLESTAKOV. I like to eat. For, you know, we live in order to pick the flowers of pleasure. What was that fish called?

ARTEMY FILIPOVICH (*running up*). Cod, sir.

KHLESTAKOV. Delicious. Where was it we ate? In the hospital, wasn't it?

ARTEMY FILIPOVICH. Exactly right, sir, in the charitable institution.

KHLESTAKOV. I remember, I remember, there were beds there. And the sick all got well? There weren't many there, it seems.

ARTEMY FILIPOVICH. Ten are left, no more; the rest have all gotten well. It's been arranged that way, that's the setup. Since I took command, it may even seem incredible to you, they all get well like flies. A sick man hardly gets into the infirmary and he's already well, and not so much because of medications as because of honesty and order.

MAYOR. And, may I be so bold as to tell you, to what the head-splitting obligations of the local town-governor extend! So many matters of all kinds, relative to cleaning, repairing, fixing alone lie on him—in a word, the most intelligent man in the world would get into difficult straits, but, thanks to God, everything goes along fine. Any other mayor, of course, would be delighted with his advantages; but, would you believe it, even when you go to bed you keep thinking: my Lord, if only I could arrange it so the authorities saw my zeal and were satisfied . . . Whether they give me a reward or not, of course, is up to them, but at least I'd be content in my own heart. If there's order in the whole town, if the streets are swept, if the prisons are well kept, if there are few drunks . . . what more can I ask for? In faith, I don't want any honors. It's, of course, tempting, but compared to virtue everything's dust and fuss.

ARTEMY FILIPOVICH (*aside*). Look at the loafer, how he paints things! What a gift of gab God gave him!

KHLESTAKOV. That's true. Must admit, I myself like to busy my mind sometimes: one time prose, next time verses come out.

BOBCHINSKY (*to* DOBCHINSKY). True, it's all true, Pyotr Ivanovich. Such remarks . . . it's obvious he studied the sciences.

KHLESTAKOV. Tell me, please: don't you have any distractions, societies, where one could, for example, play a little cards?

MAYOR (*aside*). Hey, my boy, we know whose glass house you're throwing stones at! (*Aloud*) God forbid! Here there's not even a whisper about such societies. I've never had a card in my hand: don't even know how to play these cards. Never could look at them with indifference: and if I just happen to catch sight of some kind of a king of diamonds or anything else, why such loathing comes over me, I just spit on 'em. Once it happened somehow, amusing some children, I built a house of cards, and after that I dreamed of the damned things all night. God bless those who can kill such precious time at cards.

LUKA LUKICH (*aside*). And he, the bastard, outpointed me a hundred rubles yesterday.

MAYOR. It's better I use the time for the government's benefit.

KHLESTAKOV. But, no, you remark unjustly . . . It all depends on the point of view from which one looks at a thing. If, for example, you call it quits when you ought to strike from three corners . . . why, then of course . . . No, don't say that, sometimes it's very tempting to play a bit. (ANNA ANDREYEVNA *and* MARYA ANTONOVNA *enter.*)

MAYOR. I make bold to present my family: my wife and daughter.

KHLESTAKOV (*exchanging greetings*). How happy I am, madam, that I have the pleasure of seeing you.

ANNA ANDREYEVNA. It is even more pleasant for us to see such a personage.

KHLESTAKOV (*showing off*). For goodness sake, madam, quite the contrary: it's even more pleasant for me.

ANNA ANDREYEVNA. How can it be, sir! You are pleased to say this just as a compliment. I humbly beg you to be seated.

KHLESTAKOV. To stand beside you is already happiness; nevertheless, if you so insist on it, I'll sit down. How happy I am that finally I am sitting beside you.

ANNA ANDREYEVNA. For goodness sake, I don't dare take it on myself . . . I think that, after the capital, voyagement must seem to you very unpleasant.

KHLESTAKOV. Extremely unpleasant. Having become accustomed to live, *comprenez-vous*, in society and suddenly to find yourself on the road: dirty taverns, the gloom of ignorance. If, I must say, it weren't for the occasion which . . . (*looks at* ANNA ANDREYEVNA *and poses in front of her*) has so rewarded me for everything . . .

ANNA ANDREYEVNA. In fact, how unpleasant it must be for you.

KHLESTAKOV. However, madam, at this moment it is very pleasant for me.

ANNA ANDREYEVNA. How can it be, sir, you're doing me such credit. I don't deserve it.

KHLESTAKOV. How don't you deserve it? You, madam, deserve it.

ANNA ANDREYEVNA. I live in the country . . .

KHLESTAKOV. But the country, nevertheless, also has its knolls and little streams . . . Well, of course, who could compare it to Petersburg? Ah, Petersburg! What a life, really! You, perhaps, think that I just copy things. No, the head of the department is on friendly footing with me. Slaps me on the shoulder like this: "Come on over, my friend, for dinner." I run into the department for two minutes just to say: This is like this, this is like that, and then the official for letters, just a hack, is off with his pen: tr, tr . . . They even wanted to make me a collegiate assessor, but, I thought, what for? And the doorman flies after me on the stairs with a brush: please, Ivan Aleksandrovich, he says, I'll clean your boots. (*To the Mayor*) But, gentlemen, why are you standing? Please sit down!

MAYOR. The rank's such that you can keep standing.

ARTEMY FILIPOVICH. We'll stand a bit.

LUKA LUKICH. Please don't be disturbed.

(*Together*)

KHLESTAKOV. Rank aside, I beg you to be seated. (*The Mayor and everyone sit down*) I don't like ceremony. On the contrary, I always even try to slip through unnoticed. But it's impossible to hide, impossible to hide! Just as soon as I go out somewhere they're already saying: "There," they say, "goes Ivan Aleksandrovich!" And once they even took me for the commander-in-chief, the soldiers jumped out of the guard house and presented arms. Later, an officer, who I knew very well, says to me: Well, friend, we completely mistook you for the commander-in-chief.

ANNA ANDREYEVNA. You don't say!

KHLESTAKOV. Yes, I'm known everywhere. I'm acquainted with the pretty actresses. Various vaudeville players I, also . . . See literary men often. On friendly footing with Pushkin. I've often said to him: "Well, brother Pushkin?"—"So-so, brother," he answers: "that's the way it goes" . . . Very eccentric.

ANNA ANDREYEVNA. So you write, too? How pleasant that must be for the writer. I suppose you publish in magazines, too?

KHLESTAKOV. Yes, I publish in magazines, too. There are, however, a lot of things I've written: *The Marriage of*

Figaro, Robert the Devil, Norma. I don't even remember the titles. And all by chance: I didn't want to write, but the theatrical directorate says: "Please, friend, write something." I think to myself: perhaps, brother, I will! And so one evening, it seems, I wrote it all, astounded everybody. I have an extraordinary facility with ideas. Everything that was under the name of Baron Brambeus, the *Ship of Hope,* and the *Moscow Telegraph* . . . I wrote it all.

ANNA ANDREYEVNA. You don't say, so you're Brambeus?

KHLESTAKOV. Who else? I correct all their poems for them. Smirdin gives me forty thousand for this.

ANNA ANDREYEVNA. So, I suppose, *Yury Miloslavsky,* too, is your work?

KHLESTAKOV. Yes, that's my work.

ANNA ANDREYEVNA. I just thought so.

MARYA ANTONOVNA. Oh, Maminka, it's written in it that it's Mr. Zagoskin's work.

ANNA ANDREYEVNA. Look at that: I just knew that even here she'd argue.

KHLESTAKOV. Oh sure, that's right, that's Zagoskin's exactly; but there's another *Yury Miloslavsky,* and that's mine.

ANNA ANDREYEVNA. Well, now, it's probably yours I read. How well written!

KHLESTAKOV. I, I must admit, live by literature. My house is the first in Petersburg. It's well known there: the house of Ivan Aleksandrovich. (*Turning to everyone*) Do me the kindness, gentlemen, if ever you're in Petersburg, I beg you, I beg you come see me. You know, I also give balls.

ANNA ANDREYEVNA. I think balls must be given there with such taste and splendor.

KHLESTAKOV. You simply can't imagine. On the table, for example, there's watermelon—seven hundred rubles of watermelon. The soup in the saucepan came straight from Paris by ship; they take off the lid—there's steam the like of which you'll never find in all nature. I'm at a ball every day. There we have our own foursome for whist. The Minister for Foreign Affairs, the French envoy, the German envoy, and me. And you just die from laughter playing, there's absolutely nothing like it. Just as soon as you run upstairs to your own place on the fifth floor you say to the cook just: "Hey, Mavrushka, my cloak" . . . What am I saying, I even forgot I live on the second floor. One flight's enough for me . . . And it'd be interesting to glance into my vestibule even before I've gotten up. Counts and princes are all crowded in there and buzzing, like bumblebees, you can hear just the bz, bz, bz . . . Other times the minister, too . . (*The Mayor and the rest timidly get up from their chairs*) They even address me on packages: Your excellency. Once I even ran the department. It was strange: the director left; where he went was unknown. Well, naturally, there were rumors: how, why, who'll take his place? Lots of generals were anxious for it and tried, but would they do however: no, it was odd. It would seem easy, to all appearances, but you examine it all—simply the God-damnedest thing. They see there's nothing to be done—they turn to me. And that very same minute they send out messengers, messengers, more messengers through all the streets . . . can you imagine, thirty-five thousand messengers alone? What a position to be in, I ask you? "Ivan Aleksandrovich, come run the department!" I, I must admit, was a bit confused, went out in my wrapper: wanted to refuse, but, I thought, it'll get to the sovereign; and the service record, too . . . "If you please, gentlemen, I accept the position, I accept," I says, "so be it," I says, "I accept, only under me there'll be no shilly-shallying! I have my ears open! I . . ." And that's exactly how it was: I go through the department—it's simply an earthquake—it trembles and shakes, like a leaf, the whole time. (*The Mayor and the rest tremble in fear;* KHLESTAKOV *gets more excited*) Oh! I don't like fooling around. I gave them all a warning. The State Council itself is afraid of me. And why, in fact? I'm such a man! I never look at anyone . . . I tell them all: I know who I am, I know. I'm everywhere, everywhere. I go to the Court every day. Tomorrow they'll promote me right to Field Marshal . . . (*Slips and almost hits the floor, but is supported by the officials with respect*)

MAYOR (*coming up to him and shaking all over, tries to speak*). But yo—yo—yo—yo.

KHLESTAKOV (*in a quick, curt voice*). What's that?

MAYOR. But yo—yo—yo—yo.

KHLESTAKOV (*in the same tone*). I can't make a thing out, it's all nonsense.

MAYOR. Yo—yo—yo . . . urest, excellency, wouldn't you like to rest . . . Here's the room and everything you need.

KHLESTAKOV. Nonsense: rest. If you want, I'm ready to rest. Your lunch, gentlemen, was fine . . . I am satisfied, I am satisfied. (*Declaims*) Cod! Cod! (*Enters the adjoining room, the Mayor behind him*)

BOBCHINSKY (*to* DOBCHINSKY). Now there, Pyotr Ivanovich, is a man. That's what it means, man. In all my life I was never in the presence of such a bigwig, almost died of fright. What do you think, Pyotr Ivanovich, what's he in regard to rank, now?

DOBCHINSKY. I think he's practically a general.

BOBCHINSKY. And I think a general wouldn't do to shine his shoes! Or if a general, why then he himself's generalissimo. You heard: the State Council drew back. Let's go, let's hurry up tell Ammos Fyodorovich and Korobkin. Good-bye, Anna Andreyevna.

DOBCHINSKY. Good-bye, neighbor! (*Both go out*)

ARTEMY FILIPOVICH (*to* LUKA LUKICH). It's simply terrible. But why, you don't know yourself. And we're not even in our dress uniforms. Well, so, by the time we're awake the report'll be on its way to Petersburg. (*Goes out in deep reflection together with the Superintendent of Schools, saying:*) Good-bye, madam!

ANNA ANDREYEVNA. Oh, what a nice man!

MARYA ANTONOVNA. Oh! a darling!

ANNA ANDREYEVNA. And what refined manners! You can tell right away he hails from the capital. His ways and all that . . . Oh, how fine! I love young people like that terrifically! I'm simply head over heels in love. And I must say he liked me a lot: I noticed it—he was looking at me all the time.

MARYA ANTONOVNA. Oh, Maminka, he was looking at me.

ANNA ANDREYEVNA. That's enough of your nonsense, please! It's completely out of place now.

MARYA ANTONOVNA. No, Maminka, really.

ANNA ANDREYEVNA. Look at that! God save us, you never stop arguing! You just never stop. What would he look at you for? And what'd be the point of his looking at you?

MARYA ANTONOVNA. Really, Maminka: he was looking all the time. And when he started talking about literature, he glanced at me, and then when he was telling how he played whist with the envoys, then, too, he looked over at me.

ANNA ANDREYEVNA. Well, maybe, just once, and then only just in passing. "Oh," he says to himself, "I might as well take a look at her."

MAYOR (*comes in on tiptoe*). Sh . . . sh . . .

ANNA ANDREYEVNA. What?

MAYOR. I'm not so glad I gave him drinks. What if even only half of what he said is true? (*Gets lost in thought*) How can it not be true? A man who is drunk brings everything out. Wears his heart on his sleeve. Course, he padded it a bit. But nothing's said without a bit of padding. Plays with ambassadors and goes to the Court . . . But now, really, the more you think about it . . . God only knows, you never know what goes on in a man's head. It's just as if you were standing on some sort of bell-tower or were going to get hanged.

ANNA ANDREYEVNA. But I absolutely didn't feel any kind of shyness. I simply saw him as an educated, worldly man of the highest fashion, and never minded about his rank.

MAYOR. All right, you're—women. You all get caught, just a word does it. All you want is sugar and spice! Suddenly there's some shouting for no reason. You get beaten, that's all, and your man's gone. You, dear, behaved as loose with him as if with some kind of Dobchinsky.

ANNA ANDREYEVNA. I advise you not to become anxious in this regard. We know something of that sort . . . (*Looks at her daughter*)

MAYOR (*aside*). Why talk to you! In fact, what a sudden turn of events! Couldn't pull myself together till now from fear. (*Opens the door and speaks through the doorway*) Mishka, call officers Svistunov and Derzhimorda: they're somewhere near here behind the gate. (*After a brief silence*) Now everything in the world's set up really funny: if people were only obvious, but a fellow's slim, slight—how can you find out about him, who is he? Now a fellow in the army nevertheless shows what he is, but as soon as he puts on his frockcoat—why he's just like a fly with clipped wings. Spent a long time just a while ago holding out in the tavern. Knocked off such allegories and double-talk you couldn't make out the meaning for the life of you. And now he's finally given in. And still he said more than he should have. It's obvious, he's young.

(OSIP *enters. All run to meet him and beckon with their fingers.*)

ANNA ANDREYEVNA. Come here, dear man!

MAYOR. Sh! . . . What? what? He's asleep?

OSIP. Not yet, he's stretching a bit.

ANNA ANDREYEVNA. Listen, what's your name?

OSIP. Osip, madam.

MAYOR (*to his wife and daughter*). Enough, that's enough from you! (*To* OSIP) So, now, my friend, did they feed you well?

OSIP. Fed me, thank you kindly, fed me fine.

ANNA ANDREYEVNA. So, now, tell us: an awful lot of counts and princes, I think, come see your master?

OSIP (*aside*). What'll I tell 'em? since they fed me fine now, means they'll feed me even better after. (*Aloud*) Yes, counts, too.

MARYA ANTONOVNA. Osip darling, how cute your master is!

ANNA ANDREYEVNA. But, Osip, please tell us how he . . .

MAYOR. Now please stop! You're only bothering me with these stupid speeches. So, my friend?

ANNA ANDREYEVNA. What rank has your master got?

OSIP. The usual.

MAYOR. Oh my God, you and your stupid questions still! You don't let a man have a chance to talk business. So, now, my friend, how's your master? Strict? Likes to give a good scolding, doesn't he?

OSIP. Yes, likes order. Wants everything in good working order.

MAYOR. I like your face a lot! My friend, you must be a good man. So, now . . .

ANNA ANDREYEVNA. Listen, Osip, does your master wear a full-dress coat there, or . . .

MAYOR. This is enough from you, really, you chatterboxes. Here's something important. It's all about the life of a man . . . (*To* OSIP) So, now, my friend, really, I like you very much. Never hurts, you know, to drink a last cup of tea for the road; it's cool out now. So here's a couple of rubles for you for the tea.

OSIP (*taking the money*). Humbly grateful, sir. May God give you all kinds of health; helped out a poor man.

MAYOR. Fine, fine, glad to do it myself. Now, my friend . . .

ANNA ANDREYEVNA. Listen, Osip, what kind of eyes does your master like most of all?

MARYA ANTONOVNA. Osip, darling! What a sweet little nose your master has!

MAYOR. Stop it, let me! (*To* OSIP) Now, my friend, tell me, please: what does your master pay most attention to, that is, what does he like best on the road?

OSIP. He likes it, on examination, the way he has to. Most of all he likes to be well received, that his reception's good.

MAYOR. Good?

OSIP. Yes, good. Why this's what I, a serving man now, look for, too, that it's good for me, too. Honest to God, it's happened we're driving in somewhere: "So, Osip, they treat you good?" "Bad, your honor!" "Eh," he says, "this, Osip, is a bad host." "You," he says, "remind me when I get there."—"But," I thinks to myself, "the hell with him! I'm a simple man."

MAYOR. Good, good, right to the point. Just now I gave you something for tea, so here's something on top of that for pretzels.

OSIP. Why're you so kind to me, your honor? (*Pockets the money*) I'll drink to your health.

ANNA ANDREYEVNA. Come over to me, Osip! You'll also get something.

MARYA ANTONOVNA. Osip, darling, kiss your master for me! (*A slight cough by* KHLESTAKOV *is heard in the other room.*)

MAYOR. Sh! (*Stands on tiptoe. Addresses the whole stage in a low voice*) God forbid your making noise! Go to your rooms! That's enough from you . . .

ANNA ANDREYEVNA. Let's go, Mashenka! I'll tell you what I noticed on our guest, what only the two of us can talk about between ourselves.

MAYOR. Oh, the things they'll say there! I think if you just go and listen you'd stop your ears afterwards. (*Turning to* OSIP) So, my friend . . .

(DERZHIMORDA *and* SVISTUNOV *enter.*)

MAYOR. Sh! Look at the bandy-legged bears pounding with their boots! Such thumping, as if someone were throwing forty poods out of his cart! What the hell are you thumping in here for?

DERZHIMORDA. I was by order . . .

MAYOR. Sh! (*Covers his mouth*) How the crow cawed! (*Mimics him*) I was by order! Growls like out of a barrel! (*To* OSIP) So, my friend, you go get ready there whatever your master needs. Ask for anything in the house you want. (OSIP *goes out*) And you—stand on the porch and don't move! And don't let any outsiders into the house, especially merchants! If you let in even just one of them, I'll . . . Soon as you see somebody coming to ask a favor, or even not to ask a favor, grab him by the back of his neck and give him a push! Like this! Real good! (*Shows how with his foot*) You hear? Sh . . . sh . . . (*Goes out on tiptoe behind the Policemen*)

ACT IV

The same room in the Mayor's house. Enter cautiously, almost on tiptoe: AMMOS FYODOROVICH, ARTEMY FILIPOVICH, *the Postmaster,* LUKA LUKICH, DOBCHINSKY *and* BOBCHINSKY, *in uniform and full-dress coats. The entire* [*opening*] *scene is spoken in low voice.*

AMMOS FYODOROVICH (*arranges everyone in a half-circle*). For God's sake, gentlemen, hurry up and make a circle, and be more orderly! God Almighty: goes to the Court and scolds the State Council! Formation! Get in step, don't fail, in ranks, now! You, Pyotr Ivanovich, run around this side, and you, Pyotr Ivanovich, stand here.
(*Both* PYOTR IVANOVICHES *run around on tiptoe.*)

ARTEMY FILIPOVICH. As you please, Ammos Fyodorovich, we need to undertake something.

AMMOS FYODOROVICH. What precisely?

ARTEMY FILIPOVICH. But it's obvious what.

AMMOS FYODOROVICH. Slip it under?

ARTEMY FILIPOVICH. Yes, sure, even slip it under.

AMMOS FYODOROVICH. Dangerous, my God, he might start shouting: a government man. Why not as a present from the nobility for some kind of monument?

POSTMASTER. Or: just say, here, some money came in the mail and nobody knows who it belongs to.

ARTEMY FILIPOVICH. Look out he doesn't send you off in the mail some place pretty far off. Listen, this kind of thing isn't done this way in a well-run state. What're a whole squadron of us here for? You have to introduce yourselves one at a time, confidentially and all . . . properly then; so it don't get to nobody. That's how it's done in a well-run society. So you now, Ammos Fyodorovich, you begin first.

AMMOS FYODOROVICH. Be better if you did, our esteemed visitor broke bread in your institution.

ARTEMY FILIPOVICH. It'd be better if Luka Lukich was, as the instructor of youth.

LUKA LUKICH. Can't, I can't, gentlemen. I was brought up in such a way, I must admit, that as soon as anybody even one rank higher starts talking to me I lose all confidence and my tongue's like it got stuck in the mud. No, gentlemen, not me, really, not me.

ARTEMY FILIPOVICH. But, Ammos Fyodorovich, except for you there's nobody. Whatever you say is like Cicero off your tongue.

AMMOS FYODOROVICH. What do you mean! What's this: Cicero! Look at what you've invented! Why the next time you're talking about your pack of dogs or your bloodhounds, you'll be carried away to . . .

ALL (*pressing him*). No, you don't talk only about dogs, but also about the tower of . . . No, Ammos Fyodorovich, don't let us down, be our guide and protector! No, Ammos Fyodorovich.

AMMOS FYODOROVICH. Leave me alone, gentlemen!

(*At this moment footsteps and coughing are heard from* KHLESTAKOV'*s room. All rush, vying with each other, for the door, crowd together and try to get out, which happens not without some being squeezed. Exclamations ring out in a low voice:*)

BOBCHINSKY'S VOICE. Ow, Pyotr Ivanovich, Pyotr Ivanovich! You're on my foot!

ZEMLYANIKA'S VOICE. Gentlemen, let me go in peace, I'm completely squashed.

(*Several exclamations burst out:* Ai! Ow! *At last all push their way out and the room remains empty.* KHLESTAKOV *comes out, looking sleepy.*)

KHLESTAKOV (*alone*). Seems I slept like a log. Where'd they ever get such mattresses and quilts; I even sweated. Seems they slipped me something during lunch yesterday: my head's been pounding till now. Here, I see, you can spend the time with pleasure. I like cordiality, and I like it best of all, I must say, when they try to please me from their hearts, and not so that they get back interest. And that Mayor's little daughter isn't bad at all, and the Mama's the kind you could still . . . No, I don't know, but, really, I like this life.

AMMOS FYODOROVICH (*coming in and stopping, to himself*). God, oh, God! May it end safely; why, here, I'm even weak in the knees. (*Aloud, straightening up and holding his sword close to him in his hand*) I have the honor to present myself:

the Judge of the local District Court, Collegiate Assessor Lyapkin-Tryapkin.

KHLESTAKOV. I beg you to be seated. So you're the judge here?

AMMOS FYODOROVICH. Since eighteen-sixteen I have been elected to the three-year term by the will of the nobility and have continued in my post to the present time.

KHLESTAKOV. But is it profitable to be a judge?

AMMOS FYODOROVICH. For three three-year terms I was recommended for the Vladimir, fourth degree, with approval on the part of the authorities. (*Aside*) But with the money in my fist, why my fist's all on fire.

KHLESTAKOV. I like the Vladimir. The Anna, third degree, isn't the same thing at all.

AMMOS FYODOROVICH (*pushing his pressed fist a little bit forward. Aside*). My God, I don't know where I'm sitting. As if I were on hot coals.

KHLESTAKOV. What's that in your hand?

AMMOS FYODOROVICH (*getting hopelessly confused and dropping the bills on the floor*). Nothing, sir.

KHLESTAKOV. What do you mean, nothing? I see some money fell down.

AMMOS FYODOROVICH (*shaking all over*). Not at all, sir. (*Aside*) Oh, my God! Now I'm really on the carpet! And they've sent the wagon to haul me away.

KHLESTAKOV (*picking it up*). Yes, it's money.

AMMOS FYODOROVICH (*aside*). Now, everything's done for: I'm lost! I'm lost!

KHLESTAKOV. You know what: give me this as a loan . . .

AMMOS FYODOROVICH (*quickly*). Yes, sir; of course, sir . . . with great pleasure. (*Aside*) Courage, courage! Get me out of here, Mother of God!

KHLESTAKOV. You know, I spent everything I had on the road: what with this and that . . . Besides, I'll send it to you right away from my place.

AMMOS FYODOROVICH. For goodness sake! How can you! Even without that this is such an honor . . . Of course, with my feeble powers, zeal and diligence for the authorities . . . I try to merit . . . (*Gets up from his chair, straightening up and coming to attention*) I dare not further disturb you by my presence. Will tnere not be some injunction for me?

KHLESTAKOV. What sort of injunction?

AMMOS FYODOROVICH. I presume, some injunction by you for the local District Court?

KHLESTAKOV. Why? Now, of course, there's nothing I need to do in it at all.

AMMOS FYODOROVICH (*bowing and going out, aside*). So, the town is ours!

KHLESTAKOV (*as he goes*). The judge is a good man!

(*The Postmaster enters, straightening up, in a full-dress coat, holding his sword.*)

POSTMASTER. I have the honor to present myself: the Postmaster, Privy Councilor Shpekin.

KHLESTAKOV. Ah! Come in! I very much like pleasant company. Sit down. Have you always lived here?

POSTMASTER. Exactly so, sir.

KHLESTAKOV. I like the little town here. Of course, it's not very populous—but, so what? Obviously it's not the capital. Isn't that right, it's obviously not the capital?

POSTMASTER. Absolutely right.

KHLESTAKOV. Of course it's only in the capital that there's *bon ton* and none of these provincial clucks. What's your opinion, isn't that so?

POSTMASTER. Exactly so, sir (*Aside*) Why, I must say, he's not proud at all; asks about everything.

KHLESTAKOV. But, of course, you have to admit, you can live happily even in a little town.

POSTMASTER. Exactly so, sir.

KHLESTAKOV. In my opinion, what do you need? You need only to be respected, to be loved sincerely—isn't that right?

POSTMASTER. Absolutely correct.

KHLESTAKOV. I'm delighted, I must say, that you're of the same opinion. Of course, I'm considered odd, but that's the way I am. (*Looking straight at him, talking to himself*) Now I'll just ask this Postmaster for a loan. (*Aloud*) I had such a strange experience: I spent absolutely all I had on the road. Couldn't you lend me three hundred rubles?

POSTMASTER. Why not? I would consider it the greatest good fortune. Here, sir, please. Ready to help you from the bottom of my heart.

KHLESTAKOV. I'm extremely grateful. I must say, I really don't like to deny myself anything on the road, and what for? Isn't that so?

POSTMASTER. Exactly so, sir. (*Rises, straightens up and holds his sword close*) I dare not disturb you longer by my presence . . . Will there not be some sort of observation in connection with the department for the administration of the mails?

KHLESTAKOV. No, nothing.

(*The Postmaster exchanges bows and goes out.*)

KHLESTAKOV (*lighting up a cigar*). The Postmaster, too, it seems to me, is a very good man. At least, obliging. I like people like that.

(LUKA LUKICH *enters, practically pushed through the doorway. Behind him a voice is heard saying almost aloud:* "Why are you timid?")

LUKA LUKICH (*straightening up, not without trepidation and holding his sword close to him*). I have the honor to present myself: the Superintendent of Schools, Titular Councilor Khlopov.

KHLESTAKOV. Ah, come in. Sit down, sit down. Don't you want a cigar? (*Hands him a cigar*)

LUKA LUKICH (*to himself in indecision*). Here's a fine how-d'ye-do! I didn't suspect anything like this at all. To take it or not to take it?

KHLESTAKOV. Take it, take it, it's a perfectly good cigar. Of course, not what you get in Petersburg. There, old man, I used to smoke twenty-five-kopek cigars, you'd simply smack your lips when you smoked one. Here's a light; light up. (*Hands him a candle*)

(LUKA LUKICH *tries to light up and trembles all over.*)

KHLESTAKOV. But that's the wrong end.

LUKA LUKICH (*drops the cigar in fright, spits, and giving it up as hopeless, to himself*). The hell with it all! This damned timidity's ruined me!

KHLESTAKOV. I see you're not a lover of cigars. But I must admit: they're my weakness. And in regard to the female sex, I can't be indifferent at all. What about you? Which do you like best, brunettes or blondes?

(LUKA LUKICH *is in complete perplexity about what to say.*)

KHLESTAKOV. No, tell me frankly, brunettes or blondes?

LUKA LUKICH. I don't dare know.

KHLESTAKOV. No, no, don't try to get out of it. I'd like to know your taste for sure.

LUKA LUKICH. I make so bold as to inform . . . (*Aside*) Now, I don't know what I'm saying myself.

KHLESTAKOV. Ah! ah! Don't want to say. I bet some little brunette caused you a weensy bit of trouble. Confess, did she?

(LUKA LUKICH *is silent.*)

KHLESTAKOV. Ah! ah! You blushed, see, see! Why don't you say so?

LUKA LUKICH. I got frightened, your ex . . . hon . . . illus . . . (*Aside*) I've lost my damned tongue, I've lost it!

KHLESTAKOV. Got frightened? It's true there's something in my eyes that instills timidity. At least, I know that not one woman can withstand them; isn't that so?

LUKA LUKICH. Exactly so, sir.

KHLESTAKOV. I had the strangest experience: I spent everything on the road. Can't you lend me three hundred rubles?

LUKA LUKICH (*grabs his pockets, to himself*). What if I haven't any! I do, I do. (*Pulls out the bills and, trembling, hands them to him*)

KHLESTAKOV. Humbly grateful.

LUKA LUKICH. I dare not disturb you further by my presence.

KHLESTAKOV. Good-bye.

LUKA LUKICH (*flies out almost at a run and, aside, says*). Well, thank God! Perhaps he won't look in on the classes.

(ARTEMY FILIPOVICH *enters, straightening up and holding his sword close.*)

ARTEMY FILIPOVICH. I have the honor of presenting myself: the Trustee of Social Welfare Institutions, Privy Councilor Zemlyanika.

KHLESTAKOV. How are you; I humbly beg you to be seated.

ARTEMY FILIPOVICH. I had the honor of accompanying you and receiving you in the charitable institutions entrusted to my care.

KHLESTAKOV. Ah, yes! I remember. You gave me an excellent lunch.

ARTEMY FILIPOVICH. Glad to do what I can in the service of my country.

KHLESTAKOV. I must admit, that's my weakness: I love good food. Tell me, please, seems to me as if yesterday you were just a bit shorter, isn't that so?

ARTEMY FILIPOVICH. Very possibly. (*Falls silent*) I may say that I spare nothing and zealously do my duty. (*Moves his chair closer and speaks in a low voice*) Now the local Postmaster does absolutely nothing: everything is in great neglect, packages are held up . . . Be so good as deliberately to look into this yourself. The Judge, too, who was here just before I came in, does nothing but hunt hare, keeps dogs in his offices, and is a man, if I must confess to you, which I must do for the benefit of my country, of course, is a man of the most objectionable conduct: there is a certain landowner here, one Dobchinsky, whom you have been pleased to see, and just as soon as this Dobchinsky goes away from home anywhere, why he's there sitting with his wife, I'm ready to swear . . . and look at the children carefully: not one of them resembles Dobchinsky, but they all, even the little girl, are the spitting image of the judge.

KHLESTAKOV. You don't say! and I wouldn't have thought so at all.

ARTEMY FILIPOVICH. And take the Superintendent of the local school. I don't know how the authorities can entrust such a position to him. He's worse than a Jacobin, and inculcates such corrupt principles into the young that it's hard to say what. If you would instruct me to, I would set all this forth better on paper.

KHLESTAKOV. Fine, even if on paper. It will be very pleasant for me. I so much like, you know, when things are dull, to read something entertaining . . . What's your name? I keep forgetting.

ARTEMY FILIPOVICH. Zemlyanika.

KHLESTAKOV. Ah, sure, Zemlyanika. And now, tell me, please, you have little ones?

ARTEMY FILIPOVICH. Of course, sir, five; two already grown-up.

KHLESTAKOV. You don't say: grown-up! And what are their . . . now, what are their?

ARTEMY FILIPOVICH. That is, do you not wish to ask, what are their names?

KHLESTAKOV. Yes, what are their names?

ARTEMY FILIPOVICH. Nikolai, Ivan, Elizaveta, Marya and Perepetuya.

KHLESTAKOV. That's fine.

ARTEMY FILIPOVICH. Not daring to disturb you with my presence, or to take up time set aside for sacred obligations . . . (*Bows in preparation for leaving*)

KHLESTAKOV (*escorting him*). No, it's nothing. It's all very amusing, what you've been saying. Please, some other time, also . . . I like this very much. (*Goes back and, having opened the door, shouts after him:*) Hey, you! What's your name? I keep forgetting what they call you.

ARTEMY FILIPOVICH. Artemy Filipovich.

KHLESTAKOV. Do me a favor, Artemy Filipovich, a strange thing happened to me: on the road I spent everything I had. Haven't you got four hundred rubles you can lend me?

ARTEMY FILIPOVICH. I do.

KHLESTAKOV. Really; how lucky. I humbly thank you.

(BOBCHINSKY *and* DOBCHINSKY *enter.*)

BOBCHINSKY. I have the honor of presenting myself: an inhabitant of the town here, Pyotr, son of Ivan, Bobchinsky.

DOBCHINSKY. Landowner Pyotr, son of Ivan, Dobchinsky.

KHLESTAKOV. Ah sure, I've already seen you. I think you fell then; how's your nose?

BOBCHINSKY. Thank God! please don't be disturbed: it's dried up, it's now completely dried up.

KHLESTAKOV. That's fine that it's dried up. I'm glad . . . (*Suddenly and curtly*) Haven't you some money?

BOBCHINSKY. Money? What money?

KHLESTAKOV (*loudly and rapidly*). A loan of a thousand rubles.

BOBCHINSKY. Not that much, honest to God. But don't you have some, Pyotr Ivanovich?

DOBCHINSKY. Not on me, sir. Because my money, if you wish to know, is placed in the bureau of public care.

KHLESTAKOV. Well, if you don't have a thousand, so, a hundred.

BOBCHINSKY (*rummaging in his pockets*). Don't you have a hundred rubles, Pyotr Ivanovich? All I have is forty in bills.

DOBCHINSKY (*looking in his wallet*). All I have is twenty-five rubles.

BOBCHINSKY. You look more carefully, Pyotr Ivanovich! You have a tear, I know, in the pocket on the right-hand side, so probably some somehow fell into the hole.

DOBCHINSKY. No, honestly, there's nothing in the hole, either.

KHLESTAKOV. Well, it makes no difference. I was just asking. Good, let it be sixty-five rubles. It makes no difference. (*Takes the money*)

DOBCHINSKY. I make so bold as to make a request to you in regard to a certain very delicate situation.

KHLESTAKOV. What's that?

DOBCHINSKY. A matter of a very delicate nature, sir: my older son, I beg you, was brought to birth by me even before my marriage.

KHLESTAKOV. Yeah?

DOBCHINSKY. That is, it is no more than report, but he was brought to birth by me no less completely than as if in marriage, and all this, as is proper, I subsequently concluded with the lawful bonds of matrimony. So I, as you see, want him to be completely so to speak my lawful son, sir, and be called like myself, Dobchinsky, sir.

KHLESTAKOV. Good, let him have the name! That's possible.

DOBCHINSKY. I would not disturb you but it's a pity about his abilities. A little boy like this . . . gives you great hopes: he can recite different verses by heart and if a little knife turns up he'll carve little carts right away just as artfully as a magician. Pyotr Ivanovich here knows, too.

BOBCHINSKY. Yes, he has great ability . . .

KHLESTAKOV. Fine fine: I'll try to do something about this, I'll call . . . I hope . . . it will all be done, yes, yes indeed. (*Turning to* BOBCHINSKY) And don't you have something to tell me?

BOBCHINSKY. Of course, I have a very humble request.

KHLESTAKOV. What? What about?

BOBCHINSKY. I most humbly beg you, when you get back to Petersburg, to tell all the different nobles there, the senators and admirals, that you know, your eminence, or excellence, there lives in such-and-such a town one Pyotr Ivanovich Bobchinsky. Just say that: there lives one Pyotr Ivanovich Bobchinsky.

KHLESTAKOV. Very good.

BOBCHINSKY. And if you happen to see the sovereign, so tell the sovereign, too, that you know, say, your imperial highness, in such-and-such a town there lives one Pyotr Ivanovich Bobchinsky.

KHLESTAKOV. Very good.

DOBCHINSKY. Excuse us for having troubled you so by our presence.

BOBCHINSKY. Excuse us for having troubled you so by our presence.

KHLESTAKOV. Not at all, not at all. It was very pleasant for me. (*Shows them out. Alone:*) There are lots of officials here. Seems to me, I must say, they take me for some government man. I suppose I cut a fine figure in front of them yesterday. What a stupid game! I'll write to Tryapichkin in Petersburg all about it. He scribbles little articles. Let him give them a good punch in the nose. Hey, Osip! bring me some paper and ink! (*Osip looks around the door, saying:* "Right away") To Tryapichkin indeed, if anyone's to get it in the teeth—look out, he won't spare his own father for a witty remark and he loves money, too. Nevertheless, these officials are good people: it's a nice gesture on their part that they lent me money. I must look and see just how much I have. Three hundred from the judge. From the postmaster three hundred, six hundred, seven hundred, eight hundred . . . What greasy paper! Eight hundred, nine hundred! Oho! it's topped a thousand! . . . So now, Captain! Now if I run into you, we'll see who gets who! (OSIP *enters with ink and paper*) So you see, you idiot, how they receive me and regale me! (*Begins writing*)

OSIP. Sure, thank God! Only you know what, Ivan Aleksandrovich?

KHLESTAKOV (*writes*). What?

OSIP. Get away from here. Honest to God, it's time.

KHLESTAKOV (*writes*). Nonsense! What for?

OSIP. Here's why. The hell with all of them. You've had a good time here two days now—that's plenty. Why get involved with them long? Spit on them! Can't count on this: maybe some other fellow'll show up. Honest to God, Ivan Aleksandrovich! And the horses here are great: they'd take off just like that!

KHLESTAKOV (*writes*). No. I'd like to stay on here a bit. Let's go tomorrow.

OSIP. What do you mean tomorrow! Honest to God, Ivan Aleksandrovich, let's go. Even though you get lots of honor here and all, it'd be better, you know, to get out in time . . . See, they took you, really, for somebody else, and your old man'll be angry that you stayed on too long . . . so, really, we could get going famously! And they'd give us fine horses here.

KHLESTAKOV (*writes*). All right. Just take this letter down ahead, and take the order for coach horses with it. And be sure the horses are good. Tell the drivers I'll give them a ruble apiece, so they send off a courier, and sing songs! (*Continues writing*) Tryapichkin will die laughing, I can just see it . . .

OSIP. I'll send it off with the man here, sir, and myself do the packing so no time's lost.

KHLESTAKOV (*writes*). Good. Only, bring me a candle.

OSIP (*goes out and speaks offstage*). Hey, listen, pal! Take this letter over to the post office and tell the postmaster that he accepts it for nothing, and tell him to have 'em send round to my master right away the very best troika, an express one; but my master don't pay the traveling expenses, tell him. The traveling expenses, see, tell him, are paid by the government. And be quick about it, or, see, my master'll get mad. Wait, the letter's not ready yet.

KHLESTAKOV (*continues writing*). It'd be interesting to know: where does he live now—in Post-Office Street or in Pea Street. I know he, too, likes to move around from place to place and not pay up. I'll take a guess and send it to Post-Office. (*Folds it up and addresses it*)

(OSIP *brings a candle.* KHLESTAKOV *seals the letter. At this moment* DERZHIMORDA'*s voice is heard:* "Where you going, beardy? I'm telling you, nobody's 'lowed in.")

KHLESTAKOV (*gives* OSIP *the letter*). So, take it.

VOICES OF THE MERCHANTS. Let us in, sir! You cannot not let us in. We have come on business.

DERZHIMORDA'S VOICE. Go on, get out! He ain't seeing no one, he's asleep.

(*The noise increases.*)

KHLESTAKOV. What's going on there, Osip? Go see what the noise is.

OSIP (*looking out the window*). Some kind of merchants want to come in, but the policeman won't let 'em. They're waving papers; must be, they want to see you.

KHLESTAKOV (*going over to the window*). What do you want, good people?

MERCHANTS' VOICES. We have recourse to your kindness. Let us in, sir, and receive our petition.

KHLESTAKOV. Let them in, let them in! They may come in; Osip, tell them: they may come in.

(OSIP *goes out.*)

KHLESTAKOV (*takes the petitions in through the window, unfolds one of them and reads:*) "To His Most Noble Eminence the Gentleman of Finances from the merchant Abdulin" . . . God knows what this is: and there's no such rank! (*The merchants enter with a basket of wine and loaves of sugar*) What do you want, my good men?

MERCHANTS. We implore your kindness.

KHLESTAKOV. And what would you like?

MERCHANTS. Don't ruin us, sir! We endure offenses completely unjustified.

KHLESTAKOV. From whom?

ONE OF THE MERCHANTS. Always from the local Mayor. There never was such a Mayor, sir, anywhere. He does such wrongs you can't describe them. He's starved us out with quartering soldiers in our houses, so you might as well hang yourself. He doesn't go according to what you do. Grabs you by the beard and says: "Ah you, you Tartar!" Honest to God! If somehow, I mean, we didn't show him the proper respect; but, as it is, we always do what's right: what he needs for clothes for his spouse and daughter, we don't object to that at all. No, you see, that's not enough for him—honest! Comes into the shop and whatever he stumbles on takes it all: catches sight of a piece of goods and says: "Hey, my friend, this is good goods; send it over to my place." So you send it, and the piece is practically fifty arshins.

KHLESTAKOV. Not really? Oh, what a swindler!

MERCHANTS. Honest to God! Nobody remembers there ever

being such a mayor. You go hide in the back of your shop all the time when you see him coming. That is, not speaking with any kind of refinement, he takes any kind of junk: prunes that've been lying seven years in the barrel that my helper won't eat, but he puts his whole fist in. His nameday's St. Anthony's Day and you take everything to him, he doesn't need anything anyway. But, no, you give him more, and, he says, his nameday's on St. Onufry's Day, too. What can you do? You take it over on Onufry's Day, too.

KHLESTAKOV. He's really a robber.

MERCHANTS. Honest to God! And just you try to contradict him, he'll quarter a whole regiment in your house. And if you lock the door on him: I won't, he says, subject you to corporal punishment or trial by fire and water—that's against the law, he says, but I'm going to make you eat dirt.

KHLESTAKOV. Oh, what a swindler! Why, for that he should go straight to Siberia.

MERCHANTS. Sure, wherever your kindness sends him, it's all fine, just so long, that is, as it's far from us. Don't disdain, guardian of us all, our bread-and-salt: we greet you with some sugar and a little basket of wine.

KHLESTAKOV. No, don't think of such a thing. I don't take any kind of bribes at all. Now, if you, for example, offered me a loan of three hundred rubles, why that's something completely different: loans I can accept.

MERCHANTS. Please, guardian of us all. (*They take out money*) But what's three hundred! You better take five, only help us.

KHLESTAKOV. As you please: loans—I won't say a word, I'll take it.

MERCHANTS (*they take the money to him on a silver tray*). Please, and take the little tray, too.

KHLESTAKOV. All right, the tray, too.

MERCHANTS (*bowing*). And just this once take some sugar, too.

KHLESTAKOV. Oh, no: I never take any kind of . . .

OSIP. Your excellency! Why don't you take it? Take it! Everything's a help on the road! Here, gi' me the loaves and the bag! Gi' me everything! It'll all come in handy.

What's that? A string? Gi' me the string, too! The string, too, 'll come in handy on the road: if the cart falls apart or something else you can tie it up.

MERCHANTS. So do us the favor, your eminence, if you can't, that is, help us in our request, why we don't know what'll happen: simply go hang ourselves.

KHLESTAKOV. Certainly, certainly. I'll do what I can.

(*The merchants go out; a woman's voice is heard:* "No, don't you dare not let me in! I'll complain to him himself about you. Don't you push me so hard!")

KHLESTAKOV. Who's there? (*Goes over to the window*) What do you want, good woman?

TWO WOMEN'S VOICES. I beg your kindness, sir! Let us in, my lord, to hear what we have to say.

KHLESTAKOV (*out the window*). Let her in.

(*The Locksmith's Wife and the Non-Commissioned Officer's Wife come in.*)

LOCKSMITH'S WIFE (*bowing to the ground*). I beg your kindness!

N.C.O.'S WIFE. I beg your kindness . . .

KHLESTAKOV. What kind of women are you?

N.C.O.'S WIFE. Non-commissioned officer's wife Ivanova.

LOCKSMITH'S WIFE. The locksmith's wife, a local townswoman: Fevronya Petrova Pashlepkina, my father . . .

KHLESTAKOV. Wait; you speak first. What do you want?

LOCKSMITH'S WIFE. I beg your kindness: I implore your favor against the Mayor! May God do him all kinds of harm, so neither his children, nor himself, the swindler, nor his uncles, nor his aunts never get nothing good from nothing.

KHLESTAKOV. Why?

LOCKSMITH'S WIFE. Why he ordered my husband, now, to be called up into the army and it wasn't our turn, such a swindler he is! And besides it's illegal: he was married.

KHLESTAKOV. How could he do that?

LOCKSMITH'S WIFE. He did it, the swindler, he did it: I hope God lays him low both in this world and the next! And I hope all kinds of dirty tricks happen to him and to his aunt, if he has a aunt, and I hope his father, if he has one living, and himself, the dog, die or choke once and forever, such a swindler he is. The tailor's son was supposed to be took, and a drunkard he was, but the parents give a rich present, so he fastens on to merchant Panteleyeva's son, and Panteleyeva sends three bits of cloth over to his wife, so he comes to me: "What y'need," he says, "a husband for, he's no good for you anyway." I know myself whether he's no good or not, that's my business, you swindler, I says. "He," he says, "is a thief: even if he hasn't stolen nothing yet, it makes no difference," he says, "he will, so even without that, next year he joins the recruits." And what's it like for me without my husband, you swindler! I'm a weak woman, you bastard! I hope all your relatives go to hell, and if you got a aunt, I hope your aunt . . .

KHLESTAKOV. All right, all right. Now, what about you? (*Escorts the old woman out*)

LOCKSMITH'S WIFE (*going out*). Don't forget, dear sir! Be merciful!

N.C.O.'S WIFE. I come, sir, about the Mayor . . .

KHLESTAKOV. Well, so, what about him? Come to the point.

N.C.O.'S WIFE. Flogged me, sir.

KHLESTAKOV. How?

N.C.O.'S WIFE. By mistake, dear sir. Some of the women started scrapping in the market place, but the police didn't get there in time, so they grabbed me. They gave me such a good going over I couldn't sit down for two days.

KHLESTAKOV. So what's there to do about it?

N.C.O.'S WIFE. There's nothing, 'course, to do about that. But now you order him to pay a fine for this mistake. I got no reason to turn down my good fortune, and the dough'd come in real handy right now.

KHLESTAKOV. All right, all right! Go on, go on. I'll take care of it. (*Hands with petitions reach in through the window*) Who else is there? (*Goes over to the window*) I don't want it, I don't want it! Don't, don't need it! (*Going away*) Fed up, god damn it! Don't let them in, Osip!

OSIP (*shouts out the window*). Go on, go home! Too late, come tomorrow!

(*The door opens and some sort of figure steps forward in a shaggy cloak, with an unshaven beard, puffed lips and bandaged cheek. Behind him several others are shown in perspective.*)

OSIP. Go on, get going! What're you coming in for? (*Puts his hands against his belly and pushes him out in front of himself into the vestibule, slamming the door behind*)

(MARYA ANTONOVNA *enters.*)

MARYA ANTONOVNA. Ah!

KHLESTAKOV. Why did you get frightened, madam?

MARYA ANTONOVNA. No, I didn't get frightened.

KHLESTAKOV (*showing off*). Goodness, madam, it's very pleasant for me that you took me to be such a man as . . . Dare I ask you: where were you thinking of going?

MARYA ANTONOVNA. Really, I wasn't going anywhere.

KHLESTAKOV. Now why, for example, weren't you going anywhere?

MARYA ANTONOVNA. I was wondering, isn't Maminka here . . .

KHLESTAKOV. No, I'd like to know why you weren't going anywhere.

MARYA ANTONOVNA. I've disturbed you. You were busy with important things.

KHLESTAKOV (*showing off*). But your eyes are better than any important things . . . You can't possibly disturb me; in no way possible; on the contrary, you can bring me great pleasure.

MARYA ANTONOVNA. You talk as they do in the capital.

KHLESTAKOV. For such a beautiful person as you. Dare I be so fortunate as to offer you a chair? But no, you should have not a chair but a throne.

MARYA ANTONOVNA. Really, I don't know . . . I *did* have to go. (*Sits down*)

KHLESTAKOV. What a lovely little kerchief you have!

MARYA ANTONOVNA. You scoffers, you just laugh at provincial people.

KHLESTAKOV. How I wish, madam, I were your little kerchief that I might embrace your lily-white neck.

MARYA ANTONOVNA. I don't understand what you're talking about at all: some sort of kerchief . . . The weather's very odd today.

KHLESTAKOV. Your little lips, madam, are sweeter than any weather.

MARYA ANTONOVNA. You keep saying such things . . . I'd like to ask you rather to write some sort of verses in my album to remember you by. You, I suppose, know lots.

KHLESTAKOV. For you, madam, anything you want. Just tell me, what sort of verses would you like?

MARYA ANTONOVNA. Any sort like that—good ones, new ones.

KHLESTAKOV. But what verses! I know lots.

MARYA ANTONOVNA. Well, tell me, which are you going to write me?

KHLESTAKOV. Why tell you? I know them anyway.

MARYA ANTONOVNA. I just love them . . .

KHLESTAKOV. I have lots of different kinds. So, if you like, I'll just give you this: "O, man, why vainly in thy grief dost grumble at our God . . ." Well, and others . . . I can't remember now; besides it doesn't make any difference. Better than that I offer you my love, which from your glance . . . (*Moving his chair closer*)

MARYA ANTONOVNA. Love! I don't understand love . . . I've never known what this love is . . . (*Moves her chair away*)

KHLESTAKOV (*moving his chair closer*). Why do you move your chair away? It's better for us to sit close to each other.

MARYA ANTONOVNA (*moving away*). Why close? It's all the same far away.

KHLESTAKOV (*moving closer*). Why far away? It's all the same close.

MARYA ANTONOVNA (*moving away*). What's this for?

KHLESTAKOV (*moving closer*). Why it seems close to you, but you just think of it as far. How happy I would be, madam, if I could press you in my arms.

MARYA ANTONOVNA (*looking out the window*). What's that there, that just flew away? A magpie or some other bird?

KHLESTAKOV (*kisses her shoulder and looks out the window*). It's a magpie.

MARYA ANTONOVNA (*rises in indignation*). No, this is too much . . . Such impudence!

KHLESTAKOV (*holding her back*). Forgive me, madam: I did it from love, precisely from love.

MARYA ANTONOVNA. You think I'm such a provincial girl . . . (*Tries to get away*)

KHLESTAKOV (*continuing to hold her back*). Out of love, really out of love. I was only teasing, Marya Antonovna, don't get angry! I'm ready on my knees to beg your forgiveness. (*Falls on his knees*) Forgive me, forgive me. You see, I'm on my knees.

(ANNA ANDREYEVNA *enters.*)

ANNA ANDREYEVNA (*catching sight of* KLESTAKOV *on his knees*). Ah, what a scene!

KHLESTAKOV (*rising*). Damn it!

ANNA ANDREYEVNA (*to her daughter*). What does this mean, madam, what way to behave is this?

MARYA ANTONOVNA. Maminka, I . . .

ANNA ANDREYEVNA. Get out of here! You hear, out of here, out of here! And don't dare show your face! (MARYA ANTONOVNA *goes out in tears*) Excuse me, I, I must confess, have been thrown into such confusion . . .

KHLESTAKOV (*aside*). And she's very luscious, too, not bad at all. (*Throws himself on his knees*) Madam, you see, I am burning with love.

ANNA ANDREYEVNA. What, you're on your knees! Oh, get up, get up, the floor here's completely dirty.

KHLESTAKOV. No, on my knees, absolutely on my knees, I must know what is fated for me: life or death.

ANNA ANDREYEVNA. But please, I still don't fully understand the meaning of your words. If I'm not mistaken, you're making a declaration of love with regard to my daughter.

KHLESTAKOV. No, I am in love with you. My life hangs by a hair. If you do not crown my unalterable love, then I am unworthy of earthly existence. With my heart on fire I ask your hand.

ANNA ANDREYEVNA. But let me note: I'm in a certain sense . . . I'm married . . .

KHLESTAKOV. That doesn't matter. For love there is no distinction, as Karamzin said: "The laws condemn." We'll withdraw beneath the canopy of the streams. Your hand, I ask your hand.

(MARYA ANTONOVNA *suddenly runs in.*)

MARYA ANTONOVNA. Maminka, Papinka said you should . . . (*Catching sight of* KHLESTAKOV *on his knees, screams:*) Ah, what a scene!

ANNA ANDREYEVNA. Well what's wrong with you? What's that for? Why? What sort of thoughtlessness is that! You just suddenly run in like a singed cat. Well what did you find so surprising? What popped into your head? Really, like a little three-year-old child. Doesn't seem, doesn't seem, absolutely doesn't seem she's eighteen at all. I don't know when you're going to be more sensible, when you're going to behave like a well-brought-up young lady. When you're going to know what the right rules are and proper conduct.

MARYA ANTONOVNA (*in tears*). Really, Maminka, I didn't know . . .

ANNA ANDREYEVNA. There's always some old draught blowing around in your head; you follow the example of Lyapkin-Tryapkin's daughters. What do you look at them for, there's no point in your even looking at them. There are other examples for you to follow: your mother's right in front of you. That's the kind of examples you should take after.

KHLESTAKOV (*grabbing the daughter by the hand*). Anna Andreyevna, don't oppose our happiness, but give your blessing to our unalterable love.

ANNA ANDREYEVNA (*in amazement*). So you love her?

KHLESTAKOV. Decide: life or death?

ANNA ANDREYEVNA. You see, you fool, you see, all because of you, you worthless girl, our guest's on his knees; and you just suddenly run in like a madwoman. Really, it'd be worth it if I refused on purpose: you're not worthy of such happiness.

MARYA ANTONOVNA. I won't do it, Maminka; honest, I'll never do it again.

(*The Mayor enters, in a rush.*)

MAYOR. Your excellency! Don't ruin me! Don't ruin me!

KHLESTAKOV. What's happened to you?

MAYOR. The merchants have complained to your excellency. I swear on my honor, not half of what they said is true. They themselves swindle the people and cheat them. The non-commissioned officer's wife lied straight to your face, pretending I'd flogged her. She's lying, honest to God, she's lying. She flogged herself.

KHLESTAKOV. Let the non-commissioned officer's wife drop dead. I've nothing to do with her!

MAYOR. Don't believe them, don't believe them! They're such liars . . . Even such a child won't believe them. They're known all over town as liars. And about the swindling, if I may be so bold as to tell you: they're such swindlers the likes of which the world never saw before.

ANNA ANDREYEVNA. You know what honor Ivan Aleksandrovich has done us? He's asking for our daughter's hand.

MAYOR. What! what! You're crazy, Mother! Please don't get angry, your excellency, she's just a bit crazy, that's the way her mother was, too.

KHLESTAKOV. Indeed. I am expressly asking for her hand. I am in love.

MAYOR. I can't believe it, your excellency.

ANNA ANDREYEVNA. Even when you're told?

KHLESTAKOV. I'm talking to you seriously . . . I may go crazy from love.

MAYOR. I don't dare believe it, I'm unworthy of such honor.

KHLESTAKOV. Indeed. If you don't agree to give me Marya Antonovna's hand, why God only knows what I'll do.

MAYOR. I can't believe it; you're joking, your excellency.

ANNA ANDREYEVNA. Oh, what a numbskull, really! when people keep on telling you.

MAYOR. I can't believe it.

KHLESTAKOV. Give me her hand, give me her hand—I am a desperate man, I will do anything: if I kill myself, you'll get taken to court.

MAYOR. Oh, my God! In faith I'm not at fault in thought or deed. Please don't be angry! Please do what your Worship pleases! Really, my head now . . . I myself don't know what's going on. I've been such a fool now as I've never been in my life before.

ANNA ANDREYEVNA. So, give them your blessing.

(KHLESTAKOV *goes up to him with* MARYA ANTONOVNA.)

MAYOR. May God bless you, it's not my fault.

(KHLESTAKOV *and* MARYA ANTONOVNA *kiss.*)

MAYOR (*looking at them*). I'll be God damned! Really! (*Rubs his eyes again*) They're kissing. Oh, saints alive, they're kissing! A real bridegroom! (*Shouts; jumping up and down in delight*) Hey, Anton! Hey, Anton! Hey, you Mayor! Look how everything's turned out!

(OSIP *enters.*)

OSIP. The horses are ready.

KHLESTAKOV. Ah, good . . . Right away.

MAYOR. What, are you going?

KHLESTAKOV. Yes, I'm going.

MAYOR. But when, that is . . . You yourself made a suggestion about, I think, a wedding.

KHLESTAKOV. Only a moment . . . Only one day to my uncle's—a rich old man, and tomorrow I'll be back.

MAYOR. We dare not detain you in the hope of your safe return . . .

KHLESTAKOV. Of course, of course, I'll go immediately. Good-bye, my love . . . No, I simply can't say it. Good-bye, sweetie! (*Kisses her hand*)

MAYOR. But don't you need anything for the road? You, perhaps, are short of funds?

KHLESTAKOV. Oh no, what for? (*Having reflected a bit*) On the other hand, why not?

MAYOR. How much would you like?

KHLESTAKOV. Well, then you gave me two hundred, that is, not two hundred but four. I don't want to take advantage of your error—so, please, the same amount now, so it'll be exactly eight hundred.

MAYOR. Right away! (*Takes it out of his wallet*) Besides, as if on purpose, in the newest, crispest bills.

KHLESTAKOV. Ah, fine. (*Takes the bills and examines them*) This is fine. It's good luck, they say, when it's new money.

MAYOR. Exactly so, sir.

KHLESTAKOV. Good-bye, Anton Antonovich! I'm much indebted to you for your hospitality. I've never had so fine a reception anywhere. Good-bye, Anna Andreyevna; good-bye, my sweetie, Marya Antonovna. (*They go out*) (*Offstage.*)

KHLESTAKOV'S VOICE. Good-bye, angel of my soul, Marya Antonovna.

MAYOR'S VOICE. What's this you're doing? You're going straight by the regular stagecoach?

KHLESTAKOV'S VOICE. Yes, I'm used to doing it this way. I get a headache from carriages with springs.

COACHMAN'S VOICE. Whoa!

MAYOR'S VOICE. But at least something to put over you, even if only a little laprobe. Wouldn't you like me to have them give you a laprobe?

KHLESTAKOV'S VOICE. No, what for? It's nothing. On the other hand, why not; let them give me a laprobe.

MAYOR'S VOICE. Hey, Avdotya! Go into the storeroom; get out a rug, the very best, the one with the light-blue background, the Persian one, hurry!

COACHMAN'S VOICE. Whoa!

MAYOR'S VOICE. When may we expect you?

KHLESTAKOV'S VOICE. Tomorrow or the day after.

OSIP'S VOICE. Ah, that's the rug? Give it here, put it this way! Now put some hay on this side.

COACHMAN'S VOICE. Whoa!

OSIP'S VOICE. Here on this side! Here! More! Good. That'll be great! (*Beats the rug with his hand*) Now sit down, your honor!

KHLESTAKOV'S VOICE. Good-bye, Anton Antonovich.

MAYOR'S VOICE. Good-bye, your excellency!

THE WOMEN'S VOICES. Good-bye, Ivan Aleksandrovich!

KHLESTAKOV'S VOICE. Good-bye, Maminka!

COACHMAN'S VOICE. Hey, now, your fliers!

(*The little bell rings. The curtain falls.*)

ACT V

The same room. The Mayor, ANNA ANDREYEVNA *and* MARYA ANTONOVNA *on stage.*

MAYOR. Well, Anna Andreyevna? so? Have you thought anything about that? What a windfall, the rascals! Admit it frankly: you never even dreamed of such a thing: simply a little Mayor's girl and suddenly, ugh! the rascals, what a devil she's related to!

ANNA ANDREYEVNA. Not a bit of it. I knew it long ago. It's a marvel to you 'cause you're a simple man; you've never seen respectable people.

MAYOR. I'm a respectable man myself, Mother. But really, what do you make of it, Anna Andreyevna: what big shots you and I've become now! hey, Anna Andreyevna? Way up; I'll be God damned! Just you wait, I'll give it hot to all these lovers of petitions and secret reports. Hey, anybody there? (*A Policeman comes in*) Oh, it's you, Ivan Karpovich; call the merchants over here. I'll give it to them, the cheaters. So they complained on me! You see, it's the damned Jews. Just you wait, my boys! Before, it was just child's play, but now I'll give it to you man to man. Keep a list of everybody who just went to complain about me and above all these pencil-pushers, the pencil-pushers who rolled out the petitions for them. And tell everybody so they know: look now, tell them, what honor God has sent this mayor, that he's not giving his daughter's hand to just any simple fellow, but to someone like there never was before, who can do everything, everything, everything, everything! Tell everybody so they all know. Shout it out all over town, ring the bells, God damn it! When there's a triumph, let's be triumphant! (*The Policeman goes out*) Isn't that the way, Anna Andreyevna, hey? How about us now, where'll we live? Here or in Peter?

ANNA ANDREYEVNA. Naturally, in Petersburg. How can we stay here!

MAYOR. Well, so, if Peter, then in Peter. But it'd be good here, too. But, you know what I think, Anna Andreyevna, the hell with being mayor, hey?

ANNA ANDREYEVNA. Naturally, what's being a mayor!

MAYOR. What do you think, Anna Andreyevna, you know I could get me a really high rank now, because he's really close to all the ministers and goes to the Court. And then on account of that, you can make such a production of it that, in time, you wind up a general. What do you think, Anna Andreyevna: can I make general?

ANNA ANDREYEVNA. What do you mean! Of course you can!

MAYOR. Oh, God damn it, it'd be great to be a general! They'd hang a sash across your shoulder. Which sash is the best, Anna Andreyevna? The red or the light-blue?

ANNA ANDREYEVNA. Why of course light-blue's best.

MAYOR. Hey? Look what you want! The red's good, too. You know why I want to be a general? Because maybe you have to go some place—couriers and adjutants gallop on ahead everywhere: horses! And at all the stations nobody's getting them, they're all still waiting, all these titulars and captains and mayors, but you, you don't give a damn; you dine some place with a governor and then: Hold it, mayor! Heh, heh, heh (*bursts out and dies of laughter*), that's what's enticing, you cheats!

ANNA ANDREYEVNA. Still you like everything vulgar. You must remember that we have to change our life completely, that your friends aren't going to be some kind of an old dog-lover judge who you go out and poison rabbits with, or Zemlyanika. On the contrary your friends are going to be people with the finest manners: counts and all the best society . . . Only, really, I'm afraid for you you're sometimes going to drop words you don't even hear in polite society.

MAYOR. So? A word does no harm.

ANNA ANDREYEVNA. It was all right as long as you were mayor. But there, see, life'll be completely different.

MAYOR. True. There, they say, they have two fish: lake salmon and smelt so good you start drooling as soon as you start to eat them.

ANNA ANDREYEVNA. And he's still talking just about fish! I don't want our house to be anything but the first in the capital, and so there's such a fragrance in my room you can't come in and just have to squint. (*Squints and sniffs*) Ah! How good!

(*The Merchants enter.*)

MAYOR. Ah! Hello, my dear boys!

MERCHANTS (*bowing*). Your good health, sir!

MAYOR. So, boys, how are you doing? How're things selling? What're you complaining about, you teapot-traders, you weighers and measurers? You arch-swindlers, you huge monsters, you biggest thieves in the world, you complaining? Hey? Hauled in a lot? See, they think, now they'll put him in jail! Do you know, seven devils and a witch get after you, that . . .

ANNA ANDREYEVNA. Oh, my God, what language you use, Antosha!

MAYOR (*with displeasure*). It's not a question of language now! Do you know that that same official whom you complained to is now going to marry my daughter? What about that? hey? What do you say now? Now I'll get you! ooh! cheat the people . . . You make a contract with the town treasury, swindle it out of a hundred thousand by giving rotten cloth, and then donate twenty arshins, and then you think you're going to get a reward for that? If you only know, how you're . . . And you stick your bellies out: I'm a merchant, don't touch me; the nobility, you say, has nothing over us. Sure, the nobility . . . ah, you, you plug-ugly! The noble studies serious things: if he gets whipped in school it's so he'll know something useful. But what do you do? You start out swindling, your master beats you because you don't know how to cheat enough. Even as boys you don't know the Lord's Prayer but you're already underweighing, and as soon as your belly puffs out, you line your pockets and you're already on your high horse. Damn you, you're unbelievable! What, you put on such airs 'cause you guzzle down sixteen samovar-fulls a day? Why, I spit on your heads and all your importance!

MERCHANTS (*bowing*). Guilty, Anton Antonovich!

MAYOR. You complaining? And who helped you cheat everybody when you built the bridge and wrote down twenty thousand for wood when there wasn't even a hundred rubles' worth? I helped you, you goat beards! You've forgotten that. If I'd told on you about that, I could have taken you off to Siberia, too. —What do you say to that, hey?

ONE OF THE MERCHANTS. Guilty before God, Anton Antonovich. The devil mixed us up. And we swear to stop complaining from now on. Anything you want, only don't get mad!

MAYOR. Don't get mad! *Now* you're falling around my feet. Why? Because my side's won, but even if I'm just a bit on yours, you, you cheats, want to pull me down into the mud and even cover me up with a log.

MERCHANTS (*bowing to the ground*). Don't ruin us, Anton Antonovich!

MAYOR. Don't ruin us! Now you tell me: don't ruin us! What was it before? I ought to . . . (*Waving his hand*) Well, let God forgive you! Enough! I'm not malicious; only now be careful, keep your eyes and ears open! I'm giving my daughter away to no just ordinary nobleman. So there's congratulations . . . you get me? not just to get through with it with some cured sturgeon or a loaf of sugar . . . well, God be with you.

(*The Merchants go out.* AMMOS FYODOROVICH *and* ARTEMY FILIPOVICH *enter.*)

AMMOS FYODOROVICH (*still in the doorway*). Can one believe one's ears, Anton Antonovich? You've been showered with extraordinary good fortune.

ARTEMY FILIPOVICH. I have the honor of congratulating you on your extraordinary good fortune. I was sincerely delighted, when I heard. (*Goes over to kiss* ANNA ANDREYEVNA'*s hand*) Anna Andreyevna! (*Goes over to kiss* MARYA ANTONOVA'*s hand*) Marya Antonovna!

RASTAKOVSKY (*enters*). I congratulate Anton Antonovich, may God grant you and the new couple long life and bless you with numerous descendants, grandchildren and great-grandchildren, Anna Andreyevna! (*Goes over to kiss* ANNA ANDREYEVNA'*s hand*) Marya Antonovna! (*Goes over to kiss* MARYA ANTONOVNA'*s hand*)

(KOROBKIN *and his wife and* LYULYUKOV, *enter.*)

KOROBKIN. I have the honor of congratulating Anton Antonovich! Anna Andreyevna! (*Goes over to kiss* ANNA ANDREYEVNA'*s hand*) Marya Antonovna! (*Goes over to kiss her hand*)

KOROBKIN'S WIFE. I heartily congratulate you, Anna Andreyevna, on your new happiness.

LYULYUKOV. I have the honor of congratulating you, Anna Andreyevna! (*Goes over to kiss her hand and then, having turned toward the audience, clicks his tongue with a look of boldness*) Marya Antonovna! I have the honor of congratulating you! (*Goes over to kiss her hand and turns to the audience with the same boldness*)

(*A great number of guests in frockcoats and morning coats come in and first kiss* ANNA ANDREYEVNA'*s hand, saying:* "Anna Andreyevna," *and then kiss* MARYA ANTONOVNA'*s, saying:* "Marya Antonovna!" BOBCHINSKY *and* DOBCHINSKY *push their way through.*)

BOBCHINSKY. I have the honor of congratulating you.

DOBCHINSKY. Anton Antonovich! I have the honor of congratulating you.

BOBCHINSKY. On the happy event.

DOBCHINSKY. Anna Andreyevna!

BOBCHINSKY. Anna Andreyevna! (*Both go over to her at the same time and bump their foreheads together*)

DOBCHINSKY. Marya Antonovna! (*Goes over to kiss her hand*) I have the honor of congratulating you! You will have great, great joy and will wear a gold dress and will sip various rare soups and will pass the time very amusingly.

BOBCHINSKY (*interrupting*). Marya Antonovna, I have the honor of congratulating you! May God give you all kinds of prosperity, ten-ruble bills and a little son just so (*Shows the size with his hand*) big so you can sit him on your hand. Yes, sir: the little boy'll cry all the time: wah! wah! wah! (*Several more guests enter, going up to kiss their hands;* LUKA LUKICH *and his wife enter.*)

LUKA LUKICH. I have the honor . . .

LUKA LUKICH'S WIFE (*runs in ahead*). Congratulations, Anna Andreyevna! (*They kiss*) I'm so delighted, really; I've been told: Anna Andreyevna's marrying her daughter. —Ah, my God! I thinks to myself, and I'm so delighted I says to my husband: Listen, Lukanchik: how happy Anna Andreyevna is! Well, I thinks to myself, thank God, and I says to him: I'm so excited I'm just burning with impatience to tell Anna Andreyevna personally . . . Ah, my God, I thinks to myself: Anna Andreyevna was just waiting for a good match for her daughter and now here it is: turned out just exactly as she wanted and, really, I was so delighted I couldn't say a thing. I cried and cried, just simply sobbed. Luka Lukich says to me: "What're you crying for, Nastinka?" "Lukanchik, I says, I don't know myself, the tears're just coming down in a stream."

MAYOR. I humbly beg you to be seated, ladies and gentlemen. Hey, Mishka, bring in some more chairs.

(*The guests sit down. The Chief of Police and Policemen enter.*)

CHIEF OF POLICE. I have the honor of congratulating you, your excellency, and wishing you prosperity for years to come.

MAYOR. Thank you, thank you! I beg you, be seated, ladies and gentlemen!

(*The guests take seats.*)

AMMOS FYODOROVICH. Now tell us, please, Anton Antonovich, how did all this get started: the step by step development of the whole thing.

MAYOR. The way the thing developed is extraordinary: he himself made the proposal.

ANNA ANDREYEVNA. In a very respectful and most refined manner. Said everything extraordinarily well; he says: "I, Anna Andreyevna, only out of respect for your merits . . ." And such a handsome, well-educated man, of the most noblest principles. "For me, believe me, Anna Andreyevna, for me life's not worth a kopek. Only because I respect your rare qualities."

MARYA ANTONOVNA. Ah, Maminka! You know he said that to me.

ANNA ANDREYEVNA. Stop it, you don't know anything, and don't butt into what isn't your business! "Anna Andreyevna, I'm overcome . . ." He showered such flattering words on me . . . and just as I was about to say: We can never dare hope for such an honor, he suddenly fell on his knees and in that same noblest manner says: "Anna Andreyevna, don't make me the most unhappy man! Agree to answer my feelings, or else I'll end my life with death."

MARYA ANTONOVNA. Really, Maminka, he said that about me.

ANNA ANDREYEVNA. Sure, of course . . . it was about you, too, I don't deny any of it.

MAYOR. And he got me so scared, said he was going to shoot himself. I'll shoot myself, I'll shoot myself, he says.

MANY OF THE GUESTS. You really don't say!

AMMOS FYODOROVICH. What a thing!

LUKA LUKICH. Really something, the way fate set it up.

ARTEMY FILIPOVICH. Not fate, sir, fate's a chicken. Merit brought it about. (*Aside*) Such a pig always has all the luck.

AMMOS FYODOROVICH. If you want, Anton Antonovich, I'll sell you that hound you wanted to get.

MAYOR. No: I've no time for hounds now.

AMMOS FYODOROVICH. Well, if you don't want it, we can agree on another dog.

KOROBKIN'S WIFE. Ah, Anna Andreyevna, how happy I am over your good fortune! You can't imagine.

KOROBKIN. Where, may I ask, is our celebrated guest now? I heard that he left for some reason.

MAYOR. Yes, he left for a day on an extremely important matter.

ANNA ANDREYEVNA. To his uncle to get his blessing.

MAYOR. To get his blessing; but tomorrow already . . . (*Sneezes; all the "God-bless-you's" become one dull roar*) Deeply grateful! But tomorrow already back again . . . (*Sneezes. A dull roar of "God-bless-you's." Other voices are more audible:*)

CHIEF OF POLICE'S. We wish you good health, your excellency!

BOBCHINSKY'S. A hundred years and a bag of ten-ruble bills.

DOBCHINSKY'S. May God grant you live for years and years!

ARTEMY FILIPOVICH'S. Hope you drop dead!

KOROBKIN'S WIFE. Go to hell!

MAYOR. I humbly thank you! And wish you the same.

ANNA ANDREYEVNA. We now plan to live in Petersburg. Here, I must say, the air is such . . . much too countryish . . . I must say, very disagreeable . . . And my husband now . . . He will receive a general's stars there.

MAYOR. Yes, I must admit, ladies and gentlemen, God damn it, I very much want to be a general.

LUKA LUKICH. And God grant you get it.

RASTAKOVSKY. Man can do nothing, but God can do everything.

AMMOS FYODOROVICH. Great ships need deep waters.

ARTEMY FILIPOVICH. Honor according to deserts.

AMMOS FYODOROVICH (*aside*). That'll be a good trick, when he's really made a general! The stars'll fit him like a saddle on a cow! No, friend, that part of the song's still far off. There are cleaner hands than yours here, but so far yet they aren't generals.

ARTEMY FILIPOVICH (*aside*). What now, God damn it, but he's bucking for general. I'm afraid that maybe he'll be a general at that. He's got enough importance, the devil himself won't touch him. (*Turning to him*) But, Anton Antonovich, don't forget us later.

AMMOS FYODOROVICH. And if anything happens, if, for example, we need something here, don't take away your protection.

KOROBKIN. Next year I'm going to take my son to the capital to serve the government, so do me the favor, give him your protection, take the place of a father for the poor little orphan.

MAYOR. I'm ready, for my part, ready to do what I can.

ANNA ANDREYEVNA. Antosha, you're always ready to make promises. First, you won't have time to think about this. And how can you, and why should you, burden yourself with such promises?

MAYOR. Why not, my dear: sometimes it's possible.

ANNA ANDREYEVNA. It's possible, of course, but you know you mustn't give your protection to all the small fry.

KOROBKIN'S WIFE. Did you hear what she called us?

GUESTS. So what, she was always like that. Let a peasant just sit at the foot of your table and he'll try to climb to the head.

(*The Postmaster rushes in with an unsealed letter in his hand.*)

POSTMASTER. An amazing thing, ladies and gentlemen! The official who we thought was an inspector general wasn't an inspector general.

ALL. What do you mean, wasn't an inspector general?

POSTMASTER. Absolutely wasn't an inspector general; I found it out from a letter.

MAYOR. What're you saying? What're you saying? What letter?

POSTMASTER. Why from his very own letter. A letter comes to me at the post office. I look at the address, I see: Post-Office Street. I'm stupefied. Well, I think to myself, I bet he found something wrong in the Post-Office Department and is informing the authorities. So I took it and opened it.

MAYOR. How could you?

POSTMASTER. Don't know myself: an unnatural power drove me. I was just about to call the courier to send it off by relays—but curiosity got the better of me such as I never felt before. I can't, I can't, I hear myself saying I can't, but I'm being pulled, being pulled so. So in one ear I keep hearing: now don't open it, you'll ruin yourself once and for all like a chicken; but in the other it's like some kind of demon's whispering: open it, open it! open it! And as I press down the wax, flames go through my veins, and when I open it, I'm like ice, honest to God, like ice. My hands're trembling, and everything's all mixed up.

MAYOR. But how did you dare unseal the letter of an important person with such authorization?

POSTMASTER. That's just it—he's not authorized and he's not an important person.

MAYOR. Well, what is he then, to your way of thinking?

POSTMASTER. Neither this nor that; God knows what.

MAYOR (*vehemently*). What do you mean neither this nor that? How can you dare call him neither that nor this, nor God knows what? I arrest you . . .

POSTMASTER. Who? You?

MAYOR. Yes, me.

POSTMASTER. Try and catch me!

MAYOR. Do you know that he's going to marry my daughter, that I'm going to be a noble myself, that I'll stuff you into Siberia itself?

POSTMASTER. Oh, Anton Antonovich! What's Siberia; Siberia's far away. Let me read it to you instead. Ladies and gentlemen! May I read you the letter?

ALL. Read it, read it!

POSTMASTER (*reads*): "I hasten to inform you, dear Tryapichkin, of the wonders that have happened to me. An infantry captain cleaned me out on the road, so that the innkeeper was about to send me to jail when suddenly, on account of my Petersburg appearance and my clothes, the whole town took me for a governor-general. Now I'm staying at the Mayor's, living on the fat of the land, and running wild after his wife and daughter; only I haven't decided which to begin with—I think, first with the mother, because, it seems, she's ready right now to do everything . . .

"Remember how we were poor together, ate as catch can, and how the baker once grabbed me by the collar because of the pies we ate and charged up to the king of the English? Now it's completely the other way round. Everybody gives me loans as big as I like. Really queer people. You'd die laughing. You write little articles, I know: put them into your writings. First: the Mayor—stupid as a horse's ass . . ."

MAYOR. It can't be! That's not there.

POSTMASTER (*shows the letter*). Read it yourself.

MAYOR (*reads*). "As a horse's ass." Impossible; you wrote this yourself.

POSTMASTER. What would I have started writing for?

ARTEMY FILIPOVICH. Read it!

LUKA LUKICH. Read it.

POSTMASTER (*continuing to read*). "The Mayor is as stupid as a horse's ass . . ."

MAYOR. Oh God damn it! He had to repeat it again! As if it wasn't good enough the first time.

POSTMASTER (*continuing to read*). Hm . . . hm . . . hm . . . hm . . . "horse's ass. The Postmaster also is a good fellow . . ." (*Stopping reading*) Well, here he expressed himself indecently about me, too.

MAYOR. No, read it!

POSTMASTER. But what for?

MAYOR. No, God damn it, if you're going to read it, read it! Read it all!

ARTEMY FILIPOVICH. Let me, I'll read it. (*Puts on his glasses and reads*) "The Postmaster is an exact replica of the department's watchman Mikheyev; a bastard, too, I bet, drinks like a fish."

POSTMASTER (*to the audience*). Well, a nasty boy who ought to be whipped; nothing more!

ARTEMY FILIPOVICH (*continuing to read*). "The Supervisor of the Charitable Insti . . . tu . . . tu . . . to . . ." (*Hiccoughs*)

KOROBKIN. What did you stop for?

ARTEMY FILIPOVICH. But the illegible pen . . . Besides, it's clear he's a scoundrel.

KOROBKIN. Give it to me! Now I have, I think, better eyes anyway. (*Takes the letter*)

ARTEMY FILIPOVICH (*not giving the letter*). No, this place can be skipped, but further on it's legible.

KOROBKIN. But, come on, I know already.

ARTEMY FILIPOVICH. The reading I can do myself; further on, really, it's all legible.

POSTMASTER. No, read it all! It's all read up to here.

ALL. Hand it over, Artemy Filipovich! Give him the letter. (*To* KOROBKIN) Read it!

ARTEMY FILIPOVICH. Right away. (*Hands him the letter*) Now please . . . (*Covers it with his finger*) read on from here. (*All press close to him.*)

POSTMASTER. Read it! Read it! Nonsense, read it all!

KOROBKIN (*reading*). "The Supervisor of Charitable Institutions Zemlyanika: absolutely a pig in a yarmulka." [2]

ARTEMY FILIPOVICH (*to the audience*). Not even witty. A pig in a yarmulka! How can a pig be in a yarmulka?

KOROBKIN (*continuing to read*). "The Superintendent of Schools reeks of onion."

LUKA LUKICH (*to the audience*). Honest to God, I've never had an onion in my mouth.

AMMOS FYODOROVICH (*aside*). Thank God, at least there's nothing about me.

KOROBKIN (*reads*). "The Judge . . ."

AMMOS FYODOROVICH. Here you are! (*Aloud*) Ladies and gentlemen, I think the letter's very long. And what the hell's in it: just a lot of junk to read.

LUKA LUKICH. No!

POSTMASTER. No, read it!

ARTEMY FILIPOVICH. No, go on read it!

KOROBKIN (*continues*). "The Judge Lyapkin-Tryapkin is in the worst degree mowvaiz-tone . . ." (*Stops*) Must be a French word.

AMMOS FYODOROVICH. God only knows what it means. It's all right if it's just swindler, but maybe it's something worse still.

[2] *yarmulka*—skullcap in Yiddish.

KOROBKIN (*continuing to read*). "But on the other hand the people are hospitable and good-natured. Good-bye, dear Tryapichkin. I myself, following your example, want to do some writing. It's hard, my friend, to live like this, you finally want some real nourishment for the soul. I see exactly: one must do something grand. Write to me in Saratov province, and from there to the village Podkatilovka." (*Turns the letter over and reads the address*) "To His Excellency, Noble Sir, Ivan Vasilevich Tryapichkin, St. Petersburg, Post-Office Street, number 97, turning toward the yard on the third floor, on the right."

ONE OF THE LADIES. What an unexpected reprimand!

MAYOR. When he cuts your throat he cuts it! I'm dead, dead, completely dead! I don't see a thing. I see a whole lot of pigs' snouts instead of faces; but nothing else . . . Catch him, bring him back! (*Waves his hand*)

POSTMASTER. How can you catch him! As if on purpose I ordered the stationmaster to supply the very best troika, and the devil himself made me send the order on ahead.

KOROBKIN'S WIFE. Now, *there* is an extraordinary mess!

AMMOS FYODOROVICH. But I must admit, God damn it, ladies and gentlemen, he borrowed three hundred rubles from me!

ARTEMY FILIPOVICH. And three hundred rubles from me.

POSTMASTER (*sighs*). Oh! And three hundred from me.

BOBCHINSKY. From Pyotr Ivanovich and me sixty-five in bills. Yes, sir.

AMMOS FYODOROVICH (*spreading his arms in perplexity*). How's it possible, gentlemen? How come we really made such a big mistake?

MAYOR (*pounds his forehead*). How *did* I? Really how did *I?* damned old fool! Lost my wits, stupid old goat that I am! . . . Thirty years in the service; not a merchant, not a contractor could pull it off; I played swindlers off against swindlers, such old foxes and cheaters they were all set to rob the whole world, but I kept hooking them; cheated three governors! what governors! (*Waves his hand in disgust*) There's no point in talking about governors!

ANNA ANDREYEVNA. But this just can't be, Antosha: he promised to marry Mashenka . . .

MAYOR (*angrily*). He promised! Thumbed his nose—that's "he promised" for you! Rubbing it in with this promise!

(*In a frenzy*) Just look, look, all you world, all Christianity, all of you just look how the Mayor's been made a fool of! He's been made a fool, a fool, the old bastard! (*Threatens himself with his fist*) Hey you, fat-face! You thought a drip, a rag, was a big shot! And here he's now pouring it out everywhere all along the road, in the fastest troika! He'll spread the story around the world. It's not enough you're a laughingstock—some line-stuffer, some paper-waster will put you in a comedy. That's what's insulting: he won't spare rank or title and everybody'll show their teeth and pound their palms. What're you laughing for? You're laughing at yourselves! Oh, you! (*Stamps his feet furiously on the floor*) I'd give it good to all these paper-wasters! oh! line-stuffers, damned liberals! seed of the devil! I'd tie you all up in a bundle, soak you all in flour, and go stuff you in the devil's hat! (*Gestures with his fist and pounds his heel on the floor. After a brief silence:*) I still haven't come to. Here's really how God when he wants to punish you takes away your sense first. So, what was there in this weathercock that resembled an inspector general? There was nothing. He wasn't even half your little finger's worth of resemblance—and suddenly everybody shouts: inspector general! Now, who was the first who let out he was an inspector general? Answer me.

ARTEMY FILIPOVICH (*spreading his arms*). I can't explain how it happened for the life of me. As if some kind of fog knocked us out, the devil mixed us up.

AMMOS FYODOROVICH. Now who let it out, there's who let it out: these heroes! (*Points to* DOBCHINSKY *and* BOBCHINSKY)

BOBCHINSKY. Honestly, not me, I didn't even think . . .

DOBCHINSKY. I didn't think anything, absolutely nothing . . .

ARTEMY FILIPOVICH. Of course, it was you!

LUKA LUKICH. Goes without saying. Ran in like madmen from the tavern: "He's come, he's come and he doesn't pay for anything . . ." You found a big wig!

MAYOR. Naturally, you! Town gossips, damned liars!

ARTEMY FILIPOVICH. The hell with you with your inspector general and your stories.

MAYOR. You just scour the town, get everyone embarrassed, you damned chatterboxes, sow scandal, you short-tailed magpies.

AMMOS FYODOROVICH. Damned dabblers!

LUKA LUKICH. Fools!

ARTEMY FILIPOVICH. Potbellied wisps!

(*All move back from them.*)

BOBCHINSKY. Honest to God, it wasn't me, it was Pyotr Ivanovich.

DOBCHINSKY. Ah, no, Pyotr Ivanovich, you know you were the first to . . .

BOBCHINSKY. Now not a bit; you were first.

(*A Gendarme enters.*)

GENDARME. The inspector who has just arrived from Petersburg by special command demands your presence immediately. He has stopped at the hotel.

(*The words astound everyone, like thunder. A sound of amazement flies from all the ladies' lips unanimously; the whole group, having suddenly shifted its position, remains petrified.*)

THE PANTOMIME

The Mayor in the middle in the form of a pillar with outspread arms and his head thrown back. On his right: his wife and daughter with their whole bodies reaching toward him; behind them the Postmaster, turned into a question mark, facing the audience; behind him Luka Lukich, bewildered in the most innocent way; behind him on the very edge of the stage, three ladies, guests, leaning on each other with the most satiric expression on their faces, facing directly toward the Mayor's family. On the Mayor's left: Zemlyanika, tilting his head somewhat to the side, as if listening to something; behind him the Judge, with his arms spread wide, moving his lips as if he wanted to whistle or say: "Now here we go round again!" Behind him Korobkin, turned to the audience with squinting eyes and a look of caustic reproach at the Mayor; behind him, on the very edge of the stage, Bobchinsky and Dobchinsky with their hands reaching out toward each other, gaping mouths and eyes popped out at each other. The other guests stand simply like statues. For almost a minute and a half the petrified group keeps this position. The curtain falls.

The Storm

A DRAMA IN

FIVE ACTS

Aleksandr Nikolayevich Ostrovsky

DRAMATIS PERSONAE

All the characters except Boris are dressed in the Russian fashion.
—[Author's note]

Savel Prokofyevich Dikòi, a merchant, an important figure in the town
Boris Grigoryevich, his nephew, a young man, well educated
Marfa Ignatyevna Kabanova (Kabanikha), a rich merchant's widow
Tikhon Ivanych Kabanov, her son
Katerina, his wife
Varvara, Tikhon's sister
Kuligin, a bourgeois, self-taught watchmaker seeking the perpetuum-mobile
Vanya Kudryash, a young man, Dikòi's clerk
Shapkin, a bourgeois
Feklusha, an itinerant holy woman
Glasha, a maid in the Kabanov's house
The Lady with two valets, an old woman of seventy, half-crazy
Townspeople of both sexes

The action takes place in the town of Kalinovo on the Volga in summer. Ten days elapse between the third and fourth acts.

A NOTE ON THE PLAY

The Storm was begun by Ostrovsky in July, 1859, and finished less than three months later, on October 9. That same month he read it to the actors of the Maly Theater in Moscow. Their committee on scripts approved it for performance on the twenty-fourth; the censor passed it on October 31; and the première occurred on November 16, 1859, in the Maly Theater with Nikulina-Kositskaya in the role of Katerina. License to publish the play was granted on December 9, and the play appeared in the magazine *Biblioteka dlya chteniya*, No. 1, 1860. In March, 1860, it was published separately, and it has been regularly performed and reprinted ever since. At first received hostilely by conservatives but warmly by liberals, the play has come to be considered Ostrovsky's greatest work and a fixture in the Russian classical repertoire.

The text of the play translated here is that of the second edition of Ostrovsky's collected works, issued during his lifetime, found in A. N. Ostrovsky, *Sochineniya*, vol. III, St. Petersburg, 1867, and, reprinted, in A. N. Ostrovsky, *Polnoe sobranie sochinenii*, vol. II, Moscow, 1950.

ACT I

A public garden high on the banks of the Volga; a view of the village with its church beyond the Volga; two benches and some bushes on stage.

KULIGIN *is sitting on a bench and looking across the river,* KUDRYASH *and* SHAPKIN *are walking around.*

KULIGIN (*sings*). "Flat in the middle of the valley, on the smooth and level height—" (*Stops singing*) Marvelous, truly got to admit it's marvelous! Kudryash! Here, now, my friend, I've been looking across the Volga every day some fifty years and I still can't look at it enough.

KUDRYASH. What about it?

KULIGIN. An unusual view! Beautiful! You feel happy all over.

KUDRYASH. What do you mean!

KULIGIN. Exciting! And you with your "what do you mean"! You've got used to it, or else you don't understand how much beauty's spread through nature.

KUDRYASH. But that's hardly something to talk to you about! You're our old queer chemist.

KULIGIN. Mechanic, a self-taught mechanic.

KUDRYASH. It's all the same.

(*Silence.*)

KULIGIN (*pointing to one side*). Look there, Kudryash my friend, who's that there waving his arms so?

KUDRYASH. That? That's Dikòi giving his nephew hell.

KULIGIN. Chose the right place!

KUDRYASH. He's got a place everywhere. He doesn't care about anyone. Boris Grigorich fell into his hands and so he's riding him all the time.

SHAPKIN. You'll never find such a curser as our own Savel Prokofich! He'll take a man apart for nothing.

KUDRYASH. A sharp man!

SHAPKIN. Kabanikha's all right, too!

KUDRYASH. Yeh, but she, at least, does it all pretending repect, but he's like if he just got out of prison.

SHAPKIN. No one can quiet him down, so he goes right on fighting!

KUDRYASH. We haven't got many fellows who'd do it with me, or we'd teach him to stop his dirty tricks.

SHAPKIN. And what would you do?

KUDRYASH. Give him a good scare.

SHAPKIN. How?

KUDRYASH. Four or five of us together would give him a good talking-to all alone in an alleyway some place so he'd come to be as quiet as a lamb. He wouldn't say a word to anyone about what we taught him, though, but just go on his way and look back over his shoulder.

SHAPKIN. It wasn't for nothing he wanted to send you off to the army.

KUDRYASH. Wanted to, but he didn't, so it makes no difference, doesn't matter. He won't send me off, 'cause he smells with that big nose of his that I won't sell my head cheap. He frightens you, but I know how to talk to him.

SHAPKIN. Since when?

KUDRYASH. What do you mean, since when? I'm considered vulgar. What else's he keeping me on for? Must be he needs me. So, therefore, I'm not afraid of him, but let him be afraid of me.

SHAPKIN. As if he wouldn't give you hell.

KUDRYASH. How can he help it? He can't live without doing it. But I don't give in, either. He says one word, and I say ten. He spits and goes on. No, I'm not going to be going down on my knees for him.

KULIGIN. What, follow his example! It's better to be patient.

KUDRYASH. So, if you're so smart, you teach him civility first and then us! It's a shame his daughters are all teen-agers, not one of them's grown up.

SHAPKIN. What if they were?

KUDRYASH. I'd play up to him. I'm a terrible man with the women!

(DIKÒI *and* BORIS *go by.* KULIGIN *tips his cap.*)

SHAPKIN (*to* KUDRYASH). Let's go over here, or he'll really latch on to us.

(*They go aside.* DIKÒI *and* BORIS *enter.*)

DIKÒI. You came here just to twiddle your thumbs, didn't you? You sponger! The hell with you!

BORIS. It's a holiday. What's there to do at home?

DIKÒI. You can find something if you want to. Told you once, told you twice: don't you dare let me see you out. Still set on it, hey? Haven't got enough room, hey? No matter where a man goes, there you are. Damn you! What're you standing around like a statue for, hey? Someone talking to you or not?

BORIS. And I'm listening, what more do you want?

DIKÒI (*looking hard at* BORIS). Go to hell! I'm not going to talk to you any more, you double-talking Jesuit. (*Leaving*) What a pain in the neck! (*Spits and goes out*)

(KULIGIN, KUDRYASH, *and* SHAPKIN *return.*)

KULIGIN. What do you have to do with him, sir? We can't understand at all. Why would you want to live with him and take his abuse?

BORIS. Want to, Kuligin! I have no choice.

KULIGIN. Why have you no choice, sir, if I may ask you? Please tell us, sir, if you can.

BORIS. Why not? You knew our grandmother, Anfisa Mikhailovna?

KULIGIN. Why sure!

KUDRYASH. Who didn't?

BORIS. She didn't like it that my father married a noblewoman. On account of which mother and father lived in Moscow. Mother used to tell me she couldn't get used to her relatives for three days, it all seemed so strange to her.

KULIGIN. Strange isn't all! What can I say! One must have gotten really accustomed, sir.

BORIS. Our parents brought us up in Moscow well, spared nothing for us. Sent me to the Academy of Commerce and my sister to boarding school, but then they both suddenly died during an epidemic of cholera, and my sister and I were left orphans. Next we heard that our grandmother here had died, too, and had left a will that said our uncle should pay us the share due us when we reach majority, but on the condition—

KULIGIN. What condition, sir?

BORIS. That we're respectful to him.

KULIGIN. That means, sir, you'll never see your inheritance.

BORIS. That's not the half of it, Kuligin. He'll first make all kinds of trouble for us, curse us out in every way possible as much as he feels like, and it'll still end up by his giving us nothing or, you know, some little thing. And he'll start saying, too, that he gave it out of charity, that even that wasn't coming to us.

KUDRYASH. That's the way the merchants do things. And then, even if you were respectful to him, who's going to prevent his saying that you weren't?

BORIS. That's it. Even now, already, every so often, he says: "I have my own children; why should I give money away to others'? That way I must slight my own!"

KULIGIN. That means, sir, that things're going badly for you.

BORIS. If only I were alone, it wouldn't matter! I'd drop everything and go away. But that'd be hard on my sister. He even used to write for her, but my mother's relatives didn't let her go, wrote that she was sick. What kind of a life would she have had here?—it's frightening to think of it.

KUDRYASH. That goes without saying. As if they had any manners!

KULIGIN. How do you get on in his house, sir—what's your position?

BORIS. Why, none. "Stay with me," he says, "do what you're told, and take what I give you." That is, at the end of a year he'll figure it out the way he feels.

KUDRYASH. That's the way he does things. Not one of us dares pipe up about our wages or he'd curse the world down to its foundations. "How do you know," he says, "what I have on my mind? No chance your knowing what goes on inside me! And maybe I'll take it into my head to give you five thousand." Now you try to talk to him! Only, in all his life so far he hasn't once gotten into such a frame of mind.

KULIGIN. What can you do, sir? You have to try to play up to him somehow.

BORIS. That's the point, Kuligin, that it's impossible. Even his own family can't possibly please him, never mind someone like me!

KUDRYASH. Who's going to please him as long as his whole life is one round of cursing after another? And mostly because of money; not one account can be settled without argument. The other fellow's glad to give in just to get free of it all. And what trouble there is if somebody crosses him in the morning. He picks on everybody all day long.

BORIS. Every morning my aunt with tears in her eyes begs

everybody: "My dears, don't get him angry! Darlings, don't get him angry!"

KUDRYASH. Not a chance of saving yourself! If he happens to go to the market, it's the end! He curses out all the peasants! And even if you're willing to take a loss, still you can't avoid the swearing. And then he's at it the rest of the day.

SHAPKIN. There's just one word for him: warrior!

KUDRYASH. And what a warrior!

BORIS. And what trouble there is when he's affronted by someone he doesn't dare give hell to; then people in his house—hang on!

KUDRYASH. My God! What a joke it was! One day a hussar gave him hell when he was on the ferry on the Volga. What he didn't do!

BORIS. And in the house afterwards! For two weeks after that everybody hid in the attic and the larders.

(*Several figures go by at the back of the stage.*)

KULIGIN. What's happening? Are they already out of vespers?

KUDRYASH. Come on, Shapkin, let's go get a drink! What're we standing here for?

(*They bow and leave.*)

BORIS. Ah, Kuligin, it's very, very hard for me here, not being used to it! Everyone looks at me somehow strangely, as if I were superfluous here, as if I were bothering them. I don't know the local customs. I know that all this is ours, is Russian—but still I just can't get used to it.

KULIGIN. And you never will, sir.

BORIS. Why not?

KULIGIN. The way people live in our town, sir, is savage. Among the merchants, sir, you'll never see anything but crudeness and naked poverty. And we can never, sir, break through this shell! Because by honest work we can never earn more than our daily bread. And whoever has money, sir, tries to enslave the poor in order to pile up even more money through their honest labor. Do you know what your uncle, Savel Prokofich, answered the mayor? Some peasants went to the mayor to complain that he hadn't paid up a single one of them honestly. The mayor began to tell him: "Listen," he says, "Savel Prokofich, you pay your peasants properly. They come complaining to me every day!" Your uncle slapped the mayor on the shoulder and said: "Is it worth our while, your excellency, for you and me to be talking about such trifles? A lot of people pass through my hands in the course of a year. Understand me now: if I don't pay each of them just a little kopek apiece, for me it means thousands saved, so it works out fine for me!" That's how it was, sir! But among themselves, sir, how they live! They undercut each other's business, not so much for profit as out of envy. They war on each other; they lure drunken clerks into their tall mansions, such clerks, sir, there's nothing human about their looks at all, their human appearance is gone. And for a little handout these clerks scribble them out on official stationery malicious intrigues against their relatives and neighbors. And then the trial and procedures begin, sir, and there's no end to the torment. There's trial after trial here, and they even take it to the provincial capital, where they're already waiting for them and clapping their hands in joy. But it's easier said than done: they lead them on, and on, and drag it out and out; and they're even delighted with all this delay, which was just what they wanted. "Myself," they say, "I'll lose all my money, but it'll cost him his last kopek, too." I wanted to try to express all this in verse . . .

BORIS. You can write poetry?

KULIGIN. In the old style, sir. I've read a good deal of Lomonosov, Derzhavin . . . Lomonosov was quite a man, a discoverer of the natural world . . . And, you know, he, too, came from among us, from just plain people.

BORIS. You ought to write it down. It would be interesting.

KULIGIN. If I can do it, sir! I'll be eaten alive for it! As it is, sir, I get it in the neck for talking so much; but I can't help it. I like to talk about one thing and another. I still was meaning to tell you, sir, about family life here, but some other time. You'd be interested to hear.

(*Enter* FEKLUSHA *and another woman.*)

FEKLUSHA. Splendor, my dear, splendor! Glorious beauty! What more can you say! You live in the promised land! And the merchant class are pious people, a people endowed with many virtues! With generosity and great charity! I'm so pleased, my dear, pleased all through. For all we received may their bounty increase, and especially the Kabanovs' house.

(*They go out.*)

BORIS. The Kabanovs'?

KULIGIN. A terrible hypocrite, sir. She gives presents to beggars but has completely crushed the people in her own house. (*Silence*) If only, sir, I could find the perpetuum-mobile!

BORIS. What would you do?

KULIGIN. What not, sir! The English will give a million, you know. I would use all the money for the people, for public support. You have to give work to the merchants. Otherwise you have hands and nothing to work on.

BORIS. And you really hope to find the perpetuum-mobile?

KULIGIN. Absolutely, sir! Only have to raise some money for models now. Good-bye, sir. (*Goes out*)

BORIS (*alone*). It would be a shame to disillusion him! What a good man! Dreams his dream and is happy. But, it seems, there's nothing I can do about wasting my youth in this hole. I already go around completely dead, and my head is getting filled with more and more nonsense. What it's come to! Have I got to start being tender? At bay, outdone, on top of it all I even foolishly took it into my head to fall in love. With who! With a woman I can never even get a chance to talk to. (*Silence*) And still I can't get her out of my head for love or money. There she is! She and her husband, and the mother-in-law with them! Am I not a fool! Take a peek from around the corner and then head home. (*Goes out*)

(KABANOVA, KABANOV, KATERINA *and* VARVARA *enter.*)

KABANOVA. If you want to obey your mother, then, as soon as you get there, you do what I told you.

KABANOV. But how could I disobey you, Mama!

KABANOVA. Elders aren't much respected nowadays.

VARVARA (*to herself*). How *not* do what you say!

KABANOV. I don't think, Mama, I've ever made a move against your will.

KABANOVA. I would believe you, my dear, if I hadn't seen and heard for myself what sort of respect parents get now from their children! We just have to remember how many troubles mothers endure from their children.

KABANOV. Mama, I . . .

KABANOVA. If the mother sometimes says something insulting to your pride, why, I think, you still have to put up with it. What do you think?

KABANOV. But, Mama, when haven't I put up with it from you?

KABANOVA. Your mother is old and slow-witted, but you young people are clever and you mustn't expect so much from us fools.

KABANOV (*sighing, aside*). O, Lord! (*To his mother*) Could we even dare think of it, Mama!

KABANOVA. But, you know, sometimes parents are strict with you out of love, give you scoldings out of love, always trying to teach you what's good. Well, that's not much liked nowadays. And the children go spreading it to everyone their mother's a grumbler, that their mother's always after them worrying them to death. And, the Lord save us, some little word doesn't please the daughter-in-law and it's already going around that the mother-in-law has completely crushed her.

KABANOV. Really, Mama, who's talking about you?

KABANOVA. Haven't heard a thing, my dear, haven't heard a thing, don't want to tell stories. If I had heard, my dear, why then I'd hardly be talking to you like this. (*Sighs*) Ah, what burdens we have! And the next thing you know you sin again! The conversation draws you in, and you get angry, you sin. No, my dear, say what you want about me. You can never prevent a person from talking; what they don't dare say to your face they say behind your back.

KABANOV. May the tongue shrivel . . .

KABANOVA. Stop, stop, don't swear! It's a sin! I've long ago noticed that your wife is dearer to you than your mother. Ever since you got married, I haven't felt your old love for me.

KABANOV. Mama, what makes you feel this?

KABANOVA. Everything, my dear! What a mother doesn't see with her eyes she can feel with her heart, for her heart knows. But if it's your wife's taking you from me, now, I don't know.

KABANOV. But no, Mama! For goodness sake!

KATERINA. For me, Mama, you're just the same as my own mother, and Tikhon, too, loves you.

KABANOVA. You'd do well to keep quiet, I think, until you're asked something. Don't take his part, dear; I won't insult him, don't worry! He's my son, too; don't you forget it! Why did you jump forward to make a fuss in front of me? So I would see, hey, how much you love your husband? I know, I know, you show this off in front of everyone.

VARVARA (*to herself*). What a place she picked for her lecture.

KATERINA. You're talking about me unfairly, Mama. Whether in front of people or not, I'm still the same, and I'm not showing off anything about myself.

KABANOVA. But I didn't want to talk about you, and here we've started.

KATERINA. Even if we have, what are you insulting me for?

KABANOVA. What a fine-feathered hen! Already insulted!

KATERINA. Nobody likes to have to listen to false accusations!

KABANOVA. I know, I know my words don't sit well with you, but what can I do, I'm no stranger to you, my heart aches for you. I saw long ago you'd like to be free. Well, so, wait a while, you'll live freely when I'm gone. And then you can do what you want, when there are no more elders over you. And maybe you'll think of me.

KABANOV. But, Mama, we pray to God for you day and night, that God will give you, Mama, health and every kind of blessing and success in business.

KABANOVA. Stop it, enough, please. Perhaps you loved your mother when you were unmarried. What am I to you now? You have a young wife.

KABANOV. One doesn't interfere with the other: my wife is one thing, and the respect I have for my mother is something else.

KABANOVA. So, will you exchange your wife for your mother? I won't believe that for a moment.

KABANOV. But what should I change for? I love them both.

KABANOVA. Oh, all right, spread it thick! I see I'm already in your way.

KABANOV. Think what you want; you can do as you please. Only I don't know why I ever was born such an unfortunate man never to be able to please you.

KABANOVA. What are you pretending to be an orphan for? What are you whimpering about? What kind of a husband are you? Look at yourself! Is your wife going to have any fear of you after this?

KABANOV. What should she be afraid for? It's enough for me that she loves me.

KABANOVA. What do you mean be afraid for! What do you mean be afraid for! Are you mad? If she has no fear of you, so much the less she'll have of me. And then what kind of order will there be in the house? After all, I believe, you're living with her in lawful marriage. Or, to your way of thinking, doesn't lawful marriage mean anything? If you're harboring such absurd thoughts in your head, you'd better not be chattering away in front of your sister, in front of a young girl; she, too, has to get married. She'll get an earful of your chatter, and then afterwards her husband'll thank us a lot for the lesson. You see the way you still take things, and you keep wanting to live independently.

KABANOV. But, Mama, I don't want to live independently. What would I live independently for!

KABANOVA. So, the way you think, you still have to be all tenderness to your wife? And not raise your voice at her, or threaten her?

KABANOV. But, Mama, I . . .

KABANOVA (*heatedly*). Even if she takes a lover! Well? This, too, maybe, the way you think, isn't anything? Well? Say something!

KABANOV. But, Mama, honest to God . . .

KABANOVA (*with complete composure*). Fool! (*Sighs*) How can you talk to a fool! It's just a waste of time. (*Silence*) I'm going home.

KABANOV. We're going right away, too, only we'll walk along the avenue once or twice more.

KABANOVA. As you want, only be sure I don't have to wait for you! You know I don't like that!

KABANOV. Yes, Mama, God forbid!

KABANOVA. That's right! (*Goes out*)

KABANOV. There you are, that's what I always get from Mama, thanks to you. That's what my life's like!

KATERINA. How is it my fault?

KABANOV. Whose fault it is I don't really know.

VARVARA. How could you know!

KABANOV. And she kept insisting all the time: "Get married, get married, I want to see you married!" But now she's always nagging and after me all the time—all thanks to you.

VARVARA. It's hardly her fault! Your mother pounces on her, and then you, too. And you keep saying you love your wife. I'm sick and tired of seeing you. (*Turns away*)

KABANOV. No use talking about it! What can I do?

VARVARA. Know what you have to do—keep quiet, if you can't do anything better. What are you standing around for, shifting from one foot to the other? I can see by the look in your eyes you've got something on your mind.

KABANOV. Well, what?

VARVARA. It's obvious what. You want to go over to Savel Prokofich's and have a drink with him. Isn't that right?

KABANOV. You guessed it, friend.

KATERINA. Come back soon, Tisha, or Mama will get mad at us again.

VARVARA. You be quick, in fact, or you know what!

KABANOV. I certainly do!

VARVARA. We haven't got any great desire to have to take a whole lot of abuse on account of you.

KABANOV. I'll just be a second. Wait for me! (*Goes out*)

KATERINA. So, Varya, you feel sorry for me?

VARVARA (*looking aside*). Of course, it's pitiful.

KATERINA. So you like me? (*Kisses her warmly*)

VARVARA. Why shouldn't I like you?

KATERINA. Thank you! You're such a nice person; myself, I like you terrifically. (*Silence*) You know what I thought of?

VARVARA. What?

KATERINA. Why don't people fly?

VARVARA. I don't understand what you're talking about.

KATERINA. I mean: why don't people fly like birds? You know, sometimes I think I am a bird. When you stand on a mountain, you long to fly. I'd take a running jump like this, lift my arms, and fly. Might try it now? (*Is about to run*)

VARVARA. What are you making up?

KATERINA (*sighing*). How lithe I was! Here among you I've completely lost it.

VARVARA. You think I don't see it?

KATERINA. What I was like! I lived without longing for anything, like a bird in the sky. Mama doted on me, dressed me up like a doll and didn't make me work; whatever I used to want to do I did. You know how I used to live as a girl? Wait, I'll tell you. I used to get up early; if it was summer, I'd go down to the spring, get washed, carry a pail of water back with me and water all, all the flowers in the house. I used to have lots and lots of flowers. And then Mama and I would go to church, and all the holy women, too—our house used to be full of holy women and pilgrims. And we'd come back from church and sit down to some work, usually some kind of fine embroidery, and the holy women would start telling about where they'd been, what they'd seen, different ways of life, or they'd sing verses. That's how the time would pass until dinner. Then the old women would lie down to take a nap and I'd take a walk in the garden. Then to vespers, and in the evening again more stories and songs. How good it was!

VARVARA. It was the same with us, you know.

KATERINA. But here everything is done under compulsion. And I liked going to church terrifically! It was just as if I were entering Heaven, and I didn't see anyone, and didn't count the time, and didn't even hear when the service was over. Just as if it all took only a second. Mama used to say that everyone used to look at me and wonder what was going on! But you know: on a sunny day such a bright shaft of light used to fall from the cupola and the smoke used to hover in the column like clouds, I used to imagine I saw angels flying in the column and singing. And when I was a girl I used to get up at night—we, too, had icon-lamps burning everywhere—and pray somewhere in a corner until morning. Or I'd go out into the garden early in the morning, when the sun was just beginning to come up, and fall on my knees and pray and cry, not knowing myself what I was praying for or what I was crying about, and that's the way they'd find me. And what I prayed for then, what I asked for, I don't know; I didn't need anything, I had enough of everything. And what dreams I had, Varenka, what dreams! Either golden temples or some kind of extraordinary gardens, and invisible voices would be singing all the time, and it would smell of cypress, and the mountains and trees didn't seem like ordinary ones but the way they are drawn in icons. It was as if I was flying, flying through the air. And even now I sometimes dream, but rarely, and not that.

VARVARA. What?

KATERINA (*after a pause*). I'm going to die soon.

VARVARA. Stop it, what are you talking about!

KATERINA. No, I know I'm going to die. Oh, my dear, something evil is happening to me, some kind of wonder! Nothing like it has ever happened to me before. There's something extraordinary inside me. As if I were beginning life all over again, or . . . I really don't know.

VARVARA. What kind of thing's happening to you?

KATERINA (*takes her by the hand*). It's something, Varya, that seems somehow sinful! Such fear has come over me, such fear has come over me! As if I were standing on the edge of an abyss and someone were pushing me over and there's nothing for me to hold on to. (*Holds her head with her hand*)

VARVARA. What's wrong with you? Are you all right?

KATERINA. I'm all right . . . It would be better if I were sick, for it's no good this way. A kind of wild dream is creeping into my head. And I can't get away from it. I start to think—I can't collect my thoughts at all; to pray—and I can't get through the prayer at all. I mumble the words with my tongue, but my mind's on something else altogether: as if the devil himself were whispering in my ear all the time about such awful things. And I imagine such things I get feeling really guilty. What's happening to me? Some kind of trouble is coming! I can't sleep at night, Varya; I keep thinking I hear some kind of whisper all the time: someone is ever so tenderly talking to me, as if fondling me the way a pigeon coos. I don't dream any more, Varya, like before, of the heavenly trees and mountains; but it's as if someone were embracing me passionately, hotly, and taking me somewhere, and I'm going after him, going . . .

VARVARA. Yes?

KATERINA. But what am I telling you all this for? You're a girl.

VARVARA (*looking around*). Say it all! I'm worse than you.

KATERINA. What can I say! I'm ashamed.

VARVARA. Say what you want, there's nothing to fear.

KATERINA. It's getting so unbearable for me, so unbearable at home, I could run away. And the thought comes over me that, if I were free, I'd sail down the Volga now in a boat, singing, or in a fine troika, in the arms. . . .

VARVARA. As long as it's not your husband.

KATERINA. How do you know?

VARVARA. How can I help it?

KATERINA. Oh, Varya, the thought is sinful! How much I've cried, and what I haven't already done to myself! There's no way I can get away from this sin. There's no place to go. Isn't it bad, isn't it a terrible sin, Varenka, that I love someone else?

VARVARA. Who am I to judge you? I have my sins.

KATERINA. What can I do? I haven't the strength. Where can I go? I'll do something to myself out of despair!

VARVARA. What are you talking about! What's got into you! Wait a little, my brother'll leave tomorrow, we'll think of something; perhaps it'll even be possible for you to see each other.

KATERINA. No, no, we mustn't! What are you talking about! What are you talking about! God forbid!

VARVARA. What are you so scared of?

KATERINA. If I meet him just once, I'll run out of the house and won't go home for anything in the world.

VARVARA. Wait a little, and then we'll see.

KATERINA. No, no, don't talk to me about it, I don't want to listen.

VARVARA. How can you want to waste away! Even if you die of despair, nobody's going to feel sorry for you! So, wait it out. What's the need of torturing yourself so!

(THE LADY *enters with a cane and followed by two valets in tricornered hats.*)

THE LADY. Well, my beauties? What are you doing here? Waiting for your young men, your beaux? Having a good time? A good time? Your beauty make you happy? That's where beauty takes you. (*Points to the Volga*) There, there, into the dark pool itself. (VARVARA *smiles*) What are you laughing for? Don't you be happy! (*Stamps her cane*) You all will burn in unquenchable fire. You all will boil in inextinguishable pitch! (*Going*) There, there, that's where beauty takes you. (*Exits*)

KATERINA. Oh, how she scared me—I'm all trembling, as if she prophesied something about me.

VARVARA. I hope you get it in the neck, you old hag!

KATERINA. What did she say that for? What did she say?

VARVARA. Nonsense every bit. A lot we needed to hear the nonsense she says. She prophesies like that to everyone. She went about sinning all her life from the time she was young. Ask anyone what's said about her! Now she's afraid of dying. What she's afraid of herself she scares others with. Even all the little boys in town hide from her—she threatens them with her cane and shouts (*imitating her*): "You all will burn in fire!"

KATERINA (*shutting her eyes*). Ah, ah, stop! My heart's sinking.

VARVARA. She isn't something to be afraid of! An old crazy woman . . .

KATERINA. I'm afraid, terrifically afraid. She still seems to be standing in front of me.

(*Silence.*)

VARVARA (*looking around*). Why doesn't my brother come; look, there's a storm coming.

KATERINA (*in terror*). A storm! Let's run home! Quickly!

VARVARA. What's wrong with you, you out of your mind?! How can you show up at home without my brother?

KATERINA. No, we must go home, go home. God be with him!

VARVARA. But you're already very afraid and the storm's still a long way off.

KATERINA. Well, if it's far away, let's wait a bit, if you want, but really it would be better to go. We'd better go!

VARVARA. But you know if there's going to be anything, you won't hide from it at home either.

KATERINA. Still it would be better, a lot more peaceful: at home I can pray to the icons and to God!

VARVARA. I didn't know you were so afraid of storms. I'm not afraid.

KATERINA. How can you not be afraid, child! Everyone must be afraid. It's not terrible that it might kill you but that death will suddenly catch you as you are with all your sins, with all your evil thoughts. I'm not terrified of dying, but when I think that I will suddenly appear before God just the way I am now in front of you, after all we've said—that's what is terrifying! What's going on in my head! What sinfulness! It's terrible to say it! (*Thunder*) Ah! (KABANOV *enters.*)

VARVARA. Here comes my brother. (*To* KABANOV) Run faster! (*Thunder.*)

KATERINA. Oh! Faster, faster!

ACT II

A room in the KABANOVS' *house.* GLASHA *puts clothes in bundles;* FEKLUSHA *enters.*

FEKLUSHA. Dear girl, you're always at work! What're you doing, dear?

GLASHA. Getting the master ready for the road.

FEKLUSHA. Why, is he going somewhere, our fair boy?

GLASHA. He is.

FEKLUSHA. Going for long, dear?

GLASHA. No, not for long.

FEKLUSHA. Well, may he have a fine journey! What, is the mistress going to wail or not?

GLASHA. I don't know how to tell.

FEKLUSHA. Has she before?

GLASHA. I never heard her.

FEKLUSHA. I really like to hear it, dear, when someone wails good! (*Silence*) And you, girl, keep your eye on a poor woman so she don't filch something.

GLASHA. Whoever can make you all out, you're always slandering each other. How come you don't get on peaceably? Seems you can't get on at all among us, you wanderers, but you're all the time arguing and bickering. You aren't afraid of sin at all.

FEKLUSHA. Can't get on, dear, without sin; we live in this world. Now let me tell you, dear: just one devil upsets any one of you, you simple people, but we, we wandering people, we get six against us, or twelve, and then we have to fight them all down. It's tough, dear!

GLASHA. What do you get so many for?

FEKLUSHA. That, dear, is what the devil does out of hatred against us, 'cause we lead such a righteous life. But, dear, I'm no cantankerous fool, that's not one of my sins. I have got one sin, though, it's true; I know what it is myself. I love to eat sweets. Well, so what! God punishes my weakness.

GLASHA. But, Feklusha, have you been wandering far?

FEKLUSHA. No, dear. On account of my weakness I ain't travelled far. But as for hearing things—I've heard a lot.

They say there are such lands, dear girl, where there's no Orthodox tsars but sultans rule the earth. In one land the Turkish sultan Mahnut sits on the throne and in the next, the Persian sultan Mahnut; and they make judgments, dear, over all the people and no matter what they judge, it's all unjust. And they can't, dear, judge one thing righteously, they got such limitations on them. Our law is righteous, but theirs, dear, is unrighteous. It comes out one way according to our law, but according to theirs just the opposite. And all their judges in their countries are all unrighteous, too; so, dear, they address them in their requests: "Judge me, unrighteous judge!" And then there's also a land where all the people have heads like dogs.

GLASHA. How come, like dogs?

FEKLUSHA. For infidelity. I'm off, my dear, I'll go around among the merchants, see if they haven't got something for a poor woman. Good-bye for the while!

GLASHA. Good-bye. (FEKLUSHA *goes out*) Really, what lands there are! What miracles, what miracles there are in this world! But here we sit and don't know nothing. It's a good thing that there are these good people; 'cause then you hear what's going on in the wide world; or else we'd all die fools. (KATERINA *and* VARVARA *enter.*)

VARVARA (*to* GLASHA). Put the bundles in the cart, the horses have come. (*To* KATERINA) They married you off young, you didn't have a chance to have a good time as a girl; so, you see, your heart isn't tired out yet.

(GLASHA *goes out.*)

KATERINA. And it never will be.

VARVARA. Why?

KATERINA. That's the way I was born, with a passionate nature! I was barely six, no more, when I did something really! I got offended by something at home, and it was close to nighttime and already dark. I ran out to the Volga, jumped in a boat and pushed off from the shore. They found me the next morning more than ten versts away!

VARVARA. Well, and did the boys keep looking at you?

KATERINA. Indeed they did!

VARVARA. What about you? Really didn't you love one?

KATERINA. No, I just laughed.

VARVARA. But, of course, Katya, you don't love Tikhon.

KATERINA. What do you mean I don't! I feel very sorry for him!

VARVARA. No, you don't love him. If you feel sorry for him, you don't love him. And no reason to, to tell the truth. And there's no use your trying to hide your feelings from me! I long ago noticed that you love another man.

KATERINA (*in fright*). How did you notice?

VARVARA. How silly you talk! I'm hardly a little girl! Here's the first sign: as soon as you see him your whole expression changes. (KATERINA *looks down*) There's little . . .

KATERINA (*looking away*). Well, who?

VARVARA. But you yourself know, why should I say his name?

KATERINA. No, say it! Say his name!

VARVARA. Boris Grigorich.

KATERINA. It's him, Varenka, him! Only, Varenka, for God's sake . . .

VARVARA. Of course! You yourself be careful not to let it slip out somehow.

KATERINA. I don't know how to deceive; I can't conceal anything.

VARVARA. But you can't do otherwise. Just remember where you're living! Our whole house is based on deceit. I, too, wasn't a deceitful woman, but I learned to be when I had to. I was out walking yesterday and happened to see him, talked to him.

KATERINA (*after a short silence, looking down*). Well, so?

VARVARA. Told me to say hello to you. It's a shame, he says, there's no place to meet.

KATERINA (*lowering her head still further*). No place to meet! Besides, what for . . .

VARVARA. The other's so dull . . .

KATERINA. Don't talk to me about him; do me the favor, don't talk! I don't want to know him! I will love my husband. Tisha, my darling, I won't leave you for anyone! I didn't want to think about it, but you're getting me confused.

VARVARA. Then don't think. Who's making you?

KATERINA. You don't spare me anything! You say: Don't think; but you yourself remind me. Is it really I who want to think about him? What can I do if he won't go out of my head? No matter what I start thinking about, there he stands as if in front of me. I want to keep my feelings in, but there's no way I can. Do you know that last night again the devil caught me? You see, I was on my way out of the house.

VARVARA. You're such a queer one, God bless you! But the way I see it: do what you want, only so it's on the sly.

KATERINA. I don't want it that way. What's the good of it? I'd rather suffer as long as I can.

VARVARA. And when you can't, what will you do?

KATERINA. What will I do?

VARVARA. Yes, what will you do?

KATERINA. What I just feel like, that's what I'll do.

VARVARA. Do it, try it, and then they'll eat you alive here.

KATERINA. So what? I'll run away; indeed, that's the way I was.

VARVARA. Where'll you go? You're a married woman.

KATERINA. Oh, Varya, you don't know what I'm like! God forbid it, of course! But if I get sick to death of everything here, then nothing will hold me back. I'll throw myself out a window, I'll hurl myself into the Volga. I don't want to go on living here, and I won't, even if you cut me to pieces! (*Silence.*)

VARVARA. You know what, Katya! As soon as Tikhon has gone, let's sleep in the garden, in the pergola.

KATERINA. What for, Varya?

VARVARA. Isn't it all the same?

KATERINA. I'm afraid to spend the night in a strange place.

VARVARA. What's there to be afraid of? Glasha will be with us.

KATERINA. Still, it's sort of frightening! But, all right, I will.

VARVARA. I wouldn't have asked you, but Mama won't allow me to alone, and I have to.

KATERINA (*looking at her*). Why do you have to?

VARVARA (*laughing*). We'll tell each other's fortunes there.

KATERINA. You must be joking?

VARVARA. Sure, I'm joking. And why not?
(*Silence.*)

KATERINA. Where's Tikhon now?

VARVARA. What do you want him for?

KATERINA. Nothing, just wondering. I guess he'll be going soon.

VARVARA. He and Mama are sitting locked in her room together. She's grinding him down now, the way rust does iron.

KATERINA. What for?

VARVARA. No reason, just teaching him some sense. He'll be two weeks on the road, out of her sight! Judge for yourself! Her heart is still pining away because he gets around independently. So now she's loading him down with orders, each more fierce than the last, and then she'll lead him up to the icon and make him swear that he'll do everything exactly as he was told to.

KATERINA. And when he's on his own he's as if bound-and-tied.

VARVARA. What do you mean bound-and-tied! As soon as he's out, he starts drinking. Now he obeys her, but he's thinking, how can I get out of it quickest?

(KABANOVA *and* KABANOV *enter.*)

KABANOVA. Well, do you remember everything I told you? Be careful, remember! Tie a string on your finger!

KABANOV. I remember, Mama.

KABANOVA. Well, now everything's ready. The horses have come; I just have to say good-bye to you, and God bless you.

KABANOV. Yes, Mama, it's time.

KABANOVA. Well!

KABANOV. What would you like?

KABANOVA. What are you just standing there for, as if you didn't know what to do? Give your orders to your wife, what she's to do while you're gone.

(KATERINA *has lowered her eyes.*)

KABANOV. But she herself, I'm sure, knows what to do.

KABANOVA. Go through it again! Well, well, give your orders! So I can hear that you've given her orders! And then when you get back you can ask whether or not she's done everything.

KABANOV (*stepping in front of* KATERINA). Obey Mama, Katya!

KABANOVA. Tell her not to be rude to her mother-in-law.

KABANOV. Don't be rude!

KABANOVA. To honor and respect her mother-in-law like her own mother!

KABANOV. Honor and respect Mama, Katya, like your own mother!

KABANOVA. Not to sit with her hands in her lap like a lady!
KABANOV. Do some work while I'm gone.
KABANOVA. Not to stare out the window all the time!
KABANOV. But, Mama, when she . . .
KABANOVA. Come on, come on!
KABANOV. Don't look out the window!
KABANOVA. Not to keep looking at the young men while you're gone!
KABANOV. Now, really, Mama!
KABANOVA (*severely*). Don't try to be difficult! You must do everything your mother tells you. (*With a smile*) It's all a lot better when it's spelled out.
KABANOV (*embarrassed*). Don't look at other men!
(KATERINA *looks at him severely.*)
KABANOVA. Well, now have a talk between yourselves about whatever you need to. Let's go, Varvara.
(*They go out.* KATERINA *stands as if benumbed.*)
KABANOV. Katya! (*Silence*) Katya, you aren't cross at me?
KATERINA (*after a short silence, shaking her head*). No!
KABANOV. What are you this way for? Forgive me!
KATERINA (*still in the same position, slightly shaking her head*). God bless you! (*Covering her face with her hands*) She insulted me!
KABANOV. If you take everything to heart you'll soon have a stroke. What do you listen to her for! She's just got to keep talking! So let her, and you let it go in one ear and out the other! Well, good-bye, Katya!
KATERINA (*throwing herself on her husband's neck*). Tisha, don't go! For God's sake, don't go! Darling, I beg you!
KABANOV. Impossible, Katya. When Mama sends me, how can I not go?
KATERINA. Well, take me with you, take me!
KABANOV (*freeing himself from her embrace*). Impossible.
KATERINA. Why impossible, Tisha?
KABANOV. A lot of fun it would be to travel with you! The two of you have already turned me into a complete workhorse here. I don't see how to get away from it, and on top of it all you're inviting yourself to go with me.
KATERINA. Have you really lost your love for me?
KABANOV. No, I haven't; but for some kind of reason a man has to run away from any lovely bride! Think about it:

whatever I may be, I'm still a man. You see, if you've lived your life like this, why then you'll run away from your wife, too. Knowing now that for two weeks there won't be any storm over my head and these fetters won't be on my legs, what do I want a wife for?

KATERINA. How can I love you, when you say such things?

KABANOV. Words are words! What else am I supposed to say? Who knows what you're afraid of? Besides, you won't be alone, you'll be staying with Mama.

KATERINA. Don't talk to me about her, don't torture me! Ah, it's my bad luck, bad luck! (*Cries*) Where can a poor woman like me go? Who can I get to help me? Saints alive, I'm perishing!

KABANOV. Oh, stop it!

KATERINA (*goes up to her husband and presses close to him*). Tisha, darling, if you stay or if you take me with you, I'll love you so, I'll caress you so, my darling. (*Caresses him*)

KABANOV. I can't figure you out, Katya! One minute I can't get a word out of you, nevermind caresses. And the next you're chasing after me.

KATERINA. Tisha, who you are leaving me to! There'll be trouble while you're gone! There'll be trouble!

KABANOV. But it's impossible; there's nothing to be done about it.

KATERINA. Then do this! Make me swear some terrible oath . . .

KABANOV. What kind of oath?

KATERINA. Something like this: while you're gone not to dare be seen anywhere, nor to talk to any stranger, nor to see any, and not to dare think of anyone but you.

KABANOV. What's that for?

KATERINA. Set my soul at rest; do me such a favor!

KABANOV. How can you promise about yourself; there's lots of things that can enter your head!

KATERINA (*falling to her knees*). Not to see my father or mother! To die without confession if I . . .

KABANOV (*lifting her up*). What are you doing! What are you doing! What a fuss! I don't want even to listen to it!

KABANOVA'S VOICE: "It's time, Tikhon!"

(KABANOVA, VARVARA *and* GLASHA *enter.*)

KABANOVA. Well, Tikhon, it's time. God be with you! (*Sits*

down) Everyone sit down. (*All sit down. Silence*) Well, good-bye! (*Gets up, and all get up*)

KABANOV (*going up to his mother*). Good-bye, Mama!

KABANOVA (*gesturing to the ground*). To the ground, to the ground! (KABANOV *bows down to the ground, then kisses his mother*) Say good-bye to your wife.

KABANOV. Good-bye, Katya!

(KATERINA *throws herself on his neck.*)

KABANOVA. What are you clinging to his neck for, you shameless creature! You aren't saying good-bye to your lover! He's your husband, your master! Or don't you know how to behave? Bow down to the ground!

(KATERINA *bows down to the ground.*)

KABANOV. Good-bye, Sister! (*Kisses* VARVARA) Good-bye, Glasha. (*Kisses* GLASHA) Good-bye, Mama! (*Bows*)

KABANOVA. Good-bye! Long good-byes are wasted tears.

(KABANOV *goes out, followed by* KATERINA, VARVARA *and* GLASHA.)

KABANOVA (*alone*). What youth is! They're silly just to look at! If they weren't mine, I'd laugh myself sick. They don't know anything, how to do anything. Don't know how to say good-bye to each other. A house is well off that has older people in it, for they hold it together, as long as they live. And the stupid things, too, want their independence, and when they get it, they get all mixed up to the dismay and amusement of good people. Of course, some feel sorry, but generally everyone laughs. It's impossible not to; they invite guests, don't know how to seat them, or even, think of it!, leave out one of the family. It's simply absurd! The old days are gone. You don't want to go into someone else's house any more. Or if you do, you spit and get out as fast as you can. What will happen when the old people have all died off, what the world will be like, I have no idea. Indeed, it's even a good thing that I won't see any of it.

(KATERINA *and* VARVARA *enter.*)

KABANOVA. You were just boasting about how much you love your husband. Now I see what your love is like. Any other good wife, seeing her husband off, wails for an hour and a half and lies on the porch. But, obviously, this means nothing to you.

KATERINA. No point in it. Besides, I can't. Just to make people laugh!

KABANOVA. That's not very clever. If you loved him, you'd learn to. Even if you can't do things as they ought to be, you could have set an example. It's more decent. As it was, obviously, it was just words. Well, I'm going to go pray. Don't bother me.

VARVARA. I'm going out.

KABANOVA (*tenderly*). What do I care! Go ahead! Have a good time while you can. You'll have plenty of time to sit in. (KABANOVA *and* VARVARA *go out.*)

KATERINA (*alone, lost in thought*). Well, now quiet will reign in our house. Ah, what boredom! If only there were some children! What sadness! I have no little children. I'd sit with them all the time and amuse them. I love to talk to children—they're like angels. (*Silence*) If I'd died when I was little, it would have been better. I'd look down on the earth from Heaven and delight in everything. And I'd fly invisibly wherever I'd want to. I'd fly out into the field and fly on the wind from cornflower to cornflower, like a butterfly. (*Gets lost in thought*) This is what I'll do: I'll begin some kind of work, as I promised; I'll go to the stores, I'll buy some linen, and I'll make some underclothes and give them to the poor. They will pray to God for me. Varvara and I will sit down and sew and we won't notice the time pass. And then Tisha will be back.

(VARVARA *enters.*)

VARVARA (*covers her head with a kerchief in front of the mirror*). I'm going out for a walk now; and Glasha is going to make up our beds in the garden; Mama said it's all right. In the garden, behind the raspberries, there's a wicker gate; Mama keeps it locked and hides the key. I took it and put another there so she wouldn't notice. Here. Perhaps we'll need it. (*Gives her the key*) If I see him, I'll tell him to come to the gate.

KATERINA (*in fright, rejecting the key*). What for? What for? Don't do it! Don't!

VARVARA. You don't need it, but I will. Take it, it won't bite you.

KATERINA. What have you started, sinner! How can you!

Have you thought what you're doing? You mustn't! You mustn't!

VARVARA. I don't like to talk a lot; besides, I have no time. It's time for me to go. (*Goes out*)

KATERINA (*alone, holding the key in her hands*). Why is she doing this? What is she thinking up? Crazy, really, she's crazy! This is the end! This is it! I should throw it away, throw it far away, hurl it into the river so they would never find it. It burns my hands like a hot coal. (*Thoughtfully*) This is the way we women are lost. Who can be happy held down! Lots of things enter your head. A chance comes, another woman's glad: and headlong she flings herself in. How is it possible, without thinking, without reasoning it out! It doesn't take long to fall! And afterwards you weep all your life, you torture yourself; you seem held down even more! (*Silence*) Being held down is bitter, so bitter! It'll make anyone cry! And most of all, us women. Take me, now. I'm living, suffering, and I see no ray of hope. And it seems I never will! The longer I live, the worse it is. And now there's this sin over me. (*Gets lost in thought*) If it weren't for my mother-in-law! She's crushed me . . . Because of her I'm sick to death of the whole house; even the walls are hateful. (*Thoughtfully looks at the key*) Throw it away? Of course, I ought to. How come it ever got into my hands? For temptation, for my downfall. (*Listens*) Someone's coming. My heart's pounding. (*Hides the key in her pocket*) No! . . . No one! . . . Why did I get so scared? And hide the key! Well, it seems that's where it should be! Apparently, fate itself wants it that way! Indeed, where's the sin in looking at him once, from a distance! Even if I talk to him, that's no shame. But how can I face my husband! But he himself didn't want to. And maybe there won't be another such chance my whole life. Then I'll be sorry for myself: I had the chance but didn't take it. What am I talking for, what am I trying to deceive myself for? I must see him even if it kills me. Who am I trying to fool? Throw the key away? Not for anything in the world! It's mine now . . . Whatever happens, I'll see Boris! Oh, if only night would come sooner . . .

ACT III

SCENE 1

The street. The gate in front of the KABANOVS' *house, a bench in front of the gate.* KABANOVA *and* FEKLUSHA *are sitting on the bench.*

FEKLUSHA. The end of the world, Marfa Ignatyevna, the end, by all the signs, the end. You still have peace and quiet in your town, but in other towns it's simply Sodom, dear: noise and bustle and never-ending coming-and-going! The people are all running around, some here, some there.

KABANOVA. We have nowhere to hurry, my dear, so we get on without rushing around.

FEKLUSHA. No, dear, there's peace and quiet in your town 'cause there are lots of people, like yourself, for example, adorned with virtues, like with flowers, so everything's done easy and pious. What's all this bustling mount up to, dear? It's all vanity, y'know. Like in Moscow: the people are running back and forth nobody knows what for. That's vanity for you. A vain people, Marfa Ignatyevna, and they're running and running. They got the notion they're running for something. Poor man, he's rushing along, don't recognize people, thinks he sees somebody waving to him, but he goes to the place and it's completely empty, nobody there, it was all just a dream. And so he goes away downcast. And another gets the idea he's catching up with a friend. Someone new to the place can see from the side right away that there's nobody there, but this man thinks all along on account of his vanity that he's catching up. Vanity, y'know, is something like a fog. Like with you, now, such a beautiful evening hardly nobody comes out to sit a while outside the house; but in Moscow now there's such a din and rattle and in the streets there's such roaring and ranting going on. Marfa Ignatyevna, what did they start harnessing the iron horse for?—all, you see, on account of speed.

KABANOVA. I heard about it, my dear.

FEKLUSHA. But I saw it, dear, with my own eyes. 'Course, others don't see nothing on account of their rushing around, so it looks like a machine to them, and they call it a machine; but I saw how it goes like this (*spreads out her fingers*) with its paws. Oh, and the noise that good people have to put up with.

KABANOVA. You call it all kinds of things you want as long as you call it a machine. People are stupid, they'll believe anything. But even if you shower me with gold, still I won't go.

FEKLUSHA. What wild thoughts, dear! God save you from such misfortune! And there's another, Marfa Ignatyevna, another certain vision I had in Moscow. I'm going along early in the morning, it's just barely daylight, and I see on a high, high house, upon the roof, somebody's standing there, all black in the face. Y'already know who it is. And he's making with his hands as if he was scattering something, but nothing's being scattered. Then I figured out that he's scattering darnels, and during the day the people don't see 'em in all their rushing around and pick 'em up. On account of which they run around so, on account of which all the women among 'em are so thin, their bodies don't put on no weight, and they look like they'd lost something, or was looking for something; and their faces are so sad, it's even pitiful.

KABANOVA. Everything's possible, my dear! In our time, how can you wonder about anything!

FEKLUSHA. Times are hard, Marfa Ignatyevna, times are hard. Already the time's begun to come into belittling.

KABANOVA. What do you mean, my dear, into belittling?

FEKLUSHA. 'Course, not us; what can we see in our vanity! But, now, clever people's been noticing that the time's getting shorter with us. Used to be, summer and winter'd go on and on, y'couldn't wait till they was over; but now y'don't notice them passing at all. Seems like days and hours stayed just the same, but time, on account of our sins, is getting shorter and shorter. That's what clever people are saying.

KABANOVA. There'll be worse things than that, my dear.

FEKLUSHA. Only hope we never live to see it.

KABANOVA. Maybe we will.

(DIKÒI *enters.*)

KABANOVA. What are you doing, neighbor, out walking around so late?

DIKÒI. And who'll stop me!

KABANOVA. Who'll stop you! Who needs to!

DIKÒI. Well, I've got nothing to talk about. What, am I under somebody's orders, maybe? What are you still here for? What kind of a swamp rat's still here!

KABANOVA. Don't you open your big mouth too much! You go find someone cheaper than me! For you, I'm dear! Go on out the way you came. Feklusha, let's go home. (*Rises*)

DIKÒI. Stop, neighbor, stop. Don't get mad. You'll still manage to be in your house; your house isn't over the hill. It's there!

KABANOVA. If you got business, don't shout, but talk sense.

DIKÒI. There's no business, but I'm a bit drunk, that's what.

KABANOVA. What do you want me to do, praise you now for it?

DIKÒI. Don't praise, don't scold. I mean, I'm drunk. That's all there is to it. Until I sleep it off, there's nothing you can do about it.

KABANOVA. So, go sleep.

DIKÒI. Where'll I go?

KABANOVA. Home. Where else?

DIKÒI. But if I don't want to go home?

KABANOVA. Why's that, let me ask you?

DIKÒI. Because there's a war on there.

KABANOVA. Who's there to fight with? Why you're the only warrior there.

DIKÒI. Well, so what, so I'm a warrior? What of that?

KABANOVA. What? Nothing. That's no great honor, because all your life you've been warring with women. That's what.

DIKÒI. Well, I mean, they *have* to give in to me. Am I going to give in to them, hey!

KABANOVA. I rather marvel at you! so many people in your house and they can't please the one of you.

DIKÒI. You go there!

KABANOVA. What do you want from me?

DIKÒI. Here's what: talk to me, so I feel better. Only you alone in the whole town know how to talk to me.

KABANOVA. Go on, Feklusha, tell them to get something ready to eat. (FEKLUSHA *goes out*) Let's go inside.

DIKÒI. No, I'm not going inside, inside I'm worse.

KABANOVA. What made you angry?

DIKÒI. Right the first thing this morning.

KABANOVA. They asked you for money, I bet.

DIKÒI. We agreed exactly, damn them; then one, then the other is after me the whole day.

KABANOVA. Must mean you have to, if they were after you.

DIKÒI. I understand it. What do you want me to do with myself when I feel this way! I know I have to give it back, but still I can't in a friendly way. You're my friend, and I have to pay you back, but if you come asking—I'll call you names. I'll give it to you, I'll give it to you, but I'll give you hell, too. Because just you mention money to me, my whole insides get kindled up, my whole insides get all on fire, that's all there is to it; and at a time like that I'll give a man hell for nothing.

KABANOVA. You have no parents over you, so you start bullying.

DIKÒI. No, neighbor, you be quiet! You listen to me! Here's the kind of thing that's happened. Round about Lent once, I was fasting when all of a sudden the devil slips a little peasant in on me: he's come for money, brought some wood along. And didn't he come to add to my troubles at just such a time! Here's the mistake I made: I swore at him till I was blue in the face, you couldn't do better, damned near hit him. That's the kind of feelings I have! Afterwards, I begged his forgiveness, bowed down to the ground, really, just like that. I'm telling you the truth, I bowed to the man's feet. That's what my feelings get me into: here on the street, right in the mud, I bowed down to him; right in front of everybody I bowed down to him.

KABANOVA. But why do you deliberately provoke yourself? That's bad, neighbor.

DEKÒI. What do you mean deliberately?

KABANOVA. I've seen, I know. As soon as you see that someone wants to ask you for something, you deliberately pick out one of your own people and let yourself go at him in order to get angry. Because you know that nobody's going to come near you when you're angry. That's it, neighbor!

DIKÒI. So what? Who doesn't grudge his own goods!

(GLASHA *enters.*)

GLASHA. Marfa Ignatyevna, dinner is served, if you please.

KABANOVA. So, neighbor, come on in! Have a bite of what God has given us.

DIKÒI. All right.

KABANOVA. Please do, welcome. (*Lets* DIKÒI *go ahead and goes out after him*)

(GLASHA, *arms folded, stands by the gate.*)

GLASHA. Boris Grigorich is really coming. Maybe to fetch his uncle? Or maybe just out for a walk? Must be, he's just out for a walk.

(BORIS *enters.*)

BORIS. Isn't my uncle here?

GLASHA. He's here. You want him?

BORIS. They sent me from home to find out where he is. But if he's here, let him stay: nobody wants him. At home they're just awfully glad he's gone.

GLASHA. If our mistress was married to him, she'd soon make him stop. But what'm I standing here with you for, like a fool! Good-bye. (*Goes out*)

BORIS. O, Lord! If only to take a peek at her! I can't go in the house; uninvited people don't come here. That's life for you! We live in the same town, almost next door, and we meet once a week, and then in church, or on the street, and that's all! Here if a woman gets married or buried it's all the same. (*Silence*) I shouldn't see her at all: it would be easier! This way I see her only in snatches, and only when others are around at that, and a thousand eyes are staring at you. It breaks your heart. And you can't even stand yourself. You go out for a walk, and you keep finding yourself always here at this gate. What do I come here for? It's never possible to see her, and if ever, maybe, there was some kind of conversation, you'd be leading her straight into real trouble. What a place I've come to! (*He goes;* KULIGIN *comes to meet him*)

KULIGIN. Well, sir? You out for a walk?

BORIS. Yes, walking by myself; the weather's lovely today.

KULIGIN. Very fine, sir, for taking a walk now. It's peaceful, the air's splendid, you can smell the flowers from the meadows across the Volga, the sky's clear . . .

A chasm opened, full of stars—
An endless chasm, endless stars.

Let's go over to the avenue, sir, there's not a soul there.

BORIS. Let's!

KULIGIN. This is the kind of hole we live in, sir! Made an avenue and nobody walks on it. They go out for a walk just on holidays and then they all alike pretend they're taking a walk, but actually they go there to show off their finery. You won't meet anybody but a drunk clerk dragging himself home from the tavern. The poor, sir, have no time to take walks; they have to work day and night. And they don't sleep but three hours out of twenty-four. But what do the rich do? You think they're out walking and taking in the fresh air? Not a bit. All their gates have long been locked and the dogs let loose. You think they're attending to their business or praying to God? No, sir. And they haven't locked up on account of thieves, either, but so others don't see how they nag at their servants and tyrannize their family. And what tears are spilled behind those locked doors, unseen and unheard! How can I tell you, sir! You can judge by your own experience. And besides, sir, behind those tightly locked doors what dark vice there is, and drunkenness! And it's all covered up and hid—nobody sees anything, nobody knows anything, only God alone! You see me, the man says, among others on the street, but you got nothing to do with my family; for this, he says, we got locks and doors and big watchdogs. The family, he says, is a secret, mysterious! We know these big secrets! What with these secrets, only he himself has it good, and all the others howl like wolves. And what's the secret? Who doesn't know it! To rob orphans, relatives, nephews, and to beat the servants so that no matter what he does, nobody'll dare speak up. That's the whole secret. Well, God bless them! But you know, sir, who of us goes out for walks? Young boys and girls. They filch a little hour or two from sleeping and go out walking together. Look, here's a couple.

(KUDRYASH *and* VARVARA *appear. They kiss.*)

BORIS. They're kissing.

KULIGIN. There's no law against it.

(KUDRYASH *goes out, but* VARVARA *goes up to the gate of her house and beckons to* BORIS. *He goes over to her.*)

KULIGIN. I'm going over to the avenue, sir. I don't want to be bothering you. I'll wait there.

BORIS. Fine, I'll be right there.

(KULIGIN *goes out.*)

VARVARA. (*covering her head with her kerchief*). You know the ravine behind the Kabanovs' garden?

BORIS. I do.

VARVARA. Come there in a little while.

BORIS. What for?

VARVARA. How slow you are! You come, then you'll see what for. Well, hurry up, they're waiting for you. (BORIS *goes out*) He really didn't recognize me! Let him think about it now. But I already know Katerina can't wait, she'll come running out. (*Goes out through the gate*)

SCENE 2

Night. The ravine, covered with bushes. Above, the fence of the KABANOVS' *garden and the wicker gate; a path leads down.*

KUDRYASH (*enters with a guitar*). Nobody here. What's she doing there! Well, let's sit down and wait. (*Sits down on a stone*) And sing a song to pass the time. (*Sings*)

As the Cossack, Don Cossack, was off to water his horse,
The young man already was standing by the gate.
Was standing by the gate and thinking his thoughts,
Thinking his thoughts, how he'd kill his wife.
And his wife, now, his wife was begging her man,
Was bowing down to him, down to the ground:
Now you, dear man, you dear, gentle friend!
Don't you kill me, don't kill me at evening!
If you kill me, kill me when midnight comes!
Give my little children time to fall asleep,
My little children, and all my dear neighbors.

(BORIS *enters.*)

KUDRYASH (*stops singing*). Well, look! A quiet man, quiet, but has also come out to have a good time.

BORIS. Kudryash, is that you?

KUDRYASH. It's me, Boris Grigorich!

BORIS. What are you doing here?

KUDRYASH. Who, me? Must be, I have to be, Boris Grigorich, since I'm here. Wouldn't come if I didn't have to. Where're you headed?

BORIS (*looking around*). Well, Kudryash, I'm supposed to stay here, but, I think, probably it's all the same to you, and there's another place you can go.

KUDRYASH. No, Boris Grigorich, I see it's your first time here, but this is already *my* place; I've been here a long time and beaten the path down well. I like you, sir, and am ready to do you any favor I can, but don't let me meet you on this path at night—so that, God forbid, nothing terrible happens. It's better to agree beforehand.

BORIS. What's wrong with you, Vanya?

KUDRYASH. What's this: Vanya! I know I'm Vanya. But you go your way, that's all. Get your own yourself and go have yourself a good time with her, and nobody'll bother you. But don't you touch someone else's! It isn't done here, or the boys'll break your leg! I'll stand up for mine . . . and I can't even say what I'll do! I'll rip your throat open!

BORIS. No point your getting angry: It hasn't entered my head to try to cut you out. I wouldn't have come here if I hadn't been told to.

KUDRYASH. Who told you to?

BORIS. I couldn't make out, it was dark. Some girl stopped me on the street and told me expressly to come here, behind the Kabanovs' garden, where the path is.

KUDRYASH. Who could it have been?

BORIS. Listen, Kudryash. Can I talk to you frankly, you won't tell?

KUDRYASH. Go ahead, don't be afraid! With me it's just as if you never said it.

BORIS. I don't know how anything is done here, neither your manners nor morals; but such a thing . . .

KUDRYASH. You've fallen in love, hey?

BORIS. Yes, Kudryash.

KUDRYASH. Well, that's all right. It's pretty free here on that score. The girls have themselves a good time, as they like, and the mother and father don't butt in. Only the older women sit shut up indoors.

BORIS. That's my misfortune.

KUDRYASH. You mean you've fallen in love with a married woman?

BORIS. With a married woman, Kudryash.

KUDRYASH. Ah, Boris Grigorich, you've got to get rid of her!

BORIS. It's easy to say—get rid of her! It's all the same to you, probably; you get rid of one and pick up another. But I can't do that! Since I've already fallen in love . . .

KUDRYASH. But that means, now, you're about to ruin her completely, Boris Grigorich!

BORIS. God forbid! God save me from that! No, Kudryash, how could I? I want to ruin her! I'd only like to see her somewhere, I don't want anything else.

KUDRYASH. How can you answer for yourself ahead of time, sir? And you know what people here are like! You know yourself. They'll eat you up, they'll drive you into your grave.

BORIS. Don't say that, Kudryash, please don't scare me!

KUDRYASH. But does she love you?

BORIS. I don't know.

KUDRYASH. Did you ever meet?

BORIS. I was at their house just once with my uncle. But I've seen her in church, we've met on the street. Kudryash, if you could only see the way she prays! What an angelic smile on her face, and her face itself seems lit up.

KUDRYASH. You mean young Kabanova?

BORIS. Yes, Kudryash.

KUDRYASH. Right! So that's how it is! Well, allow me to congratulate you!

BORIS. What for?

KUDRYASH. Why, sure! It means everything's going fine for you, if you were told to come here.

BORIS. She herself really told me?

KUDRYASH. Who else?

BORIS. No, you're joking! That's impossible. (*Holds his head*)

KUDRYASH. What's wrong with you?

BORIS. I'll go mad with joy!

KUDRYASH. See! There *is* something to go mad for! Only you be careful—don't make any fuss or you'll lead her straight into real trouble! Even if her husband's a fool, that mother-in-law is really fierce.

(VARVARA *comes through the gate.*)

VARVARA (*sings by the gate*).

My Vanya's walking by the river,
There my Vanyushka goes . . .

KUDRYASH (*continues*). Buying things. (*Whistles*)

VARVARA (*comes down along the path and, having covered her head with a kerchief, goes up to* BORIS). You wait, fellow. There's something coming. (*To* KUDRYASH) Let's go down to the Volga.

KUDRYASH. What took you so long? Always waiting for you! You know I don't like it!

(VARVARA *puts her arm around him and they go out.*)

BORIS. It's as if I were living a dream! This night, the singing, the lovers' meeting! They go with their arms around each other. It's so new for me, so good, so gay! And here I'm waiting for something! But what I'm waiting for—I don't know, and can't imagine; only my heart is pounding and every little vein throbs. I can't even think of what to say to her now, it takes away my breath, I'm all weak in my knees! What a foolish heart I have, it gets all excited suddenly, and nothing will calm it down. Here she comes. (KATERINA *quietly comes down the path, her head covered with a large white kerchief, her eyes fixed on the ground. Silence*) Is that you, Katerina Petrovna? (*Silence*) I don't know how to thank you. (*Silence*) If you only knew, Katerina Petrovna, how much I love you! (*Tries to take her hands*)

KATERINA (*in fright, but not raising her eyes*). Don't touch me, don't touch me! Oh!

BORIS. Don't be angry!

KATERINA. Go away from me! Go far away, you cursed man! Do you know, I can't atone for this sin, I can never atone! You know it will lie like a stone on my heart, like a stone.

BORIS. Don't drive me away.

KATERINA. What did you come for? What did you come for, my destroyer? You know I'm married, you know I have to live with my husband until the grave . . .

BORIS. You yourself told me to come . . .

KATERINA. But, understand me now, my enemy: until the grave!

BORIS. It would be better if I didn't see you!

KATERINA (*with emotion*). You know what I have in store for myself. Where's there a place for me, do you know?

BORIS. Calm yourself! (*Takes her hand*) Sit down.

KATERINA. What do you wish my ruin for?

BORIS. How can I wish your ruin, when I love you more than anything in the world, more than my own self?

KATERINA. No, no! You've ruined me!

BORIS. Am I really some sort of criminal?

KATERINA (*shaking her head*). Ruined me, ruined me, ruined me!

BORIS. God save me! Let me rather die myself!

KATERINA. How haven't you ruined me, if I, forsaking my house, come to you at night?

BORIS. You chose to do it.

KATERINA. I have no choice. If only I had my own choice, I wouldn't have come to you. (*Raises her eyes and looks at* BORIS. *A brief silence*) Your will rules me now; don't you see that! (*Throws her arms around his neck*)

BORIS (*embracing* KATERINA). My life!

KATERINA. You know what? Just now I suddenly wanted to die!

BORIS. Why die, if it's so good for us to be alive?

KATERINA. No, I mustn't live! I know even now that I mustn't live.

BORIS. Don't say such things, please, don't make me sad . . .

KATERINA. It's easy for you, you're a free man, but me!

BORIS. No one will ever know about our love. Don't you think I'll protect you?

KATERINA. Oh! Why protect me, nobody's to blame—I came myself. Don't spare me, ruin me! Let everyone know, let everyone see, what I'm doing! (*Embraces* BORIS) If for you I'm not afraid of sin, will I be afraid of others' judgment? They say it's even easier sometimes when you've suffered much for some sin here on earth.

BORIS. But why think about this when it's so good for us now!

KATERINA. True! I'll have plenty of time to think about it and cry my fill when I've nothing else to do.

BORIS. And I started to get scared; I thought you were going to send me away.

KATERINA (*smiling*). Send you away! How! The way we feel! If you hadn't come, why, I think, I'd have gone to you myself!

BORIS. I didn't even know you loved me.

KATERINA. I've loved you a long time. As if you came here to lead me into sin. As soon as I saw you, I wasn't myself any more: the very first time, had you beckoned to me, I think, I would have followed you. Go to the end of the world, if you want—I'll follow you and I won't look back.

BORIS. Did your husband go for long?

KATERINA. Two weeks.

BORIS. Oh, what a good time we'll have! There's plenty of time.

KATERINA. We'll have a good time. And then . . . (*Gets lost in thought*) If I'm locked in, it's death! But if I'm not, I'll find a chance to see you!

(KUDRYASH *and* VARVARA *enter.*)

VARVARA. Well, are you agreed?

(KATERINA *hides her face against* BORIS' *chest.*)

BORIS. We are.

VARVARA. Go on, take a little walk, and we'll wait. When it's time, Vanya will shout.

(BORIS *and* KATERINA *go out.* KUDRYASH *and* VARVARA *sit down on a rock.*)

KUDRYASH. This is a great trick you two thought up, to climb in through the garden gate. It's just fine for us.

VARVARA. My idea.

KUDRYASH. They'll get you for it. But your mother hasn't missed you?

VARVARA. Oh, this is beyond her! It won't enter her thick head.

KUDRYASH. But if there's trouble?

VARVARA. She sleeps soundly at first; toward morning she wakes up.

KUDRYASH. But how can you be sure? Suddenly the devil will get her up.

VARVARA. Well, so! We have the gate between us and the yard locked on the inside, on the garden side; she'll knock and knock and then go away. And in the morning we'll say that we slept soundly and didn't hear. Besides, Glasha's watching out; if there's anything, she'll shout. You can't do anything without being careful! How could you! You just have to watch out you don't get into trouble!

(KUDRYASH *plays several chords on the guitar.* VARVARA *leans against* KUDRYASH' *shoulder. He, paying no attention, plays quietly.*)

VARVARA (*yawning*). How can we find out what time it is?

KUDRYASH. One.

VARVARA. How do you know?

KUDRYASH. The watchman beat it on his board.

VARVARA (*yawning*). It's time. Call them. We'll come earlier tomorrow, so we can have a longer walk together.

KUDRYASH (*whistles and starts singing loudly*).

Always home, always home!
But I don't want to go.

BORIS (*offstage*). Right away!

VARVARA (*gets up*). Well, good-bye! (*Yawns, then kisses him coldly, as an old friend*) Tomorrow be sure to come earlier! (*Looks to the side of the stage where* BORIS *and* KATERINA *have come*) Enough saying good-bye; you're not parting forever; you'll see each other tomorrow. (*Yawns and stretches*)

(KATERINA *runs in; behind her,* BORIS.)

KATERINA (*to* VARVARA). Well, let's go, let's go! (*They go up the path;* KATERINA *turns around*) Good-bye!

BORIS. Tomorrow!

KATERINA. Yes, tomorrow! Tell me what you dream! (*Goes up to the gate*)

BORIS. For sure.

KUDRYASH (*sings to the guitar*).

Go out, young girl, the whole time
Until the evening sundown!
Keep up your hope the whole time
Until the evening sundown.

VARVARA (*by the gate*).

But I, young girl, the whole time
Until the morning light,
Keep up my hope the whole time
Until the morning light!

(*Goes out*)

KUDRYASH. And as the dawn caught fire
So I started off for home, etc.

ACT IV

In the foreground, a narrow arcade with old, nearly crumbling vaults. Here and there grass and bushes. Beyond the arches, the shore and a view of the Volga. A number of promenaders of both sexes pass behind the arches.

1ST. It's starting to rain, as if a storm were gathering.

2ND. Look, it is.

1ST. We're lucky we have some place to hide in.

(*All go in under the arches.*)

A WOMAN. And how many people on the avenue! It's a holiday, everybody came out! The women are all dressed up!

1ST. They'll duck in somewhere.

2ND. Look, they're all going to crowd in here!

1ST (*looking around at the walls*). You know, my friend, at some point, now, there were paintings on these walls. You can still even see it in places.

2ND. Well, of course! Goes without saying there were paintings. Now, y'see, it's all empty, starting to cave in, overgrown. They didn't fix it after the fire. But you don't remember the fire, that was forty years ago.

1ST. Whatever it was, my friend, there were paintings here. It's rather hard to figure them out.

2ND. That's the fire of Gehenna.

1ST. Really, my friend!

2ND. And every sort of person's on his way there.

1ST. Right, right, now I understand.

2ND. And every rank.

1ST. Even Arabs?

2ND. Even Arabs.

1ST. And this, my friend, what's this?

2ND. That's the Destruction of Lithuania. A battle! You see? How our men fought with Lithuania.

1ST. What's this Lithuania?

2ND. It's just Lithuania.

1ST. But they say, my friend, it fell down on us from Heaven.

2ND. I can't tell you. If from Heaven, well, then, from Heaven.

A WOMAN. Go on! Everybody knows it came from Heaven;

and where there was such a battle with it, there are burial mounds all over to remember it by.

1ST. That's it, my friend! You know, that's just it.

(DIKÒI *enters followed by* KULIGIN *without a cap. Everyone bows and assumes a respectful position.*)

DIKÒI. Just look, got all wet. (*To* KULIGIN) Leave me alone! Get away! (*With feeling*) Stupid!

KULIGIN. Savel Prokofich, you know, your honor, it would be of use to all the people in town in general.

DIKÒI. Go away! What use! Who needs this use?

KULIGIN. Why even just for yourself, Savel Prokofich, your honor. You could put it up, sir, on the avenue, in an open place. And what's the cost? Practically nothing: a stone column (*shows by gestures the size of each thing*), a copper plate, a round one like this, and a stud, a straight stud (*indicating by a gesture*), the simplest. I'll put all this together and cut out the numbers myself. Then you, your honor, when you want to take a walk, or others, out walking, can go right up and see what time it is. The place is just fine, with a view and all, but somehow so empty now. Also, travelers come here, your honor, go there to look at our sights; it'd be an ornament, something more pleasant to the eye.

DIKÒI. What're you coming to me for with all kinds of nonsense! Maybe I don't even want to talk to you. You ought to have found out first if I feel like listening to you, you idiot, or not. What am I to you—your equal, hey? Look at you—what a mighty big thing you found! So you come right up with your big fat mug and start spouting.

KULIGIN. If I have importuned with my own private business then I'm at fault. But I was talking about the public good, your honor. When it's a question of the public good, what do some ten rubles mean? It wouldn't require more, sir.

DIKÒI. But maybe you're figuring on robbing me. Who knows you!

KULIGIN. If I'm willing to contribute my labor for nothing, what can I steal, your honor! Besides, everyone here knows me; nobody will say anything bad about me.

DIKÒI. Well, so they know you, but I don't want to.

KULIGIN. Why, sir, Savel Prokofich, do you wish to insult an honest man?

DIKÒI. What, am I going to give you an accounting, is that it? I'm not accountable to anyone, even people more important than you. If I want to think of you this way, I will. For others you're an honest man, but I think you're a robber, and that's all there is to it. Is that what you wanted to hear from me? Well, listen! I tell you, you're a robber, that's it! What, are you going to take me to court, is that it? Remember, you're a worm. If I want to, I'll spare you; if I want to, I'll crush you.

KULIGIN. God protect you, Savel Prokofich! I'm a little man, sir, it's easy to insult me. But I'll tell you this, your honor: "Virtue is virtue in poverty, too."

DIKÒI. Don't you dare be rude to me! You hear!

KULIGIN. I'm not being rude to you at all, sir, but I'm telling you this because, perhaps, sometime you'll want to do something for the town. You have plenty of means, your honor; you need only the will to do a good deed. Take right now, for example: we have frequent storms, but we don't put up any lightning rods.

DIKÒI (*haughtily*). More nonsense!

KULIGIN. How is that nonsense, when there have been experiments made?

DIKÒI. What kind of these lightning-rod things have you got?

KULIGIN. Steel.

DIKÒI (*in anger*). Well, what else?

KULIGIN. Steel poles.

DIKÒI (*getting more and more angry*). I heard poles, you viper! Now what else? He's fixed things up: poles! Well, what else?

KULIGIN. Nothing else.

DIKÒI. So what do you think a storm is, hey? Well, say it!

KULIGIN. Electricity.

DIKÒI (*stamping his foot*). What's electricity got to do with it! Of course, you're a fraud. A storm is sent to us as a punishment so we know it, but you want to fence us off, God save us, with some kind of poles and horns. What are you, a Tartar, hey? You a Tartar? Well? Speak up! You a Tartar?

KULIGIN. Savel Prokofich, your honor, Derzhavin said:

My body will turn into dust,
My soul will rule the thunderstorms.

DIKÒI. I ought to take you to the mayor for saying such

things; he'll give it to you! Hey, good people! Listen to what he says!

KULIGIN. Can't be helped, have to resign myself to it! But when I have a million, then I'll talk. (*Waving his hand in disgust, he goes out*)

DIKÒI. What, are you going to go rob someone, is that it? Grab him! What a fake peasant! With these people what kind of a person have you got to be? I don't know. (*Turning toward the crowd*) And you, damn you, will get anyone in trouble! Here I didn't want to get mad today, but he, as if on purpose, got me all mad. Hope he drops dead! (*Angrily*) The ràin stop, hey?

1ST. Seems it stopped.

DIKÒI. Seems! You, you idiot, go on out and take a look. Seems!

1ST (*going out from under the arches*). It's stopped!

(DIKÒI *goes out and everyone after him. The stage is empty for a short while.* VARVARA *quickly runs in under the archway and, having concealed herself, looks out.*)

VARVARA. Seems it's he! (BORIS *goes by well upstage*) Pss-sst! (BORIS *looks around*) Come here. (*She waves her hand.* BORIS *comes in*) What can we do about Katerina? For pity's sake, say something!

BORIS. What's happened?

VARVARA. There's just trouble. Her husband came back, did you know? He wasn't expected, but he came.

BORIS. No, I didn't know.

VARVARA. She's simply not in control of herself.

BORIS. I lived only the ten short days he wasn't here. And now I won't see her again!

VARVARA. Ah you, what a man! Listen to me! She's all trembling, as if she had a terrible fever. She's so pale, rushes around the house as if looking for something. Her eyes are like a mad woman's! She's been crying every morning now for a long time, and sobbing. God in Heaven! What can I do about her?

BORIS. But, maybe, she'll get over this.

VARVARA. Hardly. She doesn't dare look at her husband. Mama has begun to notice this, goes around after her all the time looking at her like a dragon. And from all this she's getting worse and worse. It's simply torture to look at her! I'm afraid, too.

BORIS. What are you afraid of?

VARVARA. You don't know her! She's a strange one. Anything's possible with her. She'll do such things, that . . .

BORIS. My God! What can we do! You have a long talk with her. Really, won't she be persuaded?

VARVARA. I've tried. She doesn't listen to anything. You'd better not go near her.

BORIS. Well, what do you think she can do?

VARVARA. I'll tell you what: fall down at her husband's feet and blurt everything out. That's what I'm afraid of.

BORIS (*in fright*). Is that possible!

VARVARA. Anything's possible with her.

BORIS. Where is she now?

VARVARA. Right now she's gone for a walk on the avenue with her husband, and Mama with them. Go, too, if you want. No, better not, or perhaps she'll lose control of herself completely. (*In the distance, sounds of thunder*) A storm? (*Looks out*) Rain already. And here's a crowd coming. Hide yourself there somewhere and I'll stay in sight here so they don't think anything.

(*Several people of different ranks and sex come in.*)

1ST. Must be the butterfly's awful afraid to rush off so fast and hide.

A WOMAN. How's it going to hide! If that's the way you're born, why you can't get away.

KATERINA (*running in*). Varvara! (*Grabs her hand and holds it tightly*)

VARVARA. Stop it, what are you doing!

KATERINA. It's the end for me!

VARVARA. You think again! Pull yourself together!

KATERINA. No! I can't! I can't do anything. My heart's broken.

KABANOVA (*entering*). Exactly, exactly, one must live so as to be ready for everything. And then there wouldn't be any such fear.

KABANOV. But, Mama, what kind of special sins can she have? Just the same as all the rest of us, but it's her nature to be afraid like this.

KABANOVA. And how do you know? The human heart is a mystery.

KABANOV (*joking*). Maybe something happened without me, but nothing since I'm back.

KABANOVA. Yes, perhaps without you.

KABANOV (*joking*). Katya, 'fess up, friend, if you're at fault in anything. You know you can't hide from me! No, none of your tricks! I know everything!

KATERINA (*looking straight at* KABANOV). My darling!

VARVARA. What do you keep after her for! Don't you see how hard it is for her without you?

(BORIS *comes out of the crowd and bows to* KABANOV.)

KATERINA (*cries out*). Ah!

KABANOV. What are you scared for? You thought him a stranger? This is our friend! Is your uncle well?

BORIS. Thank God.

KATERINA (*to* VARVARA). What more does he want from me? Or isn't it enough for him that I'm tortured like this? (*Leaning on* VARVARA, *she sobs*)

VARVARA (*loudly, so her mother hears*). We've run our legs off, we don't know what to do about her, and on top of it all, here strangers come bothering us. (*Makes a sign to* BORIS, *who goes over to the exit*)

KULIGIN (*comes out center stage, turning to the crowd*). What are you afraid of, for Heaven's sake, tell me! Every blade of grass now, every flower is enraptured, but we are hiding, we are afraid, as if of some disaster! The storm will kill us! This isn't a storm, but a blessing! Yes, a blessing! But everything is a storm for you! When the Northern Lights shine, you should enjoy them and marvel at the majesty: "Dawn arises from the midnight lands!" But you get terror-stricken and try to think whether it means war or plague. When a comet falls, I can't take my eyes off it! It's beautiful! You've got used to the stars, they're always the same, but this is something new; you should look and enjoy it! But you're frightened even to glance at the sky, and tremble all over. You've made everything into scarecrows for yourselves. What people! Look, I'm not afraid. Let's go, sir!

BORIS. Let's go! It's more frightening here!

(*They go out.*)

KABANOVA. Just look at the reasoning he used! What a thing to listen to; there's absolutely nothing to say! What times we've come to, what kinds of teachers have appeared! If an old man thinks like that, what must we expect of the young!

A WOMAN. The sky is all covered over. It's covered us over just like a hat.

1ST. Look, my friend, the cloud is whirling up just like a ball, just as if something living is turning around in it. And it's creeping up on us, it's creeping up, as if it were alive.

2ND. You mark my words. This storm won't pass without something happening. I'm telling you the honest truth: 'cause I know. Either it'll kill somebody, or burn down a house; you'll see: 'cause, look! it's an extraordinary color!

KATERINA (*listening*). What are they saying? They're saying that it will kill someone.

KABANOV. It's obvious they're just saying whatever pops into their heads.

KABANOVA. Don't you judge your elders! They know more than you! Older people know the signs in everything. An older man doesn't just talk to the wind.

KATERINA (*to her husband*). Tisha, I know who it's going to kill.

VARVARA (*quietly to* KATERINA). You just keep silent!

KABANOV. How do you know?

KATERINA. It's going to kill me. Pray for me then!

(THE LADY *with two valets enters.* KATERINA *cries out and hides.*)

THE LADY. What're you hiding for? Nothing to hide for! It's clear you're afraid: you don't want to die! Want to live a bit! Who doesn't want to! Look at her, what a beauty! Ha, ha, ha! Real beauty! But you pray to God now, so He'll take away your beauty. Beauty, see, 's the end of us! You ruin yourself, you deceive people, and then you know the delight of this beauty of yours! You lead lots and lots of people into sin! The weather cocks come out to duel and stick each other with their spurs. A grand time! The old timers, the pious people forget all about death, lured on by this beauty! And who's going to answer for it? Sooner or later you've got to answer for everything. Better right into the pit with this beauty! Quicker, quicker! (KATERINA *hides*) What're you trying to hide for, foolish girl! You can't get away from God! You're all going to burn in unquenchable fire! (*Goes out*)

KATERINA. I'm dying!

VARVARA. What are you torturing yourself for, in fact! Go aside and pray a little, and you'll feel better.

KATERINA (*goes up to the wall and falls on her knees, then quickly jumps up*). Hell! Hell! The Gehenna of fire! (KABANOV, KABANOVA *and* VARVARA *surround her*) My heart has been torn to pieces! I can stand it no longer! Mama! Tisha! I am guilty toward God and toward you! Didn't I swear to you that I'd look at no one while you were gone! You remember, remember! But do you know what I did, wicked woman, while you were gone? The very first night I left the house . . .

KABANOV (*beside himself, in tears, tugs at her sleeve*). Don't, don't; don't talk! What're you doing? Mama's here!

KABANOVA (*severely*). Well, go on, say it, since you've started.

KATERINA. And the whole ten nights I went out . . . (*Sobs*) (KABANOV *tries to embrace her.*)

KABANOVA. Don't touch her! With whom?

VARVARA. She's not making any sense; she herself doesn't know what she's saying.

KABANOVA. You be quiet! This is something! Well, with whom, now?

KATERINA. With Boris Grigorevich. (*A clap of thunder*) Ah! (*Falls unconscious into her husband's arms*)

KABANOVA. So, my boy! What independence won't lead to! I told you so, but you wouldn't listen. Now you've got what you asked for!

ACT V

The setting of Act I. Twilight. KULIGIN *sits on a bench.* KABANOV *is walking along the avenue.*

KULIGIN (*sings*). The heavens were covered with the darkness of night
And everyone shut their eyes in peace, etc.

(*Catching sight of* KABANOV) How are you, sir! You going far?

KABANOV. Home. Did you hear what happened to us? The whole family has been thrown into chaos.

KULIGIN. I did, I heard about it, sir.

KABANOV. I went to Moscow, did you know? Mama gave me orders for the road, gave me a list of what to do, but as soon as I got away I started drinking. I was terribly glad to get out on my own. And I drank the whole trip, and kept drinking in Moscow the whole time, a whole lot, this much, you never saw anything like it! So I could fill up for the year. Didn't think about home even once. And even if I had, I still wouldn't have had any idea of what went on. Did you hear?

KULIGIN. I did, sir.

KABANOV. I'm a wretched man now! I'm being ruined for nothing, for a song!

KULIGIN. Your mama is terribly stern.

KABANOV. Sure. She's the whole cause of everything. But what am I being ruined for, can you tell me please? I just dropped in on Dikòi and we had some drinks. I thought it'd be easier, but it's worse, Kuligin. What my wife did to me! Nothing could be worse . . .

KULIGIN. A tricky business, sir. It's hard to judge you all.

KABANOV. No, wait! It's a lot worse than that. It's not enough to kill her for it. As Mama says, we ought to bury her alive so she would repent. But I like her, and I'd hate to lift a finger against her. I beat her a little, but Mama made me do that. I feel very sorry just looking at her, don't misunderstand me, Kuligin. Mama is making life a burden for her, but she just goes around like a shadow, never answering. She just cries and melts, like wax. Me, too, I'm just overcome with grief, looking at her.

KULIGIN. Somehow, sir, the whole thing ought to be patched up! You would forgive her, and never mention it again. Yourself, now, I believe, you've been sinful, too.

KABANOV. That's perfectly true!

KULIGIN. Well, so, there should be no reproach from a drunk! She would go on being a good wife to you, sir; look at her—better than any.

KABANOV. But don't get me wrong, Kuligin: I wouldn't be against it, but Mama now . . . You can never get her to agree!

KULIGIN. It's high time, sir, you started to think for yourself.

KABANOV. What'll I do, divide myself up? Nobody has a mind of his own, they say. This means, you have to live with somebody else's. So I'll take the last bit of whatever there is and drink it away. Let Mama then look after me, like after an idiot.

KULIGIN. Oh, sir! What a business, what a business! And Boris Grigorevich, sir, what about him?

KABANOV. He's being sent off to Tyakhta, to the Chinese, the bastard. His uncle's sending him there to work in the office of some merchant he knows. For three years.

KULIGIN. Well, how does he take it, sir?

KABANOV. Runs around like mad; cries. His uncle and I let go at him not long ago, gave him hell, hell and more hell—and he didn't say a word. Just as if he's turned into some kind of wild man. Do what you want with me, he says, but don't torture her! He, too, feels pity for her.

KULIGIN. He's a good man, sir.

KABANOV. He's gotten everything together, and the horses are ready. He's miserable; a real shame! I can see how much he wants to say good-bye to her! But that's enough of that! We've had enough from him. See, he's my enemy, Kuligin! I ought to chop him up into pieces, so he'd know . . .

KULIGIN. We must forgive our enemies, sir!

KABANOV. Wait, you talk to Mama and see what she'll say to that. So, friend Kuligin, our whole family is now completely torn apart. We're not like relatives any more, but like real enemies. Mama was preying on Varvara and preying on her, but she couldn't take it, that's just the way she is—so she up and left.

KULIGIN. Where did she go?

KABANOV. Nobody knows. They say she ran off with Kudryash, with Vanka Kudryash, and nobody can find him, either. Kuligin, got to say right away that all this is on account of Mama, because she began tyrannizing her and locking her indoors. "Don't lock me in," she says, "it'll only be worse!" And that's how it turned out. What can I do now, you tell me! Teach me how to live now! I'm sick to death of home, I'm ashamed in front of others, I start to do something—and my hands just hang at my sides. Here, now I'm going home; going for the joy of it, am I? (GLASHA *enters.*)

GLASHA. Tikhon Ivanych, sir!

KABANOV. Now what?

GLASHA. There's trouble at home, sir!

KABANOV. Lord! If it isn't one thing, it's another! Tell me, what is it now?

GLASHA. Your lady . . .

KABANOV. What? Is she dead?

GLASHA. No, sir; she's gone out somewhere, and we can't find her any place. We've worn our legs off looking.

KABANOV. Kuligin, my friend, got to go look for her. You know what I'm afraid of? That out of despair she'll lay hands on herself! She's so sad, so sad, oh! Breaks your heart just to look at her. Weren't you all watching her? Is she gone long?

GLASHA. Not very long, sir. It's our fault, we didn't look in on her. But you have to admit, you can't be watching all the time.

KABANOV. Well, what are you standing around for, run on! (GLASHA *goes out*) And we'll go, too, Kuligin.

(*They go out. The stage is empty for a short while. From the opposite side* KATERINA *comes in and quietly walks around the stage.*)

KATERINA (*alone*). [*She speaks the entire soliloquy and all the following scenes drawing her words out and repeating, deeply thoughtful and as if unconscious.—Author's note*] Nowhere, he's nowhere! Poor man, what's he doing now? Just want to say good-bye to him, and then . . . and then just die.

What did I get him into trouble for? It didn't make anything easier for me! I alone should perish! But I ruined myself, ruined him, disgraced myself, humiliated him forever! Yes! Disgraced myself, humiliated him forever. (*Silence*) I wish I could remember, what did he say? Did he feel sorry for me? What were the words he said? (*Holds her head*) I don't remember, I've forgotten everything. The nights, the nights are terrible for me! Everyone goes to bed, and I go, too; they all think nothing of it, but for me it's like the grave. It's so terrible in the darkness! There's some kind of noise, and there's singing just like at a funeral, only so quietly you can barely hear it, far, far away from me . . . You become so happy when it gets light! But you don't want to get up; just the same people again, the same conversations, the same torment. What do they look at me like that for? Why don't they kill me now? What have they done this for? In olden times, they say, people killed you. They would have taken me and thrown me into the Volga; and I would have been glad. "Have to punish you hard," they say, "to take away your sin, or you'll be tortured all your life by your sin." And how I have suffered! Must I go on being tortured for long? What am I living for now, what for? I don't need anything, I don't like anything; and even God's world is hateful to me!—but death doesn't come. You call it, but it doesn't come. Whatever I see, whatever I hear, it just hurts here (*pointing to her heart*). If I could live with him, maybe I would have some joy . . . What difference would it make: I've already destroyed my soul. How much I miss him! How much I miss him! So now, though I don't see you, hear me from the distance at least! You wild winds, carry my sad longing to him! O God, it's depressing, depressing! (*Goes up to the shore, and loudly, at the top of her voice:*) My joy! My life, my soul, I love you! Answer me! (*Cries*)

(BORIS *enters.*)

BORIS (*not seeing* KATERINA). My God! It's her voice! Where is she? (*Looks around*)

KATERINA (*runs up to him and throws her arms around his neck*). So I've seen you! (*Cries on his chest*)

(*Silence.*)

BORIS. So we have wept together, as God ordained.

KATERINA. You haven't forgotten me?

BORIS. How could I! What are you talking about?

KATERINA. No, nothing, nothing! You aren't angry?

BORIS. Why should I be?

KATERINA. Forgive me. I didn't mean to do you wrong; I wasn't in control of myself. What I said, what I did, I didn't know what I was doing.

BORIS. Stop it, what are you saying! What are you saying!

KATERINA. What's it like for you? What will you do now?

BORIS. I'm leaving.

KATERINA. Where are you going?

BORIS. Far away, Katya, to Siberia.

KATERINA. Take me with you!

BORIS. Impossible, Katya. I'm not going of my own free will: my uncle is sending me, and the horses are ready; I just begged my uncle to let me have a minute, for I wanted to say good-bye to this place where we met.

KATERINA. God bless you and keep you! Don't grieve for me. Only at first you'll be lonely, my poor dear, but then you'll forget.

BORIS. Why talk about me! I'm a free man. What's it like for you? What about your mother-in-law?

KATERINA. She torments me, locks me in. Tells everyone and tells my husband: "Don't trust her, she's cunning." And they follow me around all the time all day long and laugh right in my face. Any time I say something they keep reproaching me with you.

BORIS. And your husband?

KATERINA. Sometimes kind, sometimes angry, but drinking all the time. He's repulsive to me, repulsive; his kindness is worse than a beating.

BORIS. It's terrible for you, Katya!

KATERINA. So terrible, so terrible, it would be easier to die!

BORIS. Who could have known that we'd both suffer so because of our love! It would have been better had I run away then!

KATERINA. It only brought trouble that I ever saw you. I've had little joy, but what sorrow, what sorrow! And how much more ahead! But what's the point in thinking about what will come! Now I have seen you; they can't take that from me; and there's nothing else I need. All I wanted was to see you. Now it's a lot easier for me, as if a weight had been taken off my shoulders. And all the time I thought that you were mad at me, cursing me . . .

BORIS. What are you saying, what are you saying!

KATERINA. No, I'm not saying it right at all, not what I wanted to say! I've missed you terribly, that's it; but, here, I've seen you.

BORIS. As long as they don't catch us here!

KATERINA. Stop, stop! I wanted to tell you something! Now I've forgotten! I had to tell you something! I'm all mixed up, I can't remember anything.

BORIS. It's time for me, Katya!

KATERINA. Wait, wait!

BORIS. Well, what did you want to say?

KATERINA. I'll think of it right away. (*Reflecting*) Yes! As you travel along, don't let a single beggar go by without giving him something and telling him to pray for my sinful soul.

BORIS. Oh, if only these people knew how painful it is for me to say good-bye to you! My God! God grant it be as sweet for them sometime as it is for me now. Good-bye, Katya! (*Embraces her and starts to go*) You criminals! Monsters of cruelty! If only I had the power!

KATERINA. Stop, stop! Let me look at you for the last time. (*Looks into his eyes*) Well, that's all for me! Now, go, and God be with you. Go on, hurry, go on!

BORIS (*moves off a few steps and stops*). Katya, something isn't right! You haven't made some plan? I'll be tormented the whole way, thinking of you.

KATERINA. Nothing, nothing! God keep you safe. (BORIS *starts to go up to her*) You mustn't, you mustn't, enough!

BORIS (*sobbing*). God bless you! I can only beg God for one thing, that she die soon, so she doesn't suffer long! Good-bye! (*Bows*)

KATERINA. Good-bye!

(BORIS *goes out.* KATERINA *follows him with her eyes and stands for a short while lost in thought.*)

KATERINA (*alone*). Where to now? Go home? No, whether I go home or to my grave, it's all the same. Yes, whether home or to my grave! . . . or to my grave! It's better in the grave . . . A little grave under a tree . . . How fine! The sun will warm it, the soft rain will moisten it . . .

In spring grass will grow on it, such soft grass . . . Birds will fly into the tree, and they will sing, children will come there, and little flowers will bloom—yellow, red, blue . . . all kinds (*gets lost in thought*) all kinds. So quiet, so good! It seems easier already! I don't want to think about life. To live again? No, no, I don't want to . . . it's bad! And people are hateful to me, and home is hateful, and even the walls are hateful! I won't go there! No, no, I won't go! You go to them and they go on walking and talking, and what's all that to me? It's grown dark! And again they're singing somewhere! What are they singing? You can't make it out . . . Now's the time to die . . . What are they singing? It's all the same whether death comes itself or whether myself I . . . but I can't go on living! It's a sin! Won't they pray? The one who loves me will pray . . . They fold your hands crosswise . . . in the grave! Yes, so . . . I remember now. But if they find me and take me home by force . . . Ah, quickly, quickly! (*Goes to the shore. Loudly:*) My friend! My joy! Good-bye! (*Goes out*)

(KABANOVA, KABANOV, KULIGIN *and a laborer with a lantern enter.*)

KULIGIN. They say they saw her here.

KABANOV. But is that true?

KULIGIN. Looked right at her, they say.

KABANOV. Well, thank God, if they saw her alive.

KABANOVA. And you got all scared and cried and cried! All for nothing. Don't worry: we've still got a long struggle with her ahead of us.

KABANOV. Who could have known that she would come here! There are so many people here. Who'd ever get the idea of hiding here?

KABANOVA. You see what she'll do! That's the kind of love-potion she is! And how she tries to be strait.

(*People with lanterns come on from several sides.*)

ONE OF THE CROWD. What, did you find her?

KABANOVA. Not at all. It's as if she dropped out of sight.

SEVERAL VOICES. What's all this! What an event! Where could she have gone?

ONE OF THE CROWD. She'll turn up.

ANOTHER. She's got to!

A 3RD. Look, here she comes herself.

A VOICE BACKSTAGE: "Hey, a boat!"

KULIGIN (*from the shore*). Who's shouting? What's there?

VOICE: "A woman threw herself in the water!"

(KULIGIN *runs out with several others behind him.*)

KABANOV. My Lord, it must be her! (*Starts to run.* KABANOVA *holds him back by the arm*) Mama, let me go, for God's sake! I'll pull her out, or myself . . . What's left for me without her!

KABANOVA. I won't let you go, and don't try it! To drown yourself for her, as if she were worth that! She caused us shame enough, without thinking up more tricks!

KABANOV. Let me go!

KABANOVA. There are enough without you. I'll curse you if you go.

KABANOV (*falling on his knees*). I just want to take a look at her!

KABANOVA. They'll pull her out; you'll see her.

KABANOV (*gets up; to the crowd*). Well, good friends, haven't you seen anything?

1ST. It's dark below, you can't see anything.

(*Noise backstage.*)

2ND. As if they were shouting something, but you can't make nothing out.

1ST. That's Kuligin's voice.

2ND. They're going with the light over there along the shore.

1ST. They're coming this way. And they're carrying her.

(*Several people return.*)

ONE OF THEM. What a fellow, Kuligin! Right close here, in a little pit near the shore. With the light you can see deep down in the water. Caught sight of her dress and pulled her out.

KABANOV. Alive?

ANOTHER. How could she be alive! Threw herself down from way up; here's the cliff, and, looks like, fell on an anchor, hurt herself good, poor thing! But, fellows, just like she's alive! Only on her temple there's a little cut, and only one, just one, little drop of blood.

(KABANOV *starts to run off;* KULIGIN *and a crowd, carrying* KATERINA, *meet him.*)

KULIGIN. Here's your Katerina. Do what you want with her! Her body's here; take it. But her soul isn't yours now; it's now before its Maker, Who is more merciful than you! (*Puts her on the ground and runs out*)

KABANOV (*rushes toward* KATERINA). Katya! Katya!

KABANOVA. Enough of that! It's a sin even to cry about her!

KABANOV. Mama, *you* killed her! You, you, you . . .

KABANOVA. What are you talking about? You forgetting yourself? You've forgotten who you're talking to!

KABANOV. You killed her! You did! You!

KABANOVA (*to her son*). Well, I'll have a talk with you at home. (*Bows deeply to the crowd*) Our thanks to you, good people, for all you've done!

(*All bow.*)

KABANOV. It's all right for you, Katya! But why am I left in this world to live and suffer! (*Falls on his wife's body*)

The Power of Darkness

OR

"If One Claw is Caught, the Whole Bird is Lost"

A DRAMA IN

FIVE ACTS

Lyov Nikolayevich Tolstoy

But I say to you that every one who looks at a woman lustfully has already committed adultery with her in his heart.

If your right eye causes you to sin, pluck it out and throw it away; it is better that you lose one of your members than that your whole body be thrown into hell.

—Matthew, V: 28, 29

DRAMATIS PERSONAE

Pyotr, a rich peasant, forty-two years old, married for the second time, morbid, ailing
Anisya, his wife, thirty-two years old, a dressy woman
Akulina, Pyotr's daughter from his first marriage sixteen years old, hard of hearing, simple-minded
Anyutka, his second daughter, ten years old
Nikita, their hired man, twenty-five years old, a dandy
Akim, Nikita's father, fifty years old, an insignificant, uncomely, God-fearing peasant
Matryona, his wife, fifty years old
Marina, an orphan girl, twenty-two years old
Anisya's neighbor, ["Auntie," Anyutka's godmother]
People
Mitrich, an old, hired hand, a retired soldier
Another neighbor
A Matchmaker, a sullen peasant
Marina's husband
First girl
Second girl
Policeman
Cabman
The best man
Akulina's bridegroom
The headman
Guests, women, girls, people at the wedding

A NOTE ON THE PLAY

The basis for the subject of the play was the trial of a peasant of the province of Tula, Efrem Koloskov, which took place in the Tula District Court, October 21, 1880, and which Tolstoy was told about by his close friend N. V. Davydov, the court prosecutor.

Tolstoy started to work on the play in October, 1886, after he had received a letter from M. V. Lentovsky, organizer of the Moscow National Theater "Skomorokh." In the letter, Lentovsky asked Tolstoy to help set up a theater for producing "popular and universally accessible plays." Tolstoy worked on his play a little over three weeks.

In November, 1886, Tolstoy submitted his manuscript to the censor for clearance and to the publishing house "Posrednik" for publication. In December he completed the rewriting of the last four scenes of Act IV, which those who had read the play found unsuitably realistic for stage presentation.

From the outset, the play met with sharp opposition from the censorship. At first it was forbidden. Then, after much inquiry and agitation in high government circles, it was allowed to be published but not to be staged.

The play was first published in February, 1887, by the publishing house "Posrednik." It was at the same time included in *The Works of Count L. N. Tolstoy, Part Twelve. Works of Recent Years*, 3rd edition, Moscow, 1886. The text of this edition, checked and corrected against the manuscripts of the play, is the text printed in Volume 26 of the jubilee edition of the *Complete Collected Writings of L. N. Tolstoy* and also in the edition from which the present translation was made: L. N. Tolstoy, *Sobranie khudozhestvennykh proizvedenii*, Vol. IX, Moscow: Pravda, 1948.

In September, 1895, permission to stage the play was granted. Its long theatrical history began with the play's world première the next month.

ACT I

The action takes place in the fall in a large village. The scene is PYOTR'*s spacious peasant cottage.* PYOTR *sits on a bench mending a horse collar.* ANISYA *and* AKULINA *are spinning and singing a duet.*

PYOTR (*looks out the window*). Again the horses are out. I'm scared they'll kill the foal. Nikita, hey, Nikita! [1] He's deaf! (*Listens. To the women*) That's enough, can't hear a thing.

NIKITA'S VOICE (*from the yard-side of the house*). What?

PYOTR. Bring in the horses.

NIKITA'S VOICE. I'll bring 'em in, gimme time.

PYOTR (*shaking his head*). These hired men! If I was well, I wouldn't keep 'em on a minute. Give you only trouble. (*Stands up and again sits down*) Nikita! Never hear you. You go, huh, one of you. Akul, go bring 'em in.

AKULINA. What, the horses?

PYOTR. What else?

AKULINA. Right away. (*Exits*)

PYOTR. He's a slacker, that fellow, waste of money. Turns his back on you, just turns it.

ANISYA. You yourself're right smart—you get off the stove and onto the bench. Expect others to do it all.

PYOTR. Expect nothing from you; you aren't home all year. Ah, what people!

ANISYA. You hand out ten jobs at once and then curse. Lying on the stove it's easy to give orders.

PYOTR (*sighing*). Ah, if it wasn't for this ailment bothering me, I wouldn't keep him a day!

AKULINA'S VOICE (*backstage*). Pse, pse, pse . . .

(*One can hear the foal neigh and the horses run in through the gate. The gate squeaks.*)

PYOTR. Chatter—that's all he does. Really, wouldn't keep him.

ANISYA (*mimicking him*). Wouldn't keep him. You yourself get a move on, then you could talk.

[1] In the original, Nikita is usually called *M*ikita by his family and other peasants. For clarity in this translation, the form *N*ikita has been used except for certain diminutives.

AKULINA (*enters*). It was hard to get 'em in. Always the roan—

PYOTR. And where's Nikita?

AKULINA. Nikita? Standing in the street.

PYOTR. What's he standing for?

AKULINA. What's he standing for? He's standing round the corner, he's chatting.

PYOTR. You can never get any sense out of her. And who's he chatting with?

AKULINA (*not having heard*). What?

(PYOTR *waves his hand at* AKULINA [in disgust]; *she sits down at her spinning.*)

ANYUTKA (*runs in. To her mother*). Nikita's mother and father've come after him. Taking him home to stay, give him a rest a while.

ANISYA. Go on!

ANYUTKA. It's a fact! Cross my heart! (*laughs*) I'm passing by, and Nikita himself says: good-bye, he says, good-bye now, Anna Petrovna. Come dance at my wedding. I'm leaving you, he says. And he laughs.

ANISYA (*to her husband*). They don't seem to need you so much. Here, he's picking up to go. "I'll drive 'em in," he says.

PYOTR. And let him go; can't I find others?

ANISYA. But the money you advanced . . . ?

(ANYUTKA *goes up to the door, listens to what they say, and exits.*)

PYOTR (*frowns*). As for the money, he can serve it off next summer.

ANISYA. You're glad to let him go—so's you don't have to feed him. And the winter comes and I have to do it all by myself, work like a horse. The girl's got no great desire to work, and you'll lie on the stove. I know you.

PYOTR. If you don't know what you're saying, what do you jabber on for?

ANISYA. The yard's full of stock. You didn't sell the cow and you let in all the sheep for the winter, you ain't setting out fodder and water for 'em—but you want to let the hired man go. I'm not going to do no man's work! I'll lie down, just like you, on the stove—let everything go. Do what you want.

PYOTR (*to* AKULINA). Go get the fodder, huh—it's time.

AKULINA. Get the fodder? Oh, all right. (*Puts on her coat and takes a rope*)

ANISYA. I ain't going to work for you. Enough, no more. Work yourself.

PYOTR. Yeah, enough. What're you so mad for? You're anyone's piece of meat.

ANISYA. And you're a mad dog! Nobody gets any work out of you, and no pleasure neither. You just nag all the time. A big threatening stud-dog, that's you.

PYOTR (*spits and dresses*). Damn you! God forgive me! Got to go find out what's up. (*Exits*)

ANISYA (*after him*). Stinking devil! big-nosed!

AKULINA. What're you scolding Pa for?

ANISYA. Go to hell, you old fool. Shut up.

AKULINA (*goes up to the door*). I know what you're scolding for. You're an old fool yourself, you're a bitch. I'm not scared of you.

ANISYA. You what? (*Jumps up and looks for something to hit her with*) Look out, I'll smash you.

AKULINA (*having opened the door*). You're a bitch, a devil, that's what you are. Devil, bitch, bitch, devil! (*Runs off*)

ANISYA (*alone reflectively*). Come, he says, to my wedding. What's that they've thought up? To marry him? Look out, Nikita: if this's your doing, why I'll—I can't live without him. I won't let him go.

NIKITA (*enters, looks around. Seeing that* ANISYA *is alone, goes quickly up to her. In a whisper*). What a lot of trouble, little one. The old man came, wants to take me away—orders me home. Once and for all, he says, we're going to marry you, and you live at home.

ANISYA. So, get married. What's it to me?

NIKITA. Well, so—all right. I was figuring on how to work the whole thing out best, but she just says: Go get married. What's up? (*Winks*) You ain't forgot?

ANISYA. So get married, it's real nec—

NIKITA. And what're you snorting for? Look at her, she won't even turn around. What's going on?

ANISYA. What's going on is you want to leave me. And you want to leave me, well, and I don't need you. That's all there is to it.

NIKITA. Stop it, Anisya. Really, do I want to forget you?

Not on my life. I ain't never, that means, going to leave you for good. But I figure it this way: so I get married, so I'll come back to you; as long as they don't drag me home.

ANISYA. I'd sure need you an awful lot married.

NIKITA. Yeah, but how, my little one—a person can never get out from what his father wants.

ANISYA. You turn it all on your father, but it's all your idea. You've been making eyes at that doll of yours, that Marinka, a long time now. It's her got you to do this. Didn't run over here the other day for nothing.

NIKITA. Marinka!? I need her like a—! As if there was few of them like that who go hanging around with men!

ANISYA. What'd your father come for then? You told him to! Deceived me, you did! (*Cries*)

NIKITA. Anisya! you believe God, or not? I didn't see any of this even in a dream. I don't know a thing, really, I don't know nothing. My old man thought the whole thing up in his head.

ANISYA. As long as you yourself don't want to, then who's going to drag you into it, like as if you were an ass?

NIKITA. Also, I figure, a man can't do much contrariwise to his father. And I got no desire to.

ANISYA. Stand up to him, that's all there's to it.

NIKITA. I know a fellow stood up like that, so he got hauled off to the local judge's and got a real going-over. It's very simple. Besides I don't like it. They say it tickles—

ANISYA. Stop the joking. You listen, Nikita: if you go and take Marina for keeps, I don't know what I'll do to myself—I won't go on living! I sinned, I broke the law, and now there's no turning back. Just you as much as go away, I'll do something—

NIKITA. Why should I go? If I wanted to go, I'd of gone long ago. Not long ago Ivan Semyonych asked me to be coachman for him— What kind of life's that! Didn't go. So I figure I'm good enough for everyone. If you didn't love me, why then it'd be different.

ANISYA. But just remember. If not today then tomorrow the old man'll die, I expect—we'll cover up all our sins. I'll have a church wedding, I've been thinking, and you'll be the master.

NIKITA. Ah, there's no point guessing. What's it to me?

I work here the way I would for myself. And the master likes me, and so his old woman, too, likes me. And if the women like me, well, it's not my doing. Simple as that.

ANISYA. Will you keep on loving me?

NIKITA (*embraces her*). Like this! You've always been so close to me—

(MATRYONA *enters and for a long time crosses herself in front of the icon;* NIKITA *and* ANISYA *move away from each other.*)

MATRYONA. So what I saw I didn't see, what I heard I didn't hear. He was chasing a butterfly—well, so? Why the calf, too, see, he, too, plays around. Why not play around? It's what you're young for. But the master out in the yard's asking for you, son.

NIKITA. I came in for the axe.

MATRYONA. I know, I know, my dear, for which axe. Most of the time the women have got that axe.

NIKITA (*bends over, takes the axe*). Say, Ma, is it really true you're going to marry me off? I figure it's all for nothing. And, besides, I got no desire to.

MATRYONA. Hey-ey! Sweetie, why marry? Just go on as you are. It's all your old man's doing. Go on, my dear, we'll work it all out without you.

NIKITA. It's really queer: first you got to marry, then you don't. For sure I can't figure nothing out. (*Exits*)

ANISYA. So, Auntie Matryona, is it really true you want to marry him off?

MATRYONA. What have we got to marry him with, sweetie! You know how much we have? Not much; my old man's just babbling: marry him, marry him. This business is beyond him. Horses don't go roaming off from their oats, see, and you don't leave the good to look for the good—and that's just the way it is here. Don't I see (*winks*) what it's all leading up to?

ANISYA. So how can I, Auntie Matryona, keep it from you. You know everything. I sinned, I fell in love with your son.

MATRYONA. Now, that's something. And Auntie Matryona just didn't know. Ah, dearie, Auntie Matryona's been around, been around, been all over. Auntie Matryona, I tell you, sweetie, can see a yard through the ground. I know everything, sweetie! I know what young wives want to give sleeping powders for. Brought some. (*Unties the knot in her kerchief, takes out a packet of powders)* What I have to I see; what I don't have to, why I don't know nothing, nothing at all. That's how it is. Auntie Matryona was young, too. Had to be knowing how to get on with her own fool, too, see. Know all seventy-seven ways around. I see, sweetie, your old man's worm-eaten, all worm-eaten. What have you got to live with? Poke him with a pitchfork, no blood'll come out. You'll see, you'll bury him by spring. And you'll have to hire a man for the yard. And why's my son not a good man? No worse'n others. So what would I get by taking him away from what's coming to him? Am I my own boy's enemy?

ANISYA. Just so he don't leave us.

MATRYONA. And he won't leave, sweetie. It's all stupid. You know my old man. He's got a regular good head, but then he'll get set on something as if it was nailed in for keeps and you can't beat it out.

ANISYA. And how did all this get started?

MATRYONA. Well, you see, sweetie—you know yourself, the fellow's got a way with women, he's a good-looker, admit it. Well, he was living, see, on the railroad, and there was this orphan girl—working as a cook. Well, and she set her cap for him, this girl did.

ANISYA. Marinka?

MATRYONA. That's the one, I hope she drops dead. Well, and was there something or wasn't there, only my old man hears about it. From others maybe, or she herself squealed on him to him.

ANISYA. What a bold bitch!

MATRYONA. And so my old man, the old crackpot, ups and says: marry him, he says, marry him, cover up the sin. Let's fetch the fellow home, he says, and marry him. I argued every way. What can you do? Well, I think to myself, all right. I'll try another way. You got to handle them fools just right, sweetie. As if all has agreement. But when it really comes down to it, then you right away stand up for your own. The old woman, see, flies down from the stove, thinks over seventy-seven schemes, see, so how is he ever to figure it out. Well, I says, old man, it's a good deal. Just got to think it over. Let's go, I says, see the boy and have a talk with Pyotr Ignatich. What'll he say? Well, so here we are.

ANISYA. O-oh, Auntie, is that how it is? And what's his father tell him?

MATRYONA. Tells him? And shove what he tells him up a dog's ass. Just don't you worry, this thing'll never come off, I'm going right now to sift and sieve the whole thing with your old man and there'll be nothing left. Why I came with him just to make it look good. Why here's my son living happily, expecting happiness, and I'm going to try to marry him off to a whore? What, am I an old fool, huh?

ANISYA. She came running after him even here, this Marinka. You believe me, Auntie, when I heard he was going to get married it was like a knife went through me, through my heart. I think his heart's with her.

MATRYONA. Hey, dearie! What's he, a fool, huh? He's going to love a homeless slut, huh? Mikishka, see, he's a smart fellow, too. He knows who to love. But don't you worry, sweetie. We won't take him away for the life of us. And won't marry him neither. And you just let us have a little money, and let him go on.

ANISYA. It seems if Nikita goes I won't go on living.

MATRYONA. That's how it is when you're young. I know what you mean! You're a woman full of life, to live with such an old man—

ANISYA. Believe me, Auntie, he's hateful, he's hateful to me, the old long-nosed dog; I can't no more look him in the eye—

MATRYONA. Yeah, that's how it is. Here, look here. (*In a whisper, looking around*) I was at the old man's, see, for some powders. He give me two handfuls of drugs. Look here. This, he says, is a sleeping powder. Give, he says, just one—he'll fall into such a sleep you could walk on him. And this, he says, is such a drug, give it to him, he says, in what he drinks—there's no trace at all, but its power's great. Seven times, he says, a pinch at a time. Just give it the seven times. And the freedom, he says, will come to her soon.

ANISYA. O-o-o-o. What is it?

MATRYONA. There won't be a mark, he says. He took a ruble.

Can't do it for less, he says. 'Cause, see, you got to be smart to get 'em. I paid him myself, sweetie, out of my own pocket. I was thinking, she will, she won't, I'll take 'em to Mikhailovna.

ANISYA. O-o-o! But can something bad come from them?

MATRYONA. What should there be something bad for, sweetie? It'd be one thing if your man was strong, but as it is, why it's something he's alive. He's not long for this world, see. There're lots like him.

ANISYA. Oh, oh! my aching head! I'm scared, Auntie, there's something sinful in this. No, what is this?

MATRYONA. It can go back again.

ANISYA. What are they, and how do you, what, dissolve 'em in water?

MATRYONA. In tea, he says, it's better. Nothing, he says, is noticeable, not a trace of 'em, nothing. He, too, he's a clever man.

ANISYA (*takes the powders*). Oh, oh, my aching head! I couldn't have come to such a thing if this life wasn't so unbearable.

MATRYONA. But don't forget the ruble, too, I promised the old man I'd leave it off with him. He, too, went to some trouble.

ANISYA. Sure he did. (*Goes to the chest and hides the powders*)

MATRYONA. And you, sweetie, keep 'em real tight, so nobody knows. And if someone, God forbid, does touch 'em, 'course they're for cockroaches— (*Takes the ruble*) It also works for cockroaches— (*Suddenly stops talking*)

AKIM *enters, crosses himself in front of the ikon.*)

PYOTR (*enters and sits down*). So what d'you think, Uncle Akim?

AKIM. It'd be better, Ignatich, be a bit better, now, it'd be better— Somehow it isn't a— The mischief, I mean. I'd like it, now, I'd like the fellow, I mean, to stick to the job. But if you could, now, a— It'd be better so—

PYOTR. All right, all right. Sit down, let's talk about it. (AKIM *sits*) So what is it? So you want to marry him off?

MATRYONA. The marrying can wait a spell, Pyotr Ignatich. We have nothing, you know yourself, Ignatich. How can he marry? We can't keep our souls in our bodies. So how *can* he?

PYOTR. Judge for yourselves what's best.

MATRYONA. Then, too, there's no hurry to marry him. It's that kind of thing. It's not something that'll spoil.

PYOTR. Well now, if he gets married—that's a good thing.

AKIM. I'm for it, I mean— 'Cause for me, I mean, now— A bit of work in town, a bit of work turned up, a good job, I mean—

MATRYONA. But what work! Cleaning pits. Came home the other day, he did, and I just threw up, threw up, Lord!

AKIM. Exactly so. At first she—just exactly so, the smell sort of, I mean, hit her, but you get used to it—it's nothing, it's all the same, it's the leftovers, and, I mean, now, it's a good job— And the smell, now— It can't bother a fellow like us. You can change your clothes, too. So I'd like Nikitka home. Let him clear himself, I mean. Let him clear himself at home. And I'll keep on in town.

PYOTR. You want your son to stay home. Just right. But how'll the money be paid back?

AKIM. That's true, that's true, Ignatich, you said this, now, very justly, 'cause a man who's hired has already agreed—let him finish out his time, I mean, but, now, just let him get married. For a little while, that is, let him go, can't you?

PYOTR. Well now, I could.

MATRYONA. Yeah but the thing ain't agreed on between us. I'll be open with you, Pyotr Ignatich, just like as with God. You just judge me and my old man. He keeps harping on get him married, well, get him married. But get married to who, you ask him! If it was a real bride, would I be against my own child?—but this is a girl with a bad—

AKIM. Now that's wrongful. You're taking on, now, about this girl wrongfully. Wrongfully. 'Cause she, this girl herself, now, suffered injury from my son; I mean, there's an injury there. To the girl, that is.

PYOTR. What kind of injury's that?

AKIM. Why it turns out, I mean, it was my son Nikitka. It was Nikitka, I mean, now.

MATRYONA. You hold on a bit, I got a smoother tongue, let me tell it. This young fellow of ours lived, 'fore he came to you, you know yourself, on the railroad. And there this girl latches onto him, you know, a simple girl, Marinka they call her, worked as a cook for the gang there. And so this girl, this very same girl, points to our son, see, our son, making out as if he, Nikita, as if he tricked her.

PYOTR. There's nothing good about this.

MATRYONA. Yeah, she's a bad lot, hangs around with all sorts. A slut.

AKIM. Again you aren't right, now, old woman, you still aren't right, now, still aren't right—

MATRYONA. See, that's all the speeches you get from my eagle, my own, see—right, now, right, now, right, now—and what's right, now, you don't know yourself. You, Pyotr Ignatich, don't ask me, ask other people about the girl, anybody'll tell you the same. Just a foot-loose girl with no home.

PYOTR (*to* AKIM). Well now, Uncle Akim, if that's the way things are, why there's no point in getting him married. See, it's not like an old shoe, you can't just slip it off, being a daughter-in-law.

AKIM (*getting excited*). False, the old woman was, I mean, about the girl, now, it's all false. 'Cause the girl, she's really fine, just a really fine girl, I mean. I'm sorry, sorry, now, for this girl.

MATRYONA. Why, he really weeps for the world and lets his own go begging. Sorry for the girl but not for his son. Stick her on your neck and go through the world with her. Stop talking hot air.

AKIM. No, it's not hot air.

MATRYONA. Don't you take off, you let me talk.

AKIM (*interrupts*). No, it's not hot air. I mean, you take it all your way, 'bout the girl or 'bout yourself, you take it your way, the way it seems better to you, but God, I mean, now, He'll turn it all his way. This, too, that is.

MATRYONA. Ah, a person just wears down his tongue talking to you.

AKIM. The girl's a hard worker, real decent and, I mean, now, round her there are, I mean— And on account of our being poor, that's just what we can manage, I mean: and a wedding's not that much. But what's the most of all is the wrong there is to this girl, I mean, an orphan girl, she is, see. And she's been wronged.

MATRYONA. Any one of 'em, they all say—

ANISYA. You, Uncle Akim, listen closer to the women. They'll tell you some stories!

AKIM. But God, our God! Ain't she a person, this girl? I mean for God, too, she's a person. And what do you think?

MATRYONA. Ah, you keep harping—

PYOTR. And, you know what, Uncle Akim, you know, you can't believe these girls. And the fellow's alive. Why just right there! Send him in and ask him what this all means, right? Won't do no harm. Call the boy. (ANISYA *gets up*) Go, tell him, his father wants him.

(ANISYA *exits.*)

MATRYONA. Now you've decided this, dear, like pouring oil on troubled waters. Let the boy himself speak up. Besides, too, the way things are done now, you don't force 'em to marry. You also got to ask the fellow. He'll never in the world go marrying her and shame himself. The way I figure it, let him live at your place and work for you. No point in taking him just for the summer; we can add on someone. But you give us ten, huh, and let him stay on.

PYOTR. That talk's too soon; got to take things in order. Finish one thing, then take up the next.

AKIM. I want to add to this, I mean, Pyotr Ignatich, 'cause, I mean, now, that's the way it worked out. You work things out, I mean, the way it's best for you, and 'bout God, now, why you clean forget. You figure it's better—you do it your way, you look, and you've brought it all down on your own head, I mean. You figured how it was best, but it's a lot worse, without God.

PYOTR. Everyone knows that! You got to remember God.

AKIM. You look, it's no good, but doing it the right way, God's way, it all somehow, now, it makes you glad. Seems like that, I mean. So, I figured to myself, I'll marry the boy off, so there's no sin, I mean. He'll be home, now, just like it ought to be by the law, and I, why I'll be busying myself over town. It's a pretty nice job. A good job. God's way, I mean, now, why it's better. Then, she's an orphan, you know. Like for example, last summer they took some wood from the estate steward like that. Figured they'd trick him. Well, they tricked him, but God, now, they didn't trick, and now this—

(NIKITA *and* ANYUTKA *enter.*)

NIKITA. You wanted me? (*Sits down, takes out his tobacco*)

PYOTR (*quietly, reproachfully*). What're you doing, don't you know how to behave? Your father's calling you, but you keep fussing with your tobacco and even sit down. Come over here, get up!

(NIKITA *stands by the table, overly familiarly leaning on it and grinning.*)

AKIM. There's been made, I mean, now, seems like against you, Mikishka, a complaint, a complaint, I mean.

NIKITA. Complaint by who?

AKIM. The complaint? By a girl, by an orphan, I mean, the complaint's by her. By her, and a complaint against you, by Marina, by herself, now.

NIKITA (*chuckling*). It's terrific, really. What kind of complaint is this thing? And who was it told you; herself, huh?

AKIM. Now, I'm doing the asking now, and you, I mean, you must do the answering. Did you say you'd get married to this girl, I mean, that is, did you say you'd get married to her, I mean?

NIKITA. Makes no sense to me, what you're asking.

AKIM. I mean, nonsense, I mean, was there any nonsense between you and her, any nonsense, that is?

NIKITA. Little, indeed. You get bored and joke with the cook and play the accordion and she dances a bit. What other kind of nonsense is there?

PYOTR. You, Nikita, don't talk back, but what your father asks you answer sensibly.

AKIM (*portentously*). Nikita! You can hide from people, but you can't hide from God. You, Nikita, now, think, don't try to lie! She's an orphan, I mean, can be hurt. The orphan, I mean. You tell us a little better now, how it was.

NIKITA. Well, but, there's nothing to say. I've been telling you absolutely everything there was, and so there's nothing to say. (*Getting excited*) She won't say what was. Talk as you want, like about the dead. Why didn't she talk about Fedka Mikishkin? Does this mean, the way things're going now, I mean, you can't joke around? But she's free to talk.

AKIM. Ai, Mikishka, watch yourself! A falsehood'll show itself up. Was there something or not?

NIKITA (*aside*). They're really after me. (*To* AKIM) I'm telling you I know nothing. There was nothing between her and me. (*Spitefully*) The Lord's right there, let me die on the spot. (*Makes the sign of the cross*) I know nothing about nothing. (*Silence;* NIKITA *continues more heatedly*) What put it into your head to marry me to her? It's in fact, really, a scandal on me. Nowadays there's no such rights so you could force a fellow to marry. It's that simple. And then I swore—I know nothing about nothing.

MATRYONA (*to her husband*). What'd I tell you, you with your thick old bean, stupid. Whatever gossip he hears, why he believes it all. It's all for nothing you embarrassed the boy. And it's better the way he's been going, so let him stay on with his boss. The boss'll give us ten now to help us out. And the time'll come and we'll marry him.

PYOTR. Well, what do you think, Uncle Akim?

AKIM (*clucking his tongue; to his son*). Watch yourself, Nikita, the tears of the injured, now, don't just pass by, but every time fall on a man's head. Watch yourself, so it don't come to that.

NIKITA. As for the watching, you yourself watch out. (*Sits*)

ANYUTKA. Got to go tell Mama. (*Runs out*)

MATRYONA (*to* PYOTR). That's the way it always is, Pyotr Ignatich. He's stirred up, my old man is, gets something into his old head and you can't knock it out nohow. Only we get you all alarmed for nothing. And the way the boy's been going, let him keep on. Keep the boy—he's your servant.

PYOTR. So what do you think, Uncle Akim?

AKIM. So, well, now, I, wasn't forcing the boy, only oughtn't to be so. I was just wanting, I mean, now—

MATRYONA. You're all mixed up and you yourself don't know it. Let him stay on the way he was. The boy himself's got no desire to leave. And as far as it concerns us, we'll manage ourselves.

PYOTR. One thing, Uncle Akim: if you take him back for the summer, I don't need him for the winter. If he stays, it's for the year.

MATRYONA. So he'll be bound the year. We at home, when things are at their height, if we need someone, we'll hire him on, but let the boy stay on, and you just now—ten for us—

PYOTR. So what do you think, for another year?

AKIM (*sighs*). Yeh, well, it's pretty clear, the way it is, I mean, it's already pretty clear.

MATRYONA. Again for a year, from 'Mitry Saturday. You won't be grudging the price, and give us the ten now. Help us out now. (*Rises and bows*)

(ANISYA *and* ANYUTKA *enter.* ANISYA *sits on the side.*)

PYOTR. Well now? If it's that way, that's the way it is—let's go to the tavern and have a treat. Let's go, Uncle Akim, and have a little glass of vodka.

AKIM. I don't drink it, the liquor, I don't drink.

PYOTR. Well, you'll drink some tea.

AKIM. I'm fond of tea. Tea, just tea.

PYOTR. And the womenfolk'll drink some tea. You, Nikita, look sharp, drive in the sheep and pick up the straw.

NIKITA. All right. (*All exit except* NIKITA. *It gets dark.* NIKITA, *alone, lights a cigarette*) See, they kept pestering, come on tell us how you went after the girls. It'd take a long time to get these stories told. Marry her, he says. Yeh and marry 'em all—there'd be a real collection of wives. Yeh, I really need to get married, and since I don't live no worse than a married man, people envy me. And how did it happen someone sort of pushed me, like, so I crossed myself in front of the icon? So I wound up the proceedings right away doing that. It's terrible, frightening, they say, to swear to a lie. It's all just stupid. It's nothing, just talk. It's really simple.

AKULINA (*enters in her coat, puts down a rope, takes off her coat and goes to the larder*). You could have at least put the light on.

NIKITA. To look at you? I see you this way.

AKULINA. Go to hell.

ANYUTKA (*runs in; to* NIKITA *in a whisper*). Nikita, hurry out of here, someone's asking for you, sure as I'm living.

NIKITA. What sort of fellow?

ANYUTKA. Marinka from the railroad. Standing round the corner.

NIKITA. Go on!

ANYUTKA. Sure as I'm living.

NIKITA. What's she after?

ANYUTKA. She told you to come. I just got to say a word,

she says, to Nikita. I began asking, but she wouldn't say. Only she asked: Is it true that he's leaving you? But I says: It's not true, his father wanted to take him off and marry him, but he refused, he's going to stay on with us another year. And then she says: send him out to me, for the Lord's sake. I absolutely got to tell him something, she says. She's been waiting a long time now. Go see her.

NIKITA. The hell with her. What should I go for?

ANYUTKA. She says, if he won't come, I'll go into the house to him myself. Sure as I'm living, I'll come, she says.

NIKITA. Probably she'll stand around and then go away.

ANYUTKA. Are they fixing, she says, to marry him to Akulina?

AKULINA (*goes over to* NIKITA *to get her distaff*). Marry who to Akulina?

ANYUTKA. Nikita.

AKULINA. Just like that? Who says so?

NIKITA. It's clear, people are talking. (*Looks at her, laughs*) Akulina, really, would you marry me?

AKULINA. Marry you? Maybe I would of before, but now I wouldn't.

NIKITA. Why wouldn't you now?

AKULINA. You wouldn't love me.

NIKITA. Why wouldn't I?

AKULINA. They wouldn't allow you to. (*Laughs*)

NIKITA. Who wouldn't allow me?

AKULINA. My stepmother. She's cursing all the time, all the time looking at you.

NIKITA (*laughs*). Hey now! But you got your eyes open!

AKULINA. Me? What's there for me to see? Think I'm blind? Today she was really after Pa, really after him. She's a fat-faced witch, that's what she is. (*Exits to the larder*)

ANYUTKA. Nikita! Take a look! (*Looks out the window*) She's coming. Sure as I'm living, it's her. I'm going. (*Exits*)

MARINA (*enters*). What're you trying to do to me?

NIKITA. What'm I doing? I'm doing nothing.

MARINA. You want to get rid of me?

NIKITA (*getting up angrily*). So, is this what you came here for?

MARINA. Ah, Nikita!

NIKITA. You're all really wonderful. What'd you come for?

MARINA. Nikita!

NIKITA. Well, what about Nikita! Here's Nikita. What do you want? Get out of here.

MARINA. So, I see, you want to get rid of me, want to forget.

NIKITA. What's there to remember? See, she don't know herself. You stood around the corner, sent Anyutka in, I didn't go out to you. Means, I don't need to see you, simple as that. So, go on.

MARINA. Don't need me? Now I've become not needed. And I believed you that you'd keep on loving me. And you deceived me, and now I've become not needed.

NIKITA. And all this talk's getting nowhere, don't make no sense at all. You already told all this junk to my father. Go away, do me the favor.

MARINA. You know yourself I never loved no one but you. If you marry me or not, I wouldn't get offended. I'm not guilty of anything to you. What'd you stop loving me for? What for?

NIKITA. There's no point in you and me just talking hot air. Go away. You all make no sense.

MARINA. It doesn't hurt me so much that you deceived me, promised to marry me, but you stopped loving me. And it doesn't hurt so much that you stopped loving me as that you swapped me for another—and who for I know!

NIKITA (*spitefully going up to her*). Eh! A fellow talks to girls like you but they don't understand no kind of reasoning. Go away, I tell you, 'fore you make me do something evil.

MARINA. Something evil? What, are you going to beat me? Go ahead, beat me! What'd you turn away for? Eh, Nikita.

NIKITA. People'll come, it'll look bad, of course. And why keep talking about nothing?

MARINA. So it's the end, means that what was is gone. You tell me to forget! Well, Nikita, remember. I valued my maiden honor more than eyesight. You ruined me for nothing, deceived me. Didn't pity an orphan (*cries*), got rid of me. Killed me, you did, but still I don't have it in for you. God be with you. You find someone better, you'll forget; find someone worse, you'll remember. You'll remember, Nikita. Good-bye, even so. And I loved you, I did. Good-bye for keeps. (*Wants to embrace him and takes his head*)

NIKITA (*tearing himself away*). Hey! There's just talk between us. If you don't want to go, I'll go myself, you stay here.

MARINA (*yells*). You beast! (*In the doorway*) God won't make you happy! (*Exits crying*)

AKULINA (*comes out of the larder*). You're a dog, Nikita.

NIKITA. Why?

AKULINA. How she howled! (*Cries*)

NIKITA. What's that for?

AKULINA. What for? You wrong-ed her— You'll hurt me the same way—you're a dog. (*Exits into the larder*)

NIKITA (*alone, after a silence*). It's all somehow mixed up. I love these women like sugar, but if you go too far with them—there's trouble!

ACT II

The setting is the street in front of PYOTR*'s peasant cottage. On the audience's left is the cottage in two sections, the entranceway, with the porch in the center; on the right is the gate and edge of the yard. At the edge of the yard* ANISYA *is scutching hemp. Six months have passed since Act I.*

ANISYA (*alone, stops, listening to something*). Again he's mumbling something. Must be he climbed off the stove. (AKULINA *enters with buckets on a yoke*) He's calling. Take a look, what does he want? How he's shouting!

AKULINA. But what about you?

ANISYA. Go on, I tell you.

(AKULINA *goes into the cottage.*)

ANISYA (*alone*). He's worn me out. Won't let on where the money is, that's the thing. He was in the hall the other day, must be he hid it there. Now I myself don't know where it is. Lucky he fears parting with it. It's still in the house. If only I could find it. It wasn't on him yesterday. Now I myself don't know where it is. He's worn me out completely. (AKULINA *enters, tying her kerchief on her head*) Where you going?

AKULINA. Where? He told me to call Aunt Marfa. Call my sister, he says. I'm going to die, he says, I got to tell her something.

ANISYA (*to herself*). He's calling his sister. Oh, my aching head! Oh-oh! Must be he wants to give it to her. What am I going to do? Oh! (*To* AKULINA) Don't go! Where you going?

AKULINA. For my aunt.

ANISYA. Don't go, I tell you, I'll tell her myself, and you take the wash down to the stream. Or else you won't get it done before dark.

AKULINA. But he told me to.

ANISYA. Go where I tell you. I'll go get Marfa myself, I tell you. Bring the shirts in off the fence.

AKULINA. The shirts? But I bet you won't go. He *told* me to.

ANISYA. I told you I'll go. Where's Anyutka?

AKULINA. Anyutka? She's looking after the calves.

ANISYA. Send her in, they won't run away.

(AKULINA *picks up the wash and exits.*)

ANISYA (*alone*). If I don't go, he'll get mad; if I do, he'll give his sister the money. All my work'll be lost. I don't know myself what to do. My head's splitting. (*Goes on working*)

(MATRYONA *enters with a stick and a bundle as if for traveling.*)

MATRYONA. God bless you, sweetie.

ANISYA (*looks around, drops her work, and claps her hands in joy*). Didn't expect *this*, Auntie. God sent just the right guest in time.

MATRYONA. Well?

ANISYA. Oh, I'm all mixed up. It's terrible!

MATRYONA. What do they say, he's alive?

ANISYA. Don't talk about it. He's neither living nor dying.

MATRYONA. He didn't hand the money over to someone?

ANISYA. He's sending for Marfa now, for his own sister. Must be about the money.

MATRYONA. That's clear. He hasn't already slipped it to someone?

ANISYA. Nobody. I've been watching over him like a hawk.

MATRYONA. Well, where is it?

ANISYA. Won't say. And I can't find out nohow. He keeps hiding it away in different places. And I can't find out from Akulka neither. A real half-wit, yet she's always spying, always watching. Oh my aching head! I'm worn out.

MATRYONA. Ah, sweetie, he'll hand his bit of money on beyond your reach and you'll weep for ages. You'll get kicked out of the house empty-handed. You've suffered, my dear, you've suffered all your life with a heartless man, and when you're a widow you'll go around with a cup.

ANISYA. Don't talk about it, Auntie. I'm sick at heart, and I don't know where to turn, and I got no one to talk to. I was talking to Nikita. But he's scared, doesn't want to get mixed up in it. Told me just yesterday it's under the floor.

MATRYONA. Well, did you crawl under?

ANISYA. Couldn't—he was there. I've noticed he sometimes carries it with him, sometimes hides it away.

MATRYONA. Listen, my girl, remember: once you miss your chance, you'll never get it again. (*In a whisper*) Well, did you give him the strong tea?

ANISYA. Oh-oh! (*She wants to answer, sees a neighbor, stops talking*)

(A NEIGHBOR *passes the cottage, listens to a shout in the cottage. To* ANISYA:)

NEIGHBOR. Neighbor! Anisya, oh, Anisya! Your man seems to be calling.

ANISYA. He coughs like that all the time, like he was shouting. He's already very bad.

NEIGHBOR (*goes up to* MATRYONA). Greetings, friend, where you from?

MATRYONA. From my own place, my dear. Came to call on my son. Brought some shirts. Also got to look after my boy, you know.

NEIGHBOR. That's the way it is. (*To* ANISYA) I wanted to whitewash the house, neighbor, but, I thought to myself, it's too early. Others haven't started yet.

ANISYA. What's the hurry?

MATRYONA. Have you told the priest?

ANISYA. 'Course. He was here yesterday.

NEIGHBOR. I looked in on him yesterday, too, dearie, and he can scarce keep body and soul together. He's become just skin and bones. Why just the other day, dearie, he was as good as dead, they had to put him under the icons. They'd already finished keening, and were getting ready to wash him.

ANISYA. He came to life—got up. Now he's wandering round again.

MATRYONA. Well, you going to have him given unction?

ANISYA. They say I should. If he's still living, we want to get the priest tomorrow.

NEIGHBOR. Oh, it's hard for you, I bet, Anisyushka. As the saying goes, it's not the pain that hurts but the hours of waiting.

ANISYA. Ah, it's so hard. If only it were just—

NEIGHBOR. That's clear, as if it was easy with him dying for a whole year now. He's got our hands tied.

MATRYONA. And it's a bitter thing to be a widow. If you're young it's all right, but in your old age who's going to feel sorry for you? It's no fun to get old. At least for me. Haven't gone so far, but I'm dead tired, my feet's numb. Where's my boy?

ANISYA. He's plowing. But you come on in, we'll put up the samovar, and you'll feel better with some tea.

MATRYONA (*sits*). I'm dead tired, my dears. And about his having extreme unction, that's got to be done. They say it's also a real help to the soul.

ANISYA. Yeh, tomorrow we'll call the priest.

MATRYONA. That's it, it'll be better. And you know, dear, we're having a wedding.

NEIGHBOR. Really, when, in spring?

MATRYONA. Yeh, sure, as the saying goes: let the poor marry, and the night'll be short. Semyon Matveyevich has taken Marinka.

ANISYA. So she's found herself happiness!

NEIGHBOR. Must be a widower, asked her for his children.

MATRYONA. Four of 'em. What real woman would do this? Well, he took her. She's even happy. They were drinking the wine, you know, wasn't a strong glass—they spilled some.

NEIGHBOR. You don't say! Was there talk? And has the fellow got anything?

MATRYONA. They're doing all right for the while.

NEIGHBOR. That's one thing, but who'd go marry a man with children? Take our Mikhailo, for example. A real fellow, dear—

A PEASANT'S VOICE. Hey, Mavra, where the hell you going? Go bring in the cow.

(*The* NEIGHBOR *exits.*)

MATRYONA (*as the neighbor goes off, speaks in a smooth voice*). They're out of sin's reach, dear; at least my old fool won't be thinking about Mikishka. (*Suddenly changes her voice to a whisper*) She's gone! Well, did you treat him to a little of that tea?

ANISYA. Don't mention it. It'd be better he died by himself. And all the same he ain't dying, and I've just brought sin down on my head. Oh, my aching head! Whatever did you give me these powders for?

MATRYONA. What powders? They're sleeping powders, dear, why not give them? No harm in them.

ANISYA. I'm not talking about the sleeping powders, but about those others, about the whitish ones.

MATRYONA. Why, those were medicating powders, sweetie.

ANISYA (*sighs*). I know, but I'm scared. He's worn me out.

MATRYONA. Well, did you use a lot?

ANISYA. I gave them twice.

MATRYONA. And so he couldn't tell?

ANISYA. I took a sip of the tea myself, just a bit bitter. But he drank them up with his tea and he says: even the tea's turned on me. And I says: everything's bitter for the sick. Oh, I got terrified, Auntie.

MATRYONA. Don't you think about it. The more you think about it the worse it gets.

ANISYA. It would of been better if you hadn't given them to me and led me to sin. Just remembering it makes you shudder. Whatever did you give them to me for?

MATRYONA. Oh, what are you saying, sweetie? The Lord be with you. What're you trying to pass off on me? You look out, dear, don't try to pass the blame off onto somebody else. If it ever comes to something, I had nothing to do with it, I don't know nothing about nothing—I'll swear on the cross I never gave no powders, never saw no powders, and never heard nothing about there ever being such powders. Figure it out yourself, dear. Just the other day we were talking about you, how she, the good soul, we were saying, is suffering. The stepdaughter is an idiot, and her man's rotten—she's got to use magic. What wouldn't you do to get out of such a life?

ANISYA. Yeh, I won't deny it. My life being the way it is, that's nothing, 'cause I either got to hang myself or strangle him. Is this what life is?

MATRYONA. That's just it. No time to just sit around, but one way or another you got to find the money and give him the tea.

ANISYA. Oh, my aching head! my poor head! Myself I don't know what I got to do now, and I'm terribly scared—it'd be better if he died by himself. And I don't like having this on my conscience.

MATRYONA (*spitefully*). And how come he's not letting on where the money is? What, is he going to take it with him, so nobody else gets it? You think that's a good thing? God save us, so much money just wasted. Wouldn't that be a sin? Why, what's he doing? Oughtn't you to be watching him?

ANISYA. I don't know no more myself. He's worn me out.

MATRYONA. Why don't you know? It's clear. If you miss your

chance now, you'll repent the rest of your life. He'll give his sister the money and you'll get left.

ANISYA. Oh-oh, and besides he's sent for her, see—I've got to go.

MATRYONA. Wait a bit before you go; the first thing's to put up the samovar. We'll give him a little tea and then we'll find the money together—we'll get our hands on it, don't worry.

ANISYA. Oh-oh! What if there's something—

MATRYONA. Like what? That's why you got to watch out. You just going to roll your eyes at the money and not get it into your hands? Now you do something.

ANISYA. So, I'll go put up the samovar.

MATRYONA. Go, sweetie, do what you got to, so as not to grieve later. That's the way it is. (ANISYA *exits*, MATRYONA *beckons to her*) One thing: don't tell Nikitka about all this. He's a bit of a fool. God forbid he finds out about the powders. God knows what he'd do. He's very soft-hearted. Often, you know, he wouldn't even kill a chicken. Don't tell him. Just be trouble; he wouldn't understand this. (*Stops in terror*)

(PYOTR *appears on the threshold. Holding to the wall, he comes crawling out onto the porch and calls in a weak voice:*)

PYOTR. Why can't you all ever hear me calling? Ah, ah. Anisya, who's here? (*Falls onto the bench*)

ANISYA (*comes from behind the corner*). What'd you crawl out for? You ought to lie down where you were.

PYOTR. So, did the girl go for Marfa? It's terrible! Ah, if only death were quicker!

ANISYA. She's busy, I sent her to the stream. Give me a minute, I'll straighten things out, I'll go over myself.

PYOTR. Send Anyutka. Where is she? Ah, it's terrible! Ah, this is my death!

ANISYA. I did call her.

PYOTR. Ah! But where is she?

ANISYA. Wherever she is, I hope she drops dead.

PYOTR. Ah, I can't stand it no longer. My inside's on fire. It's just like a drill drilling in. They've got rid of me, like a dog—and no one to give me a drink— Ah! Send me Anyutka.

ANISYA. Here she is. Anyutka, go to your father.

(ANYUTKA *runs in;* ANISYA *exits around the corner.*)

PYOTR. You go now—ah!—to Aunt Marfa, tell her: Father says he wants you to come, needs you for—

ANYUTKA. For—?

PYOTR. Stop. Got to come quick, tell her. Tell her—I'm fixing on dying. Ah-ah!

ANYUTKA. I'll just get my kerchief and go right away. (*Runs out*)

(ANISYA *enters.*)

MATRYONA (*winking*). Well, dear, remember what you got to do. Go into the house, rummage all around. Hunt like a dog hunts fleas; look through everything, and I'll search on him.

ANISYA (*to* MATRYONA). Right away. I feel a lot braver, seems, with you here. (*Goes to the porch. To* PYOTR) Don't you want me to put up the samovar for you? Aunt Matryona's come to see her son, and you can have it with her.

PYOTR. So, put it up.

(ANISYA *exits.* MATRYONA *goes up to the porch.*)

PYOTR. Hello.

MATRYONA. Greetings, benefactor. Greetings, my dear. You're still ailing, it looks. My old man, too, is terribly sorry. Go see him, he says, see how he is. Sent his regards. (*Bows once again*)

PYOTR. I'm dying.

MATRYONA. And now I look at you, Ignatich, it's clear pain don't walk in the forest but falls among men. You've wasted away, you've all wasted away, my dear, I see by looking at you. Ailment, it's clear, don't make a man pretty.

PYOTR. My death has come.

MATRYONA. Ah, so, Pyotr Ignatich, God's will, you had communion, you'll get extreme unction, God willing. Your old woman, thank God, is a smart one, and you'll get buried and have prayers said for you all in a fine style. And my boy, too, for the while at least, will keep busy round the house.

PYOTR. No one to leave it to! Wife's light-headed, busy with foolishness; you see, I know everything—I know— The girl's a half-wit, and besides, too young. I've set up a house, but there's no one to take care of it. It's a real pity. (*Whimpers*)

MATRYONA. Why, if there's money or something, you can always leave—

PYOTR (*to* ANISYA *in the entranceway*). Has Anyutka gone, hey?

MATRYONA (*aside*). See, he remembered.

ANISYA (*from the entranceway*). She went right away. Go back in the house, why don't you, I'll take you.

PYOTR. Let me sit here a bit for the last time. It's heavy in there— It hurts— Ah, my heart's on fire— If only death—

MATRYONA. As long as God don't take the soul, the soul itself won't go. In death like in life, it's God's will be done, Pyotr Ignatich. You won't figure out the time of your death, neither. Might be you'll be up and around. Like over in our village now there was a man absolutely just about to die—

PYOTR. No. I have a feeling I'll die today, I have a feeling. (*Leans back and closes his eyes*)

ANISYA (*enters*). Well, so, you going or not? A person can't wait all day for you. Pyotr? Hey, Pyotr?

MATRYONA (*steps aside and beckons* ANISYA *over to her with her finger*). Well, so?

ANISYA (*comes down from the porch to* MATRYONA). Nothing there.

MATRYONA. You really looked through everything? Under the floor?

ANISYA. Not there neither. Might be something in the shed. He crawled out there yesterday.

MATRYONA. Keep looking, keep looking best you can. Lick everything clean, like with your tongue. For I'm telling you, today's the day he'll die: his nail's blue, and the earth-color's come over his face. How's the samovar doing?

ANISYA. Ready to boil.

(NIKITA *comes in from the other side—if possible, rides up to the gate on horseback; does not see* PYOTR.)

NIKITA (*to his mother*). Hello, Ma! Everyone home all right?

MATRYONA. Thank the Lord God, nothing to complain about.

NIKITA. Well, how's the boss?

MATRYONA. Sh, sh, he's sitting there. (*Points to the porch*)

NIKITA. So what, let him sit there. What's it to me?

PYOTR (*opens his eyes*). Nikita, eh, Nikita, come here. (NIKITA *goes toward him,* ANISYA *whispers to* MATRYONA) How come you're back early?

NIKITA. Finished plowing.

PYOTR. Plow the strip other side of the bridge?

NIKITA. That's a lot farther to go.

PYOTR. Lot farther? Farther still from the house. You'll have to go special. Should of done 'em together.

(ANISYA, *without exposing herself, listens in.*)

MATRYONA (*goes up to them*). Ah, my boy, why don't you try to do what he wants? He's ailing, counts on you, you got to do it like for your own father, stretch all your muscles, but serve him right. That's what I'm ordering you to.

PYOTR. So you now—ah!—dig the potatoes, the women'll—ah!—sort 'em.

ANISYA (*to herself*). Never mind, I'm on my way, too. Again he wants to send us all away; must be the money's on him right now. Wants to hide it away some place.

PYOTR. And then—ah!—it'll come time to plant 'em, but they'll be rotted. Ah! I can't take it no longer. (*Rises*)

MATRYONA (*runs onto the porch, supports* PYOTR). You want to go in?

PYOTR. Take me in. (*Stops*) Nikita!

NIKITA (*angrily*). Now what?

PYOTR. I won't see you— I'll die today— Forgive me, for the Lord's sake, forgive me if I sinned against you— In word and deed, I sinned the time—it's done now. Forgive me.

NIKITA. Forgive how? We're all of us sinful.

MATRYONA. Oh, my boy—take it to heart.

PYOTR. Forgive me, for the Lord's sake. (*Cries*)

NIKITA (*sniffs*). God'll forgive you, Uncle Pyotr. Why, I got no reason to get offended at you. I never saw you do nothing bad. You forgive me. May be, I'm more guilty against you. (*Cries*)

(PYOTR, *sniveling, exits.* MATRYONA *supports him.*)

ANISYA. Oh, my poor, aching head! He was hiding something. He's got a plan, it's clear. (*Goes over to* NIKITA) Well, you said the money is under the floor—it's not there.

NIKITA (*does not reply, cries*). I never saw him do nothing bad, nothing but good. And what've I done now!

ANISYA. Oh, stop it. Where's the money?

NIKITA (*angrily*). And who the hell knows? Go look yourself.

ANISYA. What're you so full of pity for?

NIKITA. I'm sorry for him. I feel so sorry for him! He cried so! Oh!

ANISYA. Look, if you got to feel sorry, there's someone you can really feel sorry for. He treated you like a dog, like a dog, and just now he ordered you driven off the place. It's me you should feel sorry for.

NIKITA. And what would I feel sorry for you for?

ANISYA. He'll die, and he'll have hidden the money—

NIKITA. Most likely he won't hide it—

ANISYA. Oh, Nikitushka! He's called his sister now, wants to give it to her. It's our worry how we'll make out with him having given the money away. I'll get thrown off the place! You, too, better start worrying about this. You said he crept out to the shed last night?

NIKITA. Saw him as he was coming away from there, but where he stuck it, who the hell knows.

ANISYA. Oh, my aching head, I'll go look there myself.

(MATRYONA *comes out of the cottage, goes down to* ANISYA *and* NIKITA; *in a whisper:*)

MATRYONA. Don't go nowhere; the money's on him, I felt it, on a string.

ANISYA. Oh, my poor aching head!

MATRYONA. Bat an eye now and later you'll have to be looking up in the sky. His sister'll come—and then it's good-bye.

ANISYA. And when she comes, he'll give it to her. What'll we do? Oh, my aching head!

MATRYONA. What'll we do? Look here. The samovar's boiled up, you go make some tea and pour him some (*in a whisper*) and pour everything folded up in the letter out and give it to him. When he's drunk the cup, then grab it. Don't worry, he won't talk.

ANISYA. I'm scared.

MATRYONA. Don't you think about it, do it quickly, and I'll keep an eye on the sister, in case of something. Don't slip up. Grab the money and bring it here, and Nikita'll hide it away.

ANISYA. Oh, my head! How'll I go up to him and—and—

MATRYONA. Don't think about it, I'm telling you; do what I tell you. Nikita!

NIKITA. What?

MATRYONA. You stay here, sit out on the ground, in case there's something to do.

NIKITA (*waving his hand*). These women're cooking something up. It really gets you. Well, the hell with you. It's time I went—and dug the potatoes.

MATRYONA (*stops him by the arm*). Stay here, I'm telling you.

(ANYUTKA *enters.*)

ANISYA. Well, so?

ANYUTKA. She was at her daughter's in the garden. Coming right away.

ANISYA. When she comes, what'll we do?

MATRYONA (*to* ANISYA). Hurry up, do what I tell you.

ANISYA. Myself I don't know—don't know nothing, it's all mixed up. Anyutka! Go down, dear, to the calves; they've scattered. Oh, I can't do it.

(ANYUTKA *exits.*)

MATRYONA. Go, huh; the samovar's out, I expect.

ANISYA. Oh, my poor, aching head! (*Exits*)

MATRYONA (*goes up to her son*). Well, my boy. (*Sits beside him on the ground*) Also got to think out what you're going to do, and not just let it go.

NIKITA. What is it I'm going to do?

MATRYONA. Why, how you're going to get on in the world.

NIKITA. How I'm going to get on in the world? Others get on, so'll I.

MATRYONA. The old man, I expect, will die today.

NIKITA. He'll die, and go up to Heaven. What've I got to do with it?

MATRYONA (*all the time keeps talking and glancing at the porch*). Eh, my boy! The living think of the living. Here, too, sweetie, you got to have your wits about you. What do you think, why I've been busy all over doing things for you, got all bedraggled running round for you. So you remember, and don't forget me later.

NIKITA. But what were you running round for?

MATRYONA. For what's your business, for the way things'll work out for you. If you don't run round ahead of time, nothing'll work out. You know Ivan Moseyich? I had dealings with him, too. Stopped in the other day. I went to him, too, see, on the same business. I was sitting there and we were talking. By-the-bye, I says, how'd a man, Ivan Moseyich, figure this out? Let's say, I says to him, a widower peasant took, let's say, a second wife, and the only children, let's say, is the other wife's daughter and one by this one. What about, I says, if this peasant dies, is it possible, I says, for another man to take his place in this widow's household? is it possible, I says, for this man to marry off the daughters and himself stay on the place? It's possible, he says, only you got to make, he says, a lot of effort over it. With money, he says, you can arrange these things, but without money, he says, there's no point in even poking your nose into it.

NIKITA (*laughs*). That's what they all say, just hand 'em out money. Everybody needs money.

MATRYONA. Well, sweetie, I explained everything to him. First thing, he says, you got to get your boy registered in that village. Got to have some money for that—to give the old men a treat. After that, see, they'll sign. You got to do it all, he says, with your wits about you. Look here. (*Takes a piece of paper out of her kerchief*) Here, he wrote out a whole paper, read it, you're smart.

(NIKITA *reads*, MATRYONA *listens.*)

NIKITA. The paper, it's clear, is a judgment. There's no great brains in that.

MATRYONA. But you listen what Ivan Moseyich told me to do. More than anything else, he says, Auntie, be careful not to let go of the money. If she don't, he says, get hold of the money, they won't let her get herself another man. Money, he says, is the source of everything. So, keep your eyes open. Things're coming to a head, my boy.

NIKITA. So what? The money's hers, let her worry about it.

MATRYONA. How you judge things, boy! You think a woman can figure such a thing out? Supposing she takes the money, how's she to figure what to do with it? You know what women are, but you're a man. I mean, you can hide it and everything like that. You, 'course, got more sense, in case something happens.

NIKITA. Ah, your woman's thinking can't be counted on at all.

MATRYONA. What do you mean, can't be counted on! You

hide the money away. This woman'll be in your hands. Then in case she begins to snore a bit or something, you can give her a good one.

NIKITA. The hell with you, I'm going.

(ANISYA *runs out of the cottage, pale, around the corner to* MATRYONA.)

ANISYA. It *was* on him. Here it is. (*Points under her apron*)

MATRYONA. Give it to Nikita, he'll hide it away. Nikita, take it, hide it some place.

NIKITA. So, gimme.

ANISYA. Oh-oh, my aching head, do it myself, huh. (*Goes toward the gate*)

MATRYONA (*grabs her arm*). Where you going? They'll know you're gone, here's his sister coming; give it to him, he knows how. What a fool!

ANISYA (*stops in indecision*). Oh, my aching head!

NIKITA. So, gimme, huh, I'll stick it some place.

ANISYA. Where'll you put it?

NIKITA. Or you scared? (*Laughs*)

(AKULINA *comes in with the wash.*)

ANISYA. Oh-oh, my poor, aching head! (*Hands over the money*) Nikita, be careful.

NIKITA. What're you afraid of? I'll stick it where I won't find it myself. (*Exits*)

ANISYA (*stands in terror*). Oh-oh! What if he—

MATRYONA. So, he died?

ANISYA. Seems he's dead. I took it off him, and he didn't feel a thing.

MATRYONA. Go in the house, here's Akulina coming.

ANISYA. But, I sinned, and what's he going to do with the money—

MATRYONA. Stop it, go in the house, here's Marfa coming, too.

ANISYA. Well, I believed him. Something'll come of it. (*Exits*)

MARFA (*comes from one side;* AKULINA, *from the other. To* AKULINA). I would have come long ago, but I'd gone to my daughter's. Well, what's with the old man? Or is he fixing to die?

AKULINA (*puts down the wash*). God knows. I was down by the stream.

MARFA (*pointing to* MATRYONA). Whose woman's that?

MATRYONA. From Zuyevo, I'm Nikita's mother, from Zuyevo,

my dear. How do you do. Wasted away, your dear brother's wasted away. Came out here himself. Call my sister, he says, 'cause, he says— Oh! maybe he's already gone?

(ANISYA *runs out of the house with a shout, grabs hold of the post and begins to wail.*)

ANISYA. Oh-oh-oh, and who've you left me to, oh-oh-oh-oh, and who, oh-oh-oh, who've you left me for, oh-oh-oh-oh— unhappy widow—your clear eyes are closed, oh-oh-oh-oh, for ages and ages—

(*The* NEIGHBOR *enters. The* NEIGHBOR *and* MATRYONA *support* ANISYA *by the arm.* AKULINA *and* MARFA *go into the house. A crowd gathers.*)

A VOICE FROM THE CROWD. Call the women, got to clean up.

MATRYONA (*rolls up her sleeves*). There's water in the kettle, isn't there? Least there is in the samovar, I expect. They didn't throw it out. I'll help, too.

ACT III

PYOTR'*s cottage. Winter. Nine months have passed since Act II.* ANISYA, *carelessly dressed, sits by the loom, weaves.* ANYUTKA *is on the stove. Also* MITRICH, *the old hired man.*

MITRICH (*enters slowly, takes off his coat*). Oh, merciful Father! So the master ain't back?

ANISYA. What?

MITRICH. Nikita ain't come in from town?

ANISYA. No.

MITRICH. Went on a spree, most likely. Oh, Lord!

ANISYA. You clean up the threshing-floor?

MITRICH. Sure did. Cleared everything up like it ought to be, covered it up with straw. Don't like doing things half way. Oh, Lord! Mikola the Good! (*Picks his calluses*) It's time for him to be here.

ANISYA. What should he hurry for? He's got money, he's on a spree with the girl, I bet—

MITRICH. He's got money, so why not have a spree? But how come Akulina went to town?

ANISYA. Ask her yourself what in God's name she went for.

MITRICH. What *would* a person go to town for? There's lots of everything in town, if only you got something to pay with. Oh, Lord!

ANYUTKA. I heard it myself, Ma. I'll buy you a little shawl, he says, sure as I'm living I'll buy it, he says; you can pick it out yourself, he says. And she got herself really dressed up, put on her velveteen waist and her French kerchief.

ANISYA. As if she's all girlish shame as far as the door, but soon as she's stepped out she's forgot all about it. Shameless girl!

MITRICH. Naw! What's there to be ashamed about? You got money, go have a good time. Oh, Lord! Too early for supper, ain't it? (ANISYA *is silent*) Might as well warm up a bit then. (*Climbs onto the stove*) Oh, Lord! holy Mother of God Mikola the Sweet!

NEIGHBOR (*enters*). Your man ain't back, seems?

ANISYA. No.

NEIGHBOR. It's time. Didn't stop in at our tavern, maybe?

Sister Fekla was telling me, dear, there's lots of sledges from town standing there.

ANISYA. Anyutka! hey, Anyutka!

ANYUTKA. What?

ANISYA. Run over to the tavern, sweetie, and see if he didn't stop in there drunk.

ANYUTKA (*jumps off the stove, puts on her things*). Right away.

NEIGHBOR. And took Akulina with him?

ANISYA. Otherwise there was no point in going. On account of her; found things to do. Got to go to bank, he says, the payment's gone, but really it's just her gets him mixed up.

NEIGHBOR (*shakes her head*). What can you do. (*Silence*)

ANYUTKA (*in the doorway*). And if he's there, what'll I tell him?

ANISYA. You just take a look if he's there.

ANYUTKA. All right, I'll be back in a minute.

(*A long silence.*)

MITRICH (*growls*). Oh, Lord! Mikola the Good.

NEIGHBOR (*shudders*). Oh, you frightened me. Who's that?

ANISYA. Mitrich, the hired man.

NEIGHBOR. Oh, he gave me a real start! I'd forgotten. By the way, they were saying, neighbor, you're going to marry Akulina.

ANISYA (*comes out from behind the loom toward the table*). We'd just started arranging with Dedlovo, but it's clear there's some kind of talk has got to them, too, we'd just started arranging, but then there was silence. So the whole thing fell through. Who'd want to, anyway?

NEIGHBOR. And the Lizunovs from Zuyevo?

ANISYA. There was an offer. But that, too, didn't work out. He won't take her home.

NEIGHBOR. But you ought to be marrying her off.

ANISYA. Surely ought to. I can't figure out, neighbor, how to get her out of the house; 'deed, the whole business can't be worked out. He don't feel like it. And her, too. Hasn't finished his spree, yet, with his beauty, see, with his own girl.

NEIGHBOR. Sin, sin, sin! Couldn't make it up. And him her stepfather, too.

ANISYA. Ah, neighbor. I can't tell you how cleverly they tricked me, pulled the wool over my eyes. Foolish me, I noticed nothing, thought nothing, and so married him

Didn't suspect the littlest thing, but they'd already made an agreement between them.

NEIGHBOR. Oh, what a thing!

ANISYA. The longer we went the more there was; I saw they'd begun to shy away from me. Ah, neighbor, it makes me sick, my life's sickening. Been better if I'd never loved him.

NEIGHBOR. What can you do?

ANISYA. It's hard for me, neighbor, real hard to have to live with such a wrong. Oh, so hard!

NEIGHBOR. Why, they're saying he's even got quick to use his hand.

ANISYA. Everything's true. Used to be he was quiet when he was tight. Used to drink hard before this, and all the time I was good to him, but now just as soon as he's filled himself he takes it out on me, wants to grind me underfoot. The other day he pulled my braids for all he was worth, and I hardly got away. And the girl's worse than a snake. Only how can the earth bring forth such evil things!

NEIGHBOR. Oh-oh-oh! Neighbor, you ain't well, I can tell by looking at you! How do you stand it! Took in a beggar, and now he's making a fool of you. Why don't you let him have a piece of your mind?

ANISYA. Oh, good neighbor! What can I do the way I feel? My other old man was pretty hard, but still I twisted him round my little finger just as I wanted, but now I can't, neighbor. Soon as I see him, my heart melts. I can't get up the littlest courage to go against him. I'm all chicken-hearted when he's around.

NEIGHBOR. Oh, neighbor! It's clear someone's cast a spell on you. Matryona, they say, does things like this. Must be it was her.

ANISYA. 'deed, I think so myself, neighbor. How it hurts, you know, the second time. Seems I could tear him to pieces. But I catch sight of him—no, I can't bring myself to do a thing.

NEIGHBOR. It's clear, indeed, something's been done here. It don't take long, my dear, to spoil a man. Now just I look at you I see something's happened.

ANISYA. My legs've become just like sticks. But take a look at the half-wit, at Akulina. The girl was a tattery, sloppy thing, but now just look at her. It came from some place.

It's he dressed her up. She's got all decked out; she's all swelled up like a bubble. And then, don't matter she's an idiot, she's gotten it into her head: I'm the lady of the house, she says. The house's mine. The old man was fixing to marry him to me. And such a wicked thing, Lord save us. Gets so spiteful she'll pull the thatch off the roof.

NEIGHBOR. Oh-oh, I see what your life's like, neighbor. And there's people envy you, too. They're rich, they say. It's clear, my dear, the rich have their troubles, too.

ANISYA. There *is* something to envy. But even all our money'll just vanish into thin air. It's terrible how he's wasting money.

NEIGHBOR. But how come, neighbor, you let him have it so easy? The money's yours.

ANISYA. Seems you know it all. And so that's the one mistake I made.

NEIGHBOR. If I was you, neighbor, I'd go right to the police, to the chief himself. The money's yours. How can he waste it all? There's no such rights.

ANISYA. Nowadays they pay no attention to that.

NEIGHBOR. Ah, neighbor, I see what you're doing. It's worn you down.

ANISYA. Worn me down, dear, completely worn me down. He's worn me out. Myself I don't know nothing no more. Oh, my poor aching head!

NEIGHBOR. Ain't somebody coming? (*Listens; opens the door, and* AKIM *enters*)

AKIM (*makes the sign of the cross, kicks off his bast-shoes and takes his things off*). Peace to this house. You doing well? Hello, Auntie.

ANISYA. Hello, Uncle. Just come over? Come on in, take your things off.

AKIM. I was just thinking, now, I mean, why don't I go, now, to my boy's, I'll go see my boy. Didn't set out right away, had a bite of dinner, I mean, then set out. And there's a lot of snow, now, is heavy going, heavy, that's why I'm late, I mean. And the boy's home? My boy's in, I mean?

ANISYA. No. Over town.

AKIM (*sits down on the bench*). I've a little business with him, I mean, now, a little business. I was telling him the other day, I was telling him what I need, my little horse gave out,

I mean, the little horse. Got to hunt one up, some kind of little horse, a little horse, now. That's why I came, I mean.

ANISYA. Nikita was telling me. When he comes, you two can talk it over. (*Rises, goes to the stove*) Have some supper, and he'll be here. Mitrich, come to supper, hey, Mitrich!

MITRICH (*growls, wakes up*). What?

ANISYA. Supper.

MITRICH. Oh, Lord, Mikola the Good!

ANISYA. Come to supper.

NEIGHBOR. I'm on my way. 'Bye. (*Exits*)

MITRICH (*slides down*). Didn't even notice I fell asleep. Oh, Lord, Mikola the Sweet! Hello, Uncle Akim.

AKIM. Eh! Mitrich! What're you doing here, now?

MITRICH. I'm on here as hired man, with Nikita, with your son.

AKIM. Well, now! As my son's hired man, now! Well, now!

MITRICH. I was working for a merchant over town, but I drank myself out of there. So I came here to the village. Got no corner myself, so I hired out. (*Yawns*) Oh, Lord!

AKIM. Why, now, I mean, what's Mikushka do? There's so much, I mean, so much to do, now, he took on a man, hired a man?

ANISYA. What's he got to do? Before, he managed himself, but now, there's something on his mind, so he took on a hired man.

MITRICH. He's got money, so what's it to him—

AKIM. Now, that ain't right. Why, that ain't right at all, now. That ain't right. Being spoilt, I mean.

ANISYA. He's already spoilt, spoilt, that's the trouble.

AKIM. A man thinks, now, how it'd be better, but it comes out, I mean, worse. A man gets spoilt by money, gets spoilt.

MITRICH. A dog, too, will go mad from fat. How can't a man get spoilt from fat! How I got turned around from fat! Three weeks I drank night and day. Drank away my last pair of pants. Had nothing left, so I quit. Now I've sworn off. The hell with it.

AKIM. But your old woman, I mean, where's she?

MITRICH. My old woman, my friend, has settled down in her right place. Sits over town in the bars. A big lady, too—one eye torn out, the other black-and-blue, and her mug twisted round to the side. But she's sober, keeps her belly full of good food, never shows up.

AKIM. Oh-oh! How can that be?!

MITRICH. And what else can a soldier's wife do? She's set out in her own business.

(*Silence.*)

AKIM (*to* ANISYA). What'd Nikita go to town for, now, he took something over, to sell, I mean, took something over?

ANISYA (*sets the table and serves*). Went empty. Went for some money, to get some money at the bank.

AKIM (*eats supper*). What're you doing with it, what more do you want to do with the money, the money?

ANISYA. No, we ain't touching it. Only twenty, thirty rubles. Ran out, so had to get some.

AKIM. Had to get some? Why do you take it out, that is, the money? Today, I mean, now, you'll take it out, tomorrow you'll take it out—so, now, you'll take it all out, I mean.

ANISYA. This is a extra payment. But the money's still all whole.

AKIM. Whole? How so, now, whole? You take it out, but, now, it's whole? Like if you put a store of meal and all, now, in the bin, or in the granary, and then you take some meal out of there—what, it'll be whole? It's not, I mean. They're tricking you. You find out about that, or they'll trick you. How can it be whole? You, that is, take it out, but it's whole.

ANISYA. I don't know nothing more. Ivan Moseyich settled it for us then. Put your money, he says, in the bank—and the money'll be whole and you'll receive a percent.

MITRICH (*has finished eating*). That's right. I worked for a merchant. Everything was like that at his place. Put your money in and go lie on the stove, you'll get it.

AKIM. That's wonderful talk, now. How do you get it? You get it, now, but he, I mean, who does he get it from? The money?

ANISYA. They give out money at the bank.

MITRICH. How's that? She's a woman, she can't add or subtract. But you look here, I'll show you what it's all about. You mind now. You, for example, have money, but me, for example, spring's come to my place, the land's lying idle, there's nothing to sow with, or to pay the tax neither. So, I mean, here I come to you. Akim, I says, give me a ten and I'll clear out of my fields, I'll let you have to Pokrovo, and

I'll harvest an acre for security. You, for example, can see I got something to pledge with: a little horse, maybe, or a cow, and you says: give me two, three rubles security, and that's it. You're a millstone round my neck; I can't get rid of it. All right, I says. I'll take the ten. Fall comes, I reckon things up, take it back, and you've skinned a extra three rubles off me.

AKIM. Why that, I mean, the man does it crookedly, now, if he's forgot God, I mean. This, I mean, ain't the point.

MITRICH. Wait now. It's coming to it right away. You mind now. Now, you handled it so, skinned me, I mean, but Anisya, for example, she's got money put away. She's got no place to keep it; besides, she's a woman, don't know what to do with it. She comes to you. Can't some use, she says, be made out of my money? Sure, you says, it can. So you wait. I come again afore summer. Give me, I says, ten again, and I've got security— Now here you figure it out: if the skin still ain't all been taken off me, if you can still flay me some more, you give me Anisya's money, but if, for example, I ain't got nothing, if there's nothing to gobble up, you, I mean, figure it out, you see there's nothing to skin off me, and you says right away: Go to hell, my friend, and you keep an eye out for somebody else, give it out again, lend out both yours and Anisya's and skin that fellow. That's just what a bank is. And just like that it goes round and round. A real clever business, my friend.

AKIM (*getting angry*). What kind of thing's that? That, now, I mean, that's dirty business. If men, now, do that, why men believe that a sin. It's not in the laws, not in the laws, I mean. It's dirty business. How can educated people, now—

MITRICH. My friend, with them it's the best thing to do. But mind you now. Whoever's a bit stupid, or a woman, who can't put his money to work himself, he takes it to the bank and they, their bellies already stuffed, catch even more of this money and skin the people. A real clever business.

AKIM (*sighing*). Eh, I see, now, there's trouble, indeed, without money, but with money, now, twice as much. That's how it is. God commanded us to labor. But you, I mean, now, put money in the bank, and then go to sleep, but the money, I mean, it'll feed you fine just piling up. It's dirty business I mean; it's not in the laws.

MITRICH. Not in the laws? They don't pay no attention to that nowadays, my friend. They'll clean you out of house and home. That's the way it goes.

AKIM (*sighs*). It's already clear now. The time's come. I had a look, I mean, at the urinals, too, over in town. What we've come to. All smooth and shiny, I mean, very dressy. Done up like a tavern. And for nothing. It's all for nothing. Ah, God's been forgotten. Forgotten, I mean. Forgotten, we've forgotten God, God. Thanks, my dear, I'm full, I'm fine. (*They get up from the table;* MITRICH *climbs onto the stove.*)

ANISYA (*clears the dishes and eats*). If only his father would appeal to his conscience, but it's shameful to be telling.

AKIM. What?

ANISYA. Nothing, talking to myself.

(ANYUTKA *enters.*)

AKIM. Ah! good girl. Always busy! Got chilled, I expect?

ANYUTKA. 'deed, I'm awful cold. Hello, Grampa.

ANISYA. Well? is he there?

ANYUTKA. No. Only Adriyan from town was there; he was saying he saw him back over in town, in the tavern. Your old man's dead drunk, he says.

ANISYA. You want a bite, maybe? It's there.

ANYUTKA (*goes to the stove*). Oh, it's so cold. My hands got frozen.

(AKIM *takes off his shoes;* ANISYA *washes the spoons.*)

ANISYA. Uncle!

AKIM. What do you want?

ANISYA. Say, Marishka's all right?

AKIM. All right. Making out. Clever, peaceable little woman, now, she's making out, I mean, doing fine. All right. A little woman, I mean, serious, and all, a fine doer, and obedient-like. A little woman, I mean, all right.

ANISYA. They were saying over in your village there's a fellow, relative of Marinka's husband, they want to marry to Akulina. Did you hear anything?

AKIM. That the Mironovs? The women were chattering something. But I never paid no mind. Something in passing, I mean, I don't know, now. The old women were talking. But I don't remember things good, don't remember so good, I mean. But, why, the Mironovs, now, are good peasants, I mean, it's all right.

ANISYA. I can't figure out how to get the matchmaking done with faster.

AKIM. What for?

ANYUTKA (*listens*). They've come.

(NIKITA *enters, drunk, with a bag and a bundle under his arm and with packages wrapped in paper; opens the door and stands still.*)

ANISYA. Well, pay no attention. (*Continues washing the spoons and does not turn her head when the door opens*)

NIKITA. Anisya, hey wife! Who's come? (ANISYA *looks up and turns away. She is silent.* NIKITA, *threateningly:*) Who's here? Or have y'forgotten?

ANISYA. He'll be swaggering now. Come on in.

NIKITA (*still more threateningly*). Who's come?

ANISYA (*goes to him and takes his hand*). Well, my husband's come. Come on in the house.

NIKITA (*pulls back*). Right, y'husband. And what's y'husband called, hey? Say it right.

ANISYA. Oh, go to hell—Nikita.

NIKITA. Right! Y'cow—say my middle name.

ANISYA. Akimych. Well?

NIKITA (*still in the doorway*). Right. No, now say my last name.

ANISYA (*laughs and pulls his hand*). Chilikin. You're really bloated!

NIKITA. Right. (*Holds on to the jamb*) No, now you say which leg Chilikin steps into his house with first?

ANISYA. Oh, stop it—you'll freeze us all.

NIKITA. Say it, which leg first? Y'absolutely got to say.

ANISYA (*to herself*). I'm fed up now. Well, the left. Come on in, hey.

NIKITA. Right.

ANISYA. Take a look who's here.

NIKITA. M'father? Why, I ain't hiding from m'father. I can pay m'respects to m'father. 'Lo there, Pa. (*Bows to him and puts out his hand*) Our compl'ents to you.

AKIM (*not answering*). It's the vodka, it's the vodka, I mean, what it does. Dirty business!

NIKITA. Vodka! What, did I drink too much? Abs'lutely at fault, drank with a friend, congrat'lations.

ANISYA. Go lie down, hey.

NIKITA. M'wife, say, where'm I standing.

ANISYA. All right, all right, go lie down.

NIKITA. I'll still drink up a samovar-full with m'father. Put up the samovar. Akulina, come in, hey.

AKULINA (*all dressed up, comes in with packages. To* NIKITA). What did you strew everything round for? Where's my yarn?

NIKITA. Yarn? Yarn's there. Hey, Mitrich! You there? 'Sleep? Go put the horse away.

AKIM (*does not see* AKULINA *and watches his son*). What's he doing? The old man, I mean, he's dead tired, he was threshing all day, but he was getting loaded. Put away the horse! I'll be! Dirty business.

MITRICH (*climbs off the stove, puts on his leg wrappings*). Oh, good Lord! Horse's in the yard, hey? Dead tired, I bet. But look at *him*, the hell with him, the way he swilled it up. Brim full. Oh, Lord! Mikola the Sweet! (*Puts on his coat and goes out to the yard*)

NIKITA (*sits down*). Y'forgive me, Pa. Drank too much, 's true, but, well, what's there to do? A chicken, too, 'll drink. So, what's the difference? But y'forgive me. And Mitrich, now —he don't mind, he'll put it away.

ANISYA. Really want the samovar started?

NIKITA. Start it. M'father's come, want to talk t'him, drink some tea. (*To* AKULINA) Did y'bring in everything?

AKULINA. Everything? Brought mine, but the rest's in the sledge. Here, this one ain't mine. (*Throws a bundle on the table and puts her packages away in a chest*)

(ANYUTKA *watches how* AKULINA *packs;* AKIM *does not look at his son and puts his foot-wraps and felt boots on the stove.*)

ANISYA (*exits with the samovar*). As it is, the chest's full, and he bought more.

NIKITA (*puts on a sober expression*). Now you, Pa, don't get offended with me. You think I'm drunk. I pos'tively can do anything. It's all right to drink if you don't lose your head. You and me, Pa, can have a little talk right now. 'member everything. 'bout the money you asked, the little horse giving out—I 'member. All that can be done. All that's something we can do. If the 'mount of money wanted's pretty big, why then might put it off a bit, but otherwise I can do it all. Here!

AKIM (*continues to putter with his gear*). Ah, my lad, now, I mean, a spring road is not a real road—

NIKITA. What y'mean by that? A talk with a drunk ain't a real talk? Now don't you worry. We'll drink up some tea. And I can do everything, pos'tively can fix everything up.

AKIM (*shakes his head*). Eh, eh, eh!

NIKITA. The money, here it is. (*Reaches in his pocket, pulls out his wallet, thumbs through the bills, takes out a ten-ruble bill*) Take it for a horse. Take it for a horse, I can't forget m'father. Abs'lutely won't forget him. On account he's m'father. Here, take it. 's very simple. Glad to do it. (*Goes to* AKIM *and shoves the money at him.* AKIM *does not take the money.* NIKITA *grabs his hand*) Take it, I tell you, now I'm giving it to you; glad to do it.

AKIM. I can't, I mean, take it and I can't talk with you, I mean. On account you're, now, not yourself, I mean.

NIKITA. Won't let you. Take it. (*Stuffs the money into* AKIM'S *hand*)

ANISYA (*enters and stands still*). Sure, take it. You know he won't leave you alone.

AKIM (*takes it, shaking his head*). Ah, the vodka! He ain't a man, now, I mean—

NIKITA. Now that's better. If you give it back, so, you give it back; but if you don't—God bless you anyway. That's the way I do things! (*Sees* AKULINA) Akulina, show 'em your presents.

AKULINA. What?

NIKITA. Show 'em your presents.

AKULINA. The presents? Why show them? I already put 'em away.

NIKITA. Get 'em, I tell you. Anyutka'll be real pleased to look at 'em. Show 'em to Anyutka, I tell you. Open the little shawl. Give it here.

AKIM. Oh, it makes me sick to look! (*Climbs onto the stove*)

AKULINA (*gets it and puts it on the table*). So there! What's there to look at?

ANYUTKA. Not bad at all! Least as good as Stepanida's.

AKULINA. Stepanida's? What's Stepanida's compared to this? (*Getting animated and unwrapping*) Look here, what goods—real French!

ANYUTKA. What lovely calico! Mashutka has some like it, only a bit lighter, with a light-blue background. This is awful pretty.

NIKITA. What'd I tell you!

(ANISYA, *angry, goes by to the larder, returns with the pipe and stand [for the samovar] and approaches the table.*)

ANISYA. Look at you, showing off.

NIKITA. Take a look at this!

ANISYA. What's there for me to look at? I never saw things, hey? Put it away. (*Brushes the shawl onto the floor*)

AKULINA. Why're you throwing things around? Throw your own stuff around. (*Picks it up*)

NIKITA. Anisya! Look here!

ANISYA. What should I look for?

NIKITA. You think I've forgotten you. Look here. (*Shows her a bundle and sits on it*) Present for you. Only got to earn it. Woman, where'm I sitting?

ANISYA. That's enough bragging. I ain't scared of you. Whose money do you have your sprees with and buy presents for your fatty with? With mine!

AKULINA. What do you mean, yours! You wanted to steal it, but didn't get the chance to. Get out, you! (*Tries to get by, pushes*)

ANISYA. What're you pushing for? I'll push you!

AKULINA. Push me? All right, come on. (*Advances toward her*)

NIKITA. Hey, you two, quit it! (*Stands between them*)

AKULINA. Keeps poking her nose in. You better shut up, keep things to yourself. You think people don't know?

ANISYA. What do they know? Say it, say what they know!

AKULINA. Know something 'bout you.

ANISYA. You're a whore, you live with somebody else's husband.

AKULINA. And you poisoned yours.

ANISYA (*throws herself at* AKULINA). You're lying!

NIKITA (*holds her back*). Anisya! You've forgotten?

ANISYA. What, you threatening me? I ain't scared of you.

NIKITA. Get out! (*Spins* ANISYA *around and pushes her out*)

ANISYA. Where'll I go? I ain't going out of my own house.

NIKITA. Get out, I tell you. And don't dare come back.

ANISYA. I ain't going. (NIKITA *pushes her,* ANISYA *cries and shouts, hangs on to the door*) What's this? Am I being thrown out of my own house on my ear? What're you doing, you—

you criminal? You think the law's got nothing on you. Just you wait!

NIKITA. All right, all right!

ANISYA. I'll go to the headman, to the police.

NIKITA. Out, I tell you! (*Pushes her out*)

ANISYA (*from behind the door*). I'll hang myself!

NIKITA. I bet.

ANYUTKA. Oh-oh! Mama dearest, my Mama. (*Cries*)

NIKITA. Hey now, got real scared of her. What y'crying for? Don't worry, she'll come back. Go see how the samovar's doing.

(ANYUTKA *exits.*)

AKULINA (*gathers the packages, puts them away*). Ugh, the foul bitch, what a stink she made! You watch, I'll cut up her jacket. Really, I will.

NIKITA. I chased her out, what more d'y'want?

AKULINA. She got my new shawl dirty. A real bitch. If she hadn't gone, I would of scratched her eyes out.

NIKITA. Stop being mad. What's there for you to be mad about? What if I loved her?

AKULINA. Loved her? What a fine one to love, that fat mug! If you'd got rid of her then nothing would of happened. You would of sent her to hell. But the house's mine, anyway, and the money's mine. A housewife she calls herself, a housewife—what kind of a housewife's she for a husband? She's a murderer, that's what. She'll do the same to you.

NIKITA. Ah, you can't make a woman shut up with nothing. Y'don't know yourself what you're blabbing about.

AKULINA. I do, too. I ain't going to live with her. I'll chase her off the place. She can't live with me. I'm a housewife, too. She's no housewife, she's a jailbird.

NIKITA. Stop it. What've you got to share with her? Don't look at her. Look at me. I'm the boss. I do what I want. Stopped loving her, started loving you. I love who I want. That's my right. And jail for her. This is where she stands with me (*points to under his feet*). Ah, the accordion ain't here.

Pies on the stove,
Kasha on the stairs,
But we'll be living

And having a spree;
But death'll come
And we'll be dying.
Pies on the stove,
Kasha on the stairs—

(MITRICH *enters, takes his coat off and climbs on the stove.*)

MITRICH. The women was at it again, I see. Got in each other's hair. Oh, Lord! Mikola the Good.

AKIM (*sits on the edge of the stove, gets his foot-wraps and felt boots and puts them on*). Climb up, climb up to the corner.

MITRICH (*climbs up*). They can't divvy everything up, that's clear. Oh, Lord!

NIKITA. Go get the brandy. We'll drink it with the tea.

ANYUTKA (*enters; to* AKULINA). Sissy-Sis, the samovar wants to be fetched!

NIKITA. But where's your mother?

ANYUTKA. She's standing in the doorway, crying.

NIKITA. All right. Call her, tell her to bring in the samovar. And, Akulina, you put the dishes on.

AKULINA. Dishes? Aw, all right. (*Assembles the china*)

NIKITA (*gets the brandy, rolls, herring*). This, now, is for me, and this is some yarn for the little woman, and the kerosene's there in the doorway. And here's the money. Wait a minute (*Takes the abacus*) I'll figure it out in a second. (*Counts*) Wheat flour eight griven, veg'table oil, Pa ten rubles. Pa! Come drink your tea.

(*Silence.* AKIM *sits on the stove and rewinds his leg-wrappings.*)

ANISYA (*brings in the samovar*). Where'll I put it?

NIKITA. On the table. So, did y'go to the headman? What'd I tell you; get it out of your system. Come on, quit being mad. Sit down, have a drink. (*Pours a small glass for her*) And here's a little present for you. (*Gives her the bundle he was sitting on.* ANISYA *takes it silently, shaking her head*)

AKIM (*slides off and puts on his fur coat; goes over to the table, puts the bill on it*). Here's your money. Put it away.

NIKITA (*does not see the bill*). Where you going all dressed?

AKIM. I'm going, going, now, for the Lord's sake, forgive me. (*Takes his hat and broad belt*)

NIKITA. What the hell's this? Where y'going to do anything at night now?

AKIM. I can't, I mean, I can't, now, stay in your house, can't stay, forgive me.

NIKITA. What're you leaving the tea for?

AKIM (*puts on his belt*). I'm leaving, 'cause, I mean, things're wrong in your place, I mean, now, wrong, Mikishka, wrong, in your house. I mean, you're living bad, Mikishka, bad. I'm leaving.

NIKITA. Oh, stop talking. Sit down and drink some tea.

ANISYA. Why, Pa, we'll be shamed in front of everyone. What'd you get offended at?

AKIM. No offense to me, now, no offense at all, I mean, but just that I see, now, my son, I mean, is headed for perdition, my son's headed for perdition, I mean.

NIKITA. What kind of perdition!? You just show me now.

AKIM. Perdition, perdition, you're all the way in perdition. What'd I tell you last summer?

NIKITA. Didn't say much, though.

AKIM. I told you, now, 'bout the orphan girl, that you wronged the orphan girl, wronged Marina, I mean.

NIKITA. Yeh, y'mentioned it. No point telling a old story twice; besides, the thing's done with.

AKIM (*getting angry*). Done with? No, my boy, it ain't done with. One sin, I mean, leads to another, pulls it on after itself, and you, Mikishka, you've got mired in sin. Got mired, I see, in sin. Got mired, got bogged down, I mean.

NIKITA. Sit down and drink some tea, that's the whole conversation.

AKIM. I can't, I mean, drink some tea. On account of your wicked ways, I mean, I feel terrible, really terrible. I can't drink tea with you, now.

NIKITA. Ah, he's dawdling. Come over to the table.

AKIM. In your pile of wealth, now, you're like in a net. You're in a net, I mean. Ah, Mikishka, your soul's in peril!

NIKITA. What kind of right you got to give me a lecture in my own house? And in fact what're you harping on? What'm I giving in to you like a kid for you to box my ears? Now that ain't done no more.

AKIM. Right, right, I've heard that nowadays they pull the fathers' beards, I mean, and that's perdition, perdition, that is.

NIKITA (*angrily*). We make out, don't ask you nothing, but here you've come over to us wanting something.

AKIM. Money? There's your money. I'll go begging, I mean, but not that, won't take that, I mean.

NIKITA. Get off it. And your getting mad's breaking up the party. (*Restrains him by the arm*)

AKIM (*screams*). Let me go, I won't stay. Be better to spend the night under a fence than in your filth. Whoo! God forgive us! (*Exits*)

NIKITA. I'll be damned!

AKIM (*opens the door*). Wake up, Nikita. Your soul's in peril. (*Exits*)

AKULINA (*takes the cups*). Well, pour it, huh?

(*All are silent.*)

MITRICH (*growls*). O, God, have mercy on my sinful soul!

(*All shudder.*)

NIKITA (*lies down on the bench*). Oh, it's hard, it's hard, Akulka. Where's the accordion, hey?

AKULINA. The accordion? So, you missed it. Why, you took it to get mended. I've poured some, drink.

NIKITA. Don't want it. Put the light out—oh, it's hard for me, so hard! (*Cries*)

ACT IV

Autumn. Evening. The moon is shining. The inside of the yard. In the center of the stage, the winter cottage and gate to the right, the summer cottage and cellar. Bits of conversation and drunken shouts are heard coming from the cottage. A neighbor comes out of the doorway and beckons to ANYUTKA'*s godmother, the* NEIGHBOR.

A NEIGHBOR. How come Akulina ain't come out?

NEIGHBOR. How come she ain't come out? 'deed she'd be glad to get out, but she ain't got a minute, you see. The matchmakers came to look the bride over, but she, my dear, is lying in the summer house and don't so much as poke her nose out, poor thing.

A NEIGHBOR. How come?

NEIGHBOR. 'Tween you and me, they say she's got cramps.

A NEIGHBOR. Not really!?

NEIGHBOR. Really. (*Whispers in her ear*)

A NEIGHBOR. So? That's real bad. And 'course the matchmakers'll find out.

NEIGHBOR. How'll they ever find out? They're all drunk. Besides, they're mostly after the dowry. It's easy enough, they're giving with the girl two fur coats, my dear, six housecoats, a French shawl, also a lot of linen and, they were saying, a couple of hundred rubles.

A NEIGHBOR. Well, and even with that money you can't be happy. It's a terrible shame.

NEIGHBOR. Shhh—the matchmaker don't know nothing.

(*They stop talking and enter the doorway. The* MATCHMAKER *comes out of the doorway alone, hiccoughing.*)

MATCHMAKER. I'm all sweaty. Awful hot. Got to cool off a bit. (*Stands, takes a big breath*) God knows what's going on—something ain't right, don't make me feel good—well, it's the way my old woman—

MATRYONA (*comes out from the same doorway*). And I'm looking all over: where's the matchmaker, where's the matchmaker? And here you are, my dear— And so, my dear, thank the Lord, it all came out right honorably. Matchmaking's not for boasting. And I never learned to boast anyways. But since you got a good deal, why, God grant it, you'll both be saying your thanks the rest of your lives. The girl, you know, is one of a kind. Can't find such a girl in the district.

MATCHMAKER. Seems not bad, the whole business, but we got to keep our eyes open about the money.

MATRYONA. Don't talk about the money. What it was her family give her it all goes with her. Nowadays it's something, too, three fifties.

MATCHMAKER. We don't mind; it's for our own child. You want everything good as you can.

MATRYONA. And I'm telling you the truth, matchmaker: if it wasn't for me, you would of never found her in your life. They got a inquiry from the Kormilins, too, but I stuck up for you. And about the money—I'll tell you the truth: when the departed was dying, may his soul rest in peace, he give orders that the widow take Nikita into the house, 'cause I know all this from my son, but the money, now, was for Akulina. Another man, you know, would of taken it himself, but Nikita gives it all to her to the last bit. Money like that now is something.

MATCHMAKER. People are talking, there was more money left her. The young fellow's a quick one, too.

MATRYONA. Babes-in-arms. Others take a huge slice; these give what there was. I'm telling you, forget all your figuring. Seal it up tight. What a girl, good as a plump bean.

MATCHMAKER. Seems not bad, the whole business. My old woman and me's been noticing something about the girl, though. How come she ain't come out? We're thinking, maybe she's ailing?

MATRYONA. Oh, oh—she's ailing? 'Deed there's none in the district like her. The girl's like iron—can't hurt her. You saw her yourself the other day. Terrific worker. Got a little deafness, that's a fact. So, a little worm-hole don't spoil a good, red apple. And why she ain't come out, now, that's, see, something 'tween you and me. Something's been done to her. And I know which bitch cast the spell. They knew there was a betrothal, see, so tried to break it. But I know a counter-charm. The girl'll be up and around tomorrow. Don't you worry 'bout the girl.

MATCHMAKER. Well, all right, the thing's settled.

MATRYONA. Right, right, you've agreed, and no backing out.

And don't forget me. I was working on this, too. Don't you be leaving—

A WOMAN'S VOICE FROM INSIDE THE COTTAGE. It's time we were going, Ivan, come on.

MATCHMAKER. Right away. (*Exits*)

ANYUTKA (*runs out of the doorway and beckons* ANISYA *over*). Mama!

ANISYA (*from there*). What?

ANYUTKA. Mama, come here, or they'll hear. (*Goes toward the barn with her*)

ANISYA. Well, what? Where's Akulina?

ANYUTKA. She went into the granary. It's terrible what she's doing there! Sure as I'm living, she says, I can't stand it no longer. I'll scream, she says, at the top of my voice. Sure as I'm living.

ANISYA. Maybe she'll wait. Let's see the guests off.

ANYUTKA. Oh, Mama! It's so terrible for her. And she's so cross. It's no use, she says, their drinking my health. I ain't going to marry, she says, I'm going, she says, to die. Mama, what if she died! It's awful, I'm scared!

ANISYA. Don't worry, she won't die; but don't you go see her. Run on.

(ANISYA *and* ANYUTKA *exit.*)

MITRICH (*alone; comes from the gate and sets about picking up the scattered hay*). Oh, Lord! Mikola the Good! The wine they swilled up! And let the smell out all over. Ah, it stinks in the yard. Ah no, not for me, the hell with him! Look how they tossed the hay around! Don't eat what's to eat—just trample on it. Look at that, a whole bundle. The smell! Gets right into your nose. Hell with him! (*Yawns*) Time for bed. But got no itch to go in the house. Gets all around and up your nose. Stinky, damned smell. (*One can hear people leaving*) So, they've gone. Oh, Lord! Mikola the Good! They're collaring themselves, too, playing tricks on each other. And all for nothing.

NIKITA (*enters*). Mitrich! Why don't you go get on the stove; I'll clean up.

MITRICH. All right. Toss this to the sheep. So, saw 'em off?

NIKITA. Saw 'em off, but something ain't right. Don't know how it'll work out.

MITRICH. Lot of nonsense! Nothing to it. There's the hos'ital for such things. There, no matter who's the cause of it all, everything's cleaned up. Give 'em whatever you want, no questions asked. Even give you money sometimes. Only you got to become a wet nurse. Nowadays it's all easy.

NIKITA. You watch out, Mitrich, so you don't babble something too much.

MITRICH. What do I care? Cover your tracks best you can. How you reek of wine! I'm going in. (*Exits yawning*) O, Lord!

NIKITA (*is long silent; sits down on a sledge*). Ah, what a mess!

ANISYA (*comes out*). Where're you now?

NIKITA. Here.

ANISYA. What're you sitting here for? No time to be waiting around. Got to carry it away right now.

NIKITA. What'll we do?

ANISYA. I told you what. So go do it.

NIKITA. Yeh, you'd put it in the foundling home, wouldn't you?

ANISYA. Go and take it yourself, if you want to. You're a dainty one for dirty tricks, I see, but pretty weak at getting out of 'em.

NIKITA. What'll I do?

ANISYA. I tell you, go in the cellar and dig a hole.

NIKITA. But you can figure out something else.

ANISYA (*mocking him*). Something else. Can't do it that way, 'parently. You ought to of been thinking about this earlier. Go where you're told.

NIKITA. Ah, what a mess, what a mess!

(ANYUTKA *enters.*)

ANYUTKA. Mama! Gramma's calling. I bet Sis's got a baby, sure as I'm living, it cried out.

ANISYA. What're you making up now; why don't you drop dead. Some kittens are whining there. Go into the house and go to sleep. Or I'll give you one—

ANYUTKA. Mama, Mama dear, it's the truth, so help me God—

ANISYA (*threatens her*). I'll give you one! And not a peep from you! (ANYUTKA *runs out. To* NIKITA) Go on, do what you're told. Or you watch out! (*Exits*)

NIKITA (*alone, is long silent*). Ah, what a mess! Oh, these women! It's no good! You, she says, ought to of been thinking earlier. When earlier to think of it? When to think 'bout it at all? Just last summer Anisya herself started making up to me. Well, so what? You think I'm a monk? The old man died, so, and I covered up my sin, like I ought to have. Wasn't all my doing. You think there aren't a lot like that? And then these powders. You think I p'suaded her to do that? Why, if I'd known, I would of killed her right then, bitch! Really, I would of killed her! Made me a partner in these dirty dealings, the dirty slut! I got sick of her right from that moment. Soon as my mother told me then, got sick of her, got sick of her, couldn't stand looking at her. How could I live with her? So, this happened! This girl started hanging round. What's the difference to me? If it wasn't me, it would of been somebody else. And now it's this far! And again it wasn't any of my doing. Oh, what a mess! (*Sits reflectively*) These women got guts—what they figured out. But I ain't going to do that.

MATRYONA (*comes out in a hurry with a lantern and a spade*). What're you sitting here for, like a chicken on an egg? What'd your old woman tell you to do? Get it ready.

NIKITA. But what're you all going to do?

MATRYONA. We know what's got to be done. And you do what you got to.

NIKITA. You're getting me all mixed up in it.

MATRYONA. What do you mean? You trying to back out? It's gone this far, and now you think you'll back out.

NIKITA. Yeh, but what a thing! A living being besides.

MATRYONA. Eh, a living being! Why, there's hardly any life in it. Besides, where you going to put it? Go ahead, take it to the foundling home—all the same it'll die, and the story'll get round, and right away they'll all be shouting about it, and we'll have the girl on our hands.

NIKITA. But if they find out?

MATRYONA. Can't a person fix things up in his own house? We'll fix it up so there won't be the littlest scent. Just do what I tell you. What we got to do is woman's work, but we can't get on without a man. Here's the spade, now, so crawl down there and fix it up. I'll hold the light.

NIKITA. Fix up what?

MATRYONA (*in a whisper*). Dig a little hole. And then we'll bring it out and quickly clean up there. Ah, there she's shouting again. Go on, go on. And I'll go see her.

NIKITA. But, is it dead?

MATRYONA. Sure, it's dead. Just you got to move quickly. 'cause people ain't turned in yet. They'll hear, they'll see— they got to know everything, the bastards. And the policeman was passing by this evening. Here, take this. (*Hands him the spade*) Crawl into the cellar. Dig a little hole in the corner there, the earth's soft, and then you can smooth it over again. Old Mother Earth won't tell a soul how the cow's licking with its tongue. Go on. Go on, my dear.

NIKITA. You're getting me all mixed up in it. The hell with you all. Really, I'm getting out of here. Do it yourselves best you can.

ANISYA (*from the doorway*). Well, did he get it dug, hey?

MATRYONA. Why'd you leave her? What'd you do with it?

ANISYA. Covered it up with a piece of burlap. Nobody'll hear it. Did he get it dug?

MATRYONA. He won't!

ANISYA (*jumping out, in a rage*). He won't! And does he want to take care of the louse in jail?! I'll go right to the police, tell 'em everything. Go down together. I'll tell everything right this minute.

NIKITA (*dumb-struck*). What'll you tell 'em?

ANISYA. What? Everything! Who took the money? You! (NIKITA *is silent*) And who gave the poison? I did! But you knew, knew, knew! I was in agreement with you!

MATRYONA. Now, now, now. Mikishka, what're you hanging back for? What're you going to do? You got some work to do. Go on, sweetie.

ANISYA. Look at him, the big saint! He won't! You've been harming me long enough. You been riding on my back, and now my turn's come. Go on, I tell you, or I'll do what I said!— Take the spade, take it! Go on!

NIKITA. Hold on, now; what do you insist for? (*Takes the spade, but hesitates*) No, I won't do it—won't go down.

ANISYA. Won't go? (*Begins to shout*) Hey, everybody!

MATRYONA (*covers her mouth*). What're you doing? You crazy?! He'll go— Go on, my boy, go on, my dear.

ANISYA. I'm going to call for help.

NIKITA. Stop it! Ah, these people! Just you better hurry up. It's all one. (*Goes to the cellar*)

MATRYONA. That's the way it is, sweetie: you knew how to

splurge, now you got to know how to cover your tracks.

ANISYA (*still all agitated*). He's been making a joke of me long enough with his lady-friend! I'm not going to be alone in this. Let him be a murderer, too. He'll find out what it's like.

MATRYONA. Now, now, you're all upset. Don't you get mad, dear; do things quietly and bit by bit; that's the best way. Go to the girl now. He'll do it. (*Follows him with the lantern*)

(NIKITA *crawls into the cellar*)

ANISYA. I'll make him smother his own stinking kid himself! (*Still all agitated*) I suffered all by myself from worriment over Pyotr's bones. Let him, too, find out what it's like. I'm not going to spare myself; I said, I'm not going to spare myself!

NIKITA (*from the cellar*). Some light, hey!

MATRYONA (*shines the lantern; to* ANISYA). He's digging. Go get it.

ANISYA. Stay with him. Or the bastard'll run away. And I'll go get it.

MATRYONA. Careful, don't forget to christen it. Or I can do it. Got a cross?

ANISYA. I'll find one, I know where it is. (*Exits*)

MATRYONA (*alone*). How bitter she's got, like a old woman. And it's wrong to be talking like that. Well, thank God, let's finish up this business, and no one'll be the wiser. We'll get rid of the girl without trouble. Then the boy'll live peaceably. They live in plenty, thank God. And he won't forget me, neither. Where'd they be without Matryona? They couldn't of figured nothing out. (*Calling down to the cellar*) Is it ready, son?

NIKITA (*crawling up, his head visible*). Is it there? Bring it over, hey! What're you dawdling for? Let's do it if you're going to do it.

(MATRYONA *goes to the doorway and meets* ANISYA. ANISYA *comes out with the baby wrapped in rags.*)

MATRYONA. Well, did you christen it?

ANISYA. Of course. Took it from her by force—wouldn't let go. (*Goes up to and gives it to* NIKITA)

NIKITA (*does not take it*). You take it down yourself.

ANISYA. You take it, I tell you. (*Throws the baby to him*)

NIKITA (*grabs it*). It's alive! Mother of God, it's moving! it's alive! What'll I do with it?

ANISYA (*grabs the baby out of his arms and throws it into the cellar*). Hurry up and smother it and it won't be alive. (*Pushes* NIKITA *down*) It's your business, you finish it.

MATRYONA (*sits down on the step*). He's soft-hearted. It's not easy for him, poor dear. Well, so what! It's his fault, too. (ANISYA *stands in front of the cellar entrance.* MATRYONA *sits down on a porch step, looks at her and thinks*) Whew, how scared he is! Well, so what? so it ain't easy, but you can't get around it. What could you do with it? Just think, too, how another time they'll be begging for children! And, look, God don't grant 'em, or they're all born dead. Like with the priest's wife. And here they don't want it, and so it's alive. (*Looks into the cellar*) Must be, it's finished. (*To* ANISYA) Well?

ANISYA (*looking into the cellar*). He's covered it up with a board, and sat down on it. Must of finished.

MATRYONA. Oh-oh! You don't want to sin, but what can you do?

NIKITA (*crawls out, trembling all over*). It's still alive! I can't! It's alive!

ANISYA. So it's alive, so where're you going? (*Tries to stop him*)

NIKITA (*throwing himself at her*). You get out of here! I'll kill you! (*He grabs her arm, she tears herself away, he runs after her with the spade.* MATRYONA *rushes to meet him, stops him.* ANISYA *runs onto the porch.* MATRYONA *tries to take the spade away.* NIKITA *threatens his mother with it*) I'll kill you, I'll kill you, too, get out! (MATRYONA *runs up to* ANISYA *on the porch.* NIKITA *stops*) I'll kill you! I'll kill you all!

MATRYONA. It's on account of his fright. Don't mean nothing, it'll pass.

NIKITA. What've they done? What've they done to me? It whined so— How it crunched under me. What've they done to me! And it's alive, still, really, it's alive! (*Stops talking and listens*) It's whining— Listen, it's whining. (*Runs toward the cellar*)

MATRYONA (*to* ANISYA). Sure, he's going to go bury it. Nikita, you need a light.

NIKITA (*without answering, listens by the cellar entrance*). Can't hear a thing. It was getting back at me. (*Walks on and stops*) And how the little bones crunched under me. Crr—crr— What've they done to me? (*Again listens*) Again it's whining, really, it's whining. What is this? Mother, oh, Mama! (*Goes over to her*)

MATRYONA. What, son?

NIKITA. Mother, for the love of God I can't do no more. Can't do nothing. Mother, my own mother, spare me!

MATRYONA. Ah, you're really scared, poor dear. Go in, go in, drink up a little vodka, maybe, to give you courage.

NIKITA. Ah, Mama, came my turn, see. What've you done to me? How these little bones crunched, and it whined so! Mother, my own mother, what you've done to me! (*Goes off and sits down on a sledge*)

MATRYONA. Go on in, dear, and have a drink. It's doing a thing at night's so scary. But give yourself time, it'll turn light, see, a day or two'll pass, and you won't think about it no more. Give us time, we'll marry the girl off and we won't think about it no more. And you go have a drink, go have a drink now. Myself I'll clean up in the cellar.

NIKITA (*rouses himself*). Is there some vodka left there? Might take a bit! (*Exits*)

(ANISYA, *who has stood all the time in the doorway, silently moves aside.*)

MATRYONA. Go on, go on, sweetie, and I'll do it myself, I'll crawl in myself and cover it up. Where'd he throw the spade now? (*Finds the spade, goes halfway down into the cellar*) Anisya, bring the light over here, will you?

ANISYA. But what about him?

MATRYONA. He's got real scared. You were real hard on him. Leave him alone, he'll come round. God help him, I'll do it myself. Put the light here. I can see. (*Disappears in the cellar*)

ANISYA (*toward the door where* NIKITA *went in*). Well, had your fun? You lived in grand style, now you wait, you'll find out yourself what it's like. You'll come down a peg.

NIKITA (*jumps out of the doorway toward the cellar*). Mother, Mama!

MATRYONA (*pokes her head out of the cellar*). What, son?

NIKITA (*listens*). Don't fill it up, it's alive. Don't you hear it? it's alive! Listen—it's whining. There distinctly—

MATRYONA. And how could it be whining? You know you flattened it out like a pancake. You smashed its whole little head.

NIKITA. What?! (*Covers his ears*) It's still whining! I've ruined my own life! Ruined it! What've they done to me?! Where can I go?! (*Sits down on the steps*)

VARIANT

The following variant may be read instead of the previous scene beginning with Anisya's speech from the doorway, "Well, did he get it dug, hey?"

The cottage of Act I. ANYUTKA, *undressed, lies on the bench under a coat.* MITRICH *sits on the top bunk and smokes.*

MITRICH. Look, now, what a stink they've made. Hope their bellies burst. They were squandering the stuff. Can't kill it with tobacco even. Gets right up into your nose. Oh, Lord! Well, bedtime. (*Goes over to the lamp to turn it out*)

ANYUTKA (*jumps up, sits*). Grampa,[1] don't put it out, dear.

MITRICH. Why not?

ANYUTKA. They were making such a hubbub in the yard. (*Listens*) You hear, they've gone into the granary again?

MITRICH. What's it to you? They're not asking for you, I expect. Lie down and go to sleep. And I'll just turn out the light. (*Turns it down*)

ANYUTKA. Grampa, sweet Grampa! don't put it all the way out. Leave just a crack, or it's scary.

MITRICH (*laughs*). All right, all right. (*Sits down beside her*) What you scared of?

ANYUTKA. Can't help it, Grampa. Sis was struggling so. She was beating her head against the floor. (*In a whisper*) See, I know— She's fixing to have a baby— Must already be born—

MITRICH. What a fidget! let the frogs hop on you. You got to know everything. Lie down and go to sleep. (ANYUTKA *lies down*) That's the way. (*Covers her*) That's the way. 'Cause if you'll be knowing a lot, you'll soon grow old.

ANYUTKA. And are you going to get up on the stove?

MITRICH. And where else? You little stupid. She's got to know

[1] An affectionate form of address; they are not related.

everything. (*Covers her again and gets up to go*) Lie down, that's it, and go to sleep. (*Goes to the stove*)

ANYUTKA. Cried just once, but now you can't hear a thing.

MITRICH. Oh, Lord, Mikola the Good! What can't you hear?

ANYUTKA. The baby.

MITRICH. But there ain't one, so there's nothing to hear.

ANYUTKA. But I heard it, sure as I'm living, I heard it. So quiet like and thin.

MITRICH. There's lots you heard. But did you hear about the little girl, just like you, and a hobgoblin stuck her in his bag, and that was the end of her.

ANYUTKA. What d'you mean, hobgoblin?

MITRICH. Why, just that. (*Climbs on the stove*) The stove's good today, it's warm. It's real pleasure! Oh, Lord, Mikola the Good!

ANYUTKA. Grampa! You 'sleep?

MITRICH. What'd you think—I'm going to sing?

(*Silence.*)

ANYUTKA. Grampa, Grampa! They're digging! Honest, they're digging! Digging in the cellar, you hear it? Sure as I'm living, they're digging!

MITRICH. What she won't think up. Digging at night. Who's digging? The cow scratches herself, and you keep saying—they're digging! Go to sleep, I tell you, or I'll put the light out right away.

ANYUTKA. Grampa, dear, don't. I'll stop, honest, I'll stop, sure as I'm living, I'll stop. I'm scared.

MITRICH. Scared? Now don't you fear nothing, and then you won't be. You get scared yourself when you get afraid. 'course you get afraid when you get scared. What a stupid little girl.

(*Silence. A cricket.*)

ANYUTKA (*in a whisper*). Grampa! Grampa! You asleep?

MITRICH. Now what?

ANYUTKA. What's the hobgoblin like?

MITRICH. He's the way he is. Like if someone like you—don't sleep, so he comes along with his bag, plop, the girl's in his bag, sticks his head in, lifts up her nightie, and gives her a spanking.

ANYUTKA. What's he spank her with?

MITRICH. Takes a switch to her.

ANYUTKA. But he can't see there in the bag.

MITRICH. Don't worry, he sees.

ANYUTKA. But I'll bite him.

MITRICH. No, dear, you won't bite him.

ANYUTKA. Grampa, someone's coming! Who is it? Ah, saints alive! Who is it?

MITRICH. Who's coming's coming. What do you care? Your mother, I expect, she's coming.

(ANISYA *enters.*)

ANISYA. Anyutka! (ANYUTKA *pretends she is asleep*) Mitrich!

MITRICH. What?

ANISYA. Why you burning the light? We're going to sleep in the summer cottage.

MITRICH. Just finished clearing up. I'll put it out.

ANISYA (*looks through the chest and grumbles*). When you need something you can never find it.

MITRICH. What're you looking for?

ANISYA. Looking for a cross. Got to christen someone. God help us, it'll die! Unchristened! A sin, see!

MITRICH. Sure, o' course, got to do the right thing— What, did you find it?

ANISYA. Found it. (*Exits*)

MITRICH. Well, there, or I would of given her mine. Oh, Lord!

ANYUTKA (*jumps up and shivers*). Oh-oh, Grampa! Don't you go to sleep, for the Lord's sake! How terrible!

MITRICH. What's so terrible?

ANYUTKA. It'll die, I bet, the little baby? Gramma christened Aunty Arina's just like that—and it died.

MITRICH. If it dies, it'll get buried.

ANYUTKA. But, maybe, it won't die, except Gramma Matryona's here. See, I heard what she said, sure as I'm living, I heard.

MITRICH. What'd you hear? Go to sleep, I tell you. Just hide your head under the blanket.

ANYUTKA. If it was to live, I'd take care of it.

MITRICH (*growls*). Oh, Lord!!

ANYUTKA. Where'll they put it?

MITRICH. They'll put it where they got to. Not your worry. Go to sleep, I tell you. Here's your mother coming—she'll scold you!

(*Silence.*)

ANYUTKA. Grampa! And the girl you were talking about, sure she didn't get killed?

MITRICH. What girl? Oh, that little girl came out all right.

ANYUTKA. Like you said, Grampa, they found her?

MITRICH. Yeh, they found her.

ANYUTKA. But where'd they find her? Tell me.

MITRICH. Found her in her own house. Came into the village, the soldiers began to rummage through the houses, and look—there's this little girl herself lying on her belly. They were going to hurt her, but I felt so sorry for her I picked her up in my arms. You know, she didn't want to at all. Was all heavy, dead weight, like if she weighed five poods. And with her hands catching at anything she could get hold of, and you couldn't get 'em free nohow. Well, I picked her up, and patted her head and patted it. She was all shaggy, like a hedgehog. Got to caress her, caress her—and she quieted down. Soaked a biscuit, gave it to her. She understood like. Nibbled it up. What could you do with her? We took her. Took her, began to feed her and take care of her, and she got used to it, and we took her along on the march, and so she went along with us. She was a nice little girl.

ANYUTKA. She wasn't christened?

MITRICH. Who knows. Used to say, not just right. On account of her people wasn't ours.

ANYUTKA. Germans?

MITRICH. Listen to you: Germans. Not Germans, Asians. They're just the same like Kikes, but not Kikes, neither. Poles, but Asians. Krudly, Krugly you call 'em. I forget now. We called the little girl Sashka. Sashka, and she was pretty. I've forgotten everything, see, but right now it's like I was looking at her herself, may she have health and a long life. That's all I remember out of all my service. How they flogged us, I remember, and that's how clear I remember this girl. She would hang on your neck, you know, and you would carry her. What a fine little girl she was, you'll never find a better. Gave her away later. Company commander's wife took her as daughter. And she came out all right. How sorry the soldiers were!

ANYUTKA. And, Grampa, I remember, too, how Pa died. You hadn't come to us then. He called Nikita in and he says to him: forgive me, he says, Nikita—and he himself started crying. (*Sighs*) It was so sad.

MITRICH. Exactly so, exactly so—

ANYUTKA. Grampa, Grampa. There they go making that noise in the cellar again. Aie, saints alive! Oh, Grampa, they're doing something to it. They're going to kill it! Such a little thing, you know—oh! oh! (*Covers her head and cries*)

MITRICH (*listens*). 'Deed they're doing something dirty, damn 'em. What dirty things these women are! You can't say much for the men, but these women— They're like wild beasts. Not scared of nothing.

ANYUTKA (*gets up*). Grampa, Grampa!

MITRICH. What now?

ANYUTKA. Not long ago a man traveling through spent the night, he was saying that when a baby dies his soul goes right straight to heaven. Is that true?

MITRICH. Who knows, must be. So?

ANYUTKA. Well, if I was to die. (*Whimpers*)

MITRICH. If you die, you'll be gone.

ANYUTKA. You're a baby still to ten, and your soul, maybe, will still go to God, but then, see, you go bad.

MITRICH. How you go bad! The whole pack of you can't help but go bad. Who teaches you? What'll you see? What'll you hear? Just only foul things. I ain't so very smart, but I do know something. Not a lot, but still nothing like a country woman. What's a country woman? Nothing but slush. There's millions of you women in Russia, and you all, just like blind moles, you don't know nothing. How to work up cow's death, all kinds of tricks, and how to put children to roost with the chickens—that's what they know.

ANYUTKA. Mama's put 'em to roost.

MITRICH. Exactly so, exactly so. There's millions of just you women and girls, and they're all like wild beasts. The way you grow up's the way you'll die. Without seeing nothing, without hearing nothing. A man—why, he, even in the saloon, or in a dungeon, maybe, or with the soldiers, like me, he finds out something. But what's a woman? Don't know nothing about God, don't even know what's the meaning of Friday, what it's all about. Friday, Friday, but you ask her what's Friday, she don't know. They go round sticking their heads into the manure, like little puppies with their eyes shut. Know just their own stupid songs: ho-ho, ho-ho. But what's this ho-ho, themselves they don't know—

ANYUTKA. But, Grampa, I know "Our Father wh'art in heaven" up to the middle.

MITRICH. You know a lot! And a person can't ask much of you all neither. Who teaches you? Just a drunken man who sometimes takes the reins to you. That's all the learning. Don't know myself who's going to answer for you. The recruits got a non-com or a sergeant to look out for 'em. But there's nobody to look out for you women. So all these women're just a herd with no pasture, the mischiefest of 'em all. Stupidest things in the world. Biggest good-for-nothings.

ANYUTKA. What can you do?

MITRICH. Do what you can. Cover yourself up, now, and go to sleep. Oh, Lord!

(*Silence. A cricket.*)

ANYUTKA (*jumps up*). Grampa! Somebody's shouting, somebody's in trouble! Honest, really, he's shouting. Grampa, dear, come closer.

MITRICH. I tell you, cover yourself up.

NIKITA (*enters with* MATRYONA). What've they done to me? What've they done to me!?

MATRYONA. Have a little drink, have a little drink of vodka, sweetie. (*Gets the vodka and puts it on the table*) What's wrong?

NIKITA. Gimme it. Take a swig?

MATRYONA. Sh! They ain't asleep. Come on, drink it.

NIKITA. What is this? What'd you think this up for? You could've taken it away some place.

MATRYONA (*in a whisper*). Sit here, sit down here; drink some more, and have a smoke. It'll clear your head.

NIKITA. Mother my own, came my turn, see. How it whined, and how the little bones crunched—crr—crr—I ain't a man no more.

MATRYONA. Phhh! What're you talking such complete nonsense for. It's just that doing a thing at night's so scary, but wait till the day comes, a day or two'll pass, and you won't think about it no more. (*Goes up to* NIKITA, *puts her hand on his shoulder*)

NIKITA. Get away from me. What've you all done to me?

MATRYONA. What's going on with you, son, really? (*Takes* NIKITA's *hand*)

NIKITA. You get away from me! I'll kill you! Nothing matters no more. I'll kill you!

MATRYONA. Ah, ah, you've got real scared! Why don't you go to sleep now.

NIKITA. Got no place to go! I'm done for!

MATRYONA (*shakes her head*). Oh, oh, got to go clean up, and he can sit here a while, and it'll pass. (*Exits*)

NIKITA (*sits, his face covered with his hands.* MITRICH *and* ANYUTKA *are completely still*). It's whining, really, it's whining, there, right there, distinctly. She's going to cover it up, really she's going to cover it up! (*Runs to the door*) Mama, don't cover it up, it's alive!

MATRYONA (*coming back, in a whisper*). What're you doing, for the Lord's sake! It's not coming back. How can it be alive! Why, all its little bones are smashed.

NIKITA. Gimme some more vodka. (*Drinks*)

MATRYONA. Go on, son. You can sleep now; don't worry.

NIKITA (*stands, listens*). It's still alive! There! It's whining! Don't you hear it? Listen!

MATRYONA (*in a whisper*). 'Course not!

NIKITA. Oh, Mother! I've ruined my life. What you've all done to me! Where can I go? (*Runs out of the cottage and* MATRYONA *after him*)

ANYUTKA. Grampa, dear Grampa, they smothered it!

MITRICH (*angrily*). Sleep, I tell you. Ah, you, let the frogs hop on you! Look out I'll switch you! Go to sleep, I tell you.

ANYUTKA. Grampa dear! Somebody's grabbing my shoulders, somebody's grabbing, grabbing with his hands. Grampa, dear Grampa, sure as I'm living, I'm coming right away. Dear Grampa, let me up on the stove! Let me up for Christ's sake— It's grabbing—grabbing— Aaaaa! (*Runs to the stove*)

MITRICH. Look how they've scared the little girl. Dirty creatures, exactly, let the frogs hop on 'em. Well! climb on up, come on.

ANYUTKA (*climbs on the stove*). Don't you go away.

MITRICH. Where would I go? Come on, come on! Oh, Lord, Mikola the Sweet, Holy Mother of God in Kazan! They scared her so. (*Covers her up*) Little fool, real little fool—Scared her, really, the dirty things, hope their bellies burst.

ACT V

SCENE 1

The threshing-floor In the foreground, a rick of grain; on the left, the threshing-square; on the right, the barn. The barn gate is open; there is straw in the doorway. The yard can be seen in the background, and songs and little bells can be heard. Two girls are going along the path by the barn toward the cottage.

FIRST GIRL. There, see, how we got through, and we didn't get our good shoes dirty, but if you go by the village!—it's real dirty— (*They stop and wipe their feet on the straw. The girl looks at the straw and sees something*) What's that there?

SECOND GIRL (*looks carefully*). That's Mitrich, the hired man here. Look, he's got real drunk.

FIRST GIRL. But he never used to drink?

SECOND GIRL. Up till today, I guess.

FIRST GIRL. Look! Looks like he came here for some straw. See, he's still got the rope in his hands, and just like that he fell asleep.

SECOND GIRL (*listens*). They're still singing the praises. Must be, they haven't done the blessing yet. Akulina, they were saying, didn't give the answering lament at all.

FIRST GIRL. Mama was saying she's going against her will. Stepfather threatened her into it, or she would of never done it in her life. What they haven't been saying about her!

(MARINA *enters, overtakes the girls.*)

MARINA. Hello, girls!

GIRLS. Hello, Auntie!

MARINA. Going to the wedding?

FIRST GIRL. It's already over. We're just going to look.

MARINA. Tell my old man, Semyon from Zuyevo, I'm waiting. You know him, don't you?

FIRST GIRL. 'course. He's some kind of relative of the groom.

MARINA. Sure, he's my husband's nephew.

SECOND GIRL. Why don't you go yourself? You got to go to the wedding.

MARINA. Don't want to, dear, besides I haven't the time. Got to go on. We weren't fixing on coming to the wedding. We were taking oats to town. Stopped to feed the horse, and they asked my old man in.

FIRST GIRL. Whose place did you stop at? Fyodoroch's?

MARINA. His. So I'll just wait here and you, dear, go call my old man. Tell him to come out, sweetie. Tell him: your old woman, Marina, says you got to go; they're hitching up.

FIRST GIRL. Well, all right, if you won't go yourself.

(*The girls exit along the path toward the yard. One can hear singing and the sound of little bells.*)

MARINA (*alone; is lost in thought*) Wouldn't matter if I went, but I don't want to, 'cause I haven't seen him since that very day when he turned me down. More than a year ago. But might just take a peek at how he's getting on with his Anisya. People are saying they got differences. She's a coarse woman, temperamental. He's probably remembered more than once, I bet. Had his sights set on a easy life. Traded me off. Well, God help him, I've got nothing against him. Then, it really hurt. Ah, it was terrible painful. But now it's worn off me—and I've forgotten. But just to take a quick look at him— (*Looks toward the yard, sees* NIKITA) Look! What's he coming for? Did the girls tell him? What'd he leave his guests for? I'm going. (NIKITA *walks at first with his head bent over and, waving his arms, he mutters*) How gloomy he is!

NIKITA (*catches sight of* MARINA, *recognizes her*). Marina! Dear friend, Marinushka! Why're you here?

MARINA. Came to fetch my old man.

NIKITA. Why didn't you come to the wedding? Could of taken a look, could of laughed at me.

MARINA. What should I laugh at you for? I came after my husband.

NIKITA. Eh, Marinushka! (*Tries to embrace her*)

MARINA (*breaks away angrily*). Oh, Nikita, you stop doing this. What's past is past. Came for my husband. He's here, ain't he?

NIKITA. Means we can't remember the past? You won't let us?

MARINA. No point to remember the past. What's past is past.

NIKITA. And don't come back, you mean?

MARINA. And don't come back. But what'd you come out for?

The man of the house, but you come away from the wedding.

NIKITA (*sits down on the straw*). What'd I come for? Eh, if you only knew, if you only knew! I'm sad, Marina, I'm so sad my eyes couldn't look no more. Just got up from the table and came out, came away from the people, just so to see nobody.

MARINA (*goes over closer to him*). What's wrong?

NIKITA. Something I can't eat up by eating, drink up by drinking, sleep off by sleeping. I feel sick, so sick! And I feel sickest of all, Marina, being alone and having nobody to share my grief with.

MARINA. But you can't live without grieving, Nikita. 'Deed I had my own spell of weeping—and it passed.

NIKITA. That was over what was, over the past. You had your spell, friend, but now it's my turn.

MARINA. But what's wrong?

NIKITA. Ah, what's made me sick of my whole life. I'm sick of myself. Eh, Marina, you didn't know how to hold on to me, and you ruined me and yourself, too! You think this is life?

MARINA (*stands by the barn, cries and tries to contain herself*). I ain't complaining about my own life, Nikita. May God give everybody as good. I ain't complaining. I told my old man everything then. He forgave me. And don't hold it against me. I don't find no fault with my life. My old man's quiet and considerate to me. I keep his children clean and dress 'em. He helps me out, too. What've I got to be bitter about? It's clear, that's the way God wanted it. But what's wrong with your life? You got money—

NIKITA. My life! Only I don't want to break up the wedding, I'd take a rope, this rope here (*picks up the rope from the straw*) and I'd toss it right over this beam here. And I'd fix up a real good loop, and I'd climb up on the beam, and put my head right in. That's what my life's like!

MARINA. You mean it? God help you!

NIKITA. You think I'm joking? Think I'm drunk? I ain't drunk. Today I ain't a bit tight. But grief, grief's eaten me up completely. Eaten me up so, that nothing seems good to me! Eh, Marinushka, the only time I lived was with you, remember, and we spent the nights together on the railroad.

MARINA. Now, Nikita, don't you hurt where it's already sore.

I got married, and you, too. My sin's forgiven, and don't you now bring back the past—

NIKITA. What can I do with my feelings? Where can I go now?

MARINA. What can you do? You got your own wife, don't make eyes at others, but take care of your own. You loved Anisya, so go on loving her.

NIKITA. Ah, this Anisya's like bitter wormwood to me, only she's wrapped herself round my legs, like witchgrass.

MARINA. Whatever she is she's your wife. What do you talk like that for! Better go back to your guests and send my husband out to me.

NIKITA. If only you knew the whole mess— But what's there to talk about!

(MARINA'*s husband and* ANYUTKA *enter.*)

MARINA'S HUSBAND (*comes out from the yard, red-faced and drunk*). Marina! M'wife! Y'old woman! Y'here, hey?

NIKITA. Here's your husband coming, calling you. Go now.

MARINA. And what'll you do?

NIKITA. Me? I'll lie here a bit. (*Lies down in the straw*)

MARINA'S HUSBAND. Where is she?

ANYUTKA. There she is, Uncle, by the barn.

MARINA'S HUSBAND. What're y'standing there for? Go on in t' th'wedding! Our hosts say y'got to come, do th'honor. Party'll be going off right 'way, an' we'll get goin'.

MARINA (*comes out to meet her husband*). But I didn't much want to.

MARINA'S HUSBAND. Go on, I tell you. Y'can drink up a little glass, 'gratulate that rascal Petrunka. Hosts'll feel slighted, but we'll get everything done all right. (*Embraces* MARINA *and, stumbling, goes off stage with her*)

NIKITA (*raises himself up and sits in the straw*). So, I saw her, and I feel worse than ever. Only time it was like living was with her. It's not just that I've ruined my whole life; I ruined my own self! (*Lies down*) Where'll I go now? Ah! Open wide, sweet mother earth!

ANYUTKA (*sees* NIKITA *and runs over to him*). Pa, oh, Pa! They're looking for you. Everybody, even the godfather, has already given their blessings. Sure as I'm living, they have. They're already getting cross.

NIKITA (*to himself*). Where'll I go now?

ANYUTKA. What? What'd you say?

NIKITA. Didn't say nothing. What're you after me for?

ANYUTKA. Pa! Let's go! (NIKITA *is silent.* ANYUTKA *pulls him by the hand*) Pa, come and bless 'em! Honest and true, they're getting cross with you and swearing at you.

NIKITA (*pulls his hand away*). Leave me alone!

ANYUTKA. Well, now!

NIKITA (*threatens her with the reins*). Get out of here, I tell you. Or I'll give it to you.

ANYUTKA. Then I'll get Mama. (*Runs off*)

NIKITA (*alone; gets up*). Now how'll I go? How'll I take the icon? How'll I look her in the eye? (*Lies down again*) Oh, if only there was a hole in the earth, I'd go in. People wouldn't see me, and I wouldn't see no one. (*Again gets up*) I won't go in— Let 'em perish! Won't go in. (*Takes off his boots and picks up the rope; makes a loop in it, throws it around his neck*) Do it like this.

(MATRYONA *enters.* NIKITA *sees his mother, takes the rope off his head and lies down again on the straw.*)

MATRYONA (*comes up in a hurry*). Nikita! Nikita! Look at that, he don't even say a word. Nikita, what's wrong with you, you drunk? Come on, Mikitushka, come on, come on, sweetie. The people're tired of waiting.

NIKITA. Ah, what've you all done to me? I ain't a man no more.

MATRYONA. What're you talking about? Come on, dear, do the blessing and all the honors and have it over with. Everybody's waiting, see.

NIKITA. How can I bless anyone?

MATRYONA. It's clear how. Don't you really know?

NIKITA. Know how, I know how. Who's it I'll be blessing? What'd I do to her?

MATRYONA. What'd you do? What a thing to think of remembering! Nobody knows: neither Peeping Tom nor the garbage man. And the girl's doing this herself.

NIKITA. How's she doing it?

MATRYONA. Of course, she's doing it out of fear, too, but she's doing it. What else is there to do? She ought t've thought about it then. She can't be jibbing now. And the matchmakers got nothing against it. Looked the girl over twice, and besides she's got some money with her. It's all sewed up, done with.

NIKITA. But what about what's in the cellar?

MATRYONA (*laughs*). What's in the cellar? Cabbage, mushrooms, potatoes, I expect. What're you remembering the past for?

NIKITA. I'd be glad not to remember. But I can't. Soon as I start thinking, I hear it. Oh, what've you done to me?

MATRYONA. And what're you, in fact, making it so hard for?

NIKITA (*turns over and lies flat on his face*). Ma! Don't you be tormenting me! I'm full right up to here.

MATRYONA. But still you got to. The people're talking anyway, and here the father suddenly goes off, won't move more, hasn't got the guts to give his blessing. They're about to kiss the icons right away. Long as you're scared, they'll guess it right away. Go in like the chief and not like a thief. Or else you're running from the wolf right into the bear. Most of all don't show no expressions, don't be scared, my boy, or they'll take it the worst way.

NIKITA. Ah, you've got me all mixed up in this!

MATRYONA. Stop it, let's go. And go on out and give 'em the blessing. Everything just as it ought to be, honor and all, and that's the end of it.

NIKITA (*lies on his face*). Can't do it.

MATRYONA (*to herself*). What's happened? There was nothing, nothing, and now suddenly this. Something unnatural, it's clear. Nikita, get up! Look, here's Anisya coming, left the guests, too.

ANISYA (*enters, dressed up, red-faced, a little high*). It's going so well, Mama! Going so well, honestly! And how pleased everybody is. Where is he?

MATRYONA. Here, sweetie, here. He's laid down in the straw, and he's still lying. Won't move.

NIKITA (*looks at his wife*). Look, drunk, too! I look at her and feel sick at heart. How can you live with her? (*Turns over on his face*) I'll kill her sometime. It's going to get worse.

ANISYA. Look where he is, crawled into the straw. Or you had too much? (*Laughs*) I'd lie down with you right here a bit, but I got no time. It's going so well in the house now! It's a joy to see. And th'accordion! The women're sparkling, it's going just fine. Everybody's drunk. It's a real honor to us, it's going so well!

NIKITA. What's going so well?

ANISYA. The wedding, it's a gay wedding. Everybody's saying there's not many a wedding like this one. So grand, so fine. Go on in. We'll go together. I've had a bit, but I'll take you. (*Takes his hand.*)

NIKITA (*pulls his hand away in disgust*). Go by yourself. I'll come.

ANISYA. What're you cross about? All our troubles're over, we got rid of what was keeping us apart, just got to live now and be happy. It's all so right, according to law. I can hardly tell you how happy I am. Just like if I was marrying you all over again. Oh, everybody's so pleased! They're all thanking us. And the guests're all so fine. And Ivan Moseyich—and the policeman, too, they've been singing praises, too.

NIKITA. So, keep sitting with them—what'd you come here for?

ANISYA. But you got to go in. Or what's it going to look like? The hosts go out and leave the guests. And the guests're all so fine!

NIKITA (*gets up, brushes the straw off*). Go in, the both of you. And I'll be right there.

MATRYONA. The night cuckoo out-cuckooed the day. Wouldn't listen to me, but runs right after his wife. (*She and* ANISYA *go*) You coming?

NIKITA. Right away. You go on, I'll follow. I'll come, I'll do the blessing— (*The women stop*) Go on—and I'll follow. Go on! (*The women exit.* NIKITA *looks after them, lost in thought*)

NIKITA (*sits down and takes off his shoes and socks*). So I got to go! How?! No, the both of you look, see if I'm not up on the beam. Slipped the loop and jumped from the beam, and now you find me. Hey, thank God, the reins're here. (*Gets lost in thought*) Anything different I could shake off. I could shake off any kind of sorrow! But this is God knows where—down in my heart, can't get it out nohow. (*Glances toward the yard*) Nohow. Someone's coming again. (*Mimics* ANISYA) "Fine, so fine! I'll lie down a bit with you!" Ah! the dirty bag! Go to hell, and hug me when they take me down from the beam. It's the only way. (*Grabs the rope, pulls it*)

MITRICH (*drunk, gets up, not letting go of the rope*). Won't let you have it. Won't let nobody have it. I'll bring it myself. Said I'd get the straw—so I'll get it! Nikita, is it you? (*Laughs*) I'll be damned! Coming for straw?

NIKITA. Gimme the rope.

MITRICH. No, you wait. The men sent me. I'll get it— (*Gets up on his feet, begins to collect straw, but stumbles, catches himself and finally falls*) Vodka's on top. It's got me—

NIKITA. Gimme the reins.

MITRICH. Told you I wouldn't. Ah, Mikishka, you're as dumb as a pig's ass. (*Laughs*) I like you, but you're dumb. You look at me 'cause I been drinking. You can go to hell for all I care! You think I need you— Just you look at me! I'm a non-com! You idiot, you don't know how to say: non-commissioned officer of grenadiers of her majesty's very first regiment. Served the tsar, served my country faith'ly and well. But who'm I? You think I'm a soldier? No, I ain't no soldier, I'm the last guy of all, an orphan's what I am, a lost sheep. Swore off drinking, I did, and now I've really hit it! What, you think I'm scared of you? How's that? Ain't scared of no one. Been drinking, so, I been drinking. Now for two weeks I'll get clobbered, give the old bottle hell. I'll drink away everything down to my cross; drink away my hat; I'll pawn my ticket and I don't fear nobody. Got flogged in the regiment so I wouldn't drink. They whipped and they whipped— "Well," they says, "will you now?" I will, I says. Why be scared of them scum? That's the kind I am! It's the way God made me. Swore off drinking. Didn't drink. Now I been drinking—I'll go on drinking. I ain't scared of nobody. And so I don't tell no lies, but things just as they are— Why be scared of the scum? Hell with you, I says, that's the kind I am! A priest was telling me once. The devil's the worst bragger of all. Soon as you begin to brag, he says, straight away you get scared. And soon as you get scared of people, straight away, *he* comes, straight away gets hold on you and sticks you away where he wants to. And since I ain't scared of nobody, it ain't so bad for me. I spit on his beard and his shovel and his pig of a mother! And he don't do a thing to me. Go stuff it, I tell him!

NIKITA (*makes the sign of the cross*). And what in fact am I? (*Throws the rope down*)

MITRICH. How's that?

NIKITA (*gets up*). Ain't you telling me not to be scared of people?

MITRICH. As if they was to be scared of, the scum. Take a look at 'em in the bathhouse. All cut from the same cloth. One's got a bigger belly, the other's got a littler, can hardly distinguish between 'em. The hell with 'em! Ain't nobody to be scared of! Hope their bellies burst!

(MATRYONA *comes out from the yard.*)

MATRYONA (*calls*). Well, you coming, or ain't you?

NIKITA. Oh! Yeh, be better that way. Coming. (*Goes toward the yard*)

SCENE 2

Change of setting. The cottage of Act I is filled with people, some standing, some sitting behind tables. AKULINA *and the groom are in the front corner. Bread and icons are on the table. Among the guests are* MARINA, *her husband, and the policeman. The women are singing,* ANISYA *is serving vodka. The singing dies down.*

CABMAN. Better go if we're going, 'cause the church's not so near.

BEST MAN. Wait, give us a minute, the stepfather's going to give his blessing. But where is he?

ANISYA. He's coming. Coming right away, my dears. Don't worry, have a little bit more to drink.

MATCHMAKER. What's taking him so long? We've been waiting enough.

ANISYA. He'll come. Right away. He'll be here before a close-cropped girl could plait a braid. Drink up, my dears. (*Serves vodka*) Be here right away. Sing some more, girls, while we're waiting.

CABMAN. But they've already sung up all their songs in waiting.

(*The women sing. In the middle of the song,* NIKITA *and* AKIM *enter.*)

NIKITA (*holds* AKIM *by the arm and pushes him in front of himself*). Go on, Pa, can't do without you.

AKIM. I don't like it, I mean, now—

NIKITA (*to the women*). That's enough, be quiet. (*Looks around at everyone in the cottage*) Marina, you here?

MATCHMAKER. Go on, take the icon, give the blessing.

NIKITA. Wait, gimme a minute. (*Looks around*) Akulina, you here?

MATCHMAKER. But what're you calling out everybody's name for? Where else'd she be? What's he so strange like?

ANISYA. Sons of God! What's he doing barefoot?

NIKITA. Pa! You here? Look at me. Orthodox commune, you're all here, and I'm here! Here I am as I am! (*Falls on his knees*)

ANISYA. Mikitushka, what's wrong with you? Oh, my aching head!

MATCHMAKER. I never!

MATRYONA. And I'm telling you: he's had too much of the French wine, too much. Pull yourself together, what's wrong with you? (*Tries to pick him up; he pays no attention to anyone, stares straight in front of himself*)

NIKITA. Orthodox commune! I'm guilty, and I'm going to confess.

MATRYONA (*plucks him by the shoulder*). What's wrong with you, you crazy? My dears, his mind's gone bad, Got to take him away.

NIKITA (*pushes her away with his shoulder*). Leave me alone! But you, Pa, you listen. First thing: Marinka, look here. (*Bends down to her feet and gets up*) I am guilty toward you, promised to marry you, seduced you. I deceived you, left you, forgive me for the Lord's sake! (*Again bows down to her feet*)

ANISYA. What're you babbling like this for? It's got nothing to do with nothing at all. Nobody's asking you for it. Get up, now, what're you playing such a dirty trick for?

MATRYONA. Oh-oh, something unnatural's come over him. What's been done? He's gone bad. Get up. What're you muttering such stupid stuff for? (*Pulls him*)

NIKITA (*shakes his head*). Don't touch me! Forgive, Marinka, the sin I did to you. Forgive for the Lord's sake.

(MARINA *covers her face with her hands and is silent.*)

ANISYA. Get up, I tell you, what a trick to play. Better think what you're doing. Stop trying to show off. It's shameful! Oh, my aching head! Why, he's completely crazy.

NIKITA (*pushes his wife away, turns toward* AKULINA). Akulina, what I've to say now is for you. You listen, Orthodox commune! I am damned! Akulina! I'm guilty toward you. Your father didn't die his own death. He was poisoned with poison.

ANISYA (*screams*). My aching head! What's he doing?

MATRYONA. Man's out of his mind. Take him away.

(*People draw closer, want to seize him.*)

AKIM (*pushes them away with his hands*). Stop! You, fellows, stop, now.

NIKITA. Akulina, I gave him poison. Forgive me for the Lord's sake.

AKULINA (*jumps up*). He's lying! I know who.

MATCHMAKER. What're you doing? You sit down.

AKIM. Oh, God! it's a sin, it's a sin.

POLICEMAN. Grab him! And get the headman and the witnesses. Got to draw up a statement. You, there, get up, come here.

AKIM (*toward the policeman*). Now you, I mean, Bright Buttons, I mean, you just wait. Let him have his say, now.

POLICEMAN (*toward* AKIM). Look out, old man, don't butt in. I'm required to draw up a statement.

AKIM. Likes of you, now. Just wait, I tell you. 'Bout a statement, now, don't say nothing, I mean. Here God's work's being done— A man's confessing, I mean, but you, now, 'bout some state—

POLICEMAN. Call the headman!

AKIM. Let God's work be done, I mean, then, you, too, do yours.

NIKITA. My sin toward you, Akulina, is still greater: I seduced you, forgive me for the Lord's sake! (*Bows down to her feet*)

AKULINA (*comes out from behind the table*). Let me go, I won't get married. He told me to, but now I won't.

POLICEMAN. Repeat what you said.

NIKITA. Just wait, Mr. Policeman, let me say it all.

AKIM (*in ecstasy*). Speak, my child, say everything, it'll be easier. Confess to God, don't fear the others. God, now— God! Here He is!

NIKITA. I poisoned the father, I, like a dog, destroyed the daughter, too. I had the power over her, destroyed her baby, too.

AKULINA. It's true, it's true.

NIKITA. I smothered her baby with a board down in the cellar. Sat on it—smothered it—and the little bones in it crunched. (*Cries*) And I dug it a hole in the ground. I did it, did it myself alone!

AKULINA. He's lying. I told him to.

NIKITA. Don't you protect me. I ain't scared of nobody now. Forgive me, Orthodox commune! (*Bows down to the ground*) (*Silence.*)

POLICEMAN. Tie him up; your wedding, of course, is put off. (*People draw up with their wide belts.*)

NIKITA. Wait, you'll have time. (*Bows down to his father's feet*) Father, my father, you too forgive me, cursed man that I am! You told me from the first, when I set out on this wicked wandering, you told me: "If one claw gets caught, the whole bird's lost," but, like a dog, I didn't listen to what you said, and it came like you said it would. Forgive me for the Lord's sake.

AKIM (*in ecstasy*). God'll forgive, my dear child. (*Embraces him*) Didn't spare yourself, he'll spare you. God, now, God, now! Here He is!

HEADMAN (*enters*). Lots of witnesses here.

POLICEMAN. We'll make the examination right away.

(*They tie and bind* NIKITA.)

AKULINA (*comes up and stands beside him*). I'll tell the truth. Ask me questions, too.

NIKITA (*tied up*). There's nothing to ask. I did it all myself, alone. It was my design and my own deed. Take me where you want to. I won't say nothing more.